heraldry

SOURCES, SYMBOLS AND MEANING

OTTFRIED NEUBECKER
MEMBER, GOVERNING BOARD
INTERNATIONAL ACADEMY OF HERALDRY

WITH CONTRIBUTIONS BY
J.P. BROOKE-LITTLE
RICHMOND HERALD OF ARMS

DESIGNED BY
ROBERT TOBLER

h

**TIGER BOOKS INTERNATIONAL
LONDON**

eraldry

SOURCES, SYMBOLS AND MEANING

First published in Great Britain 1977
by Macdonald and Janes Publishers
Reprinted 1988 by Macdonald & Co
(Publishers) under the Black Cat imprint
© 1989 EMB-Service for Publishers, Lucerne

This edition published in 1997
by Tiger Books International PLC, Twickenham

A CIP catalogue record for this book is available from the British Library

ISBN 1-85501-908-6

EMIL BÜHRER: Original graphic concept
FLOYD YEAROUT: Editor
FRANCINE PEETERS: Managing editor
CORINNA REICH: Editor of the original (German) text
FRANZ CORAY: Illustrator
WERNER LUZI: Illustrator
EDITH BÜRGLER: Picture acquisition
FRANZ GISLER: Production manager
NICHOLAS FRY: Translator of German text
DARYL SHARP: Copy editor and proofreader

Printed in Italy by Canale

THE MOSAIC OF HERALDRY

Mosaic is originally an Arabic word meaning "decorated," and indeed everything connected with arms is decoration, both the coat of arms itself and whatever is applied to it. Its unimaginable variety within a strict but flexible framework has a charm which once succumbed to can never be forgotten.

The cosmos, nature, the world of myths, and history combine in a picturesque network of

unforgettable symbols, under whose influence nations, states, organizations, races, and families are built up, exist, and die out. Figures from the distant past keep their power as signs of human achievement and aspiration, or are recreated and join the round anew. Abstract graphic motifs gain weighty significance which can govern the life and death of millions.

Stylized and naturalistic eagles with one, two, or three heads; lions which show their teeth at the observer; others with protruding tongues and two heads, or three bodies united with a single head; fearful man-eating dragons and panthers; unicorns bewitching maidens; also the noble ermine, lilies honoring the Virgin, and roses, the symbol of love; even the humble radish — everything which man can observe and express appears in coats of arms. And all this takes place within a framework established by credulous soldiers who had no idea that they were starting a continual and unending process of development. Plain and decorated crosses, couped or throughout and accompanied by other charges, painted on shields and hung on the wall; helmets topped by simple plumes or by crowns and lofty constructions, brightly patterned garments and decorated staffs — all these combine in a mosaic of innumerable symbols, both beautiful and deeply significant.

There was a time when everyone knew what a coat of arms was. This is not true today, but even now a knowledge of heraldry would be a valuable addition to one's general education, for one still meets it at every step.

The most turbulent regions of the world have produced signs sufficiently similar to the classical coats of arms for it to be worth investigating their presumed social and psychological history. It is certainly strange that in the past year the part of the world where there has been most unrest is precisely that area to which we can trace the origins of armory: the Holy Land, the heartland of the Near East with its holy places of many religions, from Damascus to Sinai. Whatever moral judgment one might make on the Crusades themselves, their historic significance as a collision and at the same time a reciprocal fertilization of two essentially different cultures remains indisputable.

The social prerequisites for the creation of heraldry had long since been in existence. But they did not have a lasting effect until they were combined with military experiences which made it necessary to be able to identify both the individual person and the nation he belonged to.

A badge of nationality was a boon for all those who after leaving their native land encountered a language barrier which could only be surmounted by the learned with the help of Latin. Even French, the main language of the educated, was little help, although it played an important role in the East.

In 1095 a rousing cry went up in Christendom, calling on its members to take up the cross and set off to liberate the holy places threatened by the expansion of Islam. But few people had any idea of the painful and dangerous adventure ahead. And the relatively rough-hewn Europeans received a considerable surprise when they came up against an advanced culture and a scientifically based technology, as well as advanced techniques of war. They drew certain lessons from this, but mostly in relation to technology. Arriving as conquerors in the Holy Land, they attempted to graft their own social structure onto the areas they had won. They created a ruling upper class which applied the rules of feudalism, more perfectly

than at home, but because it was only an upper stratum it was that much more fragile.

The combination of several different elements laid the foundation stone of a phenomenon which embraced the whole of the civilized world as known to the Europeans. This phenomenon was armory, which as a result of its later manifestations is also called heraldry.

Feudalism was based on an unbreakable relationship of mutual loyalty in which the vassal served his lord, and the latter provided him with care and protection. This feudal relationship was established for life between the king or his near subordinate and an individual. It was only extinguished on the death of one of the partners.

If the feudal lord was an institution, such as a church, the question would arise of whether the death of the institution's representative, who might be a bishop, would dissolve the feudal relationship or not. The understandable desire of a vassal to secure the advantages of a feudal benefice for his descendants led inevitably to the principle of the inheritability of a fief. In a society which was not as yet oriented toward technical progress and a money economy, the basis of existence was agriculture and husbandry – the land.

The popular migrations following the breakup of the Roman empire brought profound changes in the distribution of property, which tended to work in favor of those in power. As a result, two types of property ownership arose in central Europe. The first was the *allodium,* which was the inherited possession of land belonging entirely to its owner. And the second type was the *feudum,* a piece of land or territory which belonged to the king or a high-ranking lord, but was leased by the latter to a vassal so that he could produce his means of subsistence and fulfil the duties incumbent on him as a feudatory tenant. In a time when might tended to be right, one of his main duties was to be ready to support the feudal lord in the military pursuit of his ends, in person and by any other means.

So long as such operations were undertaken by relatively small groups of armed men, the need for specific badges was not

great; any kind of distinguishing sign would do. However, the situation immediately became different when the first Crusade opened the eyes of Europeans, and they found themselves forced to make common cause with neighbors from the same continent, but at the same time needed to keep close to their own countrymen. A sense of national consciousness was revealed, or at least encouraged, by the use of different colored signs of the cross, and at the same time the military leaders brought their feudal attitudes to the new situation. This new situation consisted initially in the collection of unusually large masses of soldiers which resulted in staggering numbers of casualties.

But experience soon bore fruit in the form of stricter organization and stronger defensive armor. The stronger defensive armor consisted in particular of a more extensive coverage of the face, which had the effect of making the soldier unrecognizable. This had the further consequence that, exactly like a present-day tank driver or aircraft pilot, he had to decorate his outer covering with some easily identifiable sign. This could take the form of some addition to his helmet, but it could also be painted on some part of his armor such as the shield or the horse trapper.

At the time, horses were of course the customary means of transport, both on the march and while fighting. The military duties of a vassal included the provision of a war-horse at his own cost.

The wholly personal relationship between the lord and his vassal also explains why in the early centuries of heraldry it was considered important that a coat of arms should indicate a particular person and not a family. A young man of knightly birth made his entry into active life not through his father but through the sponsor who made him into a knight. It was the success of the feudatories in gradually making the fief inheritable which lent a degree of permanence to the coat of arms, by now becoming a genuine symbol.

The rules developed during the first few centuries of the second millennium A.D. were formulated and carried out by an increasingly important professional body, the heralds. And these same rules have remained valid with very little alteration to this day.

For this reason,
everything connected with arms
is called "heraldic,"
and the whole complex
of armorial knowledge and art
is called HERALDRY.

The rules developed by the heralds are based on the experiences of medieval military craft. They achieved wide recognition because of the primary significance of military activity at the time. Their basis was that every person must be recognizable as quickly as possible under unfavorable conditions of visibility.

One of the main rules
was therefore that of tincture,
whereby metal cannot be used on
metal, nor color on color.

Thus either gold or silver must appear in appreciable proportions on every armorial shield. In addition to the need for visibility at a great distance, which means that it must also be reducible to a very small size, certain formal requirements must be fulfilled for a sign to be regarded as an armorial bearing.

It must be possible
to represent an armorial design
on pieces of medieval armor,
in particular a battle shield.

Several badges of modern states which are designated as arms would not fulfil this requirement, but they are allowed to count as arms since they exercise an essentially heraldic function.

Arms represent people
or groups of people
as though they themselves
were present.
The presence of a coat of arms
acts at a substitute for the person,
even after his death.

For this reason, arms are a favorite emblem on seals and stamps; they must not be completely identified with seals or stamps, however.

TABLE OF CONTENTS

While arms can look back on a history of several centuries, heraldry itself is permanently valid.

All political developments make themselves felt through heraldic forms. This can best be observed at the foundation of a new state, which will hoist a flag with solemn ceremony on the first day of its independence. Soon after, it will communicate to friendly nations its future coat of arms, as well as the badges of its national airline and air force.

The increasing independence of the lower administrative orders and smallest population groups has a natural consequence in the creation of local arms. As a result in such democratically constituted countries as Switzerland and Finland, almost every community has an heraldically irreproachable coat of arms.

The more tourism increases, the more obvious is the usefulness of heraldically marked signs which dispense with the need for knowing a foreign language and indicate from what point there is a change in currency, bureaucracy, manners, and lifestyle. It is also interesting to observe who attaches importance to this type of sign and where this happens. As an example, Bavaria is in no way divided from the neighboring federal states, but the traveler who enters the German Federal Republic through Bavaria is informed that it is not just a federal state, but the free state of Bavaria.

In earlier times, important towns endeavored to show their autonomy by displaying the arms of their ruling lord at the gates. The arms were often simply on a board, but many were carved in stone, as at the northern entrance to Toledo (right).

Despite all adverse comment, this tendency has also affected families which regard themselves as pillars of their community and wish to contribute to its cohesion. After the idea that one must be an emperor or a prince to bear arms has been overcome, there is an increasing need for coats of arms for families with a strong sense of identity and also for self-confident individuals.

Herald is my name of old,
From which my metier may be told.
Aneas Sylvius* later on related
How the heralds were incorporated
Many years before to go on missions
Visiting princes and men of high position,
And freely passing every frontier.
To the heralds should one reverence bear,
Give them gifts and jewels
and courtly clothing,
Fortify them in their lordly living,
Guide them safely and defend them,
Strictly punish whosoe'er offend them.

Epigram by Hans Guldenmundt, about 1550
* Pope Pius II (1548–1564)

the herald

What is a herald, and where does the use of the term "heraldry" for the science of arms come from? There is no obvious connection between arms and heralds, and the term "heraldry" has only been in existence for some three hundred years. In fact a herald is a messenger and maker of proclamations. His task is, in the German phrase, *des Heeres zu walten*, to "manage the troops," presumably by proclaiming the commander's orders. This would seem to be the origin of the Old High German *hariwalt,* which gradually penetrated all the European languages via the Old French form *herault.* In French poetry it appeared as early as 1285 in the form *hirau*, but the current German term *Herold* did not appear until 1367, and the English "herald" appeared about the same time.

The generally warlike nature of medieval society imposed some unusual functions on military officials. A messenger often had to be a diplomat, treading the tightrope between emissary and spy and acting as a forerunner of the present-day ambassador.

The close relationship between arms and heralds arose naturally out of the way medieval armies were organized and the nature of medieval warfare. Feudal society was constantly embroiled in feuds which were conducted according to chivalrous ritual and caused immeasurable damage to land and property. Each participant in a passage of arms, whether of a warlike or merely sporting character, wore a coat of arms on his shield, helmet, and banner and on the trappings of his horse. These were the only means of distinguishing him from other combatants. There consequently had to be people who could read these signs and tell a friend from an enemy. Such a man had to have a good memory, and he had to be reliable, since inaccurate identification could have catastrophic results. Knowledge has been power throughout history, and a group of men formed around the warlords of the day, distinguished by their possession of certain necessary qualities and knowledge. Exceptionally, the social origin of these men was considered of no importance.

Within a few decades after the first arms appeared, their use had spread so rapidly that knowledge of them and their functions became a responsibility of the heralds. And the latter, who previously, as little more than messengers, had been included among the minstrels and other camp followers, now became persons of consequence whose advice had to be taken. The first

In the ancient world, the powers of individual gods were carefully allotted; the chief god, or father of the gods, needed a mediator to proclaim his heavenly will. In ancient Egypt, the sacred bull Apis *(above)* served as the messenger, or herald, of Ptah, the highest of the gods.

Greek mythology attributed many human characteristics to its gods, including emotions ranging from love to hate, from gaiety to fits of rage. The god of cunning, and herald of the gods, was called Hermes by the Greeks and Mercury by the Romans. With his caduceus – a snake-entwined staff – and his winged hat, Hermes formed a link between the gods and men. He was honored and prayed to by all those who had to be cunning and alert in the pursuit of their profession.

One "Ruyers" king-at-arms became an important figure, not so much through the exercise of his functions as through his accumulation of heraldic knowledge. His name was Claes Heijnen or Heijnenszoon, and his official title was "Gelre" (Gelderland), since he was in the service of Jean de Chatillon, Count of Blois and sometime Duke of Gelderland. When the duke retreated to Holland in 1374, Claes Heijnen tore off his fetters, removed his tabard, and took a new master. He was Albert of Bavaria, Count of Holland from 1390, and he gave Heijnen the title "Beyeren" (Bavaria).

Opposite, left and middle: These portraits of 1671 show elaborately embroidered tabards which by then incorporated the lion of Scotland and the harp of Ireland. At that time also, pursuivants (middle) wore their tabards turned athwart.

The senior king-at-arms of England takes his title from the highest English order of chivalry, the Garter. The first Garter King of Arms, William Bruges, was appointed by the king in 1415. Here he is shown in prayer before the country's patron saint, St. George. His tabard is decorated with the fleurs-de-lis of France and the three lions of England.

This parade of English officers of arms is from a tourney book of the time of Henry VIII (1509–1547). The pursuivants in front are recognizable by the way their tabards are worn athwart. They are followed by heralds wearing the tabards normally and carrying a white wand.

recorded presence of a herald at a battle was in July 1173, when according to the chronicler Guillaume le Maréchal a herald observed the Battle of Drincourt in Normandy. But this was still only an isolated case, attended by special circumstances, and the institution was slow in adoption. English documents in the year 1250 mention a "king of heralds" in the royal service. Some forty years later we find the first official appointment of the kind which was later to become general for all heralds, when a man named Andrew was given the official title of "Norroy" (North King). At that time, ordinary men did not have family names but only used Christian names. Those in royal service, however, could be raised from the crowd by the use of official designations which in themselves formed a special hierarchy. Thus the heralds were elevated from the level of servants, minstrels, and entertainers. At their head stood a king-at-arms or king of heralds, followed by the heralds a step below and then by pursuivants (from the French *poursuivant*, a candidate for office). This situation has continued over the centuries, even persisting after the heralds' actual function, on which their public reputation was based, ceased to be of any particular significance.

In France the statutes for the *Connétable* (probably dating from the year 1309) describe this function exactly, giving a vivid picture of the activity of the heralds of the time. The *Connétable*, whose office persisted until its abolition by Richelieu in 1627, was commander-in-chief of the army of the king of France. The disposition of the various royal ensigns was an indication of the arrangement of the army; the kings-at-arms, heralds, and pursuivants had to group themselves around the king's banner entrusted to the lord chamberlain.

The number of these armorial experts was considerable. Following the bloody and decisive Battle of Crécy in 1346, shortly after the beginning of the Hundred Years' War, a list of the French knights who had been killed was delivered to the victor, Edward III of England. Five heralds were sent as messengers, their official names taken from French regions: "Valois," "Alençon," "Harcourt," "Dampierre," and "Beaujeu." A year later, King John II the Good (Jean le Bon), then still duke of Normandy, had in his pay four French kings-at-arms, one a noble, the others with official titles. He also had

a Norman king-at-arms, officially designated "Duke of the Norman heralds," and twenty-one heralds. This was not exceptional – in 1396 Albrecht Duke of Bavaria was also accompanied by twenty-one heralds on his campaign to Friesland. Undoubtedly, these heralds were mostly engaged as the occasion demanded; the troops too were called up according to the requirements of the moment. But although conscription was not replaced by standing armies until somewhat

The German jousting societies dressed their tournament officials in surcoats bearing the badges of the societies, in this case "Ass" and "Ibex," which also appeared on the banners held by the ladies. These officials were also equipped with a white wand, symbolizing their authority.

In the famous *Livre des Tournois* of King René, there is a description of how the tournament is opened

later, by the middle of the fourteenth century heralds seem to have become a fixed part of courtly establishments. Those heralds who had no permanent appointment, however, tended to be ignored.

The extensive knowledge of people required of the heralds demanded not only a good memory but also aids to memory in the form of written records. These could be laid out in a number of different ways. A truly systematic arrangement was unknown at the time, however. Summaries were drawn up according to the number of followers a knight possessed, his appearance at military parades or coronations, and other indications of his position in the military hierarchy. Other systems were also used, such as the arrangement of the different coats of arms by individual districts, particularly in England where in the following centuries the science of

by the heralds. Those with the loudest voices had to call out three times: *"Or oyez, or oyez!"* ("Hear ye, hear ye!"), which was followed by the announcement of the individual contest. In the upper part of the picture are the heralds of the two jousting partners, the lords of Gruthuyse and Ghistelle, both of whom were Flemish.

The finest tourney book is undoubtedly the collection of rules and precepts which King René of Anjou-Sicily (1409–1480) compiled and had illustrated. He was above all interested in the pomp and ceremony surrounding the tournament, which he described in detail. The progress of the tournament itself was of less importance to him.

Below and opposite, left to right: The duke of Brittany hands his king-at-arms the sword which the latter is to take to an opponent, to challenge him to a tournament. A pursuivant holds his master's cap and heraldic staff.

The representatives of the duke of Brittany deliver the sword to the duke of Bourbon.

heraldry was subjected to an especially rigid form of classification.

Military requirements not only forced the heralds to compile lists, but also imposed definite rules on their public conduct and way of life. They had to be able to cross the opponent's lines with impunity in a private feud or war and enter the enemy camp. They therefore wore an unmistakable costume consisting of an armorial surcoat, such as their lord himself wore on festive occasions, but – and this was an important difference – without sword, dagger, or staff; a coat of mail was worn underneath in battle. In this way the heralds were easily recognizable from a distance. This form of dress has persisted until today in countries where the institution of heralds has continued to exist in one form or another.

So long as the feudal system of war service remained, whereby princes, knights, and conscripted vassals were recognized by the standards round which they gathered, the heralds

Again wearing his tabard, he had to announce a truce if so ordered and bear messages to enemy commanders, to challenge them to fight, to demand that a fortress be given up, or to start negotiations for a surrender. He also had to organize individual combats between members of the opposing camps.

He could be sure of a considerable reward from the enemy leader who received his news, especially if he appeared to be the kind of man who could keep his mouth shut. On his return, a herald was not supposed to utter a word about what he had seen of the enemy's preparations, for an ambush as an example. In fact he had to act as if he had seen nothing at all. Otherwise he would be looked upon as a spy – though many a pursuivant must have preferred this to letting his lord come to harm. At the same time he was allowed to give his lord useful advice without going into specific details. The "Sicily" herald, who came to be regarded as an authority because he had written a book of rules for heralds, based this provision on the Christian duty to

They show him eight imaginary coats of arms on a roll of parchment. These represent umpires, of which he may choose four.

The umpires wear their arms on badges fastened to their headgear. A loud-voiced pursuivant proclaims the start of the tournament.

were indispensable in every country in western Europe. They had always to remain close to their lord and be ready at any time of the day or night, especially in time of war. They were therefore quartered in the prince's tents. If a princely decree had to be made known, the herald would don his tabard. A trumpeter would assemble the prince's followers with three blasts on his horn. The herald would then read out the text of the decree to the assembled company.

prevent bloodshed, a point of view which the warlike knights can hardly have shared.

There were many who did not shrink from trickery in war and were quite ready to deceive an over-talkative herald. Such was the case with the followers of the French herald Bertrand du Guesclin in October 1370, according to his biography. Their English "colleague" inadvertently let slip the position of his master's camp.

Tournaments were exceptionally expensive, being usually arranged in the grandest of styles. The kind of sumptuous display involved is shown in illustrations from the period. The decorations of the knights and horses became increasingly far removed from the old heraldic styles and tended to include personally chosen motifs.

Overleaf:
Ladies were naturally expected to play their role in these colorful proceedings. According to King René, they should be led four times past the helmets of the participants, which were placed in a row so that none might be overlooked. If any of the wearers had been heard to make disparaging remarks about the women, a lady would touch his helmet to single him out, and he would be called to account. Those who escaped such treatment took part in the dancing and revelry of the evening.

The French heralds indulged in such a lavish celebration with him that he fell into a drunken slumber instead of going home. And at first light the French, with "lowered banners," were able of Mühlberg, the emperor Charles V dubbed Peter von Brandenburg knight. The reward to the herald for such attendance consisted of all the non-military equipment of the former es-

to creep into the English camp and overpower and take prisoner the warlike Thomas de Granson.

When battle was opened in a correct and chivalrous fashion, it was the custom to dub new knights before the beginning of the fighting, and the heralds had to be present as witnesses at the ceremony. In 1547, Hainault Herald witnessed and recorded that on the morning of the Battle

quire, which could however be redeemed with a mark of silver.

Everyone must have been aware before a battle that he might not come out of it alive. One of the functions of the heralds was therefore to record last wishes, take care of valuables, and also take note of physical characteristics by means of which they could identify the fallen. John Talbot, Earl of Shrewsbury, fell in 1453 at the Battle

15

of Castillon, which ended the Hundred Years' War between England and France. The body of Talbot was so mutilated as to be unrecognizable and had already begun to decompose. His herald could only identify him by a gap in his teeth, which he felt by putting a finger in his master's mouth. A touching scene, as related by Mathieu d'Escouchy, took place over the body when the herald, finally convinced his lord was dead, leaned over and kissed him on the mouth. In tears, the herald declared that his forty years of service were at an end. To symbolize this he took off his tabard and laid it on the body.

Heralds were unarmed and in principle were not taken prisoner. As soon as the battle had begun, they had to move some distance away, but not too far from their lord's banner, and follow the progress of the fighting by watching the coats of arms; they also had to observe and report on the behavior of the combatants, including any acts of cowardice which they saw. After the armies had disengaged, the heralds of both sides would go onto the battlefield to decide between them who was the victor of the day. The side with the

A herald meets Death. He wears the tabard of the margrave of Baden, bearing the arms of Baden (a red bend on a gold field) and Sponheim. In 1415 the margraves of Baden undertook to continue the arms of Sponheim when the house of Sponheim died out. This occurred in 1437.

arms of the king of France, was requested by the king of England, Henry V, to declare him victor and tell him the name of the neighboring castle. This was done and King Henry, according to the prevailing custom, announced that the battle would be named after the castle.

Heralds or pursuivants who were the first to bring good news could count on being rewarded by the recipient with his own clothing. In 1473, however, the thrifty King Louis XI confined himself to promoting to the rank of herald the pursuivant who brought him the news that the small town of Lectoure had been taken.

Once the fighting was over the heralds also had the lengthy task of making lists of those killed, as identified by their coats of arms. They were assisted by scribes. They also had to arrange for burials, and anyone who had expressed a wish to be returned to his native land would be identified by a special label in a small box attached to his clothing. Thanks to his immunity, the herald also had access to the prisoners, but he was not allowed to divulge their names to the victor in

The unestablished, "freelance" heralds decorated their tabards with small plain armorial shields, while those officials with tabards bore the arms of their lords. On unimportant occasions the arms frequently took the form of a small pendant shield, such as was also worn by couriers carrying dispatches across the country. In Switzerland this usage was passed on to the officials known as *Weibel* or sergeant-ushers.

largest number of dead was considered to have been defeated.

Because of their exact eye-witness knowledge of events, the heralds were a valuable source of information to chroniclers and illustrators about these often historically decisive battles. The heralds of the losing side usually went to the enemy commander, congratulated him on the victory which God had granted him, and begged him to ask God's mercy for the souls of those killed in action. In addition they could render certain services to the victor: after the Battle of Agincourt in 1415, "Mountjoie," the king-at-

case the latter should be prompted to slay a defenseless man in a moment of anger. But at least he was able to indicate when a prisoner was a nobleman and should be treated according to his station. He also had to deal with the question of ransom money.

As a sign of victory, the heralds had to raise the standard of their lord immediately and make sure that the banners of the loser were handed over. And as they could not benefit in the normal way from the consequences of the battle, instead of sharing the booty they received a fully equipped house or its equivalent value in gold. In

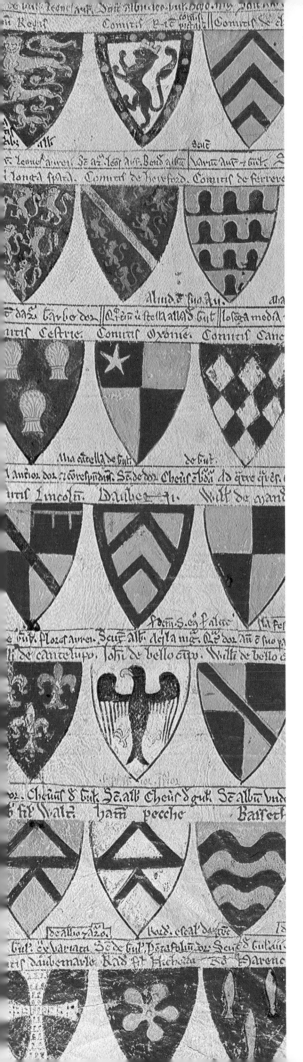

1380 the duke of Buckingham burned down the town of Vertus because the inhabitants refused to hand over their houses, which the heralds had claimed. The townspeople had taken exception to the heralds' behavior and perhaps indeed the latter had not deserved the respect normally given those of their office, for the high regard and privileges attached to their position often attracted untrustworthy people. Thus the French kings-at-arms once had to ask their king to forbid tradespeople to pass themselves off as heralds as a means of evading taxes.

Exemption from taxes was only one of the heralds' privileges. Another was the freedom to travel where they wished. This enabled them to undertake long journeys during which they could increase their knowledge of foreign lands and armory. Many of them recorded what they saw in words and pictures, and it is to this practice that we owe the armorial collections on which our knowledge of medieval heraldry is chiefly based.

There are few reports of heralds being badly

Left:
In mid-thirteenth century, Matthew Paris produced his chronicle *Historia Anglorum (History of the English).* The first two shields in the top row of this detail from the chronicle show the arms of the king of England and his brother, Richard, Earl of Cornwall, who was elected king of Romans and crowned in 1257.

Two of the heralds shown below are known to us by name. The "Sicily" Herald *(left)* served the king of Aragon (to whom Sicily then belonged) around 1420. The herald's name was Jean Courteois, and he was responsible for the most authoritative written record of the rights and duties of a herald. The pursuivant *(center)* of the elector Frederick II of Branden-

handled. In 1524 the population of Saint-Maximin in Provence killed one of Charles V's heralds, and the angry emperor razed the town. On the other hand, in 1528 the same emperor rewarded a French and an English herald who had to bring him a challenge at Burgos. He gave each a fur-lined coat and a thousand guilders. He also provided them with an escort of twenty-four archers to see them safely home.

The heralds were equally respected throughout western Europe, although the formal organization of their office in the various countries differed considerably. There were far stricter rules

burg (1413–1471) had the Christian name of Hans. His official title was "Burggraf" because his master, as a Hohenzollern, was also burgrave of Nuremberg. His personal arms are in a shield with a compony border, imitating the arms of the burgrave, which appear in the third quarter of his tabard. German pursuivants wore their tabards in the same fashion as heralds.

The French herald *(right)* comes from a far later period, as is indicated by the clothing showing beneath his tabard.

The herald represented on this playing card wears the arms of Bohemia as a badge.
The badge with the bear is that of the *Weibel* of the valley of Ursern in Switzerland.

Death as a herald. Etching by Stefano della Bolla (1610–1664).

Below, left to right:
The one-armed pursuivant of the tourneying society "Ass," Hans Ingeram, represented himself and his own coat of arms in the armorial which he compiled in 1459.

A Spanish herald from the last years of the reign of King Ferdinand I (d. 1516).

Hans von Francolin (1520–1586) was one of the first noblemen to become a herald. He was herald

west of the Rhine than in the rest of Europe, which explains the similarity of the heraldry of the Rhine with that of western Europe and particularly the Netherlands. The heralds of western Europe had clearly defined areas of jurisdiction, called marches, which had been formed from the two provinces of nobility created for the purposes of tournaments. The "Ruyers" represented the Germanic nobles and the "Poyers" the Gallic nobles – the origin of the names is not certain. Around the middle of the fifteenth century the armorial province of Ruyers was confined to the Netherlands and other imperial territories west of the Rhine; its customs were modeled entirely on those of Poyers, i.e., the French sector. The imperial king-at-arms was appointed by the duke of Brabant and Lothier in his capacity as margrave of the Holy Roman Empire; the duke was also responsible for paying him. The famous heraldic expert Claes Heijnenszoon was not only a herald with the official name of "Gelre" but also king-at-arms "de Ruyris" (of Ruyers). The "very noble and great march" of Poyers was divided geographically into three tourneying provinces: Poyers, Aquitaine, and Champagne,

empowered to grant arms and therefore had no interest in their supervision. Nevertheless these heralds were occasionally entrusted to set up tournaments, simply because of their wide variety of relevant knowledge.

A widely read book of the period (which however refers to historical events largely invented by the author) was the *Tourney Book* of the herald of the Simmern Palatinate (Pfalz-Simmern), Georg Rüxner. In his telling, it was decided as early as the year 942, at the tournament held at Rothenburg-on-Tauber, to relieve the stewards of a tournament of the burden of organizing it and to form three "tournament societies" in each district. (Although his date is much too early, his other facts seem accurate.) The stewards of these societies were empowered to choose a clearly distinguishable bird or beast as an emblem. Every steward had to make his

to the Roman emperor and to the king of Hungary, and wore respectively decorated tabards.

Swedish heralds in the funeral procession of King Johann III, 1594.

Opposite:
The duke of Lancaster was one of the first knights of the English Order of the Garter. He is distinguished from a herald by the fact that his armorial coat is cut not like a tabard but like a doublet. On top of this he wears the cloak of the Order of the Garter.

which in turn were divided into twelve marches or armorial kingdoms. Ponthieu was the chief march of the whole of Poyers, followed by Flanders, Corbie, Artois, Vermandois, central France, Normandy, Anjou, Brittany, Guyenne, Berry and Touraine (including southwestern France), and Champagne (including Bar, both Burgundies, Savoy, Dauphiné, Provence, and southeastern France). In the German empire the nobles who were sufficiently well established to take part in tournaments organized themselves independently of the princes. The heralds of the reigning princes had no cause to concern themselves with armory, since these princes were not

squire wear this badge and also wear it himself, "so that people could recognize his society. And whoever from the four countries was a tourneyer should carry the same sign round his neck, or on his cap or hat, in the district where he resided. If he was a knight he should wear it in gold or gilt, if a nobleman he should wear it all of silver, and if an esquire with the front part gilt and the rear part silver, so that the different ranks of the nobility could be distinguished from one another."

In this way the following badges were adopted for the societies in the different areas mentioned

(see page 212): Upper Rhine – swan; Middle Rhine – lion; Lower Rhine – greyhound (representing the wind – "greyhound" in German is *Windhund*); Upper Swabia – fish and falcon; Middle Swabia – ibex; Lower Swabia – mastiff or bloodhound; Upper Franconia – griffin; Middle Franconia – unicorn; Lower Franconia – ass; Upper Bavaria – bear; Middle Bavaria – horse; Lower Bavaria – peacock. Around 1480 most of these divisions still existed; a few badges such as those for Bavaria no longer appeared, while others had been added, including the Wolf society on the Rhine, and an Ibex society in the same region, which had previously belonged to Swabia. In Franconia we later find societies named after objects, such as Crown and Belt Buckle.

The organization of heralds in Great Britain reflects the country's history, in that the heralds' establishments in England and Scotland are completely different from one another. Scottish heraldry is described as the "simplest and clearest in Europe." Its purity is maintained by the leader of the Lyon Office, whose origin goes back to the fourteenth century. His official title is Lyon King of Arms, from the Scottish coat of arms, which is a lion. His powers extend far beyond those of the English heraldic establishment. The Lord Lyon is a judge who presides over a court which has jurisdiction in matters armorial, and after judicial process can prohibit the use of unregistered arms. He too has heralds and pursuivants under him. The official titles usually used for the heralds are "Marchmont," "Rothesay," and "Albany," and for the pursuivants "Kintyre," "Unicorn," and "Carrick."

Even before they were organized (in 1483–1484) as the Corporation of Kings, Heralds, and Pursuivants of Arms – shortened to The Heralds' College, or the College of Arms – the English heraldic officials formed part of the royal household. Later they came under the direction of the Earl Marshal, the duke of Norfolk. England has three kings of arms: Garter King of Arms, first created in 1415 and named after the highest English order, the Order of the Garter; "Norroy" for the area north of the River Trent; and his colleague "Clarenceux" for the area south of it. Up to 1964 there were thirty-three Garters, forty-six Clarenceuxs and sixty-eight Norroys. After the partition of Ireland, the title of Ulster King of Arms was combined with the office of Norroy in 1943.

The heralds receive their titles from the names of royal towns or counties. Thirty-eight of them in succession have carried the name "Chester," forty-three have been called "Lancaster," thirty-

Initial with a portrait of Garter King of Arms John Smart. From an initial letter of a grant of arms made by him in 1456.

Opposite:
Tabard from the reign of the Stuart Queen Anne. During her reign the parliaments of Scotland and England were combined in 1707 to form the parliament of Great Britain. This was symbolized by the lion coat of Scotland being joined to the lions of England, France being relegated to a less important place in the arms than previously enjoyed.

nine "Richmond," twenty-eight "Somerset," forty-one "Windsor," and thirty-eight "York." The names of the pursuivants are taken from royal badges. Twenty-seven have had the name "Bluemantle," thirty-six "Portcullis," thirty-seven "Rouge Croix," and fifty "Rouge Dragon." Additional heralds and "pursuivants extraordinary" may be appointed when required for special occasions, but these are not members of the College.

The building of the College of Arms in Queen Victoria street is older than the street itself, which was not laid out until 1867. It was assigned to the college in 1555 in what was then Derby Place. It was razed to the ground by fire in 1666, but was thereafter rebuilt according to plans approved in 1677. In 1956, through the generosity of an American benefactor, Mr. Blevin Davis, it was embellished with a pair of splendid iron gates saved from the demolition of Goodrich Court in Herefordshire.

ARMORIAL COAT FROM ORANGE, 1476

TABARD OF THE BURGUNDIAN HERALD
FOR THE COUNTY OF HAINAULT

TABARD WITH THE GERMAN IMPERIAL EAGLE,
FIFTEENTH CENTURY

1   The only surviving tabard from this early period.
2   The booty taken by the Swiss after their victory over Charles the Bold included this tabard.
3   The Portuguese arms in the top half of this garment date it around 1580–1640. It is the tabard of the herald of King Philip II of Spain, which was worn later by the herald of the Order of the Golden Fleece.
4–7 Each territory of the dukedom of Burgundy possessed its own herald.
8   This garment was created for the coronation of the emperor Ferdinand II as king of Bohemia on 29 June 1617. At the coronation of the emperor Leopold II in 1790 the shield on the chest was modified in accordance with territories then possessed by Austria.
9   The empty shield inescutcheon was used by the Palatinate in protest against its deprivation of the office of lord high steward of the empire on two occasions (1623 and 1714) and its uncertain possession of the office of imperial lord high treasurer (from 1648).

TABARD FOR THE HERALD OF THE GERMAN ROMAN EMPEROR

3

TABARD WITH THE FULL ARMS OF SPAIN

4

TABARD OF THE BURGUNDIAN HERALD
FOR THE DUKEDOM OF LUXEMBOURG

6

TABARD OF THE BURGUNDIAN HERALD
FOR THE COUNTY OF ARTOIS

7

TABARD OF THE BURGUNDIAN HERALD
FOR THE DUKEDOM OF BURGUNDY

9

TABARD OF THE PALATINE HERALD, BETWEEN 1714 AND 1742

10

STATE ATTIRE OF THE EMPEROR OF CHINA, NINETEENTH CENTURY

Battle scene from the *Aeneid*. The German princes who bore the lion arms around 1200 must have been very rebellious to be shown killing the bearer of the imperial eagle arms.

Below:
In the *Armorial de Gelre,* the arms of the vassals of a great lord are arranged in a row beside his own arms. They have the partly imaginary crest consisting of a curious panel opening out into a feathered end like a wing. This type is only found in the Netherlands, and because of its shape is known as *vol-banneret* ("banner-shaped wing").
The arms of Flanders appear three times: as the so-called arms of old Flanders, which still appear today in the arms of the Belgian province of Western Flanders; as the normal achievement of arms; and as the arms of the count of Cassel, differentiated by the

The armorial collections of the thirteenth, fourteenth, and fifteenth centuries are essential to a knowledge of heraldry in its heyday. The forms of that time are still considered the classical ones today, and are used as prototypes and patterns. Armorial collections include a variety of sources, first of all the colorfully executed paintings of arms which appear in large numbers on parchment rolls or in books with paper pages. In this group alone there are great differences, depending on who compiled the book and the object of the work.

Often the author or the person who commissioned him — for not everyone interested in heraldry was a competent artist — was an official such as a herald or pursuivant. In this case, within the limitations of the time, the work would generally be reliable. If the author were a private citizen, then he was dependent on the integrity of his informants and the reliability of his sources, as is the case even today. Collections of this kind were less comprehensive than those of the heralds, and less systematically put together. For the heralds, armorial collections were a daily-used tool of their trade.

Heralds gathered their knowledge of the arms in actual use as organizers of tournaments and other assemblies of knights. They noted down in lists what they saw. These lists aimed to be

according to the charges on the shield and not according to the name of the lord or lords represented by the arms. England is far richer than any other country in armorial collections of this kind. In the rest of Europe, ordinaries were made up almost solely for learning purposes, showing examples of different charges. No great interest was shown in them until the nineteenth century and the results of research are still shamefully small. Nevertheless, in the last few decades scientific evaluation of medieval armorial collec-

| COUNT OF FLANDERS | BANNER OF FRANCHE COMTÉ | OLD FLANDERS | BURGRAVE OF LILLE | DAVID VAN HALLUIN | BURGRAVE OF AUDENARDE | ROBERT, COUNT OF CASSEL | PHILIPP VAN AXEL |

thorny edge to the shield and the ermine tail on the wings. Although live figures often appear, a diving fish as a crest is rather unusual.

complete only in relation to the occasion for which they were compiled. Hence, this type of list was called an "occasional roll" in England. Also in England, official requirements produced the so-called ordinaries, which are arranged

tions of all kinds has made considerable progress.

There has been a general tendency to include with armorial collections other sources which do

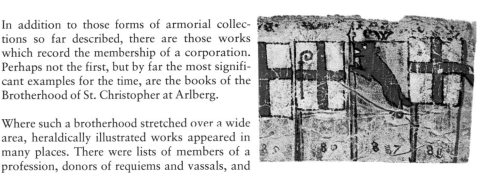

In addition to those forms of armorial collections so far described, there are those works which record the membership of a corporation. Perhaps not the first, but by far the most significant examples for the time, are the books of the Brotherhood of St. Christopher at Arlberg.

Where such a brotherhood stretched over a wide area, heraldically illustrated works appeared in many places. There were lists of members of a profession, donors of requiems and vassals, and even university matriculation registers, many of remarkable artistic quality. Such celebrated orders of knights as the Order of the Garter and the Order of the Golden Fleece, of Hubertus and of St. Michael, could afford particularly expensive and outstandingly produced armorial books. One particularly fine work is *Bruges' Garter Book,* which contains representations of the oldest knights of the Garter (see page 21). Armorial books of this kind relating to the membership of an order have in places continued right up to the present day.

Armorial collections can be technically divided into rolls and books according to their form; their use, however, varies. The term "roll," which is derived from a roll of parchment, has been kept up to the present day to designate a register with a more or less official character, as in the term "roll of trademarks."

The Zurich armorial roll makes a clear distinction between arms connected with persons and purely territorial signs. The former consist of shields, helmets, and crests, and the latter, signs of bishoprics or abbacies or of territories such as the Rhine Palatinate, are represented by banners.

not strictly deserve this name. Such sources are illustrated manuscripts, often lavishly decorated with coats of arms. Such illustrations are useful to us today, but we need to distinguish between arms which can be considered genuine and arms which were invented as purely decorative elements. (The lists in the appendix give some guidelines on this point.)

Another category of armorial collections includes those arms which have survived on buildings, either in sculpted or painted forms. In this group too are innumerable items such as tapestries and furniture decorated with coats of arms. Their value as source material is as great as that of arms painted on paper or parchment, though the latter are easier to compare. The armorial hall in Lauf near Nuremberg is just as valuable as an occasional roll, and the Wienhausen tapestries compare favorably with the first parts of the Zurich armorial roll. Less agreeable to the eye are the unillustrated lists carrying the names of the participants in an event with a description of their arms, whether it is a list of prisoners or the record of the swearing of a truce. Then there are wordy poems in which fantastic people are represented as the participants in imaginary tournaments. The arms of ruling noblemen are attributed to them and described in great detail, often the first historical record of arms still existing today. This is especially true of the legendary *Tournament of Nantes (Turnier von Nantheiz)* by Konrad von Würzburg (d. 1287). The *Clipearius Teutonicorum (List of Arms of the Germans)* by Konrad von Mure (d. 1281) restricts itself to the description of the arms themselves, but also in rhyming form. This text is rich in material for studying the development of heraldic jargon. It is clear that it spread to every country from France.

Before people thought of collecting and registering arms, heraldry had to have acquired a certain meaning. At first it seemed merely an ephemeral phenomenon, which appeared unsystematically and which historians found useful as illustrative material. Appearing around 1180, some fifty years after the first arms, the chronicles of the Sicilian campaign of the emperor Henry VI and

In the year 1334, eighteen princes united against John III of Brabant and sent him a challenge by letter. The *Armorial de Gelre* contains the text of the letter and its accompanying caricature – a boar wearing the armorial coat of Brabant. The duke of Brabant's helmet stands behind it.

Arms of the lords of Haemstede and Henevliet; the square banner signifies a feudal overlord, the three-cornered pennant a vassal-knight.

Opposite:
A page from the so-called *Wijn-bergen Armorial* which assembles the first twenty-five of the sixty-four arms of the march of Artois. This page was undoubtedly done before 1291. The author of the collection has made an effort to show groups of arms within the march, which are based partly on family relationships but also on graphic similarity.

Right:
The Franciscan monks in Munich had to read a mass every year for Duke Albrecht III of Bavaria (d. 1460) and his wife Anna of Brunswick (d. 1474). The corresponding entry in their necrology was decorated with the arms of the royal couple. The lady's arms are shown incorrectly on the heraldic right side, but turned with customary politeness towards those of her husband. The shield underneath is the device of the royal cook, which has been "heraldicized" by being transferred to a shield. As was often the case the simplest of colors are used, here black and white. The figure kneeling at prayer beneath is probably the honored Herr Glazius, the monastery's much respected patron, who died in 1524.

some illustrations to the story of Aeneas provide remarkable contemporary examples of this practice. The pictures illustrating the *Aeneid* show figures from the ancient saga in comparatively modern dress and certainly true to life. There is an unabashed representation of Aeneas seducing Queen Dido in the wood. The illustrations to the Sicilian campaign are much more informative, with pictures of the so-called Norman shields being carried through German friend and Norman foe; canting arms – a pig (*Schwein*) for the town Schweinspoint; a bend as shorthand for unknown arms; the cross as a charge on the imperial banner; the imperial eagle, still with rather variable coloring. Probably none of this was entirely authentic, since the author, Petrus de Ebulo, was a monk. His statements about heraldry are no more authoritative than would be those of most journalists in our own day.

On the other hand the authenticity of the shields shown in the illustrated manuscript of the *Aeneid* is confirmed by knights' seals from the same period. They also provide the attentive observer with information about how the shields were worn, often being shown inside out. The correspondence with the seals is so exact that they serve as a means of dating the manuscript, which has been preserved to the present day. It turns out to be a copy of the original of 1188 and cannot have been produced before about 1214. It is nevertheless one of the earliest manuscripts of its kind.

The use of coats of arms as a means of enlivening historical or mythical accounts seems to have been more popular among the Germans than in other countries. In any case, up to this point the heraldic literature of other countries contains only armorial collections, and no chronicles with heraldic illustrations are to be found. One important exception is the chronicle of the Englishman Matthew Paris (d. 1259). It contains the oldest existing record of the different families of knights, illustrated in color. The author gives the double eagle as the sign of the German empire at a time when this had yet to be established. At the time, opinion was merely becoming settled in favor of a double-headed eagle for the emperor and a single-headed one for the German Roman king (see pages 124 ff.). Links between England and the Continent were close enough then for the free exchange of information. The widow of the emperor Henry V, Mathilde, lived for more than twenty years in her former home and was known as "empress" even though two years after the death of her first husband (1125), she had married Geoffrey V Plantagenet, the heir to the English throne. Her

son's grandchild in the male line, Richard Earl of Cornwall, was elected king of Germany in 1257. Previously, her grandson in the female line – a child of Henry the Lion who had been brought up at the court of his uncle, the English king Richard I, Cœur de Lion – had been German emperor from 1209 to 1218.

The so-called *Balduineum*, which describes the emperor Henry VII's journey to Rome, is a valuable heraldic source and has been the subject of extensive research. Its most heraldically significant features are the representation of Henry before, during, and after his crowning as emperor; the still unexplained elongated red and yellow pennant, which accompanies the march to Rome (possibly the badge of Patricius of

Rome); and the fact that the author indicates by graphic means when he does not know a coat of arms, usually that of an opponent.

Later heraldically illustrated chronicles make useful source material because they contain the short-lived coats of arms used by many nobles but more particularly by members of the church. Arms such as these can be used to date other armorial collections, particularly by means of the frequently changed arms of the popes.

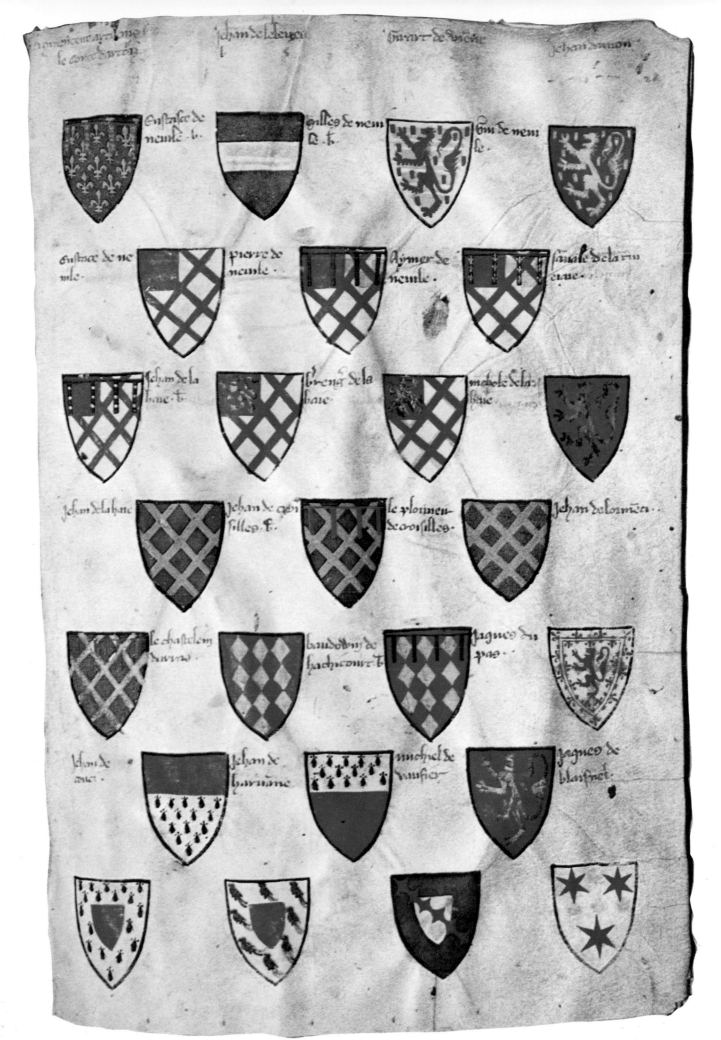

The chronicles of the fifteenth century, however, tend to lapse into fantasy. Excited by reports of journeys to foreign lands, the authors of armorial collections tended more and more to invent arms for the kings of distant countries; chroniclers invented coats of arms for the ancestors of their landlords, which have no interest as historical sources but appeal through the motifs chosen and the skill with which they are drawn. A distinction must be drawn between chronicles of this kind and the eye-witness reports of factual events. The eye-witnesses usually prove skilled in heraldry and were in most cases heralds who had acted as organizers of the events concerned. In many cases modern researchers have been the first to identify armorial rolls as lists of this kind.

Our list of such armorial items (see appendix) begins with three from the Franco-Dutch area. The first is a notable testimony to the immunity of the heralds, embracing as it does the arms of both sides. It is not named after the event but after an earlier owner of the extant copy in the seventeenth century. There is some doubt as to whether the list of the tournament of Compiègne was the earliest of its kind. Also as to the authenticity of certain tournament lists from around the same period, such as that of a tournament at Cambrai in 1267. The illustrated or written records of the arms of participants in a battle or siege are more interesting to the historical researcher than dubious tournament lists. We know of several from England, among them the roll of Caerlaverock, which because of its comprehensiveness enjoys considerable popularity and is reproduced again and again. The banners drawn in it can be bought today as cigarette cards and tin figures.

One solitary case shows the arms of some German knights who were released from prison in Italy in 1361 after having sworn an oath to keep the peace. Being little skilled in reading and writing, they could not spell their names properly, which as a result are garbled and Italianized. But they could represent their arms, which they carried on their bodies.

It was not only in a military context, however, that the herald was officially obliged to compile lists. Apart from the heraldic illustration of chronicles, we find the use of arms as decorative material in other literary accounts. Among these the "great Heidelberg song manuscript" (the *Manesse Codex*) is particularly noteworthy. Nearly every picture or scene in this is accom-

panied by the arms of the appropriate minnesinger, with in some cases so-called Minne arms instead of the actual family arms, as an expression of respect for the lady to whom the song is addressed. In the manuscripts of the *Sachsenspiegel,* on the other hand, arms play only a subsidiary role, serving to illustrate points of justice.

In the late Middle Ages, arms were introduced in many places without any idea of a collection being entailed. Works of art decorated with arms possessed aesthetic charm as well as providing information on their historical context (see pages 252 ff.). Many of these works deserved to be included among the lists of armorial collections. The armorial rolls created for some celebration such as the visit of a member of the nobility are particularly well executed. Examples

King Edward the Confessor (reigned 1042–1066), the founder of Westminster Abbey. The arms which were subsequently attributed to him are based on one of his silver coins, on which four birds are fitted into the corners of a cross. Imaginary portrait from a copy of the *Rous Roll.*

Imaginary arms of Charlemagne *(right),* which played a major part in iconography after their invention and are still used today as the arms of the cathedral chapter of Aix-la-Chapelle. Above them are the arms of the bishopric of Utrecht with the small shield in the center left free for the arms of the incumbent bishop.

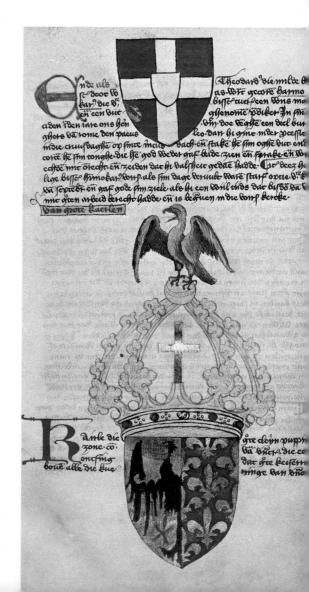

are those for the "Zum Loch" house in Zurich and the tower at Erstfelden; for the castle of Rivoli; and for the armorial hall at Lauf, where Charles IV often stayed. There is also a table from the town hall at Lüneburg which must have been decorated for some festive occasion with its allegorical medallions and coats of arms superimposed.

The custom of using coats of arms to decorate one's dwelling has an important parallel in the central European custom of putting up one's arms in the inn or lodging where one stopped. Anyone who sought a quarrel would tear down the board displaying the arms – just as the plates outside present-day embassies are often damaged by rioting crowds.

A great congress like the Council of Constance, which lasted from 1414 to 1418 and brought together several hundred thousand people, was a veritable mine of information for anyone interested in heraldry. One such person was Ulrich von Richental, who went from house to house at the time and noted down what he saw, to include it in his chronicle of the council. Unfortunately he got his notes mixed up so that his account is generally confused, especially in that part which deals with the arms of the churchmen. In addition he was given to rather too much speculation and there are many coats of arms which he could not have noted down from a lodging house, but must have made up himself. He also claims that it was possible to communicate with "Ethiopians," whom no one could have understood and who were not even able to speak Latin. The Council of Constance produced some unexpected treats for the heraldic historian. The evenings were whiled away with theatrical performances in which the arms of the three holy kings, originating in Cologne, appeared again and again. In this way they became known throughout the German-speaking world and in England.

In his efforts at comprehensiveness, Ulrich von Richental was continuing a tradition unknown to him which was already a century and a half old. This was the production of armorial collections which aimed at universal validity. The urge to produce armorial collections was prompted by either pure cultural interest or professional necessity, and in talking of general armorial collections a distinction must be drawn between those of the heralds and those of private collectors or sponsors. Both kinds first appear about the middle of the thirteenth century.

The collections of the private authors are of greater cultural interest than could be expected of those made by officials. Not only are poetic portrayals of arms often literary creations in themselves, such as the list in the German *Clipearius Teutonicorum,* or the luxurious descriptions of arms in the *Tournament of Nantes* by Konrad von Würzburg. It is also precisely these private collections which emphasize the value of a knowledge of the full armorial bearings, including crests on helmets. Helmet crests are mentioned in the *Tournament of Nantes* and in the important armorial roll of Zurich which is somewhat difficult to date – containing no arms of members of the clergy – and the armorial book *Van den Ersten.*

Apart from the Uffenbach book, which only contains energetically painted heraldic shields,

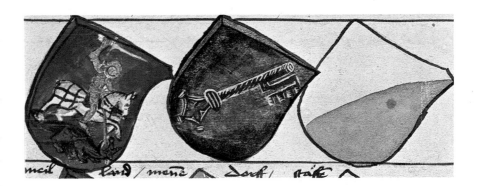

and the Grünwald book, all the armorials listed in the appendix give the full armorial bearings or "achievement" of arms. The most important German armorial by a private collector is that of Konrad Grünenberg. Also a native of Constance, although he must have lived too late to know Ulrich von Richental personally, Grünenberg adopted the work of the latter and not only extended it but also collated it in a series of powerful drawings. In 1442, Grünenberg was appointed chief architect of his home town of Constance, and three times he was mayor. He finished his comprehensive work of heraldry on 9 April 1483, and three years later set off on a six-month pilgrimage to the Holy Land. After the pilgrimage, from which he brought back the customary badges (see page 218), he lived another eight years. There are two extant copies of his armorial collection, one on paper (in Berlin-Dahlem), and another on parchment (in Munich). In 1875 it was reproduced –

The row of lion arms above comes from *Thomas Jenyns' Book* (ca. 1410), which already features chapter titles and thematic headings such as "Leones" (lions) for the section shown.

The Zurich chronicle of Gerold Edlibach devotes several pages to the arms of the vassal districts of Zurich. Here we see the St. George of Küsnacht, the key of Zollikon, and the diagonally divided blue and white shield of Zurich itself.

Overleaf:
In the convent at Wienhausen near Celle in Lower Saxony there are a number of embroidered tapestries. A few of them, like the so-called Tristan tapestry shown here, are decorated with friezes of armorial shields. They reflect the not always correct ideas held at the time of the arms of foreign countries.

TRISTRAM·DREBAT·DEN·KONING·DÆT·HEMOOTESTRIDEN·UUE

HÆVEN·MINKONINGÆRIKER·ÆLF·TRISTRÆM·DÆKERDE

ANDESKONIG·ESDÆN·º·DOGUÆMNEUORDENKONING·UND

BRÆNGIELE·UNDEURUSÆLDE·LEGNEDENÆNEINENSÆ

DOSTÆREUTÆMÆSÆEPE·DOSTUNGRÆUNDEUÆELÆDE

DOSTOTURUBRÆNIELE·UNDÆHELÆNE·URUISÆLDESÆLUE

These Japanese family signs *(mon)* show how difficult it is to work from descriptions alone when dealing with the graphic details of a particular group of motifs. The Japanese descriptions therefore do not attempt to be comprehensive. The crane in Figure 1 is merely termed *tsuru*, that in Figure 4 as fitting exactly into a circle *(schin no tsuru nu maru)*. The position of the two birds in Figure 2 is described as opposed *(mu kau)* within a circle *(no maru)*. Figure 3 is two *(ni)* cranes in a circle *(ni wa tsuru)*. It is not unusual for several families to use the same *mon*.

In the book of the Council of Constance, Ulrich von Richental included the arms of the abbots and

abbeys subject to the bishop of Constance. Some of them added their own family arms to the arms of their abbey, using both the second and third positions of the quartered shield. The red and white bend chequy in the arms of Salmansweiler and Wettingen indicates that these were Cistercian monasteries.

perfectly, for the time – with the collaboration of the then head of the heralds' office and the young heraldic expert Adolph Matthias Hildebrandt.

The armorial collections produced by heralds or other officials noticeably do not concern themselves with the helmet and crest until the middle of the fourteenth century. After that time, however, Continental heralds were forced to record the complete arms; an outstanding example of this is the armorial of the "Gelre" herald, *Armorial de Gelre*. Posterity has had some difficulty in tracing the various works which this herald produced under different official names. When he left service with the duke of Gelderland, he found a new master in the house of Wittelsbach, which then ruled Holland. Albrecht of Bavaria, Count of Holland since 1390, gave him the official name of "Bayern" (Bavaria). In addition he was king-at-arms of Ruyers; the duke of Brabant was responsible for bestowing this wide-ranging office.

Armorial lists which omitted the crest and restricted themselves to the shield clearly served as a method of quick checking – a function to which they were admirably suited. English collections of arms, in particular, very early adopted the practice of arranging the arms according to the charges on the shield.

The arrangement of the earliest heralds' armorial rolls shows clearly that they were designed for a specific purpose. There is little interest in comprehensiveness and the arms of distant foreign lands. Foreigners, even those of princely rank, tend to be included in appendices; family arms are arranged according to tourneying regions and the number of vassals held. In the fifteenth century the differences between collections start to disappear and the rolls become known by the name of the herald. Where his name is not known, researchers are obliged to adopt substitute names to designate the rolls, such as the name of the place where they were compiled. Often it is the name of a famous previous owner of the roll, who perhaps did not even possess the original, but only a copy. And we have to be content with this when, as is often the case, the original has been lost.

In the case of many armorial collections, especially in England, large numbers of copies exist in which it is simply stated that they have been copied from an old book of arms. Naturally this has not always happened without mistakes. Only in the last few decades has scientific research in archives and libraries seriously concerned itself with establishing hitherto unknown

THE ARMS OF THE KINGS OF ARAGON, FRANCE, HUNGARY, AND SCOTLAND, FROM THE *ARMORIAL DE GELRE*.

The customary arms of Aragon with the four pales gules.

Gelre's illustration of the dragon crest of Aragon negates a theory accepted elsewhere that this device was first adopted by a later king. In the course of time it developed into the bat crest of Valencia.

The arms of France became stabilized in the first third of the fourteenth century as three fleurs-de-lis (see page 132).

The arms of Hungary make reference to the epoch of the powerful King Lewis the Great (reigned 1342–1382), who was also king of Poland.

The arms of Scotland are essentially the same as those used today. It has been suggested, from the fact that the helmet mantling uses the family arms of the Bruce dynasty, whose male line died out in 1370, that Gelre used an outdated pattern. Others hold the opinion that the house of Stuart, which reigned from 1371 on-

ward, wanted to show, by keeping the arms of the Bruce family, that it had legitimately inherited the throne of Scotland.

In 1615, Louis XIII created the post of Juge Général des Armes de France, but it did little to help efforts at systematizing the bearing of arms in France. Louis XIV again raised the idea of registering arms, this time as a means of gaining extra revenue. In the meantime skilled engravers and printers had brought out printed armorials privately; a list of these is provided in the index.

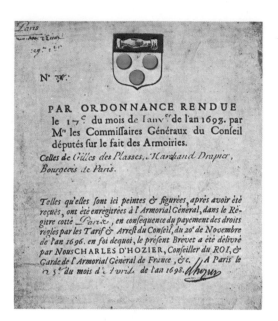

A section from the frieze of arms in the armorial hall at Lauf near Nuremberg shows the arms of the great Bohemian ruling families, including those of the von Sternbergs. When J. W. von Goethe was raised to the ranks of the nobility, he wished to use the morning star as his arms, but was forced to add a subsidiary sign because of the star of the von Sternbergs.

In the Swiss National Museum in Zurich, the beams from the "Zum Loch" house, dating from the same century, were faithfully reproduced.

exclusively devoted to the reproduction of hand-painted armorial books. Paul Adam, who died in 1964, carried out essential research for France. There is still much to be done in the other European countries.

The invention of printing in the fifteenth century introduced into the production of armorial books the use of a pre-printed template for shield, helmet, and helmet mantling. By the middle of the fifteenth century the art of copper-plate engraving had come into its own and the production of armorial books was at its height. (More information is given on this in the selected bibliography in the appendix.)

But this development did not mean the end of arms collections which were not intended for publication; we have already mentioned the armorials of orders of knights which have been continued to the present day.

One splendid but final effort on the official side was the creation of the *Armorial Général* by an edict of Louis XIV in 1696. The former Juge Général des Armes de France, Charles d'Hozier,

connections between these copies. This has been done most assiduously in England (in the series of publications entitled *Aspilogia*, Vols. I and II), partly inspired by the example of the heraldic experts von Berchem, Galbreath, and Hupp.

This team of three had a number of forerunners, including Baron Karl von Neuenstein. In the years 1892–1906 he published in Karlsruhe the monthly journal *Wappenkunde*, which was

was appointed Garde de l'Armorial Général (Keeper of the General Armorial), but at the same time made subordinate to a government official, Adrien Vannier. The purely fiscal motivation of the appointment and the disputes which arose from it in fact spoiled the whole undertaking. But in its benefits to heraldry, the event was of inestimable value.

Two pages from the armorial of the town of Como of 1593. The arms are arranged by alphabetical order of the families' names. The figures in the first three escutcheons are rooks from the game of chess, and are therefore canting arms for the names of the families – De Rochis, De Rechis, and Di Rechis.

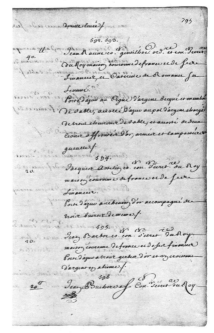

Half of the sixty-nine volumes of the *Armorial Général* in the Bibliothèque Nationale in Paris contain illustrations, and the other half the technical descriptions (or blazons as they are known in heraldic terminology). Here is a sample page *(above)*.

The only state which kept a printed official record of the arms of its noble families was imperial Russia; the work began in 1797 but was abandoned in 1840 after the printing of the tenth volume. Illustrated here are the arms of Alexander Vassilievich, Count Suvorov-Rimnikskii, which were granted him by the tsar of Russia on 11 April 1791. The arms include the German imperial eagle, which had been conferred on him by the German Roman emperor Josef II. When Suvorov became a prince of the Russian empire in 1799, his arms were "bettered" and the Russian imperial eagle was added in place of the German Roman eagle.

37

Since the fourteenth century, special attention has been devoted to the graphic design of such documents as grants of arms and patents of nobility.

The armorial documents from the last decades of the kingdom of Prussia, which perished in 1918, were bound like a book. The covers were bound with leather on which the royal emblem of the eagle was stamped and picked out in color. The corners were decorated with silver plates and the large state seal of Prussia, made from red wax, hung in a silver capsule on tasseled silver cord.

Basically, everyone is free to choose his own arms. Not everyone takes advantage of this, but a person who does so needs to have his choice ratified by an appropriate authority. The manner of this authorization depends on political circumstances. Monarchies have a stronger interest in the observation of social divisions than republics. They therefore tend to maintain the nobility as an institution, and usually have an office for issuing grants of noble status. This requires the issue of documents assigning or recognizing noble status. These documents, particularly on the continent of Europe, normally contain a grant or ratification of armorial bearings. Armorial offices are seldom empowered to assign arms to those who do not have noble status. The recording of arms and titles today is, in many countries, carried out by private, unofficial, professional associations.

Right:
In Great Britain, grants of arms have always consisted of sheets of vellum, known as Letters Patent, that is, an open document addressed to all who care to read it, with the seal or seals being attached to the bottom of it, not closing it. In them the reader is informed by the kings of arms making the grant by what authority they act and what they are granting to the recipient of the patent. Apart from the new coat of arms we also see here the standard, which as a matter of principle is not described, and the badges of Imperial Tobacco Limited. On the top edge of the document are the royal arms flanked by those of the duke of Norfolk as Earl Marshal and Hereditary Marshal of England and those of the College of Arms. In the right-hand margin are the arms of office of the three kings of arms involved (Garter, Clarenceux, and Norroy and Ulster) with their characteristic crowns. These reappear in the seals attached to the signatures at the bottom. The decoration of the document with sprigs of the tobacco plant is unusual.

T☉ ALL AND SINGULAR

to whom these Presents shall come Sir Anthony Richard Wagner, Knight Commander of the Royal Victorian Order, Garter Principal King of Arms, John Riddell Bromhead Walker, Esquire, Member of the Royal Victorian Order, upon whom has been conferred the Decoration of the Military Cross, Clarenceux King of Arms and Walter John George Verco, Esquire, Commander of the Royal Victorian Order, Norroy and Ulster King of Arms Send Greeting! Whereas Richard Anthony Garrett Esquire, Captain (retired) the 22nd Dragoons, Chairman of IMPERIAL TOBACCO LIMITED did represent unto The Most Noble Bernard Marmaduke, Duke of Norfolk, Knight of the Most Noble Order of the Garter, Knight Grand Cross of the Royal Victorian Order, Knight Grand Cross of the Most Excellent Order of the British Empire, upon whom has been conferred the Territorial Decoration, Earl Marshal and Hereditary Marshal of England and One of Her Majesty's Most Honourable Privy Council, now deceased, that Imperial Tobacco Limited was incorporated as a Limited Company on the Sixteenth day of February 1973 under the Companies Acts 1948 and 1967 That the Directors of the said Company are desirous of having Armorial Ensigns duly assigned to the Company with lawful authority and he therefore as Chairman of the said Company and on behalf of the Directors thereof did request the favour of His Grace's Warrant for Our granting and assigning such Arms and Crest and in the same Patent such Supporters and such four Devices or Badges as We may consider fit and proper to be borne & used by Imperial Tobacco Limited on Seals or otherwise all according to the Laws of Arms And forasmuch as the said Earl Marshal did by Warrant under his hand and Seal bearing date the Eighteenth day of December 1974 authorize and direct Us to grant and assign such Armorial Ensigns accordingly Know Ye therefore that We the said Garter, Clarenceux and Norroy and Ulster in pursuance of His Grace's Warrant and by virtue of the Letters Patent of Our several Offices to each of Us respectively granted do by these Presents grant and assign unto IMPERIAL TOBACCO LIMITED the Arms following that is to say:- Purpure a Bend lozengy Argent between two Coronets composed of four Tobacco Flowers raised on points above a rim Or And for the Crest On a Wreath Or and Sable A demi Maiden affronty proper crowned with a Coronet as in the Arms Or vested Purpure garnished and holding before her a bunch of Tobacco Plants Or flowered Argent, Mantled Purpure doubled Or, as the same are in the margin hereof more plainly depicted And by the Authority aforesaid We do further grant and assign the following four Devices or Badges that is to say:- (1) Three Coronets as in the Arms in triangle Or enclosing a Tobacco Flower Argent pierced Or; (2) Two Ram's Horns addorsed points downward Argent cufiled by a Coronet as in the Arms Or; (3) An open Port between two Towers Argent masoned Sable ensigned by a Coronet as in the Arms Or; (4) The Bowl of a Tobacco Pipe Or within an Annulet Argent its stem issuant from the sinister side thereof, as the same are also in the margin hereof more plainly depicted And by the Authority aforesaid I the said Garter do by these Presents further grant & assign unto IMPERIAL TOBACCO LIMITED the Supporters following that is to say:- On the dexter side a Stag and on the sinister an Unicorn both Erminois attired unguiled horned and armed the Unicorn also tufted Sable and both gorged with Coronets as in the Arms Argent attached thereto Chains reflexed over their backs also Argent standing upon a Grassy Mount Or contained by an embattled Wall Argent, as the same are also in the margin hereof more plainly depicted, the whole to be borne and used for ever hereafter by Imperial Tobacco Limited on Seals or otherwise according to the Laws of Arms In witness whereof We the said Garter, Clarenceux and Norroy and Ulster Kings of Arms have to these Presents subscribed Our names and affixed the Seals of Our several Offices this Thirtieth day of October in the Twenty-fourth year of the Reign of Our Sovereign Lady Elizabeth the Second by the Grace of God of the United Kingdom of Great Britain and Northern Ireland and of Her other Realms and Territories Queen, Head of the Commonwealth, Defender of the Faith and in the year of Our Lord One thousand nine hundred and seventy-five.

J.R.B. Walker   Clarenceux   Walter J. Verco   Norroy & Ulster

On Sunday 27 November 1975 at 12.40 p.m., Prince Juan Carlos of Spain entered the audience chamber of the Palacio de las Cortes in Madrid accompanied by his wife, Princess Sophia of Greece, and their three children. After he had taken the oath on the constitution, he was proclaimed king of Spain as Juan Carlos I. A formal coronation did not take place; the royal crown lay on a richly embroidered cushion on a low pedestal at his feet, next to the scepter and a small crucifix. Two heralds dressed in brown, with simply braided tabards, stood quietly in the background.

Together with its original constitution, the direct democracy of the Swiss has also retained its traditional outward manifestations. *Weibel* (bailiffs) ensure an orderly procedure at the *Landsge-*

Modern forms of state which are based on the possibility of an alternation of power, and control of the instruments of power by an opposition, are not conducive to the creation of pageantry and display. A prerequisite for pomp and pageantry is a degree of stability generally found only in countries with a monarchy or a directly democratic form of government.

In monarchic countries the leaders of the state are educated for their task from youth, and it is a task which normally persists even beyond the customary age limits for professional activity. In direct democracies the people are sovereign and are therefore consulted as a whole for nearly all important decisions, so that elections, which bestow full powers on those elected for specific legislative periods, scarcely influence traditional customs. Thus it is that such extremely different states as Great Britain and Switzerland, a United Kingdom and a Confederation, show in the execution of their state functions a degree of

The heraldic tradition is most continuous in Great Britain. The heralds still wear tabards which reproduce, as they always have, the armorial figures of Great Britain just as they appear on the royal coat of arms. The one exception is that in Scotland, since 1903, the quarters have been reversed so that Scotland takes precedence over England, and the arms of Scotland appear twice.

Occasions on which the entire complement of the College of Arms appear dressed in tabards are few and far between. The coronation of Queen Elizabeth II was one such occasion, when twelve of the "Officers of Arms" appeared in Westminster Abbey. In our picture opposite, some of them form an aisle together with princes and dukes, while Winston Churchill passes, bowing, resplendent in the robes of the Garter.

The five heralds nearest to him are easily recognizable. In front (with the pointed beard) is

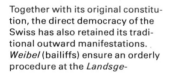

meinde, the sovereign assemblies of the people. They are dressed in the colors of the canton or the community. Here the bailiff of the half-canton of Nidwalden, flanked by those of the towns of Buochs and Wolfenschiessen, decides the result of a vote from a show of hands. The regional bailiff *(far right)* is recognizable by the shield bearing the arms of his rank which he wears on his left breast.

pageantry no longer found anywhere else in the world. It is a pageantry otherwise afforded only to the military, which on such state occasions is able to display a colorfulness which has no place in modern warfare.

The pageantry displayed by constitutional civil organs in their public appearances takes the form of official uniforms, which are identical or comparable with those of the medieval heralds.

Hugh Stanford London (1884–1959), a well-known heraldic author, Norfolk Herald Extraordinary from 1953, and next to him Dermot Morrah (b. 1896), Arundel Herald Extraordinary since 1953.

Behind the two of them is a group of three heralds. In the middle, wearing his crown of office, is Sir Thomas Innes of Learney (1893–1972), from 1945 Lyon King of Arms, the king

The heralds of Great Britain were present at the coronation of Queen Elizabeth II on 2 June 1953, contributing to the pageantry of the occasion with their splendidly colored and richly embroidered tabards *(below)*.

of arms for Scotland. On his right is Sir Richard Anthony Wagner (b. 1908), 1931 Portcullis, 1943 Richmond Herald, and since 1961 Garter King of Arms, a prolific and world-renowned heraldic author.

The heralds' tradition still lives on to a certain extent in Spain, though in a less obvious fashion. The two heralds who were present at the taking of the oath by the new king of Spain on 27 November 1975 remained quietly in the back-ground and were also fairly plainly dressed. Their brown tabards were fringed with simple braids, and on their breasts they wore merely an oval badge containing the impaled charges of the castle of Castile and the lion of León, with the same motif on their caps. On earlier occasions, however, municipal heralds have been seen with the full armorial tabard of Spain, bearing the arms of the town in question.

In the short period of his reign (20 January – 11 December 1936), King Edward VIII had to observe the traditional ceremonies. At the opening of Parliament he found himself surrounded, as were his predecessors before him, by heralds wearing tabards *(above)*. After abdicating he was given the title of duke of Windsor.

Above:
The tabards of heralds taking part in British ceremonies held in Scotland show that in that part of the United Kingdom the Scottish lion takes precedence over the English lions, as it has since 1903. Here we see a ceremony of the Scottish Order of St. Andrew, also known as the Order of the Thistle.

The importance of regional emblems is demonstrated by the ancient-Egyptian sign-bearer. He is holding the standard of his region in front of him as if in a parade or procession. The generic term "vexilloids" is used for standards of this type, which have the same function as modern regimental colors. The ram's head bearing a sun disk is a symbol of the god Amon-Ra, and can therefore be identified as the badge of Thebes.

An essentially conservative phenomenon, the world of heraldic concepts preserves many medieval notions and much of the medieval terminology. A decisive role in this was undoubtedly played by the increasing predominance of the French language over Latin in the Middle Ages. Latin was the language of the church and of learning with which heraldry had little or nothing in common. French, however, was the language of the courts and polite society, and it has remained the basic language of heraldry to the present day. Thus much English heraldic terminology is derived from medieval French (other terms are obscure for other reasons).

Some common heraldic terms are listed below. (All italicized words are defined in the list.) The index at the back of the book contains references to concepts which are explained in other parts of the book.

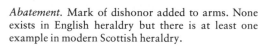

Abatement. Mark of dishonor added to arms. None exists in English heraldry but there is at least one example in modern Scottish heraldry.

Achievement. The complete armorial *ensigns.*

Addressed. Back to back.

Affronty. Facing the front.

Allerion. An eagle *displayed* but without beak and legs.

Annulet. A ring.

Antelope. The heraldic antelope has serrated horns, a beak, tufts on the body, and a lion's tail.

Apaumé. Hand or gauntlet, open and showing the palm.

Armed. Used to refer to the claws, talons, tusks, and suchlike of creatures when of a different *tincture* from the body. Also used of parts of the human body when encased in armor.

Armiger. One who bears arms. Hence "armigerous."

At Gaze. A synonym for *guardant* but only applied to members of the deer species.

Attired. Used to describe antlers when of a different *tincture* from the head or body.

Augmentation. An addition made to arms, often to commemorate a special achievement or event.

Badge. A heraldic symbol, often combined with a motto, indicating status of one kind or another (see pages 208–213).

Banner. 1. Poetic expression for flags in general. 2. In a narrower sense, an armorial flag (see page 94). 3. A hanging standard or flag (see *oriflamme*). In the strictest sense, a banner is bestowed on the bearer under specific conditions and cannot therefore be readily exchanged for a copy of the same design. For this reason it is usually fixed permanently to the staff.

Bar. An *ordinary* which runs horizontally across the shield like a *fess,* but narrower than the latter.

Bar Gemel. Two narrow *bars* close together.

Barbed. Used to refer to points of arrows and spears and the sepals of a rose.

Barre. French term for *bend sinister.*

Base. The bottom third of the shield (segments 7, 8, and 9 in the division shown on page 88).

Baton. A bendlet *couped* (see Capetian family tree, page 102); when borne from *sinister chief* to *dexter base* it is a mark of bastardy.

Bear Arms. To bear arms consists of making use of the coat of arms on all appropriate occasions.

Bend. An *ordinary* consisting of a band running diagonally across the shield from *dexter* chief to *sinister base.* A small bend is a bendlet.

Bend Sinister. A band running diagonally across the shield from *dexter base* to *sinister chief.*

Bezant. A gold *roundel* representing a coin but usually shown plain and unstamped.

Bicorporate. Having two bodies conjoined to a single head.

Billet. A *charge* consisting of a small rectangle, usually used in large numbers to cover a *field,* which is then known as *billety.*

Blazon. The technical heraldic language for describing a coat of arms. The blazon must include all the details required to enable the artist to draw an accurate coat of arms.

Bordure. A band running round and touching the edge of the shield (see page 89).

Buffalo Horns. Two bulls' or cows' horns used occasionally as a *charge* and extremely frequently as a crest in central Europe (see page 162).

Burgundian Cross. A diagonal cross formed from two crossed branches (see page 211).

Caboshed. Used of the heads of certain animals when shown affronty and cut off clean behind the ears.

Caduceus. The staff of Mercury or Hermes. It consists of a rod round which two serpents are entwined and ending in two wings at the top.

Caltrap. A *charge* derived from a kind of iron spike strewn on the ground to impale horses' hooves.

Canting Arms. Arms which make a pun or play on words involving the name of the bearer.

Canton. An *ordinary* consisting of a small square in the *dexter chief* of the shield (see page 89).

Celestial Crown. A coronet composed of eight triangular points, each ensigned with a star and set about a rim.

Chapeau. A cap of red velvet rimmed with *ermine* extending into two points at the back. Popular in England as part of a crest.

Charge. Any object used in heraldry.

Chequy. A pattern of checkers like a chessboard.

Chess Rook. A representation of the chess piece (see page 37) resembling the *cronal* of a lance.

Chevron. An *ordinary* like an inverted V emerging from the *base* of the shield (see page 89).

Chief. 1. The upper third of a shield (segments 1, 2, and 3 in the division shown on page 88). 2. A shortened form of *chief shield*.

Colors. The colors, as opposed to the metals, which make up the heraldic palette (see page 86).

Combattant. Used when two *rampant* figures face each other as if in combat.

Compartment. The ground on which supporters sometimes stand (see pages 202 f.).

Compony. Used of a *charge* which is divided into alternating rectangles of two different *tinctures*. The border of a shield so decorated would be a *bordure compony*.

Cotised. Used of certain *ordinaries* when shown with a narrow diminutive on either side. If two cotises are shown on each side it is termed double cotised.

Couchant. Lying down but with head erect.

Counterchanged. A way of describing a partitioned shield where the metal and color on one side of the partition line are reversed on the other side.

Couped. *Charges* which are untypically cut off so that they do not touch the edge of the shield.

Courant. Running.

Crined. Used of hair and tufts of hair when of a different *tincture* from the body.

Crampon. An iron clamp used by builders to strengthen walls, often used as an armorial *charge*.

Cronal. The crown-shaped steel tip of a jousting lance (see page 44).

Crown Vallery. A coronet composed of eight inverted "shield-shapes" set about a rim.

The emblems on the shield of this well-armed rider are repeated on his horse trapper and his banner.

Three types of seal, all Swedish *(from left to right):*
Armorial shield used alone as a seal; Karl Ulfsson 1373; original 25 mm. diameter.
Knight's seal showing Duke Bengt Birgersson in full armor; 1282; original 77 mm. diameter.

Chief Shield. A practical term for a large shield *quartered*, bearing one or more *inescutcheons* (see page 90).

Cinquefoil. A five-petaled figure, rose-shaped.

Clarion. An old musical instrument (see page 136).

Crozier. The *badge* of abbots and bishops, derived from the shepherd's crook.

Dancetty. A partition line composed of deep indentations (see page 89).

Deer's Attires. A favorite form of crest in Germany.

Throne seal of King Johann III of Sweden; 1571; original 110 mm. diameter. The king is flanked by the two Swedish coats of arms, which at the time were designated as the arms of the kingdom of the Swedes (crowns) and that of the Goths (lions).

At the tournament of St. Ingilbert (right) three French knights are supposed to have fought in successive engagements against thirty-six foreign opponents.

The rules of tourneying varied, and the types of weapons used differed correspondingly. Lance tips were either dangerously pointed or merely intended to give a painful jab. The last form used was called a cronal or coronel, from its likeness to a crown.

Right:
In an English miniature of the fourteenth century, St. George, the nation's patron saint since that century, is shown in the guise of a knightly sponsor handing the king the English coat of arms. Both the king and the saint are dressed in mail with an armorial tunic. They both wear the shoulder pieces known as *ailettes* which were customary at the time, bearing the same armorial designs as their tunics.

Devise. The French term for a *badge* (see pages 208 ff.).

Dexter. The heraldic term for right. (The dexter side of a shield is the right side of the bearer; i.e., the left side as seen by the spectator.)

Dimidiate. Cut in half; often used of two coats each halved vertically, the *dexter* side of one being impaled by the *sinister* side of the other.

Diadem. See pages 166 f.

Diapered (Damasked). A *field* so described has its plain surface broken up by patterns executed in a lighter or darker shade of the same color.

Disarmed. Used of an animal or bird deprived of its weapons (e.g., an eagle without beak or claws).

Displayed. A bird with wings outspread, tips upward. One also speaks of displaying arms.

Double-queued. Having two tails. This occurs almost exclusively with the lion and was characteristic of a number of arms in the classical period of heraldry (e.g., those of Bohemia and Limburg).

Double Tressure. Two narrow parallel lines forming a border within the shield. When interspersed with *fleurs-de-lis* on alternate sides it is termed "fleury counterfleury." This is a favourite *charge* in Scotland.

Dragon. A scaly, four-legged monster with batlike wings and an eagle's claws.

Ducal Coronet. A coronet similar to that of a duke but having four instead of eight strawberry leaves set about a rim. It is often used in place of a crest *wreath* but does not indicate rank (see page 162).

Eagle. One of the commonest medieval *charges* on heraldic shields, often denoting imperial sovereignty.

Eastern Crown. A crown consisting of triangular segments on a headband.

Enfile. Encircle or environ.

Engrailed. A scalloped line of partition, the points of the scalloping pointing outward.

Ennoblement. When a hitherto bourgeois family is raised to the ranks of the nobility by a reigning sovereign, it at the same time receives a coat of arms.

Ensign. Place above, as of a crown resting on a rose.

Erased. Cut off roughly, leaving a ragged edge.

Ermine. A *fur* composed of black ermine spots on white (see page 87).

Ermines. See page 87.

Erminois. A variant of *ermine,* the background being gold instead of white.

Escarbuncle. A wheel usually consisting of eight ornamental spokes radiating from a central boss and terminating in *fleurs-de-lis* (see page 63).

Family Tree. A tabular record of the ancestors of a particular person or family.

Fess. A heraldic *ordinary* consisting of a wide horizontal *bar* across the central third of the shield (see page 89).

Fess Point. The center point of the shield.

Fesswise. Running horizontally across the center of the shield.

Field. The plain ground on which a coat of arms is painted.

Field of Royal Prerogative. A completely red *field* appearing in some royal arms (see pages 53 and 165), recalling the red *banner* of feudalism.

Fitched. Pointed at the foot; used of crosses whose bottom arm ends in a point.

In the normal mace tournament, the aim was to strike off the opponent's crest; in some types of tournament it was sufficient to get in a shrewd blow with one's mace on top of the opponent's barred helmet.

Flag. The generic term for any decorative piece of material fixed loosely to a staff and not necessarily of armorial significance.

Flanks or Flaunches. The lateral thirds of a shield. (In the Continental system, described on page 88, the numbers 3, 6, and 9 represent the *sinister* flank.) English heraldic flanks are arched.

Fusil. An elongated *lozenge.*

Ghibelline Battlements. Crenelations with dovetail-shaped notches on their upper edges.

Gorged. Used of an animal wearing a collar, which may be a plain collar or also a *wreath* or a crown. The unicorn of Scotland is gorged with a crown.

LC
1509

Fleur-de-lis. A stylized form of lily; the emblem of the kings of France. Applied to a lance tip so shaped.

Flighted. Used of the feathers of an arrow, as for example when they are of a different color.

Fleury Counterfleury. See *double tressure.*

Fountain. A *roundel* barry *wavy* argent and azure.

Fret. A voided *lozenge* interlaced by a bendlet and a bendlet *sinister.*

Furs. Generic term for the stylized representation of animal pelts in heraldry (see page 87).

Goutty. Covered with drops or gouttes.

Griffin. A mythical beast whose upper body resembles that of an eagle, but with pointed ears, and the lower part that of a lion (see pages 114 f.).

Guardant. Used of heraldic animals which are looking out at the spectator.

Gyronny. Used of a shield that is divided into at least six triangular segments (gyrons) by lines radiating from the center.

Hamade. A *bar couped* (i.e., not touching the edge of the shield).

As tourneying was not only a sporting event, but treated as an opportunity to practice real situations in battle, there were group engagements which gave rise to scenes of confusion like that shown above. Important artists such as Lucas Cranach the Elder were fond of sketching such colorful scenes, which were then transferred in faithful detail to woodblocks. By Cranach's time, however, the age of tournaments such as this was practically at an end.

The heavy fifteenth-century sailing ships known as cogs were equipped with a single sail, and this was often decorated with a coat of arms or some other emblem of the king or his representative, the admiral.

Harpy. A mythical creature with a vulture's body and the head and bust of a woman.

Hatching. See page 86.

Hatchment. A corruption of *achievement* but used solely to describe an achievement painted on a *lozenge* to indicate the death of the bearer. The way the background is colored indicates the marital status of the deceased.

Haurient. Used to describe a fish shown erect.

Herald. Originally a messenger and maker of proclamations, the herald became involved with armory by necessity. His functions on the medieval battlefield combined those of ambassador and armorial expert. Outside the realms of heraldry, the concept of "herald" is connected with ideas of communication and publicity. Thus the International Herald Tribune is a newspaper, and Herald Books an English publisher.

Hexagram. A *charge* formed of two interlaced triangles, one of them inverted; also known as the star of David or the seal of Solomon.

Issuant. Used of a *charge* emerging from a line or border.

Jamb. The leg of a beast.

Knots. Knots made out of lengths of cord are very popular as family *badges* in England. A knot in the form of a figure 8 is considered a love knot, because it closes when the ends of the cord are pulled.

Label. A narrow *bar* with tabs or points pendant from it. A label of three points across the top of a shield is the distinguishing mark of the eldest son.

Langued. Almost all heraldic beasts have their tongues done in a different color, and this is known as langued. British heraldry has special rules covering this convention.

Lined. Refers to the inside of a piece of material (e.g., an armorial cloak or helmet *mantling*).

Lines of Partition. See page 89.

Lodged. A synonym for *couchant* but only used in respect of animals of the deer species.

Lozenge. A *charge* consisting of a rhombus standing on its point. In western Europe it is customary for a woman's arms to be on a lozenge (see pages 234 f.).

Lozengy. Used of a *field* divided in a diagonal crisscross pattern to give a series of *lozenges*.

Lunel. A group of four half moons with their tips turned toward one another.

Lymphad. An ancient ship with a single mast. Often shown with flags flying, sail unfurled, and oars in action.

Mantling. The decorative piece of material attached to the helmet and covering the back of the neck (see page 153).

Marshal. Draw up an *achievement* of arms showing the insignia and *quarterings* (see pages 230 f.).

Martlet. A bird resembling a house martin but having no feet; a popular *charge* in the Netherlands, and in England it is a mark of the fourth son.

Mascle. A *voided lozenge* (i.e., a lozenge with its inside cut out parallel to the edge).

Masoned. A *charge* representing masonry is said to be masoned. The joins between the blocks are assumed to be of the same shade in a darker tone unless otherwise *blazoned*.

Maunch. The sleeve of a lady's dress shown in a stylized manner (see page 137).

Melusine. A young maiden with long hair and a fish's tail (i.e. a mermaid; see page 200).

Mill-rind. A *charge* similar to a *crampon* representing the iron which supports a millstone; it is pierced in the center to take the spindle of the millstone.

Monogram. A *badge* composed of different letters or initials. An example is the monogram of Charlemagne (see page 203).

In the Mediterranean, the constant winds could not always be relied on. Larger and larger oared galleys were built and ever more richly decorated with flags and coats of arms. The above picture shows a galley of the Knights of St. John, rulers of Malta and the "police of the Mediterranean." Along each gunwale, standards bearing the arms of the grand master alternate with those of the order itself.

Hilted. Used of a sword whose hilt has a color of its own.

Impale. To place two coats side by side on a single shield, as in certain marital arms where the husband's coat is placed on the *dexter* and the wife's on the *sinister* half of the shield (see pages 234 ff.).

Inescutcheon. Used of a small shield borne in the center of another shield.

Inverted. Used of a *charge* turned through 180° from its normal position.

Irradiated. With rays of light issuing from a *charge*.

A MOST COMPLETE MONARCHIC ARMORIAL ACHIEVEMENT

At the top is an armorial banner modeled, like those of many kings, on the French oriflamme.

The royal crown is identified as that of Savoy by the crosslet botonée of St. Mauritius on the top.

The dome of the armorial tent is decorated with symbols from the collar of the Order of the Annunciata (see below).

The armorial drape, which together with the dome from which it falls forms the armorial pavilion, is held up by cords at the side.

The helmets rest on the shield, the outer pair belonging to the German arms of pretension. The central helmet carries the crown denoting royal rank, with its crosslet botonée, and above it the crest of Savoy, a winged lion's mask impaled on the tent pole.

Two lions "reguardant" act as supporters, derived from the five lions on the armorial shield between them.

The escutcheon consists of four main quarters. 1. The kingdom of Cyprus. 2. The dukedom of Saxony, derived from the supposed descent of Duke Widukind. 3. The regions of Chablais and Aosta. 4. The districts of Genevois and Montferrat. The arms of Savoy are on the inescutcheon.

Running round the shield is the chain of the "Supreme Order of the Most Holy Annunciata" *(Ordinae Sovrano della Santissima Annunziata),* of which the duke of Savoy is the grand master.

The pedestal is formed by a naturalistically represented piece of ground, in which is planted the tent pole which carries everything.

Mullet. A star, normally of five points drawn with straight lines; derives from the molet or spur-rowel.

Mural Crown or *Wreath.* An embattled crown or garland bestowed on the first soldier to scale the walls of a besieged town (see page 246).

Naiant. Used to describe a fish swimming across the shield.

Naissant. When one *charge* issues from the middle of another.

Naval Crown. A coronet composed of hulls and sails of ships set alternately about a rim.

Nebuly. One of the lines of partition (see page 89).

Nesselblatt (Nettle Leaf). The German term for a charge formed using a zigzag *bordure* (see page 134).

Nimbus or *Circle of Glory*. A synonym for halo.

Nobility. The highest social class. There are particular crowns corresponding to the different grades of nobility (see page 178).

Nombril Point. A point situated between the *fess point* and the *base* of the shield (see page 88).

Nowed. Knotted; often applied to snakes or the tails of beasts when tied in a knot.

Octofoil. An eight-leaved figure.

Ombrello. An umbrella or canopy used as a sign of dignity in church (see page 238).

Orb or *Mound*. Part of the monarch's regalia consisting of a ball surmounted by a cross, which symbolizes temporal sovereignty under the rule of Christ.

Ordinaries. A term used to refer to certain basic geometric *charges* such as the *pale*, *fess*, *chevron*, *chief*, *cross*, *bend* and *bend sinister*, *pile*, and *saltire*.

Oriflamme. 1. The imperial *banner* of France. 2. A long, pointed banner hanging on a transverse staff (see page 47).

Palisado Crown. A coronet composed of pointed stakes set about a rim; similar to a *crown vallery*.

Pallet. A narrow *pale*.

Pallium. The ecclesiastical pallium shown in the form of a Y, the top limbs issuing from the corners of the shield (see page 239, center).

Panther. A mythical beast (see page 115).

Parted. The term used to signify that a *field* is divided into different segments.

Passant. Walking along.

Pean. A variant of *ermine* composed of gold ermine spots on black (see page 87).

Pedestal. See pages 202 f.

Pegasus. The mythical winged horse which with the advent of humanism became a symbol of poetic inspiration, and also penetrated into heraldry (see page 116).

Pellet. A black *roundel*, also called an ogress or gunstone.

This section from the family tree of the French royal house illustrates the connection between the founders of the Bourbon line and Louis XIII.
The upper row contains portraits of the dukes of Bourbon with their wives. This main branch breaks off abruptly and is only temporarily replaced by subsidiary offshoots. After the murder of King Henry III in 1589, it was necessary to refer back seven generations in order to find the nearest candidate for succession to the throne. This was a

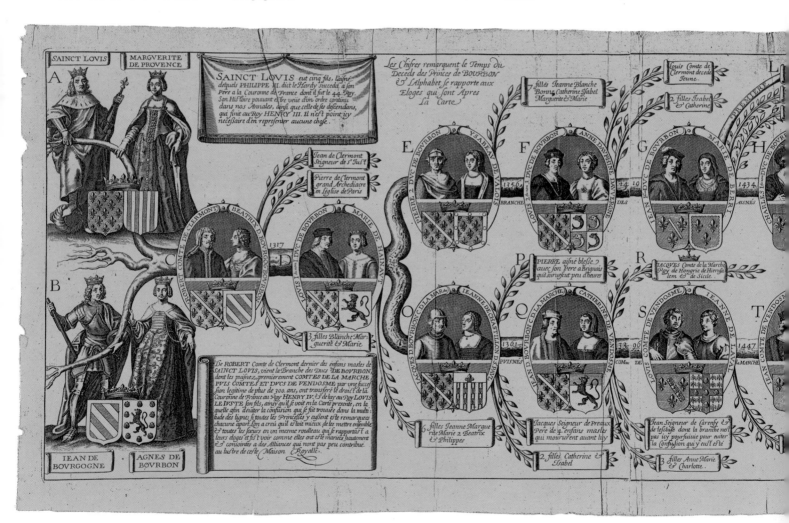

nobleman living in the Pyrenees, the duke of Vendôme, who had already inherited the title of king of Navarra through his mother and who then became Henry IV.

Orle. A *bordure* standing away from the edge of the shield by its own width (see page 89).

Over All. Used of a *charge* which is superimposed on several other charges. (See *surmounted*.)

Pale. An *ordinary* consisting of a broad vertical band down the central third of the shield (see page 89).

Pentagram. Five-pointed version of the seal of Solomon.

Per Bend, Per Bend Sinister. See page 88.

Per Fess. See page 88.

Per Pale. See pages 89 and 92.

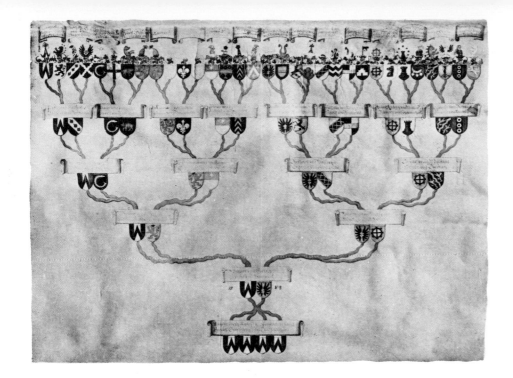

Family tree of four children of the Bernese noble family of von Erlach. It shows clearly how the number of ancestors in each preceding generation doubles with mathematical logic. An ancestral tree made as early as this rarely goes back as far as the great-great-great-grandparents. Here the mother of a pair of great-great-grandparents is missing and there is a gap in the tree.

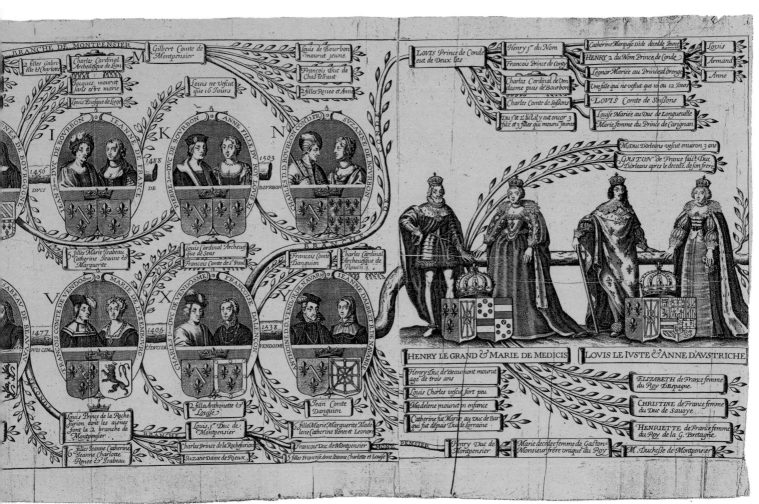

Pheon. An arrowhead.

Phoenix. A mythical bird, often depicted resembling an eagle, with outstretched wings, issuing from flames (see page 130).

Pile. An *ordinary* consisting of a triangular wedge emerging from the *chief* or, when reserved, the *base*.

Placing of Charges. Charges are described in such a way as to indicate their manner of placing on a *field*. Where three like charges are placed on a shield, two are always deemed to be in the *chief* and one in the *base* unless otherwise mentioned. Charges placed in a row across the middle of the shield are "in fess"; vertically down the middle they are "in pale."

49

The Roman eagle which Napoleon I chose in 1804 as the symbol of his empire, and lost in 1815, underwent a renaissance under his nephew Napoleon III. This time the pomp and splendor were to last eighteen years. The eagle reappeared on flag staffs, and sprigs of laurel and oak decorated the cross of the *Légion d'honneur*, as they had before.

Four years after the founding of the empire Napoleon created, by decree of 1 March 1808, a new nobility intended for a new form of heraldry. While following the traditional rules, a system based on the status of the person favored was envisaged. The knights of the *Légion d'honneur* were given the models shown here for arranging the cross of the order on their shields; the models were

Plate. A silver *roundel.*

Plume. A very popular crest composed of a bunch of feathers.

Pomeis. A green *roundel.*

Portcullis. A vertically lowered gate consisting of horizontal and vertical *bars,* the latter pointed at the bottom (see page 211).

Potent. The ancient name for a crutch, shown heraldically as a *charge* in the form of a T.

Proper. Anything depicted in its natural colors.

Quartered. See page 89.

Quartering. A segment of the armorial shield which may be smaller than an actual quarter. Each quartering represents arms inherited from a different branch of the *armiger's* family.

Quintuple Mount. A *triple mount* surmounted by two single mounts.

Rampant. Rearing up; used of beasts.

Reguardant. Used of a creature looking back over its shoulder.

Rising. Used of a bird with its wings open, ready for flight.

Sea-. Prefix to indicate a creature with a fish's tail.

Sea-monsters. Often created in heraldry by attaching a fish's tail to the top half of a creature's body. The resulting hybrids are called sea-lions, sea-unicorns, etc.

Sejant. Sitting down.

Semy. A *field* is described as semy when it is strewn with small *charges.*

Sextuple Mount. A *quintuple mount* with a sixth mount added on top.

Shakefork. Shown as a Y, the ends pointed and not touching the edge of the shield.

Sinister. The heraldic term for left. (See *dexter.*)

Slipped. Used to describe the stalk of a flower.

Spiked Mace. The correct *blazon* for a war mace covered with spikes, to distinguish it from the civic mace.

Stains. Mixed colors sometimes used in heraldry; the principle stains are murrey (mulberry color), sanguine (blood red), and tenné (orange).

Standard. A long tapering flag with the arms in the hoist and *badges,* crest, and motto on the fly (page 130).

Statant. Standing.

Surmounted. One *charge* laid over another.

Throughout. Used of a *charge* touching the edge of the shield, which does not normally do so.

Thunderbolt. Twisted bar, normally with rays of lightning behind it.

Tierced in pairle. Divided into three in the form of a Y (see page 89).

also to apply to municipal arms. We will quote just one example from the comprehensive list *(far right):* the canton on the shield serves as the position for a personal emblem. If it is to dexter and blue with a gold figure, the person is a count; if it is to sinister and is red with a silver figure, the person is a baron. Prefects and mayors bear an embattled wall, subprefects an unembattled one. With prefects the wall is surmounted by an oak sprig, with subprefects by an olive sprig. Our picture therefore indicates the rank of a "baron prefect."

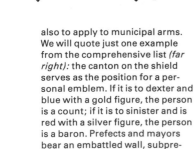

Rompu. Broken; used particularly of a *chevron,* the center broken and enhanced.

Roundel. A disk; different colored roundels have their own special names. (See *plate, pomeis,* and *torteau.*)

Salade. A medieval helmet like a broadbrimmed steel hat (see page 147).

Saltire. An *ordinary* consisting of a diagonal cross, the shape of the St. Andrew's cross (see page 107).

Scepter. A rod-shaped emblem of rank bearing a symbol of authority at the upper end (page 240).

Schirmbrett. The German term for an early type of crest (see pages 152 f.).

Tincture. The generic term for the colors in the heraldic palette, including the metals and *furs* (see page 86).

Torteau. A red *roundel.*

Trefoil. A three-leaved figure usually slipped at the *base.*

Triple Mount. A *charge* usually placed at the bottom of the shield and serving as a *base* for the armorial design itself.

Tyger. The heraldic tyger is similar to the antelope but with a lion's body and no horns. The natural tiger is usually called a Bengal Tiger.

Unguled. Used of the hooves of certain animals when of a different *tincture* from the body.

Unicorn. A mythological beast with an antelope's body, lion's tail and a bearded horse's head with a single horn on its forehead (see pages 116 f.).

Urinant. Used to describe a fish when plunging head downward.

Vair. There are two principal *furs* used in heraldry, of which vair is one. It consists of the skins of small squirrels joined head to tail (see page 86).

Vairy. A type of *fur,* a variation of *vair* (see page 86).

Visor. The movable part on the front of a helmet. In British heraldry the position of the visor denotes the rank of the bearer.

Winged. With wings attached; used of animals and monsters. A charge used in Germany, for example, consists of an animal's forepaw or eagle's talon joined directly to a single wing. Another is a clasp attached to an eagle's wing with a cloverleaf at the top.

Woman's Arms. See *lozenge.*

Wreath. 1. A wreath consisting of twisted strips of material serves as a link between the crest and the helmet, particularly in English heraldry (see page 162). 2. A wreath of leaves may be used to surround any *charge* on a shield, which is then said to be "wreathed."

Wyvern. A dragon without hind legs (i.e., more serpentine.)

Three coats of arms of the well-known diplomat and statesman Charles-Maurice de Talleyrand-Périgord, Prince of Bénévent (1745–1838). They express in heraldic forms some of the stages in his eventful life.
From left to right:
Ancestral arms of Périgord.
Arms as Napoleonic prince of

Voided. With the center cut out.

Vol. A French term for two wings joined at the base with the tips upward.

Volant. Flying.

Vulned. Wounded.

War Cry or *Cri de Guerre.* Often used as a motto by ancient families (see page 203).

Water Bouget. Symbolically depicted as two water bags pendant from a yoke (see page 156).

Wavy. One of the lines of partition (see page 89).

Yale. A very English monster, a goatlike creature with teeth like a boar, feet like a unicorn, and spots of various colors (renowned as a supporter in the arms of John Beaufort, legitimate bastard of John of Gaunt).

Yoke. A still-existing feature in the state arms of Spain (see page 210, the badge of Ferdinand I).

Zebra. Used as supporters in the arms of Botswana, as a symbol of cooperation between blacks and whites. It illustrates the tendency among newly independent nations to replace conventional European supporters with indigenous animals (see pages 186 ff.).

Bénévent, consisting of the imperial eagle in chief, and beneath it the ancestral arms and the boar of Bénévent; also the chain of the *grand aigle* of the *Légion d'honneur* and armorial drape with a prince's crown.
Arms reflecting his appointment as *Pair de France* (1815) and as duke (1817) after the Bourbon restoration; they consist of the ancestral arms together with cloak and crown.
The arms were augmented again in 1845, as a nephew had married the heiress of the Prussian title of duke of Sagan.

The consecutive arms of the former kingdom of Prussia provide an example of the changes that can take place on one coat of arms.

The first small shield *(below left)* bears the arms created in 1701 for the new title of king.

The second small shield *(below right)* contains the arms of the eleven provinces into which the kingdom of Prussia was divided after 1867 and the family arms of the reigning dynasty.

The large achievement *(opposite)* also brings together, as quarterings in one shield, the arms of fifty-two small territories, dukedoms, and counties which the king of Prussia had considered worthy of being represented in his overall title. The savage men and other decorative motifs could be changed according to circumstances, or left out altogether.

The king of Prussia normally replaced the crest with a royal crown.

The variety and richness of forms to be found in heraldry do not depend only on the endless possible combinations of geometric patterns with innumerable figures from every part of the cosmos. Combinations of several coats of arms are frequently vivid representations of great historical connections. The form and color of the various ornaments, moreover, are often highly artistic in their effect.

THE ACHIEVEMENT OF ARMS

An achievement of arms is the full armorial bearings consisting of the heraldic escutcheon, the armorial helmet, and the crest with the mantling attached to the helmet. High rank or specific personal privileges can be expressed through additional decorative devices.

SHIELD

The shield or escutcheon with its charges is the main component of a coat of arms. Until 1500 its form was governed by the shape of the shields actually used for fighting; since then graphic considerations have tended to prevail.

HELMET

The helmet is responsible for the invention of heraldry, for a closed helmet hid the wearer's face and made it necessary to invent some sign by which he could be recognized. The helmet in a coat of arms is the vehicle for displaying a crest. The helmet together with its crest may be replaced by a rank crown.

CREST

This consists of sculpted figures affixed to the top of the helmet. In some traditions the mantling forms a part of the crest, whereas in others it is a separate element which is also attached, often by means of a wreath or a coronet, to the helmet, below the crest.

SUPPORTERS

Supporters are decorative devices which do not form part of the arms proper. They usually have the form of men or animals. They are especially common in national or royal arms, among the higher nobility, and in the arms of corporate bodies. They usually stand on a pedestal, called a "compartment."

Other additional devices may include orders, mottoes, armorial cloaks and tents, banners taken in battle, and various kinds of weaponry.

GOTT MIT UNS

This assortment of badges and emblems *(right)* shows some common background shapes that have been used.

Seal of the seneschal of Flanders, Hélier von Wavrin, with the imperial eagle (ca. 1185).

Emblem of the Mamluk emir Toka Timu, Governor of Rahaba, Egypt, 1350.

Herald's coat with imperial eagle.

A representation of King Henry I of England (reigned 1100–1135). This king gave his son-in-law Geoffrey a shield with several small lions on it.

The two men bearing shields are the earliest evidence of the transferring of arms from a man to his descendants. The knight with the narrower shield is Geoffrey Plantagenet; the likeness is from the enamel portrait at Le Mans, painted in 1151. The knight with the shorter shield is William Longespée. He was in fact Geoffrey's illegitimate grandchild. His arms are not only shown on his tomb, but are also recorded in color by Matthew Paris. Both the tomb and Matthew Paris confirm that his shield contains six lions.

Although the science of heraldry spread fairly quickly, it was not created overnight. Its origin in battles where armor made friend and foe indistinguishable is reflected in the use of the word "arms" in both a heraldic and a military sense. In the German language, the congruent words *Waffen* (weapons) and *Wappen* (arms) imply the same connection. Thus the need arose for knights to distinguish themselves through combinations of shape and color. There were two possible solutions: either to divide a flat surface geometrically into at least two colored sections, or to use an already memorable or meaningful figure as a distinguishing sign. In the latter case the use of color was a secondary consideration; in the first it was indispensable.

These two possibilities were recognized by all nations as a practical solution. The development of arms in a heraldic sense was dependent on the social order of feudalism. Based on the obligation of the vassal to fight in the army of his feudal lord, this system laid the basis of the main elements which eventually formed a complete coat of arms.

There were in any case already many signs which more or less everyone knew. Unfortunately the

rules of heraldry did not begin to be written down until the fourteenth century and cannot be applied retrospectively to an earlier period. One of the most knowledgeable heraldic experts, Gustav Adalbert Seyler, referred to this era as one of primeval confusion in which basic trends could nevertheless be recognized.

The feudal system was based on mutual trust within the confines of a firmly established social hierarchy. The clothing which one wore and the degree to which one could decorate it served then as it does today as an indication of status. As the subject was dependent on the mercy of his master, he must, in order to benefit from it, show that he was worthy of this favor. He therefore needed a "certificate," a document which must obviously be genuine. So long as one could rely on the pledge of a fellow vassal, in other words as long as the latter lived, it was enough to have "witnesses" whose names are found at the end of documents recording legal transactions. To give their testimony validity they appended to the document a wax seal which if not wholly permanent would at least last several centuries. Types of seal were developed to express the social position of their owners, some of whom were extremely useful to the developing science of heraldry. This was especially true with the overwhelming majority of the nobility. Highly placed people showed themselves fullface, or in action as a soldier or huntsman. Heraldic signs were only of subsidiary importance here, a fact which has made research into the early history of arms of state a difficult task today.

The most important charges – the cross, the lily, the eagle, the lion, and the dragon, reach back into the mists of the past. It was logical that they should become the marks of royalty, for they had been this before the emergence of heraldic arms.

In researching the early history of heraldry, we are almost exclusively dependent on pictorial sources. Then, as today, nobody thought of recording in writing something which developed slowly and more or less unnoticed.

We must also test the pictorial sources for authenticity. The more time that had elapsed between the event and its depiction, the more

Mon of a Japanese family: *Hidari-mi-tsüdomoe* (triple wave spiral turning to the left).

Mon of the Tokugawa family: *Aoi go mon* (three mallow leaves in a circle).

One of the *mon* of the Minamoto family: *Maru ni futatsubiki biki* (two bars in a ring).

Emblem of the Egyptian emir Arkatây.

Badge of Egypt around 1500.

Badge of the supposed builder of the Alhambra in Granada, King Muhammad-ibn Nasr (1231–1272).

Baroque frame to an oval, 1646 (Weihenstephan monastery).

Escutcheon of the Russian Soviet Republic, created in baroque style on 26 July 1918.

this authenticity will be in doubt. Thus when Biblical kings are shown wearing a crown, the picture is not a true historical representation, but merely a translation into the terms familiar to the artist in his own day. Thus pictures are far less reliable than other kinds of testimony which speak out of their own time. And foremost among the latter are seals. Since they served for verification, they had to inspire confidence. This they did by portraying a person's customary appearance as far as armor, clothing, and bearing were concerned, if not the face. Portraitlike rendering of facial features was not achieved until the middle of the fourteenth century. The seals of mounted horsemen from early times are extremely valuable, since by showing the horse as well as the rider they offer some standard of comparison by which one can fairly positively judge the size of his armor and weapons. From such images one can also gain an idea of how the different parts of the armor fitted together. This in turn can help to elucidate other representations, such as seals on which the person in question is shown as an armed statue. In this way we can collect relatively accurate data for a period from which there are very few written accounts. Apparently insignificant signs on coins can make clear to us, for example, the difference between the cross and the eagle on the masthead of Carolingian ships. In the same way we can interpret many customs of importance in early

heraldry, such as the behavior of the Crusaders after taking a stronghold. We will return to such questions later. But now we must concentrate our attention on the shield, since this developed into the essential basis of the coat of arms.

The kings of Castile and León used canting arms on their seals (a castle and a lion) even in preheraldic times. King Ferdinand III, who became king of Castile in 1217 and of León in 1230, combined them in a revolutionary manner on the quarters of a shield, as shown in this sketch by Matthew Paris.

The illustration of St. Michael of Abraham's tapestry in the cathedral at Halberstadt (1165–1190) shows clearly how much the shields of the time were curved.

The two seals of Richard Coeur de Lion, corresponding to the two different eras of his reign, differ from one another in essential if not obvious ways. Both the helmets and the shields are different. After his delayed return from the third Crusade, Richard revoked the older seal and had himself crowned a second time, in 1194 (he had been first crowned in 1189). The introduction of a new seal was an apt measure to accompany this event.

He who would become a master in shield work, must first of all make four new pieces with his own hand, a jousting saddle,... a jousting shield, he must make them in six weeks, the masters must look at them to see if they are good... and that he can also paint them as lords, knights and squires require of him.

Extract from the
Wiener Handwerksordnung, 1410

The relationship between people and arms is expressed in the shield-shaped seals which exactly reproduced the heraldic escutcheon in its contemporary form, with the addition of an inscription referring to the bearer of the seal round the edge. The example shown above is the seal of Johann von Steglitz.

The god of the smiths, Hephaestus, called Vulcan by the Romans, forges the shield of Achilles at the

The shield became the most important bearer of what were originally simply called "signs" or badges. Later these signs developed into pictures, which could be divided into heraldic motifs and ordinary figures. But before this happened the shield underwent centuries of development as a defensive and even an offensive weapon. Primitive men soon discovered that

formed wooden planks which they held in front of them to ward off the ax-blows of an adversary. It remained to develop an attachment by which the plank could be held comfortably, leaving an arm free to wield the ax.

Remarkably enough, virtually every early shield we know of, from the most far distant past to the

behest of the latter's mother, Thetis (on the right, next to the already finished breastplate). The goddess Athene (with helmet and lance) looks on, as Hephaestus is assisted by three Cyclopes.

they had neighbors with whom they came into competition in the struggle for food. Inevitably they quarreled with them and used their most common tool, the ax, as an offensive weapon. Making use of the available materials, they

time of Christ, is round in shape. Roman sculptures of soldiers in three-quarter view show how the weapon was used. The shape of the shield, its outline, and its belled center are all evidence of the gradual refinement of weaponry, which had

A knight's shield from Seedorf, a monastery founded in 1197 on the Vierwaldstätter See. Now in the Swiss National Museum in Zurich, it was cleaned and scientifically examined in 1951. The silver lion on a blue ground represents the arms of the monastery's founder Arnold von Brienz (d. 1225). The Seedorf shield is the only "Nor-man" shield which has survived. It has been modified by cutting off the upper rounded edge close to the lion's head to achieve the shape which had become fashion-able around 1220. The leather covering which is wrapped round the shield from front to back is still visible.

The shield was the original defensive weapon. It protected its bearer against the blows of his adversary. But this function alone was not enough, it also had to frighten the enemy, as many of the Greek myths relate. The best known is the legend of Medusa (see page 70). Costly shields decorated with figures are also mentioned in the *Iliad*. An example is the shield of Achilles (see page 56). Even iconoclastic religions did not entirely renounce decoration, finding it in geometric patterns. But they naturally lacked the elements which go to make up heraldry.

of course to keep pace with that of the enemy. The predominant role which the shield was to play in heraldry can be linked with the ideal value attributed to it in ancient times by the Germans. As Tacitus relates in his *Germania* (ca. A.D. 100), the shield featured in numerous ceremonies. In puberty rites, a shield was handed to the youth to signify that he had become a man. The loss of the shield in battle was evidence of an act of cowardice, which was punished by exclusion from all worldly and religious ceremonies. When the Franks elected a king, they sat him on a shield and raised him high in the air. The spectators indicated their approval by beating on their shields. While Tacitus mentions that they used particular colors, without elucidating any further, the *Edda* (mid-thirteenth century) reports that the raising of a red shield on a ship's

land, his army consisted of mounted knights whom the Anglo-Saxons, for all their staying power, could not resist. The pictorial record of the Battle of Hastings on the famous Bayeux tapestry, and other scenes on this same work of art, show for the first time a shield which was henceforth to be known as the Norman shield. In fact it was not introduced by the Normans; they had adopted it from their numerous opponents in the south. In any discussion of the further development of the shield, therefore, it must be made clear whether we are talking about the shield of a horseman or a foot-soldier, and whether this distinction is in fact relevant. This also applies to the war shields of non-European peoples, where a distinction must be made between small shields held on the arm and large ones driven into the ground to make a wall.

Above, left to right:

Battle scene of men with axes and round shields. Rock engraving, Bohuslän, Sweden.

Cadmus slaying the dragon before founding the city of Thebes. Detail from a Laconian vase.

Persian miniature, representing Chosro II of Persia (A.D. 591).

Roman legionary. Sculpture from the Trajan column, Rome.

Germanic warrior. From the side of a font, second century, Gündestrup, Denmark.

mast was interpreted at the time as a declaration of war.

In the *Sachsenspiegel*, the different feudal estates are described as *Heerschilde* – literally "army shields." This expression indicates just how totally European life in the Middle Ages was based on the use of force. From the tenth century onward the waging of war was governed by the horse, whose rapidity in attack was amply demonstrated by the successful mounted armies of the Huns and the Moors.

When William, Duke of Normandy, afterwards known as the Conqueror, crossed over the Channel in the last successful invasion of England,

With the perfection of equestrian armor in Europe, the shield lost its military significance but acquired its function as the major item in a coat of arms.

Around 1500, graphic considerations became all-important in its design. But independently of this, shields continued to be made after the heyday of tourneying around 1500. They were masterpieces of craftsmanship, used by persons of knightly rank on ceremonial occasions.

Peoples who remained untouched by the revolution in techniques of warfare and were spared the use of gunpowder continued to fight with lances, bows and arrows, and shields until the

arrival of the colonial powers in their countries. In the last few decades some of these shields have been incorporated into national coats of arms, as for example in Kenya.

As a result of the violence which accompanies many political demonstrations today, the shields of the Middle Ages are once again in use. Classic materials such as wood and wickerwork have been joined by plastic, sometimes transparent. As well as the classical round shield, many police forces possess rectangular shields with small spyholes, with which they can form phalanxes reminiscent of the assault troops of the Middle Ages.

Thus the shield, besides being a piece of armor, became a sign of recognition, either by its size,

Japanese standing shields with archers kneeling behind. On the shields, which were known as *Tate,* are two black bars and beneath them a black *Go-san-no-kri-Mon.* Detail from a colored woodcut by the painter Sadahida showing the side of the Daimyo of Ephichigo, Uesugi Kenshin, in the Battle of the River Saigawa, 1554.

outline, or elaborate decoration. An additional aid for identification was the pennant attached to the end of a rider's lance. The fact that the pennant was made of movable material and the shield of stiff material partly explains why initially the designs on these two elements were not necessarily identical. The suitability of the shield as a basis for painted decoration or applied metalwork was governed by the arrangement of stiffening ribs and the type of handgrip used. The stiffening ribs generally extended outwards from the middle of the shield, and in the earliest shields there was a large hole to accommodate the holder's fist. This hole was covered with a massive boss, the *umbo* (literally "navel"). There was further reinforcement round the edge of the

Two heraldic seals of Duke Rudolf IV of Austria, 1360. If the knight on the seal is to be represented as turned towards the right, he must be engraved turned towards the left. But the engraver must then show the shield in a contorted position if the decorated exterior, and not merely the uninteresting inner face, is to be seen. On the other hand a knight riding towards the left can present the shield in such a way as to produce the customary heraldic combination of a slanting shield with helmet and crest above.

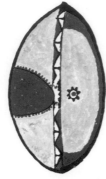

The armorial shield of Kenya *(left)* reflects the traditional shape of native warrior shields, such as that of the Masai *(below* and *left middle)*.

Many native peoples express their desire for ornamentation by painting their faces or sometimes their entire bodies. The Nuba warrior of the Sudan *(above left)* has decorated his face with a design reminiscent of those on the Masai (Kenya) shields *(above center and right)*.

shield, which had to sustain heavy blows and was considered so important that oaths were sworn by it. We know that on the earliest shields the leather arm loops and handgrips were fastened to the back with nails and screws which were driven through the wood and protruded at the front. This was an obvious invitation to the maker to decorate the ends artistically with screwed-on rosettes, as can be clearly seen on the shield of Valère (see page 127). Unfortunately no such shield has survived sufficiently intact for us

Norman soldiers crossing the Channel to invade England. The long shields make a formidable impression.

to trace the exact arrangement of the handgrip. However it would appear from various reconstructions that the mounting was not always the same and there were two possible ways of carrying the shield. One thing which is certain is that in addition to the handgrip there was a neckband or sling by which the shield could be carried on one's back while traveling. It also freed the second hand for an extra-powerful sword stroke in battle. As we have said, the screwed ends of the strap fastenings lent themselves to decoration, which explains for instance the network of chains on shields from Navarra (see page 229).

The reinforcing ribs clearly served as a basis for many armorial designs; their cross-shaped

Police marching on demonstrators with round basketwork shields, Zurich, 1973. The effect of a phalanx of men is intimidating under any circumstances.

The demonstrators in the student riots of May 1968 stormed and occupied the Théâtre de l'Odéon in Paris. They defended themselves with items from the theater's wardrobe department. The weapons from *Die Entführung aus dem Serail* came in particularly useful.

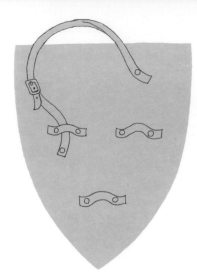

Full-length representation of Count Geoffrey of Anjou, called Plantagenet (d. 1150). He was given the nickname of "broom plant" (genet= genista) by posterity because he supposedly carried a sprig of broom on his helmet. The colored enamel portrait from his tomb in Le Mans cathedral does not show it, however. But it does show the shield which Henry I presented to him in 1127, on the occasion of Geoffrey's marriage to Henry's sole surviving daughter. The realistic rendering of the reinforcing ribs and the *umbo* make it difficult to estimate the total number of lions on the shield.

arrangement lends itself particularly well to this. The cross, after all, had been a generally accepted ideological symbol since time immemorial.

Once the sign on the shield had become the most important means of recognition, it was in the bearer's interest to make sure that it matched any others he carried. Apart from the simple pennant, which was divided geometrically, there appeared elaborate rectangular banners whose designs matched those on the shields.

Up to the fifteenth century, people were reluctant to carry armorial shields divided into more than four "quarters" or fields. But after the decorative effect of armorial designs was recognized they established a place for themselves in the graphic arts. One increasingly popular design was the arrangement of several shields around a central shield, usually divided into not more than four quarters. It was to be found on tombstones, where one could make a display of the arms of distinguished forbears, as well as on royal seals and memoranda. As the armorial escutcheon developed away from the fighting shield itself and into a shield-shaped graphic framework, so the demand for easy recognition tended to be forgotten and all the arms to be represented were brought together on the shield-shaped surface. To us today, a royal banner at first appears to be merely a brightly colored patchwork of designs, but on closer inspection it reveals a series of very real relationships. The basic principle of easy recognition still applied to the individual fields, as if they still had to be viewed from a distance.

The leather straps and loops with which the shield was hung round the wearer's neck, or carried under his arm, were fastened with screws driven through the wood. The ends protruding on the outside were decorated with ornamental plates or extended into a complete coat of arms. No original shield has survived with the straps intact. The arrangement of the straps can be reconstructed from the position of the holding screws.

With the creation of coats of arms, the reinforcing ribs of preheraldic shields mostly disappeared or became an integral part of the arms themselves.

Above, top to bottom:
1 The territory of Cleves
2 The town of Cleves
3 The town of Wesel
4 Armorial shield in Padua, 1283

The standard of Queen Mary of Great Britain (1867–1953) demonstrates the richness of effect which can be obtained with quite simple figures. This is achieved partly through the multiplication of pictorial subjects; partly through the variation of geometric patterns; and partly also through the combination of single armorial fields which in themselves are clear and distinct, but which combine to make a brightly colored patchwork, each segment having its own significance. Armorial flags are fortunately free from the constrictions imposed by the shape of a shield (opposite, top). This flag is twice as long as it is deep, and almost all the quarters can be conveniently square in shape. The individual motifs are explained in the appendix.

INFLUENCE OF THE CRUSADES

The Crusaders took their native customs with them to the Holy Land. This is particularly evident in the seals they used on their documents. In the examples shown here, only the building and the Greek inscriptions betray an Eastern influence.

Seal of the temple at the tomb of Christ.

Seal of the Order of the Knights Templar.

Seal of Hugo Archbishop of Nazareth.

Seal of Matthew Bishop of Famagusta.

Seal of Baldwin II of Flanders, Latin Emperor of Constantinople (d. 1274).

Right:
Christ leading the Christian knights.

The deep beliefs of Western Christianity, joined to a general wanderlust and desire for adventure, led to the military expeditions which are given the collective name of Crusades. The knights who set out to wrest the holy tomb of Christ and the surrounding territory from the "unbelievers" of Islam, stitched to their shoulders a cross made from a strip of material – they "took the cross." A prince who promised a pope to go on a Crusade might save his throne; to break his promise could mean excommunication.

The first Crusade, called for by Pope Urban II at the Council of Clermont in 1095, had important consequences in the years 1097 to 1099. They led to the foundation of principalities in the Holy Land, which were joined with the kingdom of Jerusalem in the last year of that century. In the new principalities, feudal attitudes were even more strongly expressed than was possible in Europe. But much was learned from the Islamic foe in the art of military communication. These experiences were exploited to the full in Europe up to the time of the second Crusade, which arose from the reconquering of Edessa by the

was nevertheless formed in the fourth decade of the twelfth century. At this time the armed groups from different regions, numbering some hundred thousand men each, created a hitherto unknown problem. The Crusaders needed to

Crusader supply ship guarded by crossbowmen. The welcoming knights await it on the left, while on the right lurk their opponents.

Turks in 1144 and was undertaken with somewhat less enthusiasm than the first. Heraldry did not develop into a systematic collection of recognition signs during the Crusades themselves, but

know in what language they could communicate with one another. In Palestine – apart from the Italians who stuck to their own language – the Crusader families spoke a kind of pidgin French.

Seal of Philip I of Flanders (b. 1243), titular emperor and son of Baldwin II.

Seal of Catherine (b. 1274), daughter of Philip I of Flanders, Countess of Valois (1320).

Seal of the Crusader Geoffrey of Méry, 1238.

This praying figure of the leader of the papal knights, Marshal Hüglin von Schöneck in St. Leonard's church in Basel, conveys a humble disposition in a knightly Crusader. His armor is lavishly decorated with his own coat of arms.

The everyday language of the natives was still Arabic, however. This situation was a major impetus to further heraldic developments.

Before the third Crusade, the kings of France (Philippe II) and England (Henry II) and Count Philip of Flanders met at Gisors in northeast France on 13 January 1188. They decided on particular colors for the crosses to be worn by their men. These were red for the French, white for the English, and green for the Flemish. After Henry II died, Richard I, Cœur de Lion, led the English participants in the Crusade. Every Crusader could now recognize by the color of the cross worn by his fighting companion what language he spoke. The often posed question of what was the "correct" shape for this or that cross cannot be answered definitively.

The surviving sources show that in the twelfth century there were many types of cross, differently shaped and with a different number of arms. In fact the wearing of the cross was not restricted to the strip of material worn by the Crusader, but extended to all possible uses.

The era of the Crusades lasted from 1096 to 1291, nearly two centuries, and is significant far beyond the actual campaigns in the Holy Land. Although politically unrewarding, the Crusades

The lodgings of the dukes of Brittany and Bourbon and their companions at a tournament, decorated with their banners and coats of arms (after the tournament book of King René).

The Lincolnshire knight Sir Geoffrey Luttrell sets out for a tournament. His ladies wish him luck and hand him the last pieces of armor

had a strong cultural influence on the Western world. The constant contact between the Crusaders and their strange surroundings was to have far-reaching consequences, even though the principalities were not rooted in the oriental population but formed a kind of garrison regime as long as they lasted. Their common sign was the cross, modified in form and color as necessity demanded. This influence has continued right up to the present day. The cross incorporated in the flags of the Scandinavian countries, for example, is directly traceable to the national crosses of the Crusaders.

The orders of knights, in particular, recognized the need to distinguish their signs from one another through differences which were not only confined to color. The arms of the states which rose on Palestinian soil were not based on the cross, since they were held in common, but rather on the family arms of the princes who had become their leaders. Therefore the oriental influence, so noticeable in the way of life of the Crusaders, is hardly to be seen in their heraldry.

The Crusades were not the only military undertakings of the Middle Ages. Petty feuds and quarrels between neighbors filled the lives of a social class whose strength was based on the

after he has been hoisted onto his horse. His wife, Agnes Sutton, holds the bucketlike helmet with its protective crest and the lance with a pennant. His daughter-in-law, Beatric Scrope, will hand him the shield last of all. All the characters are in full heraldic clothing. A notable feature of the armor is the so-called *ailettes* or shoulder pieces which were in fashion for a time.

allowed to take part in tournaments was considerably restricted. It was the aim of the established nobility, whose members could show four noble ancestors, to bar the access of rising families to their closed society. In addition there was the condition that if a man wished to take part in a tournament, a member of the same family must have taken part in another tournament in the past fifty years. The ladies, for whose favor many rode in the lists, distributed the prizes. They made the tournaments a festive social occasion in which the highest social classes took part, often as fighters but even more

A smith *(right)* finishes working a helmet on the anvil while a serving girl brings him food and drink. Herr Dietmar der Sezzer *(far right)* came from Sazze, today Soss, a village between Baden and Vöslau in Austria. The knight splits open his opponent's head with a mighty two-handed swordstroke; the latter has not had time to get in his blow and has neglected to cover himself with his shield. One can see the neutrally painted inside of the shield.

power of arms, which had therefore to be constantly exercised and tested. Opportunities for military exhibition and display were always welcome; indeed, military parades have remained popular to this day. In the Middle Ages, the public taste for such spectacles was catered for by tournaments, which literary sources mention initially in the thirteenth century.

At first designed to test the fighting capabilities of the participants, these soon developed increasingly strict rules. Eventually these rules became so refined that the circle of people

often as spectators. It was essential for a young noble to prove himself in a tournament if he was to rise above esquire and become a knight. In order to become a knight a man also had to have taken part in a campaign, which meant that he had to make a "journey" against an enemy. The need for a suitable "enemy" prevented many a peaceful settlement of petty feuds. In tournaments one did not compete against real enemies. The question of who were to be opponents was decided by lot among people of similar rank at the initial "distribution," which was combined with the inspection of helmets. At the same time

demanded proof of the right to wear a crest with a crown on it, which usually required an imperial certificate. The lists drawn up by these organizers are sometimes also illustrated with arms (see pages 26 f.) and together form a valuable category among the occasional rolls.

In the fifteenth century, tourneying reached the height of its development, only to decline very rapidly around the middle of the century. Attempts to revive it, which earned the Emperor Maximilian I the nickname of "the last knight," had no lasting effect. The fact that a German emperor was so fond of tourneying seems apt

The ceremonial use of swords. A king dubs an esquire a knight. After the latter has watched the night through in a chapel and taken a ceremonial bath, he is given new clothing and his shield and banner. A light blow on the shoulder with a sword will be the last he may receive without responding. When his own sword has been buckled onto him, he will also be given the golden spurs which are the mark of a knight.

the participants were given a genealogical test, and often turned away. The list of those rejected in tournament books is astonishingly long.

The pageantry developed in tourneying was by definition thoroughly heraldic in character. The organization lay in the hands of the "crier," who was initially called *grôgiraere* and later on the "herald" (see page 14). The heralds made sure that the heraldic rules were kept, rejected coats of arms which broke the rules of color, and

enough when one remembers that the numerous pieces of armor which were invented for all the different types of tournament game have largely German and not French names. Yet the French language was and is the basic language of heraldry throughout the world.

The further development of heraldry was decisively influenced by various changes in tournament rules. In tourneying with a mace, instead of unseating one's opponent with a lance, one had

The presence of ladies gave competitive tournaments their initial stimulus. Their contribution might consist not only of applause but also an attractive garland or a costly brooch which they would hand ceremonially to the victor of their choice.

to strike off his crest with the mace (see pages 144 f.).

An announcement had to be made before each tournament as to which kind of tourneying was allowed. Under the emperor Maximilian numerous types were conceived of, including group battles which must have resulted in the most terrible carnage. But the tournaments were basically of three kinds – mace tourneying with club and sword in special half armor; tourneying proper, a full-scale fight with lance and sword in strengthened cuirasses; and tourneying on foot with lance and sword in cuirasses. Some combattants were proficient in all three.

Medusa shield of the emperor Charles V. From ancient times both armorers and sculptors were fond of representing the shield of Athene. Renaissance artists, too, tried their hand at this ancient theme. Medusa was so beautiful that Poseidon fell in love with her and lay with her in the temple of Athene Chrysaor and Pegasus. This angered Athene, who turned Medusa's luxuriant hair into snakes and cursed her so that anyone who looked at her would be turned to stone. By looking at Medusa indirectly, in a mirror, Perseus was able to cut off her head, which Athene then fastened to her shield.

Faced with an aggressive opponent, a man is forced to defend himself. Advances in weaponry call forth advances in defensive armor and vice versa. In heraldry this double process is recorded particularly in the design of the shield.

The Romans *(right)* recognized how important it was to cover vulnerable parts of the body. They also discovered that by forming rows of straight-edged shields they could build a whole wall or even a roof, which they called a *testudo* (tortoise), under the protection of which they could overrun fortifications.

Right:
The pillaging Norsemen terrorized the whole of the Western world in their ships. We do not know for certain where they found the inspiration for the elongated shields which were named "Norman" after them. They did not invent them, but extended their area of use.

The shields of the ancient Greeks were round and gave their bearers adequate protection only in hand-to-hand fighting. Achilles fell victim to this when he was killed by an arrow in his heel.

There were many variants of the two-man fights, as reported in illustrated tournament books. Among those described are jousting with lance and sword in strengthened cuirasses; fighting on foot with all kinds of weapons in cuirasses or special "battle cuirasses"; tilting with blunted lances in special half armor (tilting armor); and also "high armor tilting" with old-fashioned equipment. In addition, there was tilting in leg armor and tilting armor; Italian tilting in Italian-type tilting armor including leg armor, with the

opponents separated by a fence; German tilting in normal tilting armor; and mixed jousting with one man on horseback against an opponent on foot.

There was also running with sharpened lances in special half armor known as running armor, usually without protection on the arms; "field running" in running armor, including arm and leg armor and with a mechanism for disengaging the shield once it had been struck; a type of field

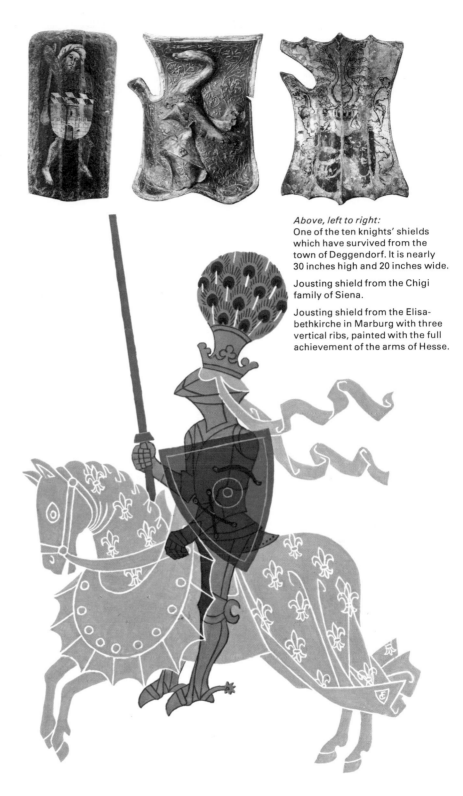

Above, left to right:
One of the ten knights' shields which have survived from the town of Deggendorf. It is nearly 30 inches high and 20 inches wide.

Jousting shield from the Chigi family of Siena.

Jousting shield from the Elisabethkirche in Marburg with three vertical ribs, painted with the full achievement of the arms of Hesse.

running, using a shield with detachable segments; "target running," a type of field running with a round shield or "target" instead of the kind with sections which would break off when struck; "shield running" in running armor with arms and jousting shield; Italian running, in complete special armor of Italian design; running in running armor with the shield firmly screwed in position; "plume running" in running armor with a mechanism for disengaging the shield when struck; a type of plume running with an arrangement of rollers instead of the plume; running in running armor with a high shield instead of helmet and plume; and running without helmet and plume, with a grill-like

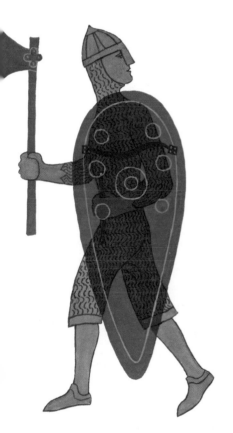

shield screwed in position. There were other variations too numerous to mention.

A tournament required considerable preparation – the challenge to an opponent and the preparation of the field, the lists, and the stands. These were tasks which fell to the heralds and their retinue. The customs and habits which they developed have been recorded more than once, most notably in the tournament book of King René the Good (see pages 13 f.). With changes in

the technology of weaponry the interest in tournaments declined. In 1439 the tournament at Landshut ended a long series. In 1479 the Frankish knights attempted to revive the practice, but the attempt ended eight years later with the last mace tournament at Worms. Here a zealous knight by the name of Siegmund von Gebsattel fought his fifth tournament in the space of scarcely three years. He had been in Stuttgart, Ingolstadt, Ansbach, and Bamberg as well as Worms. Once he was not admitted, at

The fact that a soldier could cover larger distances on horseback than on foot changed the techniques of armory. If a man did not have to carry his whole weight himself, he could be more heavily laden with iron. Thus his legs, for example, could be encased in armor as well; at the same time the shield could be made smaller.

RECONSTRUCTED
VIKING SHIELD

FUNERAL SHIELD OF
COUNT WALRAF III OF
TIERSTEIN (d. 1402)

FUNERAL SHIELD OF
BARON PETER OF
RARON, 1479

ETCHED IRON SHIELD,
VENETIAN, CIRCA 1500

FLORENTINE
ROUND SHIELD,
CIRCA 1550

The geometrically ideal form of the circle has also remained valid as an escutcheon for arms. This row shows round shields from many different epochs and cultures.

least twice his horse was borrowed, and on several occasions he was pitted against his lord. He let the latter pay his expenses, at least at Worms, and cut off his lord's crest in the tournament. But the lord had his revenge and took off his vassal's crest also. Taking part in a tournament was naturally a costly business and not within the means of most. By that time tourneying had become not only too expensive, but also useless as a form of practice. When events similar to tournaments were held in succeeding decades

knights had discovered the striking force of a couched lance held by a man fastened firmly to his horse instead of being thrown like a spear. But at Sempach in 1386 it had been proved that even foot-soldiers, spurred on by anger against their oppressors, could annihilate an army reinforced by lance-carrying riders. On that occasion the Swiss Confederation shook off the control of the duke of Austria and the landed nobility who supported him. Another revolutionary result was that of the Battle of Tannenberg in 1410 –

SHIELD IN THE STYLE
OF THE NORMAN SHIELDS,
LATE 11TH CENTURY

ELONGATED THREE-CORNERED
SHIELD WITH FAMILY ARMS,
2ND HALF OF 13TH CENTURY

ORNAMENTAL SHIELD OF
LANDGRAVE HENRY OF THURINGIA,
LATE 13TH CENTURY

STANDING SHIELD OF
THE TOWN OF ERFURT

Shields of every kind became more and more decorative as time went by. They could be used ceremonially, for example for funeral services, decorated with expensive damascening, or richly painted with full armorial bearings and whole scenes.

they were more correctly referred to as knightly games.

Real warfare, which meant the difference between political success or failure, between independence or subjection, had changed radically, especially since the opposing sides often used different tactics. When the Normans invaded England, their war-horses proved invincible to the mass of Anglo-Saxon foot-soldiers. The

the Poles call it the Battle of Grunwald after the command post of their king. Here the Germans offered battle in the customary knightly fashion, and were completely annihilated by the modern strategy of the Poles and Lithuanians.

The Battles of Sempach and Tannenberg yielded some comprehensive lists of highly interesting armorial banners and other flags taken by the winning side. After the total defeat of the oppo-

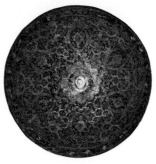

ARMORIAL FUNERAL SHIELD
OF CHARLES V,
AUGSBURG, 1558/1559

ROUND TOURNAMENT SHIELD,
ARABIC WORK FROM VENICE,
CIRCA 1600

ABYSSINIAN ROUND SHIELD,
LATE 17TH CENTURY

The arms of Christopher Beham from Nuremberg *(below)*, under which he inscribed his name in an album in 1593. The name means "man from Bohemia"; the arms are a play on words, since the

shield with its clearly marked central rib was regarded as typically Bohemian at the time.

nent there was so much booty that it was found worthwhile to make illustrated catalogues.

In the meantime gunpowder had been invented, though its use still presented some problems. Armaments technology in the fifteenth century was at first focused not so much on this as on the penetrating power of the crossbow, against which mail, however attractive an example of the armorer's art, was more or less ineffective. Nor was a shield of much use since one could

while on a campaign against the Friesians. But before the production of armor had been perfected to the point where a man was completely encased in iron, the shield was still necessary, since there was no lack of individual combatants against whom he had to measure himself.

The armed masses became larger and larger, until the vassals working out the four weeks' service demanded by their oath of fealty were

JOUSTING SHIELD
BY TADDEO DI BARTOLO,
ITALIAN, CIRCA 1300

JOUSTING SHIELD OF
KING MATTHEW CORVINUS
OF HUNGARY, PROBABLY
FUNERAL SHIELD, 1490

BURGUNDIAN PAVIS,
2ND HALF OF
15TH CENTURY

HUSSITE TYPE OF
STANDING SHIELD,
LATE 15TH CENTURY

HORSE'S HEAD ARMOR
BEARING THE ARMS OF
THE EMPEROR FERDINAND I,
AUGSBURG, 1558/1559

not see the crossbowmen, who could be hidden or covered by a wall of shields. The soldier had to be fitted out like a shield himself, completely encased in iron. The result was plate armor. This became increasingly artistic, increasingly mobile – thanks to skillfully constructed joints – but at the same time increasingly heavy. The lack of mobility had formerly cost the life of a German Roman king, Wilhelm of Holland, when in January 1256 he sank into a marsh

replaced by men enlisted and paid for longer periods. This resulted in the standing army and finally in the principle of general military service within a professional army.

The development of the kind of shield which survived in heraldry stems entirely from hand-to-hand fighting with sword and lance. The fact that sword-strokes were directed chiefly at the enemy's head had a decisive influence on the

73

design of the helmet. The lance carried on horseback was aimed at the entire body covering, but primarily the vulnerable knee. The oldest heraldic shield, the Norman shield, provides ample covering for the knee, and these shields were used both on foot and on horseback.

The classic triangular shield, named the "heater-shield" because in outline it resembles the base of a flatiron, could be smaller after the invention of the armored knee plate. But the basic form remained the same. Its elegance of shape may be the reason why it has remained the usual heraldic shield despite all changes of style, and although it does not provide enough room for arms with a multiplicity of charges.

Probably influenced by the practice of carrying a lance, a new form of shield appeared in the middle of the fourteenth century. We will refer to this as a jousting shield to distinguish it from the triangular shield. A man might well possess both types. Its distinguishing mark was a sharp indentation in the top, to the right of the bearer, which served to support the lance and was known as a lance-rest or *bouche*. In German the word *Tartsche* is used to distinguish it from the heraldic *Schild;* the former word is synonymous with the English "target" – somewhat misleadingly, since the English term refers to a small round shield and not the shape of the jousting shield. The oldest representation of a jousting shield can be found on the tomb of a knight, Ekro von Stern, who died in Würzburg in 1343.

At first the jousting shield differed from the three-cornered shield only in its outline. It was also painted with heraldic designs or decorated with relief patterns. But there was soon a development which had not taken place with the shield used hitherto. The surface of the jousting shield was painted with the full achievement of arms and even decorated with representations of whole scenes.

Departing from previous shields, which had been convex, the jousting shield tended to be more concave, a shape which could still be reinforced with ribs.

Similar to the jousting shield was the type which could be placed side by side to form a protective wall in front of foot-soldiers or crossbowmen. As these phalanxes were used principally by municipal defense forces, one finds whole sets of these shields in local museums in Germany and elsewhere.

A knight standing watch in the conventional pose of the fourteenth century. The imperial shield hangs at rest over his shoulder; his left hand rests on the pommel of his sword, the hilt of which is elongated because of the low-slung sword belt. His right hand holds a lance with a pennant bearing the Hungarian colors and a knob at the lower end enabling it to be rammed into the ground. There is no badge on the close-fitting doublet, which is delicately fringed along the lower hem. The man is armed for any untoward incident but not for battle. He wears a basinet on his head with a cloth camail beneath. Illustration from a Bohemian chess book of the second half of the fourteenth century.

Far left:
The standing shield for a crossbowman with the arms of a Roman king from the house of Austria, of the Georgian knighthood and the town of Winterthur, gives an idea of the extent to which heraldic designs can be mixed with ornamentation. It also demonstrates how the need for decoration always seems to predominate on articles of human warfare. The arms of the Roman king and the Georgian knighthood enable the shield to be dated fairly accurately. The single-headed eagle was only used by the future emperor Frederick III before he was crowned, that is, before 1452. He was also the first emperor to superimpose his own family arms on the breast of the eagle. By his renewal of the Georgian knighthood he also forged a tool which enabled him to combine family with imperial politics. The town of Winterthur at that time supported the Hapsburgs.

Left:
The cult of courtly love so abundantly cultivated by the medieval collections of lyrics was paid only lip service in reality and became the subject of open display. The theme was used to decorate items of armament such as horse trappings, crests, and even jousting shields like the one shown here. The picture appears considerably foreshortened in the illustration, because the shield bends back almost at ninety degrees. On one side is the lady, the object of adoration, in Burgundian costume. On the other kneels the love-sick knight, very young and only recently dubbed, as is indicated by the plume on his nearby jousting helmet. In the background is the figure of Death, to whom the youth will deliver himself if his suit is rejected. The scroll above spells out his sentiments as he cries, *"Vous ou la mort!"* ("You or death!")

THE NETHERLANDS
The Netherlands, including Belgium, provide some particularly early and important examples of heraldic development.

ENGLAND
In the classic (i.e., Gothic) period, the form of the armorial shield in the British Isles largely conformed to reality. The stylistic influences of the Renaissance made only an intermittent impact.
There is no proper term in English for the German *Tartsche* and it is usually refered to as a jousting or tournament shield. It is treated heraldically like other shields.

FRANCE
Here the classic form of shield has always prevailed, but artistic movements have produced some lively results in bookbinding and other fields.

GERMANY
Until around 1500, armorial shields in the German-speaking area matched the shields used for fighting. Humanism paved the way for the appearance of Italian models in heraldic art.
The knight's jousting shield had a strong influence on German heraldry. Late forms of this type of shield merge with symmetrically conceived Renaissance models.

ITALY
Italian heraldry introduced architectonic elements and typical forms into armorial art. The Italians call the last shield in the row a Samnite shield.
Italian jousting shields differ from others in that the notch which serves as a lance rest is cut in the upper edge of the shield. Shields in the form of a horse's forehead are essentially restricted to Italy

SPAIN
The half-round shield sometimes referred to in literature as the Spanish shield is correctly named, for it appears particularly early in Spain.

HUNGARY
The form of the shield in Hungarian heraldry depends very much on whether the foreign influence was more German or Italian at the time.

POLAND
The form of the shields in Polish heraldry is entirely influenced by German heraldry, which itself was exposed to Western stylistic influences and passed these on.

RUSSIA
Russian heraldry is not indigenous; as a result the forms of shield used are copied from those in the European countries lying to the west of Russia.

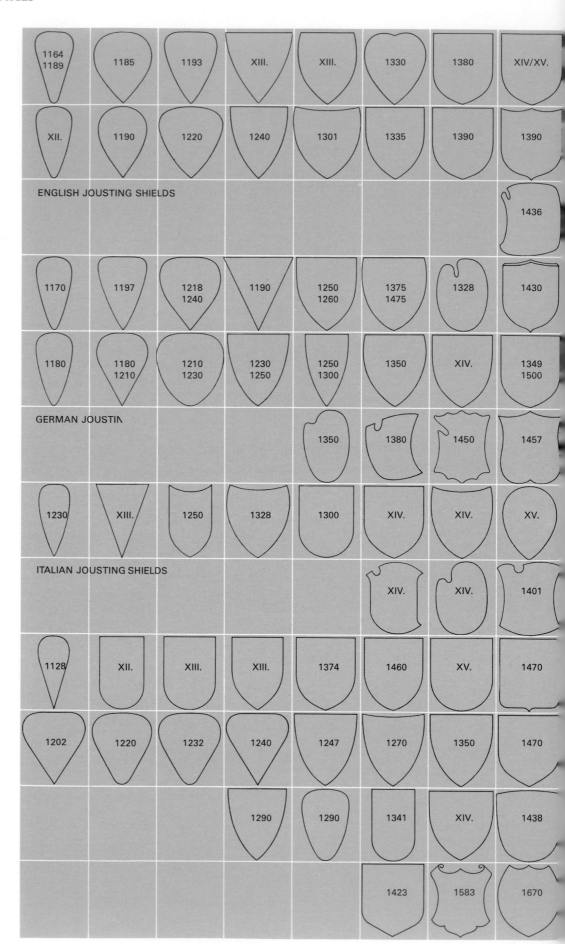

1504 1587	XVI.	XVI.	XVI.	1630	1637	1675	1688	XVIII.	1740	XX.
1467	1485	1500	1530	1648	XVIII.	XVIII.	1750 1850	1750 1850	1820	XX.
1444	1450	1450	1514	1524	1537	1533	XVIII.			
1512	1520	XVI.	1560	1520	1591	XVIII.	1700 1770	1780	XVIII./XIX.	XX.
XV.	1510	1520	1545	1580	1587	1670	1680	1768	1750	1970
1461	1470	1494	1525	1511	1520	1540				
1494	1510	1517	1570	1554	1580	1690	1738	XVIII.	XVIII.	XIX./XX.
XV.	XVI.	XVI.	1528	1550	1565	1570				
1490 1505	1493	1495	1509	1509	1515	1515	1550	1730	XVIII.	XIX.
1470	1496	1497	1507	1526	1666	1660	1680	1650	1688	XX.
1438	XV.	1504	1510	1550	XVI.	XVI.	XVI.	1579	1587	1863
1672	1688	1671	1669	1675	1695	1672	1670	1690	1800	1850

77

the sign

And God spoke unto Noah, and to his
sons with him, saying,
And I, behold, I establish my covenant
with you....
And God said, This is the token
of the covenant.....
I do set my bow in the cloud and it
shall be for a token of a covenant
between me and the earth.

Gen. 9:8–9, 12–13

Few words have so many meanings as the word "sign." This applies to all the languages of Western culture and many others. Signs can be short or long, acoustic, optical, two- or three-dimensional. Signs are the means by which men understand one another. In their most permanent form they are fashioned in or imprinted on some durable material. They enable men to become masters of their own past and pass on the benefit of their experience to later generations.

Numbers are among the oldest signs of all. Quantities may be communicated not only by letters and figures, but also by sign language. Counting starts from graphic expression and develops via the numeral until finally we have the word which represents a number and can be expressed in letters.

All written languages arose out of letters, and among them was cuneiform writing. The first attempts to record the sounds of human speech also used signs. But these could never be written down as fast as the speaker emitted them. Hence we have the development of the various kinds of stenography. The attempt to represent the outlines of nature through different formations of straight lines led to increased abstraction. This is evident in cuneiform writing, which also reflects the nature of the writing materials. The impression of a stylus on a clay tablet, which could be stored away after it had hardened, gave that elongated triangular stroke which became characteristic of the script during its three thousand year development. It acquired the name cuneiform from the shape of the stroke in the eighteenth century. Up to this time it had remained completely forgotten and was only rediscovered through excavations in the Near East.

Once cuneiform writing had lost its rebuslike character, it proved suitable as a syllabic and even alphabetic script which could render for-

eign languages and individual foreign words. Because of its laboriousness, however, in the last millennium before Christ it was completely replaced by the more flexible Phoenician-Greek-Roman alphabet. During its heyday, it retained its essential character despite the pressures of contemporary technology. On the numerous seals found its characters retain their characteristic wedge shape even when reduced to the smallest possible size. Because of its impressive

appearance, cuneiform writing retained its value as a ritual script for a long time alongside the more flexible everyday scripts; its characters had truly remained signs.

There is a near-endless number of writing systems and even today phonetic or alphabetic scripts have not penetrated everywhere.

Alphabetic scripts presuppose a general agreement on how different letters are to be pro-

Section from the impression of a Kassite cornelian cylinder seal in cuneiform writing *(left)*. The original, about 4.4 cm. (1³/₄ in.) high, is shown here enlarged about six times.

Opposite, left:
Eskimo totem pole from Alaska with an eagle and a beaver symbolizing a family community.

Opposite, right:
A man's fleeting gestures are graphically recorded in this rock drawing at Vitlyke near Tanum in Sweden. The four and three upheld fingers probably refer simply to the number seven.

Painted shield cover of the Kiowa Indians, representing a bear and the tracks it has left behind. The shields from this tribe are usually round, sand-colored, and decorated with animals and geometrical designs. Feathers are often hung from the rim. A similar shield has appeared since 1925 on the state flag of Oklahoma.

79

In the cult of Mithras the god is recognizable by his "Phrygian cap." He is shown here wearing it as he kills the bull of Mithraic legend.

nounced. Anyone who knows a foreign language, or even merely recognizes foreign words in his own language and would like to be sure of pronouncing them correctly, knows how many difficulties can be entailed by the common letter "e." These difficulties are compounded by the fact that all languages are in a constant state of development, that dialects within a country and the languages of countries with similar tongues are becoming increasingly assimilated in one another. One need only think of the German of Switzerland, Austria, and West Germany, and since 1945 of the German Democratic Republic;

Inns and lodging houses show their function by fastening to the wall signs which represent the name of the house. These signs are often masterpieces of the smith's craft. Here we see the sign of the inn "Zum Hirschen" (The Stag) in Sursee, in the canton of Lucerne.

Right:
The tradesmen's associations developed simple signs which were printed on the packing of their products to show their origin and guarantee their quality. They differ from the *Hausmarke* or merchant's marks in their preference for using letters from the Latin alphabet.

also of the English of Great Britain and the United States, or the Spanish of Castile and Argentina.

Colonial peoples who have achieved independence create written languages to fix the characteristics of their own, spoken languages. It is only a few years since Somalia was the most recent country in the world to replace three foreign languages (Arabic, English, and Italian) by a written language of its own. Here as in most cases the Latin alphabet was used as a basis, incorporating certain special signs which are not self-evident in meaning to the foreigner. Examples are double vowels, suffixes such as "e" or "h," diacritical marks such as diaereses, accents, cedillas, and also an inverted "e," reversed "a," and "i" with or without the dot. All these special signs are required to fix a "correct" language. In addition to the Latin alphabet, the Cyrillic alphabet has served as a basis for numer-

When the recognized religions erect buildings, they generally crown them with the symbol of their rites. Islam uses the crescent, Christianity the cross, which in the Eastern Orthodox Church is a three-armed cross. Another Christian symbol is the cock, which refers to Christ's prophecy in the garden of Gethsemane that Peter would deny him three times before the cock had crowed.

ous new written languages within the Russian sphere of influence.

At the same time there is a contrary tendency in favour of sign language. People in every country know the wordless signs for "ladies" and "gentlemen," for "no smoking," for overtaking and no overtaking, for stop and go. One is officially obliged to learn a large number of signs before one can drive an automobile; this is done by half the people in civilized countries, including the completely illiterate. The advantage of picture language and picture writing lies in the fact that a knowledge of the spoken language is unnecessary, and people can find their way around in foreign surroundings. But in order to make effective contact with one's fellows one also needs to know the spoken word.

Even now there are large parts of the world in which signs have yet to be ousted by an alphabetical script. This is particularly so in the gigantic area dominated by the Chinese. Though the characters of the Chinese written language with their multitude of brushstrokes may seem unintelligible to the foreigner, the fact remains that every Chinese can interpret them in a similar way whatever dialect is spoken. The unity of the Chinese People's Republic and its sphere of influence is so strongly governed by the complicated but generally used script that all efforts to Romanize the Chinese language have met with failure, and this is not only because people cannot agree on a suitable basis for transcription.

This is not the place to discuss how pictures of individual subjects gradually became ideograms, and syllabic characters for similar-sounding word parts.

Picture writing, cuneiform writing, Egyptian hieroglyphics, and Chinese characters all stemmed from the graphic representation of particular subjects. And this is true also for the Latin alphabet and other systems of writing which developed into alphabetic forms through the formation of philological principles. A further development takes place when the individual characters are given names, such as the

The increasing speed of traffic demands road signs that can be read quickly. Signs which can be understood by anyone, even illiterates, indicate what can and cannot be done, while the written language is only resorted to for qualifications of the overall rule. Sometimes a bureaucratic desire for precision leads to notices crammed with lettering which are impossible to read quickly. International agreements are a step towards making signs universally understandable.

81

Simple graphic signs have served to designate property since time immemorial. The plowman marked his plow. Sheep are given a notch in the ear. Cattle are branded with the sign of the ranch. Modern brand signs use forms taken from everyday life, such as the rocking chair of a Texan farmer included here.

Alpha and Beta from which the word alphabet is formed. The *Futhark* of the Germanic tribes is named after the first seven letters of their runic script. The Germans, too, gave their letters names with which they could be unmistakably identified, rather as one says "C for Caesar" on the telephone today. The runes were also used for prophecy, and in the twentieth century, after having interested only scholars for centuries, acquired a new and specious glory at the hands of scientific charlatans.

This sudden popularity was aroused by their formal similarity with the so-called merchant's marks *(Hausmarke)*, in which a few lines were sufficient to distinguish one mark from the next.

used in some form as a Christian symbol for nearly two thousand years. As a consequence, in Islam even an internationally known organization such as the Red Cross had to change its symbol and become the Society of the Red Crescent (the crescent being an Islamic symbol).

Today there are still secret societies which believe in the magical forces attributed to runes by the Germans. These societies play an unhealthy role in countries where an official religion such as Christianity is well established. Such signs do not have any particular foundation; they can appear to a believer in the sky and predict a victory for him, as they did for the emperor Constantine. As visions they can pro-

The invention of paper raised the question of how the manufacturer of the paper could identify himself

Numerous lists and surveys handed down from the Middle Ages show how whole professional groups – stonemasons, fishermen, merchants, and also village communities – used such signs in common. Their function was to identify the articles they produced, their tools, farm equip-

voke far-reaching decisions, like the stigmata which according to legend were shown by Christ to Pope Gregory I. But they can also fulfill a concrete function, as do flags for instance (the English term *"ensign"* is significant), when they have a genuine function as a signal and not a merely ceremonial or decorative aim. This is the case especially at sea. In Old High German, significantly, "sign" was also a synonym for "banner."

With the multiplication of different forms of life and social intercourse, both in war and in peace, language also had to produce distinguishing words. So actions are produced which are symbolic of a particular type of behavior. One throws oneself down as a symbol of submission, kneels in an attitude of begging or respect, raises the hand as a sign of blessing, and anoints a king as a sign of God's mercy on him. The signs of love are innumerable, both material and immaterial.

on his product. Trademarks and armorial devices made of fine wire, when pressed into each sheet during manufacture, made the paper appear lighter at the point of impression and thus created the "watermark."

ment, or manufactured wares so as to avoid confusion within a particular district. The big religious communities used signs to distinguish themselves from one another. The cross has been

The expression of signs in words can indicate not only their aim but also their method. A short note can be a sign of life, as a bookmark one

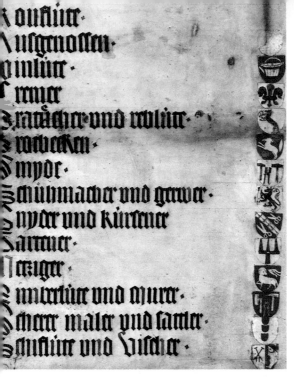

Tradesmen in nearly all medieval towns organized themselves into guilds, which adopted or were granted correct armorial bearings, especially in England and Switzerland.

lingen soon became as world-famous as the three-pronged simplification of the heraldic lily of the Fugger family — a forerunner of the type of merchant's mark now known as a "logo" (short for logogram or logotype). The logo takes the form of a striking abbreviation of or derivation from the full name of the firm, and the genre is already referred to in the publicity business in terms of the "heraldry of commerce."

John Shakespeare was granted arms in 1596 (below). The use of a spear is phonetically obvious, but etymologically doubtful.

needs only a blank strip of paper on which there is nothing to read. Brand marks are burned on, beacons use fire, illuminated signs use light. On the other hand the Latin word *signum* (plural *signa*) also had a restricted meaning which in the sixteenth century was first translated as "ban-

ner" or "ensign," words which from about 1525 were used to designate the field colors of an army.

A sign with an important place in modern life is the merchant's mark. This is the outcome of a development that began with the private ownership mark and continued through origin marks and stonemason's marks as used for calculating wages. Certain merchant's marks (see page 80) for indicating ownership or grades of quality were officially registered as early as the fourteenth century — in order, for example, that property could be claimed without difficulty from damaged ships. Such marks — they were all graphic — aimed at being as simple as possible (at least in the early days) and so easily reproducible in a variety of ways; i.e., punched in metal, stamped on sacks, printed on paper, etc.

Among German merchant's marks the wolf of Passau and the twins on knife blades from So-

There is no field more strongly associated with signs than heraldry. Both two- and three-dimensional, these signs have developed according to traditional rules into the rich profusion which exists today.

The number of species of dog known by name in the Middle Ages was not very large. Heraldry generally distinguishes only between pointers, hounds, and whippets. The hound of the counts of Toggenburg (above) is a play on the German word *Dogge*.

83

A particular feature of heraldry is the heraldic style. While rigorously formal, it is sufficiently flexible for national peculiarities to have developed. In the heyday of heraldry, between 1200 and 1500, offenses against the heraldic rules in any country were very unusual. Naturalism in heraldry is rigidly avoided.

Before heraldry acquired its name, signs existed which were so well known that they could serve as a means of recognition. These signs were subject to a traditional manner of representation which constituted the heraldic style. This was to become the outstanding feature of heraldry. The heraldic style refers to a type of representation which was subjected to fairly strict rules, but was quite flexible within those rules.

The strictness of these rules resulted from the necessity of recognizing a sign at a great distance or at high speed – the very same necessity to which heraldry owed its being. These two demands regulate the creation of national flags and traffic signs even today. The directness of the impression was initially provided by the

The stylization of the lion stemmed from the desire for symmetry. In the first picture the body forms a central axis; the strongly formed tail counterbalances the outstretched legs; the right hind leg is raised high.

As shields became wider the arrangements of the lion's limbs altered. The right hind leg is now held out horizontally.

In the late Gothic period it was more important to fill the available space than to have the lion upright. The axis is therefore inclined until the body is almost horizontal. The tail is normally curled outwards rather than inwards.

Arms of an English lord around 1390 from the chapel seat which he received as a knight of the Order of the Garter. Typical of English arms of the period are the overweighted helmet and crest and the fringed mantling falling away towards the back and ending in a thick tassel.

There are two points characteristic of Polish heraldry: a) the majority of the old arms contain figures in linear form; and b) several families without any known relationship between them can bear the same arms.

Arms of a central European noble family. The shield is broad at the bottom to accommodate numerous charges. Narrow-bodied animals (and also men) are typical of German heraldry.

Arms of an English family, the various branches of which bear the same arms in different colors. There is no contact between the upright shield and the helmet.

In Italy the jousting shield lasted longest as a part of the full achievement of arms. It is in this country that the clearest distinction was made between a jousting shield *(targa)* and the more conventional form *(scudo)*.

Claimed to be the "oldest arms in the world," these shields were transferred from one armorial collection to another and adjusted to fit the style of the time. They are shown above, after the book of the Council of Constance (1414–1418), and below in the armorial of Virgil Solis, Nuremberg 1555. Virgil Solis made a mistake in the lettering. He did not realize that the arms of the Abithay in fact contain the Hebraic letters ABT.

The difference between a natural flower and its heraldic representation can be considerable. Indeed, it has been doubted whether the fleur-de-lis is based on the lily at all.

contrast between light and dark colors. However, the contrasting patches of color soon proved insufficient to indicate the necessary differences, and therefore pictures had to be added which could be recognized by their silhouette. This is where the heraldic style appears most clearly. One of its requirements is that the figures should fill the available space as far as possible. The skill of the heraldic painter lies especially in his ability to strike a balance between the superimposed figure and the pattern formed by the surrounding background colors.

The backgrounds available for a coat of arms can be greatly varied. Historically, however, one starts with the three-cornered field which approximates the three-cornered shield of the medieval knight. The next basic form is the rectangle, sometimes long, sometimes wide, and sometimes square. The fitting of the armorial picture or "charge" into the outline of the background may require considerable adjustment, and the most frequent figures are often distorted in one way or another for this purpose. Such distortion became increasingly prevalent, and obvious examples are the figures of the Bohemian lion (below), and the eagles (see pages 124–128). A different kind of distortion – one of the hallmarks of the heraldic style – is the altered coloring of certain parts of an animal's body. The claws and tongue of the lion, the claws and beak of the eagle, also the antlers of the deer, and the hooves and horns of other animals can be colored differently from the rest of the body.

Below:

The arms of the kingdom of Bohemia in different styles *(from left to right)*:

The oldest careful representation of the arms of Bohemia in the colors of the folding table of Lüneburg, 1328 (see pages 154–155). Note the quilted covering on the helmet.

Schematic drawing of the same arms from the armorial roll of Zurich (ca. 1340). The helmet is very cursorily treated.

Representation in the Flemish style by the Gelre herald (ca. 1380). The lion is highly ornamental, almost grotesque. An elaborate plume forms the crest, while the mantling blends in with the latter. The cross on the helmet's crown may be an allusion to the imperial crown of Charles IV, who was also king of Bohemia.

Illustration from the armorial of Konrad Grünenberg, Constance, 1483. In it the arms of Bohemia take up a whole large page. In the German style the lion becomes somewhat less grotesquely distorted, but it is still drawn very much so as to fill out the field.

Illustration from the armorial of Virgil Solis, 1555. The colors of the mantling match those of the shield. The drawing aims for maximum symmetry. The chain is that of the Order of the Golden Fleece. Whoever was king of Bohemia was at that time also a knight of that order.

Arms of Pope Pius II, 1458–1464. The so-called horse-head shield is a result of striving in the Renaissance for symmetrical forms. The tiara at the top gives a more pleasing effect than the helmet and crest.

Arms of the head of a Portuguese family around 1500. The idea that each coat of arms had to represent a particular person persisted in Portugal beyond the end of the Middle Ages. The arms of the head of the family were labeled with the appropriate word *(chefe)*.

The arms of a conquistador granted by Charles I of Spain in 1546. The arms bestowed on the conquerors of South America show a poverty of invention and graphic skill which reflects the decline of Spanish heraldry, hitherto cultivated to a high degree.

Before the adoption of the hatching used today to denote colors in black and white representations of coats of arms, printed outlines were used in wood or copper engraving which could then be colored in by hand. Small letters were used as a key, on or beside the area to be painted, usually the initial letters of the colors in the language of the country concerned. Black was usually printed either as a solid (with wood

blocks) or as very close hatching (with copper engravings). This was later to lead to numerous mistakes, with close horizontal hatching, for example, being mistaken for blue instead of black. The letters generally used were:

In French and English:
O = *Or*: gold
A = *Argent*: silver
G = *Gueules* or *gules*: red
B = *Bleu*: blue
S = *Sable*: black
V = *Vert* or *verte*: green
P = *Pourpre* or *purpure*: purple
Pr = *Propre*: natural color

In German:
G or g = *Gelb* or *golden*: yellow or gold
W or w = *Weiss*: white or silver
R or r = *Rot*: red
B or b = *Blau*: blue
S or s = *Schwarz*: black
Gr or gr or ♀ = *Grün*: green
Br or br = *Braun*: purple

There is no such thing as a coat of arms without colors, but at times the colors may be difficult to recognize. Nowadays there is no problem, for we have either color printing or the accepted conventions of hatching to represent differences. But this is only a relatively recent development. Many early representations of arms on seals, tombs, weapons, and furniture and the like have survived without any coloring. We do know the coloring of many early coats of arms thanks to the sense of duty of the compilers of armorial rolls or collectors' enthusiasm. Even though it is not expressly mentioned by the earliest authors, one quickly realizes when looking at these collections that in heraldry there are as few colors as there are on modern traffic signs. There are in fact six: yellow, white, red, blue, black, and sometimes green; very occasionally we also find a purple tint, a mixture of red and blue known as purpure.

The basic rules for heraldic painting stem from the function of arms as a recognition sign on the battlefield. In every coat of arms, gold or silver – almost invariably represented by yellow and white – must appear at least once. These are the "metals," which in the classic heraldic traditions of medieval chivalry were always used alternately with the "colors." The colors in order of frequency of their appearance are red, blue, black, and green. They can be used for the ground of a shield or the coloring of a charge, but in each case the remaining parts should be in metal. It is equally correct for a field carrying some geometric pattern to be done partly in metal and partly in a color.

The rule cannot of course be strictly applied when for one reason or another a coat of arms shows three different colors, as when the field is divided into three sections, or when the charge covers a dividing line without the colors being "counterchanged."

Since, to follow our comparison, there are many more coats of arms than there are traffic signs, many more variations must be thought up to come nearer to the object of making one coat of arms look as little like another as possible. This is in fact an impossible aim which at best can only be achieved within a limited regional framework. A certain amount of tolerance is therefore called for when applying the rules of heraldry regarding color on color or metal on metal. Indeed, these rules change from country to country. For banners and flags, the rules of heraldry are generally relaxed. This was true even in the early days. The color green, which at first was seldom used, is frequently found on the banners of the high Middle Ages. It was the flut-

Planet: Sun. Precious stone: topaz. Symbol of: understanding, respect, virtue, majesty. Hatching: small dots.

GOLD = YELLOW = OR

Planet: Moon. Precious stone: pearls. Symbol of: cleanliness, wisdom, innocence, chastity, joy. Hatching: none.

SILVER = WHITE = ARGENT

Planet: Mars. Precious stone: Ruby. Symbol of: eagerness to serve one's fatherland. Hatching: vertical lines.

RED = GULES

Planet: Jupiter. Precious stone: sapphire. Symbol of: fidelity, steadfastness. Hatching: horizontal lines.

BLUE = AZURE

Planet: Saturn. Precious stone: diamond. Symbol of: mourning. Hatching: combination of the lines for red and blue, or solid black.

BLACK = SABLE

Planet: Venus. Precious stone: emerald. Symbol of: freedom, beauty, joy, health, hope. Hatching: diagonal lines "in bend."

GREEN = VERT

Planet: Mercury. Precious stone: amethyst. Symbol of: majesty. Hatching: diagonal lines "in bend sinister."

PURPLE = PURPURE

No planet sign. No precious stone. Symbolism: indefinite. Hatching: combination of red lines and gold spots.

ORANGE

Interior of planet, dragon's head. Prec. stone: hyacinth. Symbol of: nature's colors. Hatching: comb. of the lines for red and green.

BROWN = TENNÉ

tering of the flag in the wind which drew the observer's attention and not so much the color or even the pattern on the fabric.

In heraldry proper, the pattern of the material is of no significance. To add an air of luxury to the execution, the single color of a field may be patterned or "diapered," and this is not mentioned in the blazon, since the pattern remains a matter for the discretion of the artist. Diapering was also used to enliven the flat surface of armorial seals. There is no rule as to whether diapering was supposed to represent a particular metal or color. If there had been, many medieval seals would be less of an enigma than they are.

There seems no sense in trying to recognize particular colors in the pattern of diapering or small figures strewn across a field, even though it remains possible that an inventive maker of seals may once have used such a system in his practice.

One must distinguish diapering from the "furs," which are subject to strict rules. There are two types, ermine and vair. In English heraldry, which is well known for its non-realistic figures, there are, in addition to ermine itself, erminois (ermine tails on a gold field), ermines (a reverse ermine, with white tails on a black ground), and pean (gold tails on black). The gold ermine has an unreal effect, since the black tails stand out

arrangements of color are preferred or avoided by one race or another; thus, in France blue and gold predominate, while the Germans are very fond of black and gold. And in popular belief the colors still mean what they used to: red stands for love, blue for fidelity, black for mourning, green for hope or freedom.

Thus color is a major element in heraldry, and

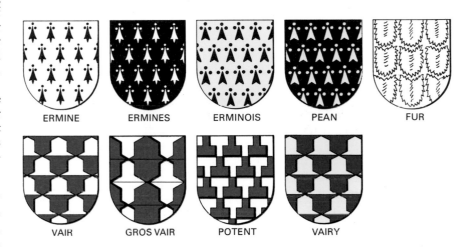

ERMINE   ERMINES   ERMINOIS   PEAN   FUR

VAIR   GROS VAIR   POTENT   VAIRY

the optically necessary restriction of the number of colors makes certain combinations essential. A particularly clear impression is made if a color

best against the white fur as they were originally intended. And the reverse version gives entirely the effect of a photographic negative.

In the Middle Ages and in early modern times, emotive values were attached to the colors. This seems no longer to be the case in modern heraldry. However, the fact remains that certain

in the technical sense always stands adjacent to a metal (or to a yellow or white). Exceptions from this rule are known as "puzzle arms." Only the king of Jerusalem was considered by custom to be absolved from the strict rules of color. He bore gold crosses on a silver shield. The division of the colors and the metals took place through "lines of partition." The basic divisions are those

DIVIDED PER PALE

PER FESS

PER BEND

PER BEND SINISTER

QUARTERLY

PER SALTIRE

The aim of all blazon is to make an unequivocal statement about the way in which the armorial shield should be arranged. It may consist of an undivided field containing one or more charges. Or it may be divided in a number of different ways. The "lines of partition" take their names from the basic charges known as "ordinaries," which themselves serve to divide the shield and provide additional quarters for charges.

CHIEF

BASE

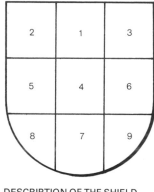

DESCRIPTION OF THE SHIELD

An armorial shield can be divided up into different areas and points, which are explained below. When the shield is divided so as to accommodate several different coats of arms (see page 90) this is done by "quartering." The system of numbering shown is traditional in Continental heraldry, and the areas it delineates are named as follows: 1–3, Chief; 4–6, Fess; 7–9, Base; 2–8, Dexter; 3–9, Sinister; 1–7, Pale.

The midpoint of the line connecting 1 and 4 is known as the honor point. The center of 4 is the fess point. And the midpoint of the line connecting 4 and 7 is the nombril or navel point.

Right:
A sample from the so-called Redinghoven armorial in the Bavarian State Library, Munich, named after its discoverer, the archivist of Jülich-Berg, Johann Gottfried Redinghoven (d. 1704). Compiled before 1440, it contains mainly southern German arms, serving here as an example of "partitions." The page shown is one of the few in this armorial containing helmets with barred visors; crowned helmets are also unusual in the book.

of the "honourable ordinaries," or as the French have it *pièces honorables*.

The lines of partition can be varied in innumerable imaginative ways. The only restriction is in the rule of alternation of color and metal. The superimposition of color upon color and metal upon metal is forbidden; so in theory are their juxtaposition, but this cannot always be avoided when for instance three different sections lie adjacent to one another (see shields opposite, "tierced in pairle" and "per fess, the upper half per pale").

Most heraldic badges have conventional names, particularly the ordinaries, which are the basic charges made up of straight lines. A line dividing a shield when only two colors are used is per fess or per pale. But if three colors are used it remains a horizontal or vertical partition. While noting this distinction, the old heraldic experts do not always make it entirely clear. Thus the first six shields on page 92 can be blazoned as follows:

1. Berchtoldshofen: Paly of four Vert and Argent (Partition)
2. Pack: Argent two Pales gules (Ordinary)
3. Trivulzio: Paly of six Or and Vert (Partition)
4. Steffen: Or three Pales Gules (Ordinary)
5. Gotschen: Paly of eight Argent and Azure (Partition)
6. Merode: Or four Pales Gules (Ordinary)

An incalculable number of variations can be achieved with combinations of partitions and ordinaries alone. Some idea of the variety is given by the tables from old books on heraldry shown on pages 92 and 93.

There we find juxtapositions of several heraldic badges, such as the silver pale with one chevron of the Swiss von Erlachs (see page 49) and next to it the pale with three chevrons of the von Nidau family, a branch of the counts of Neufchâtel. All branches of this family have pales with three or six chevrons, the chevrons either black on a gold pale in a red field or silver on a red pale against a gold ground. This is how the cousins "differenced" their arms, including the

von Badenweilers of the Black Forest. The von Erlachs, with their single chevron, were Neufchâtel vassals.

Badges that have enough space – particularly crosses and chevrons – can be and often are accompanied by smaller elements. In French heraldry, for example, chevrons between three stars occur so frequently that they no longer serve the purpose of identification.

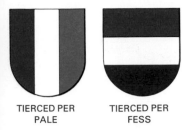

TIERCED PER PALE

TIERCED PER FESS

PALE

FESS

CHEQUY

QUARTERLY OF NINE

GYRONNY

LOZENGY

CROSS

SALTIRE

BEND

BEND SINISTER

CHEVRON

TIERCED IN PAIRLE

CANTON

BORDURE

ORLE

PER FESS, THE UPPER HALF PER PALE

 ENGRAILED

INVECTED

WAVY

NEBULY

INDENTED

DANCETTY

EMBATTLED

DOVETAILED

POTENTY

RAGULY

URDY

RAYONNÉ

"FIR TREE TOP SECTION"

"FIR TWIG SECTION"

"CLOVERLEAF SECTION"

FLEURY COUNTER FLEURY

One of the most important and at the same time most difficult tasks of the scientific armorist is the identification of uninscribed coats of arms. The systems he goes by are based either on the accompanied or traversed badge or inversely on the accompanying elements.

The first procedure was the one used by Dielitz in his *Wappenschematismus (Handbook of Coats of Arms)*, eventually printed in 1898. The illustrations that go with the book are – and have been since the Second World War – in the central archives of the German Democratic Republic in Merseburg. The reserve procedure (i.e., starting from the accompanying elements) was used by Comte Théodore de Renesse in his six-volume *Dictionnaire des figures héraldiques* (Brussels, 1894–1903), which classifies coats of arms into complete, incomplete, and quartered.

Arms of Lord Baltimore consisting of the family arms of Calvert in the first and fourth quarters and of Crossland in the second and third quarters.
The quartering of these arms which are now those of Maryland shows the variety which can be achieved by combinations of divisions and charges and different coloring.

Left:
The lines of partition on a shield can be bent or kinked in a number of ways. Most of these "sections" have conventional names. Modern commercial artists, especially in Finland, have developed new sections based on the forms of local flora.

The arms shown on the left only lasted three years and a month (1915–1918). They represent the end result of one hundred years of development. When Emperor Francis II laid down the German Roman imperial crown in 1806 and declared the Holy Roman Empire of German nations to be dissolved, he retained the outward forms of its past glory and transferred them, as from 1804, to a state of many races which previously formed only a part of the German Roman empire.

The same rules as for simple shields apply to the division of complicated ones. Complicated coats of arms are also divided into quarters and charges, which may be superimposed upon one another.

The arms of states particularly reflect political changes and upheavals. In times of continuing unrest, many a state has sought to gloss over the strife attendant on territorial rearrangements by adopting the arms of unity. Such was the case during Napoleon's troubled times in Baden, Bavaria, Hessen, and Saxony, to name only the most obvious instances.

Austria, on the other hand, carried out political change with as much care as was practical, and the gradual progress made is reflected in its arms. The shield on the breast of its double eagle grew into an armorial shield in its own right. In the center of the field the pinions of the bird were overlaid with the smaller shield of the hereditary dominions with Hungary among them. Changes were made in 1804, 1806, 1815, 1836, and 1867, bearing witness to the efforts to maintain heraldic accuracy. The arms established on 10 October 1915 brought to an end twelve years of continual experimentation. They lasted as long as the "common arms" of Austria and Hungary established at the same time.

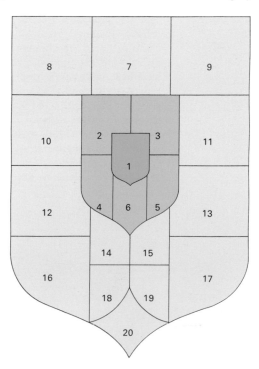

11

12

The arms of the "crown lands":
1 Archduchy of Austria
2 Archduchy of Austria below the Enns
3 Archduchy of Austria above the Enns
4 Duchy of Steiermark
5 Duchy of Kärnten
6 Duchy of Krain
7 Kingdom of Bohemia
8 Kingdom of Galicia
9 Kingdom of Dalmatia
10 Duchy of Upper and Lower Silesia
11 Duchy of Salzburg
12 Margraviate of Moravia
13 Royal county of Tirol
14 The region of Vorarlberg
15 Margraviate of Istria
16 Duchy of Bukovina
17 Bosnia and Herzegovina
18/19 Royal county of Görz and Gradiska
20 Imperial town of Trieste

Many heraldic animals were given small additional features to make them unique. The lion of Bohemia always has a double tail; the eagle of Silesia carries a half moon on its breast, usually with a cross in the center, and often with a cloverleaf at each tip. Straps bearing cloverleaves are found on many eagles. They are essential features of the Tirolean eagle.

In the heartland of Austria two coats of arms long struggled for supremacy. It was the so-called banded shield which finally won. According to a Crusader legend, Duke Leopold, after the Battle of Ptolemais in 1191, adopted a similar bloodstained tabard as his arms. The Austrian banner first appeared in 1254 in the seal of its bearer, a Count von Plain and Hardeck.

In the year 1772 Austria carved Halicz and the Vladimir region out of the kingdom of Poland, which at that time was divided up among its neighbors. She named the area Kingdom of Galicia and Lodomeria. Since no genuine ancient arms existed, three crowns in old heraldic style were established as the arms of the new kingdom.

The last three quarters of the Austrian inescutcheon concern the coastal region at the northern end of the Adriatic and reflect the

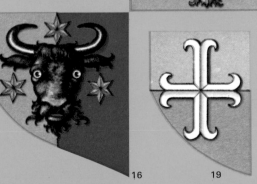

The blue shield with the five golden eagles is reputedly the standard of the margrave of Babenberg, Leopold III the Holy, and was at first gradually adopted in Lower Austria. In Upper Austria it was the arms of the lord of Machland which became the country's arms.

troubled past of this storm center of history.
When Austria collapsed in 1918, Trieste renounced the double eagle and the silver bar behind the fleur-de-lis scepter, which is actually intended to be the lance of St. Sergius.

Specimen page from one of the first great German heraldic textbooks, which at the time were still written in Latin. The author was Philipp Jakob Spener, who was also known as a pietist theologian. Born in 1635, in the Alsatian town of Rappoltsweiler, he was in close touch with the great master of heraldry at the time, Claude François Menestrier, who was only four years older than himself and whom he visited in Lyons. Previously he had concerned himself mostly with genealogy, and it was Menestrier who introduced him to heraldry. Spener produced a two-volume "heraldic work" which is divided into a general and a special section. The special section, entitled "History of Arms," gives what was for the time an unusually effective explanation of the arms of more than a hundred German and foreign families. The page shown is from the general section entitled "Heraldic Theory," and gives an idea of Spener's systematic approach. The charges are named in Latin and French. Authors derived the Latin names from the classical language. The French names were common knowledge among heraldic experts since the Middle Ages.

Opposite:
A work by a Dutchman, Jean-Baptiste Rietstap, is of inestimable value in the science of heraldry. Rietstap collected 116,000 coats of arms from the armorials available some hundred years ago and prepared them for printing with blazons in impeccable French. His *Armorial général* appeared in Gouda in 1884. It contains an introduction of several pages of text and illustrations in which the technical expressions are carefully explained and their origin documented wherever possible. Page 93 shows one of these illustrations.

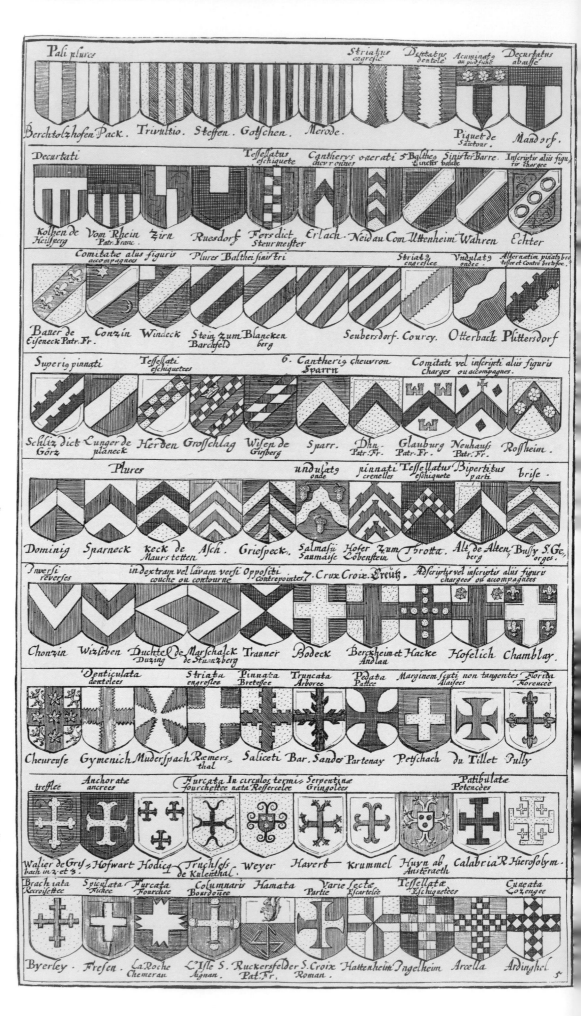

1 Chevron couped in chief
2 Chevronels
3 Chevronels disjointed
4 Bar dancetty of two
5 Three chevronels between two bendlets
6 Chevron couched sinister
7 Chevronny of four reversed
8 Two chevronels in counterpoint
9 Two chevrons interlaced, one reversed
10 Three chevronels fretted
11 Chevronny of four per pale
12 Chevronelly
13 Four chevronels palleted
14 Per chevron a crescent counter-changed
15 Tierced per pale
16 Cross between two shields in second and third cantons
17 Cross per saltire gules and azure
18 Cross surmounted by a chevron reversed
19 Cross gobony or and azure
20 Cross nebuly
21 Cross vairy
22 Cross with four knobs protruding
23 Cross fitched
24 Cross couped between four roses
25 Cross fretted between two eagles and two lions
26 Cross engrailed
27 Cross indented
28 Cross raguly
29 Cross moline
30 Cross moline fimbriated
31 Cross recercely
32 Cross fouchy
33 Cross gringoly
34 Cross fitched at all points, sur-mounted by a bar
35 Cross potent
36 Cross formy
37 Four almonds in saltire
38 Cross formy couped quarterly
39 Quarterly argent and gules four crosses formy counterchanged
40 "Key cross"
41 Cross of Toulouse
42 Potent couped and in chief a mullet
43 Patriarchal cross, the second bar rectangled sinister to the base
44 Cross potent repotent
45 Cross of nine besants
46 Saltire counter-compony
47 Saltire compony
48 Saltire gyronny of sixteen
49 Cross portate counter-compony
50 Two pales surmounted by a saltire counter-compony
51 Saltire engrailed
52 Saltire of nine lozenges
53 Pall
54 Pall couped pointed
55 Tierced per pairle
56 Pall reversed
57 Tierced per pairle reversed
58 Pile reversed in base
59 Per pile transposed
60 Per fess and per pile transposed or and azur, three roses gules
61 Quarterly and per pile transposed gules and argent counterchanged
62 Per pile reversed arched azure two fleurs-de-lis or and or a rose gules
63 Or a point pointed sable a fleur-de-lis or
64 Gules three bars and two points dexter and sinister argent
65 Gules a man and two points dexter and sinister charged each with a crescent
66 Per pile gules a pale argent, and or
67 Per pile arched gules and argent
68 Per fess azure and argent, a lozenge throughout counterchanged
69 Or a pile gules
70 Point pointed in point from sinister base to dexter chief

93

The Spanish imperial flag *(left)* is an armorial banner which corresponds exactly to the royal arms of the time (around 1500); only a strip along the top edge is added to make room for the royal crowns. It was in Spain that the method of combining arms through quartering was first employed in the thirteenth century, and there it was also developed further. When the quartered coat of arms had come to be looked upon as a single unit, it was incorporated intact into further quarterings.

The castle of Castile was initially combined through quartering with the lion of León. This was repeated as a single unit in each successive quartering until finally eight castles appeared in a diagonal line. The second and third main quarters contain the arms of the Austro-Burgundian lands, whose rulers had acceded to the Spanish throne.

Opposite:
The post-medieval English custom of inheriting arms as quarterings due to marriage with heraldic heiresses can lead to innumerable and repeated quarterings. This is particularly true of Welsh families who have multiple descents from a few traditional pre-heraldic ancestors to whom arms were attributed, mostly in the sixteenth century. Thus, many of the repeated coats in the 323 quarterings of the Lloyds of Stockton are arms attributed to Welsh chieftains living in the ninth century, or even earlier.

Anyone who becomes involved with heraldry soon becomes familiar with its rich variety of motifs. When someone asks the meaning of such and such an armorial picture, it may be of interest to know whom or what the coat of arms represents, but it is also interesting to know the origin of individual color combinations and figures. Since the thought behind the choice of a particular armorial figure can almost never be known, one's imagination often provides the only explanations. And many a heraldic "saga" is closer to the reality of life than the results of careful research.

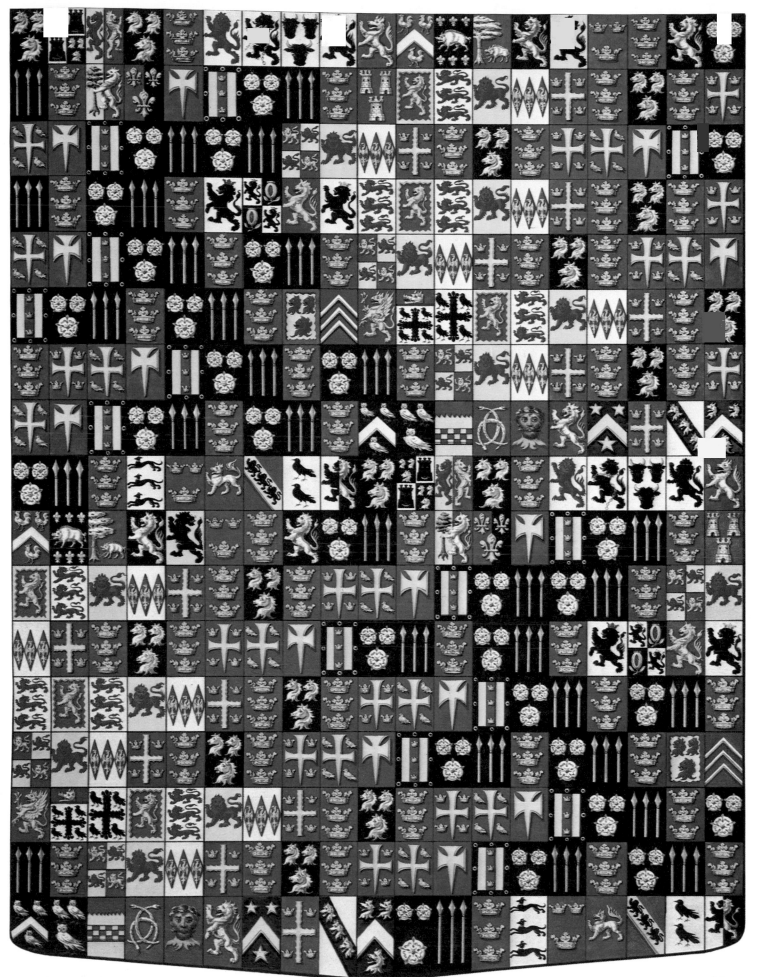

95

SIGNS OF DIFFERENCING

The reigning royal family in Great Britain goes back to Prince Albert of Saxe-Coburg, the husband of Queen Victoria, who has been justifiably called the grandmother of Europe. In 1917 the name of Saxe-Coburg was changed to Windsor. Our summary of the family tree covers all those descended in the male line from Queen Victoria. The men are usually made dukes. The titles given to them are added in brackets.

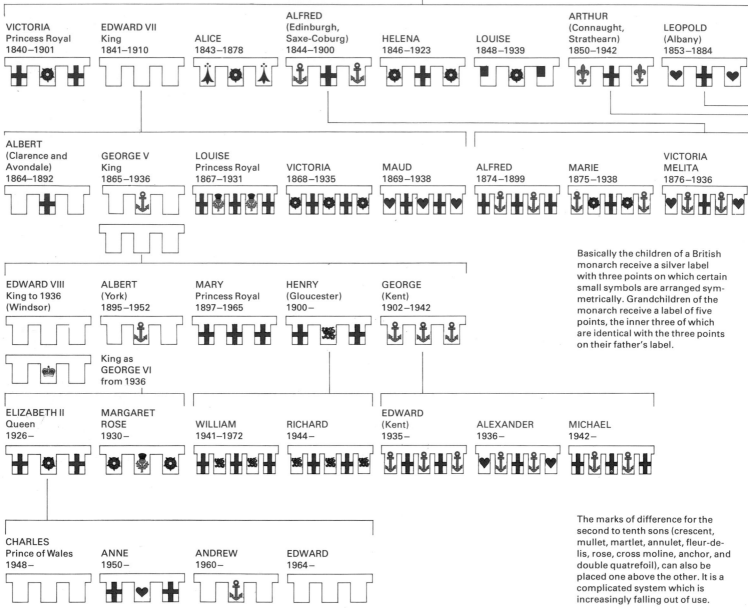

VICTORIA Queen of Great Britain 1819–1901

VICTORIA Princess Royal 1840–1901

EDWARD VII King 1841–1910

ALICE 1843–1878

ALFRED (Edinburgh, Saxe-Coburg) 1844–1900

HELENA 1846–1923

LOUISE 1848–1939

ARTHUR (Connaught, Strathearn) 1850–1942

LEOPOLD (Albany) 1853–1884

ALBERT (Clarence and Avondale) 1864–1892

GEORGE V King 1865–1936

LOUISE Princess Royal 1867–1931

VICTORIA 1868–1935

MAUD 1869–1938

ALFRED 1874–1899

MARIE 1875–1938

VICTORIA MELITA 1876–1936

Basically the children of a British monarch receive a silver label with three points on which certain small symbols are arranged symmetrically. Grandchildren of the monarch receive a label of five points, the inner three of which are identical with the three points on their father's label.

EDWARD VIII King to 1936 (Windsor)

ALBERT (York) 1895–1952

King as **GEORGE VI** from 1936

MARY Princess Royal 1897–1965

HENRY (Gloucester) 1900–

GEORGE (Kent) 1902–1942

ELIZABETH II Queen 1926–

MARGARET ROSE 1930–

WILLIAM 1941–1972

RICHARD 1944–

EDWARD (Kent) 1935–

ALEXANDER 1936–

MICHAEL 1942–

The marks of difference for the second to tenth sons (crescent, mullet, martlet, annulet, fleur-de-lis, rose, cross moline, anchor, and double quatrefoil), can also be placed one above the other. It is a complicated system which is increasingly falling out of use.

CHARLES Prince of Wales 1948–

ANNE 1950–

ANDREW 1960–

EDWARD 1964–

The form of the label in each case is established by royal decree. As the princes of Saxe-Coburg and Gotha were excluded from the British royal family in 1893, the labels chosen independently by them were not recognized in England.

One of the original guiding principles of heraldry was that a coat of arms should clearly identify a particular person while at the same time attaching some importance to the family he belonged to. This led to the creation of distinguishing signs (in French *brisures*) which while retaining the overall impression of the shield changed it to a limited degree. Certain conventions for this process were developed. In many places the crest also served as a means of differentiating individuals and as a result their own family lines. Great Britain is the only country in

the world in which the classical procedure of using a mark of difference for individuals is still customary, and this is done to the greatest extent in the royal family.

Achievement of arms of a prince of the house of Hanover, which reigned in Great Britain until 1837; its arms appear in the shield inescutcheon. Double labels are very seldom seen. In 1835 a red label with the silver horse of Lower Saxony was attributed to the Crown Prince of Hanover.

Below middle:
Four examples of marks of favor from Belgium *(left to right):* the lion from the state arms, arms of artists on the national colors, the flag of the former state of the Congo, and the initials of King Leopold III.

BEATRICE
1857–1944

ALEXANDRA
1878–1942

BEATRICE
1884–1966

MARGARET
1882–1920

ARTHUR
1883–1938

VICTORIA
PATRICIA
1886–1974

ALICE
1883–

CHARLES EDWARD
(Albany and
Saxe-Coburg)
1884–1954

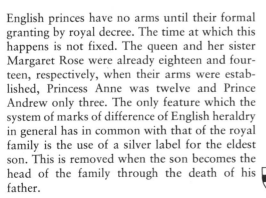

The system of a special mark of difference known as a "label" for each member of the family goes back to the time of Henry III (reigned 1216–1272), whose successor, as a prince, placed such a mark on the shield of England. Initially there was no particular system in the representation of this sign; however, no doubt on visual grounds, it was almost always white and overlaid with small figures. The number of points was not critical. Today red George Crosses, red or Tudor roses, blue fleurs-de-lis and blue anchors are chosen for preference. In addition we find red hearts, red British lions, and Scottish thistles, and occasionally the Irish shamrock. The use of the imperial crown for an abdicated king, such as the duke of Windsor, is as unusual as the occurrence itself.

The differencing of a prince's arms extends to the supporters on whose shoulders the label appears. In the arms of a prince an ingeniously devised system of crowns of rank must also be observed, which serves to indicate the relationship of generations between the prince and the sovereign.

English princes have no arms until their formal granting by royal decree. The time at which this happens is not fixed. The queen and her sister Margaret Rose were already eighteen and fourteen, respectively, when their arms were established, Princess Anne was twelve and Prince Andrew only three. The only feature which the system of marks of difference of English heraldry in general has in common with that of the royal family is the use of a silver label for the eldest son. This is removed when the son becomes the head of the family through the death of his father.

The various marks of difference of the various lines of the French royal family of the Capetians follow only the most general of patterns. They are shown on the following pages in the context of a comprehensive family tree.

A distinction must be made between the marks distinguishing the different members of a particular family and marks of favor. In almost all

countries, and particularly those with a monarchy, additional signs are granted to deserving people, and also communities, which are mostly developed from the state sign of sovereignty and appear in a chief or a canton. Thus many signs of previous monarchies survive in family arms.

In medieval times it was an Italian custom to show one's political allegiance in the chief of one's shield (see the arms of Popes Paul V, Innocence X, Innocence XI, Alexander VIII, Benedict XV, and Pius XI on pages 236–237). In the era of fascism, this custom was extended to nearly all the towns and cities of Italy *(above,* Rome).

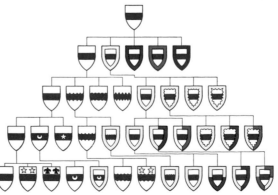

In its consistent logic the Scottish system of marks of difference reflects the concepts of the early days of heraldry. It no longer has anything in common with the English system.

THE CAPETIAN FAMILY TREE

The dynasty of the Capetians has endured the longest of any ruling house in the Occidental world. It is named after Hugh Capet (940–996, reigned 987–996), whose descendants produced all the succeeding kings of France. King Robert II (d. 1031), son of Hugh Capet, is the common ancestor of all those shown on our genealogical tree.

All kinds of heraldic development may be found there: free choice of arms; using the same colors; differencing marks for legitimate and illegitimate children; and the variations in one's arms over a lifetime. During the reign of Louis XIV, the marks of cadency were again given sophisticated attention. In recent times, the use of cadency marks has diminished.

Armorial shields in color indicate heads of houses.

BRETAGNE

Robert S.
Château-du-Loir † 1302

Pierre de Dreux
C. Bretagne † 1250

Louis VIII
R. France
1123–26

COURTENAY

Robert
C. Dreux
† 1188

DREUX

Robert I
C. Dreux

Robert II
C. Dreux
† 1218

Robert III
C. Dreux
† 1234

FRANCE

Louis VII
R. France
1137–80

Philippe II Aug.
R. France
1180–1223

ANJOU-SICILE I

Charles I, 1246 succ./ 1254 C. Anjou/ 1265 R. Sicile & 1277 R. Jérusalem/ 1246–85 (†)/ C. Provence

The rulers of the province of Dauphiné carried the title Dauphin. The last Dauphin, Anne de Viennois (right), bequeathed the title to the house of Latour-du-Pin. In 1335, the last male of this house sold the land to the king of France. Since then, the heir apparent to the throne of France has been called Dauphin.

Philippe Hurepel (left) was the first to place a mark of differencing, a label, on the royal arms. The system developed further. French princes abroad became kings and so their personal arms became new state arms.

Philippe Hurepel, C. Clermont † 1234

VERMANDOIS

Hugues
C. Vermandois
† 1102

Raoul I
C. Vermandois
† 1152

Raoul II
C. Vermandois

Louis VI
R. France
1108–37

Philippe I
R. France
1060–1108

Henri I
R. France
1031–60

Robert II
R. France
996–1031

BOURGOGNE I

Robert † 1076
D. Bourgogne

Henri de Bourgogne
† 1071/73

Eudes I
1079 D. Bourg.
† 1102

Hugues II
1102 D. Bourg.
† 1143

Eudes II
1173 D. Bourg.
† 1162

Hugues I † 1093
D. Bourgogne
1076–79

Anne Dauphine de Viennois † 1301

Jean 1270 Dauphin, C. Viennois † 1301

Henry, as "Count and Lord of all of Portugal," created an independent state from a Castilian province.

PORTUGAL

Henri † 1112
1095 C. Portugal

Guigue VII 1237 Dauphin, C. Viennois † 1270

André Guigue VI Dauphin C. Viennois † 1237

Alexandre de Bourg. S. Montagu † 1205

Eudes III 1192 D. Bourg. † 1218

Hugues III 1162 D. Bourg. † 1192

Oudard de Bourg. S. Montagu † 1333

Guillaume I de Bourg. S. Montagu † 1277

Eudes I de Bourg. S. Montagu † 1247

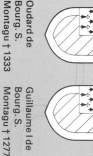

Hugues IV 1218 D. Bourg. † 1273

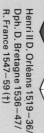

FRANCE

The French line of the Bourbons descending from Louis XIV ceased in 1883. According to the Salian rule of succession, Prince James Henry became head of the Capetians in 1941.

SPAIN

All kings of Spain derive from King Philip V, a grandson of Louis XIV. King Alfonso XIII, as head of the Capetians in 1931, at that time removed the red bordure.

After the extinction of the line of dukes of Longueville in 1707, sovereignty over their principality of Neuchâtel was successfully claimed by the king of Prussia.

The arms of the dukes of Burgundy have through illegitimate offspring also passed on to families in social decline.

On 18 February 1831, King Louis Philippe had to replace the arms of Orléans, because of the fleurs-de-lis, by the Charte of 1830.

Already at birth, the title the Duke of Anjou (indicated by the red bordure), was conferred on the second legitimate prince.

Henri II d'Orl. D. Longueville †1663

Léonor d'Orléans †1622

Henri I d'Orl. D. Longueville †1595

François C. St. Pol, 1608 D. Fronsac †1631

Léonor d'Orl. D. Longueville †1573

M. Rothelin †s.h. 1764

François III d'Orléans †1551

François d'Orl. M. Rothelin †1548

Louis II d'Orléans D. Longuev. †1537

Claude d'Orl. †1524

François Dph. 1524 D. Bret. †1536

Henri II D. Orléans 1519–36/ Dph./D. Bretagne 1536–47/ R. France 1547–59 (†)

Henri Bât. d'Ang. Grand prieur de France †1586

Henri Bât. St. Remi

Charles D. Angoulême 1523–36/ D. Orléans 1536–40/ D. Milan 1540–45 (†)

Louis D. Orléans 1549–50 †s.h.

Maximilien Bât.- Bât. C. Falais Abbé à Middelbourg †1536

S. de Bredam Bât.

Charles S. Sommerdijck †1581

Charles S. Sommerdijck †1542

Baudouin Bât. †1547

Henri III 1151 D. Anjou/ D. Orl., R. Pologne 1573/ R. France & Pol. 1574–89

François †1584 1567 D. Angoulême/1560 D. Orl.; 1567 D. Anjou/ D. Orl., R. Pologne 1573/ R. France 1573/ R. France & Pol. 1574–89

François †1584 1566 D. Orl. 1566 D. Alençon/ 1576 D. Anjou

Franç. II D. Bret. 1544–47/ Dph. 47–59/ R. Ecosse 58–60/ R. Angleterre 58–60/ R. France/ R. France 59–60 (†)

Charles IX D. Orléans 1550–59/ R. France 1560–74 (†)

Philipp Bât. de Bourg. S. Beveren †1498

Antoine Bât.

Philippe †1701 D. Anjou/ 1661 D. Orléans

Louis Philippe †1850 D. Orléans/ 1830–1848 Roi des Français

Louis Bât. C. Toulouse 1678–1737 (†)

Louis Bât. D. Maine 1670–1736 (†)

ANJOU Philippe D. Anjou 1688–91 (†)

Louis »le Grand Dph.« 1661–1711 (†)

Louis XIV Dph./ R. France 1643–1715/ 1643–52

Louis XIV Dph./ R. France 1643–1715/ C. Barcelone 1643–52

Louis François D. Anjou 1672 (†)

Louis Bât. C.Vermandois 1667–83 (†)

Nicolas d'Orléans 1607–11

Alexandre Chevalier de Vend. †1682

Henri IV 1562 R. Navarre (4 variantes)/ R. France & Navarre †1610

Louis XIII Dph./ 1610 R. France & Navarre †1643

César de Vendôme Bât. Vendôme/ D. Vendôme 1609/ 1630–65 (†)

Gaston Jean-Baptiste Anjou/ Orléans 1626–60 (†)

Antoine †1504 Le grd. Bât. Bourg.

Baudouin Bât. S. Falais †1508

Henri Bât. de Vendôme

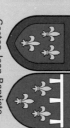
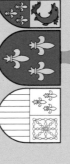
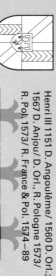

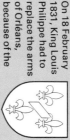

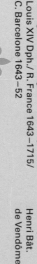

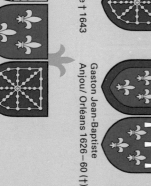

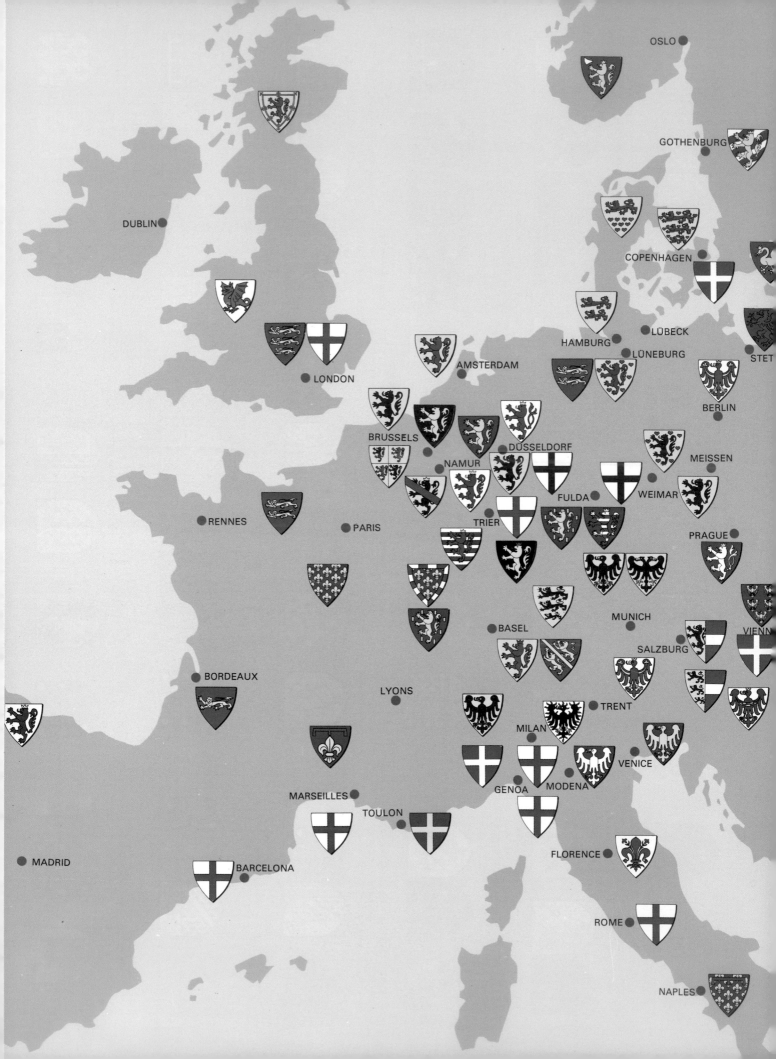

OSLO

GOTHENBURG

DUBLIN

COPENHAGEN

LÜBECK
HAMBURG   LÜNEBURG
STET

LONDON

BERLIN

AMSTERDAM

MEISSEN

BRUSSELS
DÜSSELDORF
NAMUR   FULDA   WEIMAR

PRAGUE

RENNES   TRIER

PARIS

MUNICH

VIENN

BASEL

SALZBURG

BORDEAUX

TRENT

LYONS

MILAN

VENICE

MARSEILLES   GENOA   MODENA

TOULON

FLORENCE

MADRID   BARCELONA

ROME

NAPLES

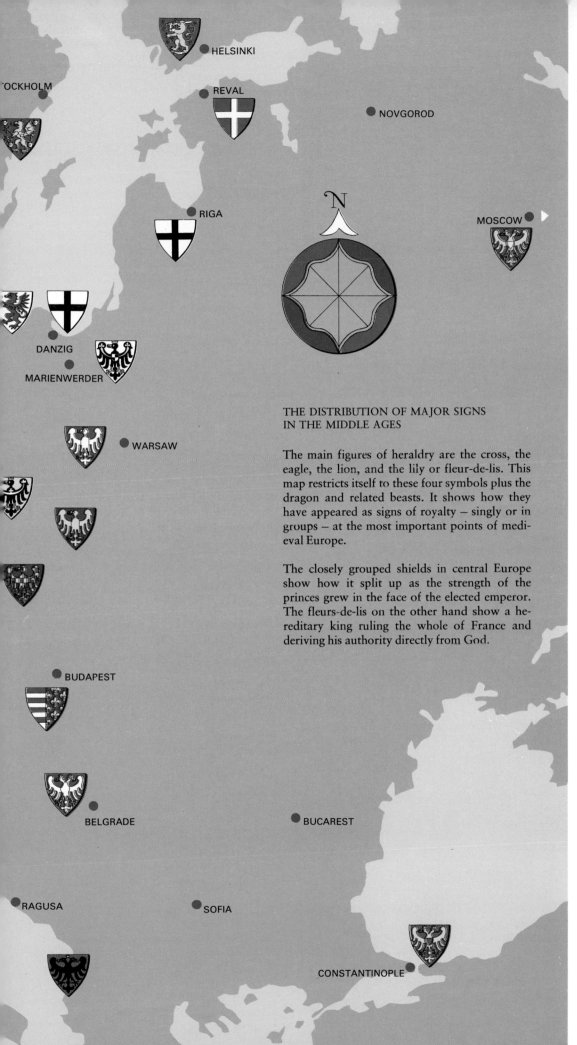

THE DISTRIBUTION OF MAJOR SIGNS
IN THE MIDDLE AGES

The main figures of heraldry are the cross, the eagle, the lion, and the lily or fleur-de-lis. This map restricts itself to these four symbols plus the dragon and related beasts. It shows how they have appeared as signs of royalty — singly or in groups — at the most important points of medieval Europe.

The closely grouped shields in central Europe show how it split up as the strength of the princes grew in the face of the elected emperor. The fleurs-de-lis on the other hand show a hereditary king ruling the whole of France and deriving his authority directly from God.

In the Middle Ages, people came to regard the West as identical with Christendom. Its sign, the cross, has not fully retained its spiritual character, but neither has it entirely lost it. The white cross on a red ground was the symbol of the Holy Kingdom, and one can perhaps interpret its adoption by the kings of Denmark and the margraves of the Savoy as evidence of their missionary zeal. The fact that the Crusaders embarked on the western coast of the Mediterranean is marked by the presence of the cross in many of the coats of arms which are found there.

The eagle had been the badge of the ancient Roman empire and was revived by Charlemagne as a symbol of world domination. Later the double-headed eagle became the personal emblem of the emperor. The loose circle of arms containing eagles indicates how the empire extended outward, consolidating its gains with a series of margraviates.

The lion is the "king of beasts" in counterpart to the king of the heavens, and clearly symbolizes the interests of the landed princes.

The lily, the symbol of the Virgin Mary, became a symbol, as the fleur-de-lis, of state sovereignty in France. A thing of beauty, it was also an emblem of political power and was carried by French princes as far as Hungary.

The dragon and its close relation the griffin are to be seen as symbols of the wind. The Welsh dragon dates back to the oriental troops used by the occupying Romans.

The Ascension of Christ with the banner of the cross, in white and red, bestowed on him by the artist as a sign of victory.

Flag of the Byzantine empire, from a major source of information on the flags of the fourteenth century, the *Conoscimiento de todos los Reinos*.
This flag of the emperor of Constantinople consists of a combination of the George Cross (red on a white ground) with the arms of the ruling family of the Paleologues. The four charges in the corners of each of the other two crosses can

be seen either as fire steles, as in the badges of the Order of the Golden Fleece, or as the Greek letter B. In the latter case they form the initial letters of the Paleologues' motto:
Βασιλεὺς Βασιλέων
Βασιλεύων Βασιλεῦσιν
"King of kings, ruling over kings."

The armorial sign of the cross is unique in Christendom. It is the first common sign under which the West gathered and at the beginning, when the first Crusade was announced, no particular significance was attached to its color. Not even the form of the cross which Christians looked up to in those times is known to us exactly.

Nor can it be said with certainty that the famous sign of victory which the emperor Constantine followed in the battle at the Milvian bridge was actually meant to represent the cross of Christ's Passion. The soldiers of the victorious emperor were given an official description so that they could paint it on their shields. The description indicates clearly that the sign was unknown to the soldiers. It consisted in fact not of a cross but

was decorated with the Christian monogram, whether carried on the end of a staff or as a flag. This is proved by innumerable coins of the emperor, who first recognized Christianity as a state religion.

Only at the beginning of heraldic times do the different forms of the cross emerge so that a particular shape or color can be ascribed to a particular group or person. The Crusader states in the Holy Land, always subject to political tensions, contributed little to the systematization of the forms of the cross. On the other hand the seals of the spiritual brotherhoods which thronged to the holy sepulcher and were only interested in the knights for their protection, provided numerous variations on that theme. The church was already using crosses fastened to the ends of staffs before there were any knights to paint them on their shields. Thus there were two lines of development: sculpted or solid crosses, and flat crosses.

The solid cross developed forms which moved with the style of the times and were characterized by the faceting of the arms, and particularly by the broadening of the ends of the arms, which were strongly reminiscent of letters. At the same time there was a multiplication of the horizontal arms, which were linked with hierarchical status. The flat cross reached basically to the

Historical paintings of the Renaissance were more concerned with dramatic effect than with historical accuracy. This painting of the school of Raphael somewhat anticipates reality, for in addition to carrying the *labarum,* the whole army is equipped with crosses on their standards. It had previously been predicted to Constantine that he would defeat his opponent Maxentius under the sign of Christ in this battle at the Milvian bridge outside Rome.

Opposite:
A particularly fine example of a "cross recercely" is found in a window in Chartres cathedral bearing the shield of Henry, Lord du Mez, who was found worthy of bearing the *oriflamme,* the imperial banner of France.

of two letters. One of them at least consisted of two crossed shafts, but this cross lay diagonally and was not the upright cross which we know. Nevertheless, in the time which followed, the true form of the cross did appear in the depiction of the monogram of Christ. In any case it is established that after Constantine's victory over Maxentius in A.D. 312, an old Roman banner, the *labarum,* served as an imperial standard and

edge of the ground on which it was painted, while the solid cross, as it was free-standing, could have highly ornamented arms. The ends of the arms were also extended on the flat cross, but elaborately ornamented crosses seldom appear as charges on an armorial shield, and tended to be used for preference as free-standing badges. We will have more to say about this in the context of knightly orders.

1 Cross
2 Cross fillet
3 Cross per fess
4 Cross per pale
5 Cross quartered
6 Cross gyronny
7 Cross gyronny of sixteen
8 Cross faceted
9 Cross counter-compony
10 Cross fretty
11 Cross double voided
12 Cross cotised
13 Cross fimbriated
14 Saltire or St. Andrew's cross
15 Cross couped
16 Saltire couped
17 Passion cross
18 Passion cross with both bars
   the same length
19 Patriarchal cross
20 Patriarchal cross with third bar
21 Russian cross
22 Cross formy
23 Cross pattée concave
24 Cross formy couped
25 Cross potent
26 Jerusalem cross
27 Cross crosslet
28 Cross degraded
29 Cross calvary
30 Cross moline
31 Cross recercely
32 Cross moline quarter-pierced
33 Maltese cross
34 Cross fleuretty
35 Cross of any Iberian order of
   knighthood
36 Cross gringoly
37 Cross fourchy
38 Cross fitchy
39 Cross bottony
40 Cross pommy
41 "Key" cross
42 Cross of Toulouse
43 Cross barby
44 Cross formy fitchée couped
45 Cross fitchée double
46 Cross indented
47 Cross engrailed
48 Cross invected
49 Cross bretessed
50 Cross embattled-counter-
   embattled
51 Cross raguly
52 Cross raguly counter raguly
53 Cross raguly and trunked
54 Cross wavy
55 Swastika couped in saltire
56 Fylfot
57 Fylfot clubbed
58 Celtic cross
59 Tau cross or cross of
   St. Anthony
60 Egyptian cross

Gonfalon or banner of the de Blonays, a prominent family in Vaud. Dating from the late fourteenth century and still in possession of the family, this fragment measures 45 by 27 centimeters. It represents a combination of the arms of the dukes of Savoy with the family arms of the de Blonays. The combination has no genealogical basis. The gonfalon expresses the interlinking of the interests of the house of Savoy with the revenues and spiritual endowments of the house of Blonay. For our purposes, the piece gives an example of the possible variations of background pattern on an empty quarter. The upper cross is diapered with triangles interspersed with fleurs-de-lis, the other with lozenges containing crosses crosslet. The "crosses crosslet fitched" surrounding the lions of the de Blonay family are an essential component of the arms, which have undergone little change during the course of the centuries.

Opposite:
Banner of Frauenfeld, the chief town of the Swiss canton of Thurgau. This charming scene, in which the pensive looking lady holds the rampant lion lightly on a chain, has been the official form of the arms and banners of the town of Frauenfeld since the fifteenth century. Originally, on the oldest municipal seal dating from the thirteenth century, the lion and the lady had their backs to one another, the latter holding a bunch of flowers. But when the lady turned round, she also discarded the flowers and took the lion on a leash. Scholars are undecided as to whether it is the lion of the Kiburgs or the Hapsburgs, for at the critical moment Frauenfeld was changing masters. To judge from the color of the lion it is a Hapsburg beast, for the latter is red.

THE LION

The heraldic stylization of the lion has its roots in its natural home. The Greeks and Persians represented it with a heavy mane in

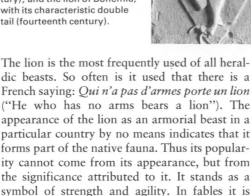

Examples of the stylization of the heraldic lion *(left to right):* a lion cub in carved stone from the monastery of Steingaden (Bavaria, twelfth century); seal of the counts of Gleichen (Thuringia, fourteenth century); and the lion of Bohemia, with its characteristic double tail (fourteenth century).

profile, as against the leopard, which was shown with less of a mane and looking at the observer. An example of such a lion's mane is on this coin from the Greek city Kyzikos in Asia Minor (394 B.C.).

Wall-hanging from the sumptuous baggage of Duke Charles the Bold, which he lost in 1476 at the Battle of Grandson. His arms are repeated on it several times; it

The lion is the most frequently used of all heraldic beasts. So often is it used that there is a French saying: *Qui n'a pas d'armes porte un lion* ("He who has no arms bears a lion"). The appearance of the lion as an armorial beast in a particular country by no means indicates that it forms part of the native fauna. Thus its popularity cannot come from its appearance, but from the significance attributed to it. It stands as a symbol of strength and agility. In fables it is described as "noble"; it is the king of the beasts, but not of the birds, over whom it has no control.

This antagonism between the two animal kingdoms is paralleled by a heraldic antagonism which makes the eagle the symbol of imperial power and the lion the symbol of royal sovereignty, as is shown by our map on pages 104–105. There must have been a strong underlying sense of this antagonism in the Middle Ages, for in the heroic poem by Heinrich von Veldeke based on the story of Aeneas, the bearer of the

sions, particularly to the powerful duke of Bavaria and Saxony, Henry the Lion of the house of Welf. Duke Henry did not bear arms in the technical sense, but he used a naturalistic picture of a lion as a seal and erected a monumental and lifelike bronze lion outside his castle of Dankwarderode in Brunswick. It was left to his descendants to adopt a formal coat of arms,

12 13 14

which was derived from the arms of England. Henry referred to himself in Latin as *Henricus Leo,* but he had two German names, Heinrich der Löwe (Henry the Lion) and Heinrich Welf. *Welf* or *Welp* was a young beast of prey, cognate

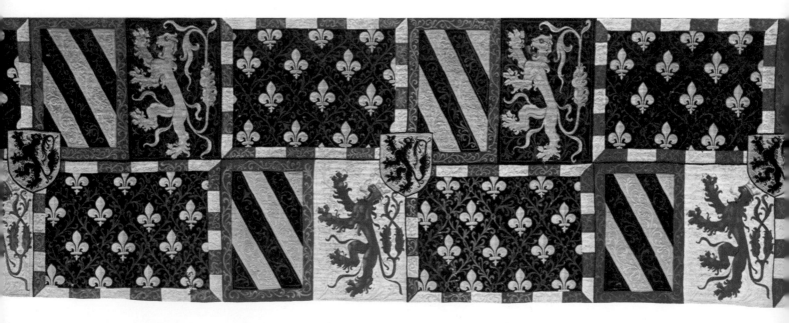

shows the new and old Burgundian fields (fleurs-de-lis and panels divided bendwise) together with some excellent examples of heraldic lions in the Netherlandish style – the golden lion of Brabant, the black lion of Flanders and the double-tailed red lion of Limburg.

arms of a lion is set against the bearer of the arms of an eagle. If one takes the latter to be the historical and geographical forerunner of the Holy Roman emperor, then the bearer of the lion represents the unruly feudal lords, to whom the emperor had to make more and more concessions

with the word for a young dog, whelp, which is used in English today.

In a society which prized the noble but fierce behavior which was the essence of knightly virtues, the lion, the king of the beasts, was a

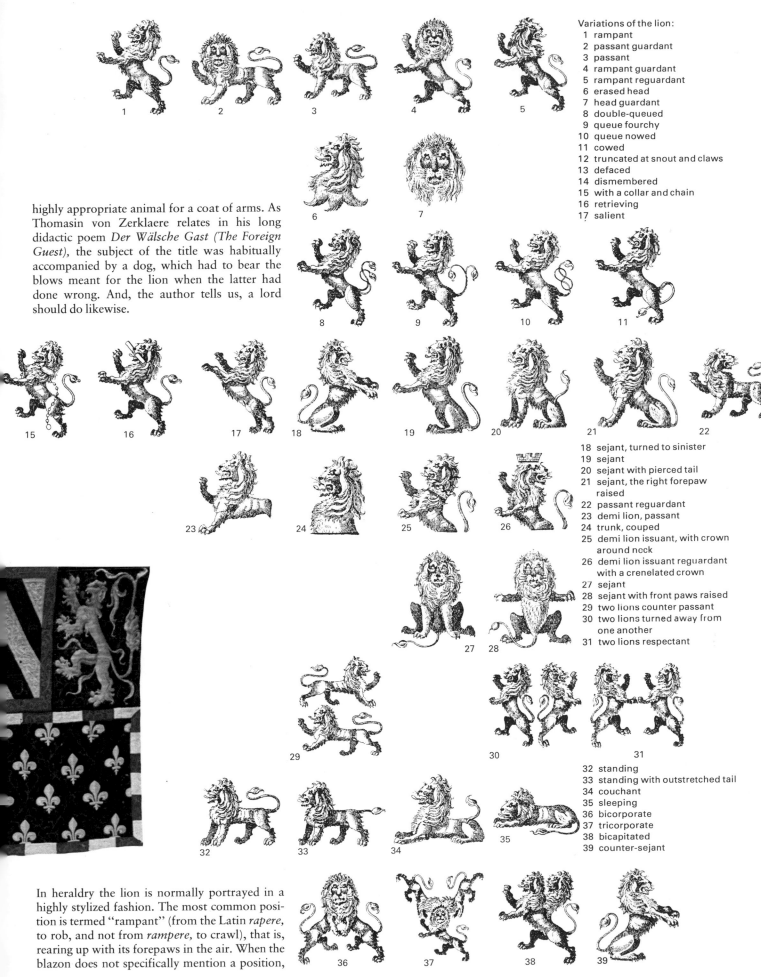

Variations of the lion:
1 rampant
2 passant guardant
3 passant
4 rampant guardant
5 rampant reguardant
6 erased head
7 head guardant
8 double-queued
9 queue fourchy
10 queue nowed
11 cowed
12 truncated at snout and claws
13 defaced
14 dismembered
15 with a collar and chain
16 retrieving
17 salient

highly appropriate animal for a coat of arms. As Thomasin von Zerklaere relates in his long didactic poem *Der Wälsche Gast (The Foreign Guest)*, the subject of the title was habitually accompanied by a dog, which had to bear the blows meant for the lion when the latter had done wrong. And, the author tells us, a lord should do likewise.

18 sejant, turned to sinister
19 sejant
20 sejant with pierced tail
21 sejant, the right forepaw raised
22 passant reguardant
23 demi lion, passant
24 trunk, couped
25 demi lion issuant, with crown around neck
26 demi lion issuant reguardant with a crenelated crown
27 sejant
28 sejant with front paws raised
29 two lions counter passant
30 two lions turned away from one another
31 two lions respectant

32 standing
33 standing with outstretched tail
34 couchant
35 sleeping
36 bicorporate
37 tricorporate
38 bicapitated
39 counter-sejant

In heraldry the lion is normally portrayed in a highly stylized fashion. The most common position is termed "rampant" (from the Latin *rapere*, to rob, and not from *rampere*, to crawl), that is, rearing up with its forepaws in the air. When the blazon does not specifically mention a position,

111

Opposite:
The arms of the kingdom of Belgium contain so many lions on the shield and the nine banners that the title of "Leo Belgicus" seems fully justified.

Right:
The crests of the kingdoms of Scotland *(left)* and England.

40 winged, standing
41 St. Mark's lion sejant
42 St. Mark's lion from the Ionian islands
43 sea lion with raised tail
44 sea lion with lowered tail, standing
45 sea lion with lowered tail, upright
46 sea lion with a dragon's tail
47 chimera

the lion may be assumed to be rampant. If he is in a different position, other terminology must be used, referring to the position of his head and limbs. An early heraldic convention found in medieval blazons uses the distinction between a lion and a leopard previously employed by the ancient Greeks. In antiquity, the lion, having a heavy mane, was generally shown in profile, while the leopard, having less hair, was shown looking towards the observer. A lion looking towards the observer therefore came to be given

40   41   42

43   44   45   46

47   48   49   50

48 lion with a man's face
49 lion with a satyr's face
50 chimera guardant

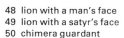

Section from a Venetian flag with the lion of St. Mark standing half on land, half on water.

the name of the animal usually shown in that pose. Some of the possible combinations are as follows. The current English heraldic terms are followed by the Old French terminology.

For a lion with both forepaws raised: lion rampant – *lion rampant.*

For a lion walking along with one forepaw raised and looking at the observer: lion passant guardant – *léopard.*

For a lion walking along and looking to the front: lion passant – *lion léopardé.*

For a lion with both forepaws raised and looking at the observer: lion rampant guardant – *léopard lionné.*

Note that the *léopard* can be recognized by the fact that it is always looking at the observer; it is always "guardant."

L'UNION FAIT LA FORCE

A popular theme in the history of art is the Macedonian King Alexander the Great's journey to heaven. In the Middle Ages, Alexander was honored as one of the nine great heroes of the world. Here two griffins, duped by a suitable bait, rise into the air, taking with them a basket containing Alexander.

Below:
Among the strange creatures included in the *Physiologue* is the basilisk, a gigantic bird with a swan's neck and a snake's tail. The head is that of a hen.

But these distinctions are only the beginning. Any armorial figure can be painted in any of the six heraldic colors, and the lion naturally offers the most examples. Animals can be shown holding anything capable of being held, usually in the right forepaw. Naturally in the case of a lion this is often a weapon – in the arms of the Grand Duchy of Hessen a sword – or the attribute of a saint, such as the ax of Saint Olaf of Norway. Alternatively it may be a peaceful subject such as the pear-twig of Pope Sixtus V. When a lion has

body is that of an eagle and the lower part with the hind legs that of a lion. The griffin is shown irradiated (i.e., emitting rays) as a symbol of luxury and its opposite, restraint. For this reason it became the emblem of a medieval order, the Tankard Order of the kingdom of Aragon. Via this symbolism, it finally became the supporter of the arms of the Germanic Holy Roman emperor (see page 90).

The roots of the pictorial language of heraldry stretch far back into pre-Christian times. The imaginary world of the creators of arms was strongly imprinted with the representations of the animal world contained in the so-called bestiaries. These were books of nature lore which attempted to describe both biological and inanimate subjects, especially with the aim of drawing moral conclusions from them. All bestiaries go back to one original source, the so-called *Physiologus* ("one versed in natural history"), a manuscript which may have originated in Alexandria in the middle of the second century B.C. Its forty-eight sections show a distinct relationship to certain passages in the Bible, combining warnings against heresy with admonitions towards abstinence and chastity. Innumerable idioms which are current even today can be traced back to these books which in the Middle Ages were almost as widespread as the Bible. They also gave rise to the popular

The basilisk rarely appears as an armorial charge, except in the arms of Basel where it serves as a supporter, either singly or in pairs, for the shield bearing the "crook of Basel" *(above right)*. Here it is an obvious example of canting arms.

wings it nearly always relates to St. Mark, the patron saint of Venice. In fact all the four evangelists have a winged creature as their symbol: Luke a bull, which is revered by painters, Matthew an angel, and John an eagle, which plays a significant part in Spanish heraldry.

The lion of St. Mark should not be confused with a griffin, a fabulous beast whose upper

animal fables. Who does not know the symbol of self-abnegatory parental love, the pelican, or the phoenix arising from the ashes? But in heraldry other beasts too are perpetuated. There is the stag which drowns its enemy, the snake, in its lair and therefore appears as an armorial beast with its prey in its mouth. And the fox, of whom it is said that it feigns death in front of the birds it is going to eat. On military banners it appears

Medieval artists were fond of personifying human characteristics and showing them in the garb of a knight with the appropriate accouterments. Heraldry proved extremely useful in this respect. Here "Lady Humility" bears a griffin on his banner, and "Lady Chastity" rides upon a unicorn.

In every cultural milieu there are mythical animals which the gods use to ride long distances upon. Thus it is reported that the Hindu god Vishnu rode on the "garuda." This bird has an almost human face. It is otherwise known as the sign of sovereignty of Thailand *(above)*, and is also the name of the Indonesian airline.

Until the sixteenth century English armorials were full of stylized monsters such as the dragon in the arms of Uther Pendragon, the father of the famous King Arthur, or the wingless wyverns ascribed to the king of Barbary.

We may laugh at the pedantry of a poet who is all technique and no inspiration. But as his arms show, Johann Christoph Gottsched (1700–1760) was aware that he owed his importance in the history of literature to French models. His poet's steed, Pegasus, rises above the symbol of exact measurement, the dividers.

Seal of Queen Mary Stuart of Scotland (1542–1587). Before the unification of Scotland and England, the Scottish coat of arms was supported by two unicorns.

Classical examples of unicorns and unicorn's head couped (above right), which have to be shown with their heads lowered so that the long horn will fit into the shield.

in all possible expressions of its trickery. It is shown as a preacher in front of hens; in many arms it is even shown indecently, with brush erect, running between the outspread legs of a naked woman. Some of the flights of fancy which this preaching technique indulged in are difficult for the modern mind to follow. The onager or wild ass is stated to make water eleven times in a night, and this is supposed to stand for the eleven remaining apostles of Christ. So far the onager has remained unknown in heraldry, but many fabulous creatures have become armorial beasts, and particularly supporters (see page 200) and badges (see page 210). As the zoologists have borrowed names from the bestiaries for newly discovered types of animals, we must now make a distinction between heraldic and natural antelopes, panthers, and other exotic beasts. This becomes all the more important as the native fauna of distant countries find an increasingly important place in their state and municipal heraldry.

One undisputedly mythical beast is the unicorn; whether it was originally identical with the similarly equipped rhinoceros must remain a matter for conjecture. In heraldry the unicorn usually has the body of a light horse, the tail of a lion, and the legs of an antelope. Its head is distinguished by the single horn and the short beard. The story that it can only be caught with the help of a virgin had a special appeal for artists. It has made the unicorn a favorite supporter, and a symbol of Christ.

Pegasus, the winged horse, plays an increased role in heraldry with the inception of humanism. It occurs mainly in the arms of intellectuals who also count themselves poets, although other families and institutions use it as well. (It currently adorns the Greek five-drachma piece.)

The *Physiologus* has many astonishing things to say about lions. According to it, Jacob, the

Nearly twenty-five hundred years old, the bronze statue of the Capitoline she-wolf stands in the Palazzo dei Conservatori in Rome. The wolf on the arms of the bishopric of Passau *(above right)* has become the arms of the town of the same name and the trademark of first-class steel goods.

Known for its fierceness, the wild boar is one of the oldest armorial charges anywhere. In 1194 Dietrich von Schweinspoint accompanied Emperor Henry VI on a campaign against Tancred, the Norman king of Sicily *(right)*.

The boar *(far right)* is one of the badges of King Richard III of England (reigned 1483–1485). An unscrupulous ruler, he was nicknamed the "boar" or the "hog" by his enemies.

father of the tribe of Israel, named his son Judah the lion cub, which is a kind of prophecy, for thousands of years later we find current the saying *Vicit leo ex tribu Juda* ("The lion of the

Various characteristics are attributed to the lion, distinguishing it from all other animals. According to the *Physiologus* the cubs come dead into the world, and after three days the father

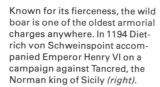

In the seal of the city of Berlin, the Brandenburg eagle appears over the back of the bear *(above)*; this was later seen as a symbol of oppression.
The seal of Bern originally contained only the bear. The imperial eagle was added around 1319 as a symbol of imperial freedom, *(above center)*, and was retained until 1714, by which time events had rendered it inappropriate *(above right)*.

In the richly wooded areas of the Carpathian mountains and East Karelia the bear in modern heraldic designs becomes a true reflection of the area's natural fauna.

tribe of Judah has triumphed"). Who the victorious lion of the tribe of Judah may be remains open to interpretation; it could be Jesus Christ, but also Haile Selassie, the late emperor of Ethiopia.

appears and breathes on them and thus they are woken and brought to life. The lion is rightly held to be the most common armorial beast on four legs. It is widely regarded as a symbol of courage, boldness, and majesty, even of Christ himself. But in some places, his position as king of the beasts has been usurped by others, notably the bull and the bear of the thick forest. Four-legged beasts are often particularly suitable as punning or "canting" arms. One did not always need to go back to the *Physiologus* to find a suitable armorial beast. A man with a name such as Cammell or Cokerell did not have to look far to find the animal of his choice. In German a man with *Schwein* or *Eber* in his name inevitably chose the wild boar *(Eber)* as his badge. Canting arms have always been popular. In many cases it may require a knowledge of philology or dialects

The bear's paw is very suitable as a representation of the whole animal. On the left is a seal of the Grisonian family von Planta; on the right are the arms of the district of the earldom of Hoya, which revives the medieval arms of the counts of Hoya.

ing, even to the extent of displacing the real significance of the arms. Such is the case with the city of Rome which traditionally owes its existence to the she-wolf's suckling of Romulus and

Switzerland is relatively rich in arms featuring bears, among them the arms of the valley community of Ursern, today part of the canton of Uri. From 1410,

The bear of St. Gallen is related to the saint who gave the Swiss town and canton their name. St. Gallus allowed a bear to help him in collecting building materials for his house. He rewarded the bear with bread, which the animal is shown holding on the town's seal *(below)*. The earliest existing impression of this seal was made on 24 May 1312. On 5 July 1475, Emperor Frederick III granted the town a

golden collar to go round the bear's neck, as can be seen on the seventeenth century banner *(left)*. The collar is an attribute often worn by heraldic bears, not usually as a symbol of help freely given, but of the subjection of a dancing bear by his tamer.

to unravel the source of the pun, for the modern form of a word may be different from that at the time when the family adopted the arms for canting reasons.

The wolf makes a suitable subject for canting arms in many languages, and the legends which often accompany it can make it doubly interest-

Remus. Wolf and fox, difficult to tell apart as heraldic animals because of their similarity of shape, are often distinguished by their attributes alone. If the animal is preying on a lamb one can assume it is a wolf; an animal with a goose or hen in its jaws is presumably a fox.

The dog, on the other hand, is easily distin-

Ursern bore a bear (in Latin *ursus*) as canting arms, with a silver cross on its back. Note the rich diapered pattern of the material of the banner.

The Indian princes imitated British customs, creating coats of arms conceived in the European style but executed with indigenous forms.

The elephant in the arms of the counts von Helfenstein is a form of canting arms.

guishable from its cousins by the fact that as a domestic animal it is nearly always wearing a collar. The boar hound is recognizable by its erect ears, the hunting dog by its drooping ones, and the grayhound by its slender body and head. Dogs are highliy suitable for canting arms, though their use may be based on other considerations than the above-mentioned characteristics, as in the case of the *Dogge* (breed of Great Dane) of the Counts of Toggenburg (see page 83).

The bear, as well, is popular for many reasons. Its tamability is recorded in all kinds of legends; many a saint has made friends with a bear. St. Corbinian did so and let him carry his baggage, a fact which is recorded in the municipal arms of Freising; St. Gallus used a bear to carry heavy weights when building a house. The phonetic associations of the word (which is pronounced in the same way in German as in English) have been used in many instances. The towns of Berlin, Bern, Bernburg, and others

in 1579. Like other heraldic beasts, the bear can be distinguished by an attribute, such as a collar, though more than one community has seen this as a symbol of oppression and had it removed, including Berlin in 1872.

There are innumerable other examples in canting arms of animals adopted directly for their names without recourse to natural histories. There is the aurochs head of Uri, the elephant of Helfenstein (a play on *Elfenbein,* the German word for ivory). There are numerous German names which, containing the syllable "herz," show a deer *(Hirsch)* or a deer's antlers in their arms. Heraldry has no objection to a bull being turned into an ox as long as it serves for a canting coat of arms. Cows are distinguished by bells round their niecks and strikingly tinctured udders. Usually, however, heraldry insists on the whole animal appearing, although the arms of the city of Coesfeld in Westphalia feature only the head, emphasized as such by the presence of a harness.

A bull's head looks fixedly at the observer. The ring through his nose is a characteristic sign to show that he has been subdued.

The crown on this bull's head of 1219 *(above right)* shows the extent to which it was venerated at the time in Mecklenburg. The different lines of the local dynasty are distinguished by the inclusion or omission of the pleated skin round the neck.

carry a bear in their arms. The Italian Prince Orsini uses a bear *(orso* in Italian) as a supporter for his arms, and the valley community of Ursern in Switzerland used the association of the Latin name *(ursus)* in adopting the bear first as a seal and then as a charge on their arms. The bear is not easy to depict graphically. The fur should be rendered clearly but not naturalistically, and the artist must be prepared to paint the animal's male organ bright red, or he may be mocked (in Switzerland at least) for having painted a shebear. This was actually the cause of a war between St. Gallen and the canton of Appenzell

The smaller the animal's size, however, the more often it is used merely for the similarity of its name and not, as in the case of the lion or the bear, because of its dominance over the other beasts of the forest.

Nor should we forget the horse. Without the horse the whole history of the Middle Ages would have been different, for thanks to the horse thousands upon thousands of men were able to move from place to place at scarcely believable speeds. The word "knight" itself is synonymous with rider or horseman in a number

The arms of the English town of Oxford are completely canting. They show an ox and a ford. The same applies to the German town of Ochsenfurt, but its arms have no helmet or crest. Such decorations are more customary with English towns than with German ones.

The arms granted to the Canadian province of Manitoba in 1905 adopted previously used emblems, consisting of the indigenous bison and the English George Cross.

When the administrations of the town and the canton of Schaffhausen were split up, the arms of the town received the house from which the ram was emerging in the original arms, while the canton's arms kept the ram.

The predominant animal on the southeast coast of the Baltic is the elk, and it was therefore the armorial beast of the old region of Semgallen. Its head appears in the arms of the town of Mitau.

of languages (German: *Ritter*; French: *cavalier*, etc.). Horses on coats of arms are not always related to this theme, however; they often refer back to preheraldic symbols. One thinks of the charger of Lower Saxony, of the horses carved in the chalk of Kent, or the legend of Hengist and Horsa, the Anglo-Saxon princes who are supposed to have settled England. The horseman appears frequently in the assimilation of a seal into an armorial charge. The rider (called the "pursuer") in the arms of Lithuania and the supposed figure of St. George in the arms of Moscow are in fact representations of the grand dukes themselves as they appear elsewhere on equestrian seals. Here they have been transferred from the seals to the coats of arms, forming early examples of a practice prevalent even today.

The human figure plays the same part on the coat of arms as the rider. Especially in communal arms there are many human figures, which originated as patron saints on seals. They are often represented by their attributes.

A deer's antlers are frequently used, particularly as a crest. The best known example is in the arms of Württemberg.

A delicately stepping bull appeared on the shield of the margraviate of Lower Lusatia as early as the fourteenth century *(far left)*. In later centuries heraldic artists tended to show it with a white belly.

The rampant bull in the arms of the city of Turin is a classic example of minimal use of color in heraldry *(left center)*. They are canting arms since the Italian for bull is *toro* and for the city itself, Torino. The crown with the nine pearls shows that the community has the status of a county. The city of Genoa, on the other hand, was compelled to renounce the king's crown included in its arms when it ceased to have royal status.

The two cows of the Pyrenean county of Béarn *(above left)* were inherited at an early date by the counts of Foix and included in a quartered shield. Today they are found in the national arms of Andorra, where they signify the continuation of the authority of the counts now exercised by the Republic of France.

The towns of Rüdesheim and Bingen, once part of the electorate of Mainz, bear practically identical arms (those of Bingen are shown). They show St. Martin on horseback, sharing his coat with the cripple.

The beaver (German *Biber*) is a canting arms for Biberach an der Riss. It is also in the arms of New York, as a reminder of the city's past.

Arms with the figures of saints have been subject to political suppression. At the time of the Third Reich arms bearing the figures of saints and even those with long-established attributes of the latter were the victims of a regular campaign of governmental regulations. This was so successful that long after the fall of the regime these "suspect" arms had to be eliminated from official publications. The patron saint of Mainz almost became a victim of this state of affairs when there were efforts to remove him from the arms of Bingen (see page 121).

121

The original arms of the kingdom of Aragon consisted of the Christian cross, through the power of which four Moorish princes had been defeated. In the struggle for the Spanish throne after 1700, the Hapsburg King Charles placed these arms on the reverse of his golden seal.

There can be many motives for the tasteful decoration of a coat of arms with human figures or parts of the body. Such coats of arms lend themselves to fanciful explanations, which are sometimes true, sometimes possible, but mostly thought up after the event. Sometimes they carry the heads of defeated enemies, as in the present-day arms of Sardinia, which are actually those of Aragon. The head of a loved one makes a more attractive subject, and on occasion may supplant the true family arms. Such is the case with the minnesinger Friedrich, a prince of the house of the margrave of Meissen (see page 234). Ethnic

Human forms in the arms of places are usually patron saints and can be recognized by their attributes. St. Fridolin appears in the banners of the Swiss canton of Glarus as a pilgrim *(right)*. He always appears with a halo and a book under his arm, usually with a knapsack, hanging from a shoulder strap, and his pilgrim's staff, which has long since been turned into an abbott's crozier.

The medieval talent for inventing variations on established coats of arms was inexhaustible. A humorous element is included in this lion with the head of a virgin wearing a bonnet, and the puppet figure conjuring small doubles of himself out of his pockets.

characteristics are often exaggerated. There is some doubt as to whether the man's torso which appears on the helmet of the same margrave of Meissen is that of a Jew. The nose appears more and more crooked in subsequent portrayals. But perhaps he was only the stepfather of Friedrich's beloved.

Whether in the form of a lady, a moor, a saint, or some other figure, central European heraldry – not only German but also Dutch and Italian – particularly favored the human figure as a crest. Parts of the body, on the other hand, predominated more on shields, leading to ingenious if not always optically appealing combinations. An example is the ancient triskelion of Sicily, which consists of three legs joined together at the upper thigh. The same sign is found as canting arms for the West German town of Füssen ("feet"). A more important case is the arms of the kings of the Isle of Man, and now of the island itself. As

Left, below:
The saintly halo attached to the head of the monk in the arms of Munich undoubtedly relates to the name of the city rather than its actual character. The city (in German, *München*) was founded by monks (German *Mönche*) in the year 1157.

Left, bottom:
Medieval heraldry did not shrink from representing naked human figures but often found ingenious ways of preserving their decency.

in the case of Sicily the figure refers to the triangular form of the island, but the arms are further elucidated by the motto *Stato quocumque jeceris* ("I will stand wherever you may throw me"). A single leg protrudes from the helmet of the king of the Isle of Man, the sole of the foot toward the sky (see page 160).

Collections of figures, especially in England, were compiled to serve as patterns for heraldic artists and workers in precious metals. Here is an English example of 1889 showing human limbs and fantastic figures with human forms and faces.

Below right:
In the Middle East, a four-legged animal with wings and a human face was considered to be a link between heaven and earth. Such a sphinx is this ivory carving found in the museum of Aleppo, Syria (ca. 900 B.C.).

Even in the real life of birds, nature favors the strongest species. The most powerful birds not only subjugate the smaller and weaker ones, they even take them from the ground as prey, together with other living beings which have only the swiftness of their feet to rely on. Thus by their very nature, the biggest birds of prey, or taloned birds *(Accipitridae)* as the zoologists now call them, are predestined to represent the divine world for men. Small wonder then, that the eagle and related birds are the most common symbols for God and heaven. This applies to every cultural area in which birds of this kind are

Ancient-Egyptian symbols of royalty *(top to bottom):*

Neck ornament of the Egyptian ruler Tutankhamen (twelfth dynasty).

Breastplate from a royal tomb in Byblos which is not only decorated with a winged falcon, but also shaped into a falcon's head at each tip.

Neck ornament consisting of the hawk of the goddess Nekhebit.

The Albanian national hero Prince Georg Kastriota, known as Skanderbeg, fought against Turkish oppression until his death in 1468. He used as his seal the double-headed eagle *(left)* of the eastern Roman empire, which was threatened by the Turks.

to be found. Unlike the lion, the next most popular armorial beast, birds of prey occur in all climates. While the armorial lion is based on a

The so-called virgin eagle of Nuremberg *(below)* was originally a German imperial eagle with a king's head; from the fifteenth century onward it was given increasingly obvious feminine characteristics.

bodies of animals and human faces – the harpies. When such a figure appears in central European heraldry, however, it is a humanistic interpretation of something quite different. The so-called *Jungfrauenadler* ("virgin eagle") in Nuremberg is actually a German imperial eagle with a king's head, and was in fact depicted in this form some decades ago. The German imperial eagle itself goes directly back to the ancient Romans. When Charlemagne was declared emperor on Christmas Day in the year 800, he erected an imperial

In South America the condor takes the place of the eagle as a symbol of sovereignty. It is nearly always naturalistically depicted and crowns the arms of the north-western countries of Colombia *(above left),* Bolivia, Ecuador, and Panama. In some of these countries the condor is expressly protected by law as a symbol of sovereignty.

medieval European notion of the animal, these birds retain a certain resemblance to nature even when strongly stylized. One can fairly easily distinguish between a falcon and an eagle by their bodily characteristics. This distinction was made in recent years by the Arab republics when they replaced the eagle of Saladin with the falcon of General Khalid ibn al-Walid from Muhammad's tribe of Koraish.

The symbolic difference between eagle, falcon, and hawk has an old tradition which goes back into prehistory. The Hittites used the double eagle as their national badge; the ancient Egyptians provided their kings with ornaments shaped like hawks and falcons which have a distinctly heraldic flavor to them. Objects of this kind have been found in the tombs of Egyptian kings. They were either hung round the neck on chains or formed breastplates fastened in some other fashion. A common feature is that they all hold spherical precious stones in their claws, representing the earth or the universe. This symbol is found in the provisional national emblem of the Republic of Egypt (1953).

Just as the ancient Egyptians tended to represent their gods as human bodies with animal faces or the heads of birds, such as eagles and hawks, so the tribes of the Balkans and the Greek islands believed in mythical winged beings with the

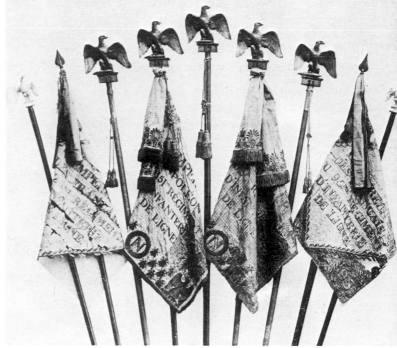

eagle on his palace in Aix-la-Chapelle. His followers "heraldicized" it so persistently that with only a few modifications due to contemporary tastes, and with one or two interruptions, it has remained the arms of Germany even into its republican era. One such interruption was from 1401, when the future emperor Sigismund confirmed that which had been generally accepted since the thirteenth century, that the emperor's eagle should have two heads, while that of the future emperor, who could only be called the German or Roman king, should only have one head. This seems to have satisfied the Hohen-

On the *signa* of the Roman legions *(above left),* which we normally refer to today as "standards," the naturalistic eagle of Jupiter appears either at the top end of the pole or on a medallion surrounded by a laurel wreath.

The Napoleonic empire's taste for Roman antiquity is seen above in its use of military colors crowned with an eagle which is typically Roman in attitude and appearance.

The minnesinger Reinmar of Zweter (now Zeutern in north Baden, Germany) formed the wing bones of his armorial eagle into a second and a third head.

Below, left to right:
Eagle on the seal of the Austrian duke of the house of Babenberg, Heinrich von Mödling (d. 1223). Impression from 1203.

Eagle from the oldest seal of the city of Vienna; impression from 1239.

Eagle holding a shield bearing the family arms of the king of Romans Richard of Cornwall (1256) in its

stauffens, although they were fond of copying the eastern Roman empire. There a double-headed eagle had become an emblem of the state and remained so. How this came about no one knows exactly, for heraldry in its western European manifestation had not taken root in the eastern Roman empire. And when the Byzantine empire lost its capital to the Turks in 1453, its heirs adorned themselves with golden double eagles on a red ground. This applied both to the genealogical heirs such as the margraves of Montferrat, or a political heir, not to say pretender or usurper such as the grand duke of Moscow, who also based his claim on close kinship.

the Russian title. Around 1700 the tzars decided to "tincture" their double eagle black on a golden field in emulation of the German Roman emperor in Vienna.

When yet a third emperor, Napoleon, now appeared on the scene, he had to find a new variant. He found it in a naturalistically drawn eagle, looked down upon by the old heraldic experts, which revived the spirit of ancient Rome. The colors he chose, gold on a blue field, were not those previously used by the kings of France, but those which he supposed to be the original colors of the German emperor, having been misinformed by his scholars.

beak. One of Richard's sons, Edmund, had this combination drawn in 1290 in memory of his father.

The eagle of Frankfurt; drawing by one of the most prolific and skillful heraldic artists of the sixteenth century, Jost Amman.

The eagle of Silesia as it appeared on the seal of Duke Bolko II in 1334. A crescent is included in the design.

The so-called burning eagle *(right)* which was the arms of the kingdom of Bohemia until the middle of the thirteenth century. From the tomb of Ottokar I (d. 1230) in the cathedral of St. Vitus in Prague, fourteenth century.

The town of Schongau formed its own arms *(right center)* from the imperial eagle and the Bavarian lozenge shield. In the arms of Wimpfen, the differentiating sign was a key *(far right)*.

The two imperial domains of Europe, the German Roman *(far right)* and the Russian *(right),* added a second head to the eagle to express their status.

The later Russian tzars only gradually came to use the title of emperor in diplomatic intercourse though the general public continued to use

But the double eagle still survives today in the arms of those towns which had it bestowed on them by the emperor Frederick III in return for help they had given him and in lieu of material compensation. It has been present also, since the time of Charles V, in the arms of Toledo and Potosí (Bolivia), and even in the arms of a people's republic, Albania. In the latter case it commemorates the national hero Skanderbeg, and the inhabitants call themselves in their own language "sons of eagles."

After Napoleon's appearance in central Europe, the double eagle lost something of its impact, but

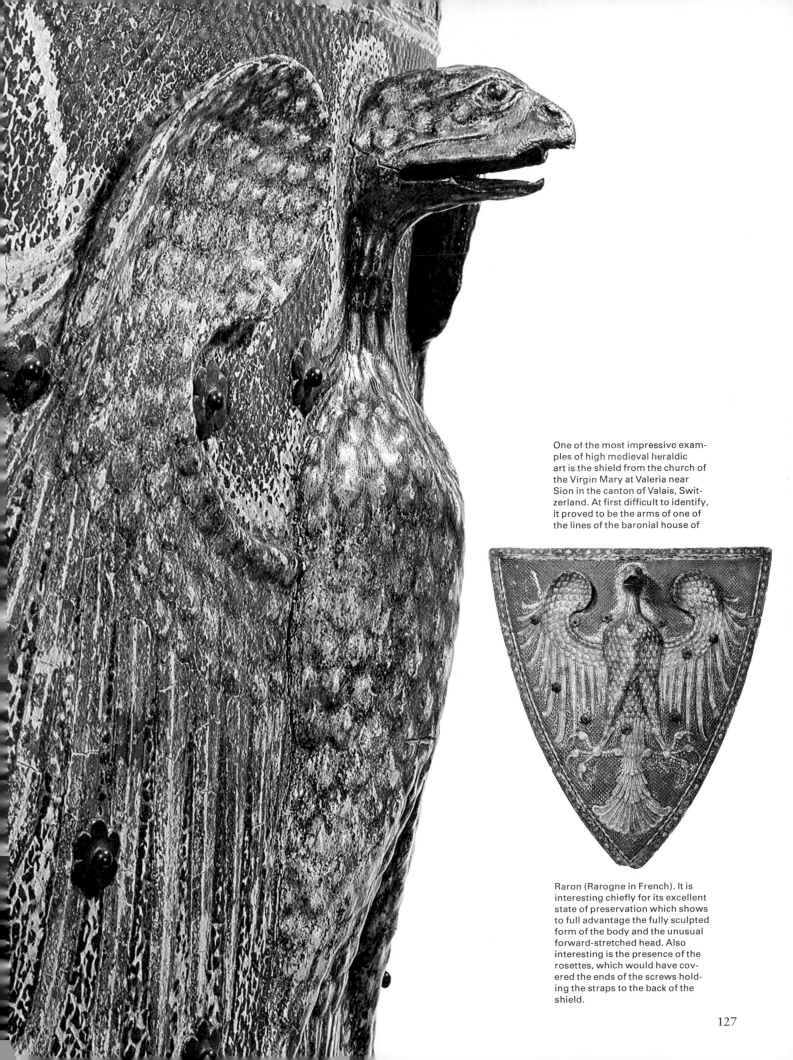

One of the most impressive examples of high medieval heraldic art is the shield from the church of the Virgin Mary at Valeria near Sion in the canton of Valais, Switzerland. At first difficult to identify, it proved to be the arms of one of the lines of the baronial house of

Raron (Rarogne in French). It is interesting chiefly for its excellent state of preservation which shows to full advantage the fully sculpted form of the body and the unusual forward-stretched head. Also interesting is the presence of the rosettes, which would have covered the ends of the screws holding the straps to the back of the shield.

The eagle is stylized in a symmetrical manner, only the head being allowed to depart from this symmetry. The wings are always set at right angles to the body and spread to a greater or lesser degree.

it was not altogether played out. A clever move on the part of the German Roman emperor Francis II saved it from extinction. As a symbol of imperial worth, it was declared the arms of the Austrian empire which was rising from the ruins of the German Roman empire. As Francis was emperor twice over, being both "elected Roman emperor" and "hereditary emperor of Austria," an Austrian eagle was laid on the breast of the "Roman" double eagle. But the former, representing a worldly title, had no halo around its head. It only received a halo again in 1934 when Dollfuss suppressed the word "republic" in Austria and changed the country into a "federal state" which had to ally itself with the Third Reich in 1938. The latter had a single-headed Roman eagle distorted in a half-heraldic, half-ancient-Roman manner.

The single-headed imperial eagle has lasted until today in those towns which were able to retain

Swiss Confederation more than for other lands, the empire was identified with the much hated and directly neighboring house of Austria.

The saying associated with the figure of the eagle, *Sub umbra alarum tuarum protege nos* ("Protect us under the shadow of thy wings"), only has a limited application for Switzerland. The motto is found particularly often above the unrealistic but widely distributed *Quaternionenadler* which was supposed to represent the unity of the empire, but more usually expressed its disintegration. In many museums one finds glass goblets with these eagles painted on them, on each of whose pinions ranks of the empire are represented by four small shields. Thus there are four counts, four margraves, four burgraves, and so on right down to the peasants.

The eagle, a classical example of heraldry's passion for symmetry, has also been used by ar-

After the emperor Frederick II was crowned king in Jerusalem, it was always one of the long-term objectives of the German emperors to win back the city of the Holy Sepulcher. In 1483 that much traveled citizen of Constance, Konrad Grünenberg, had the future imperial arms ready in his comprehensive armorial. They consisted of the imperial eagle with three heads instead of two *(above)*. However, the emperors' ambition was to remain unfulfilled.

or regain their status as "imperial towns" in the face of increasing external sovereignty. Thus the towns of Aix-la-Chapelle, Deventer, Dortmund, Goslar and Oppenheim bear the same arms as the German Federal Republic. Other former imperial towns added a further sign to the eagle, usually a small shield on the breast. After many generations of armed struggle, the Swiss gained their freedom from the empire. But its double eagle long remained a symbol of independence for them, even after 1648, when Switzerland separated from the empire completely. For the

morial artists in more natural forms. The eagle that symbolizes the house of Hohenzollern's refusal to yield to the Sun King soars above a landscape (see page 210), the sun being the attribute that identifies the bird as an eagle. In free graphic forms (e.g., on deeds of title) even the Russian and Austrian double eagles were represented as flying like ordinary birds.

Evidence of identity may also be provided by smaller creatures that only the eagle is capable of killing. But not every bird of prey necessarily

represents an eagle. For example a bird with a hood over its head and ringed legs is clearly a falcon. Some birds of the eagle type turn out to be canting arms once their local name is known; a striking example is the Saker falcon (local name: *Stocker*) in the arms of the Stocker family of Schaffhausen. An eaglelike bird tearing its breast open is in fact a pelican feeding its young in the legendary fashion. Unlike its natural counterpart, the heraldic pelican has no bill pouch.

Unlike the flat, two-dimensional shield, crests can be thought of in three dimensions and eagles can be represented more realistically, especially in their function as birds of prey. The picture above on the far right shows not an eagle but a "pelican in her piety," feeding her young with her own blood.

The political fragmentation of the medieval German empire is expressed in the imperial eagle with four coats of arms on each pinion – the so-called *Quaternionen* – each group representing one of the different ranks of the empire *(below left)*.

The independence of the Friesians on the coast of the North Sea, allegedly granted by Charlemagne, is expressed in the half imperial eagles which are included in family arms *(above)*.

The period around 1800 favored a greater naturalism in the portrayal of heraldic animals, as evidenced *(right)* by the copying of the Roman eagle under Napoleon.

In designing their eagle in 1782, the founders of the United States believed that they could and should get away from conventional heraldry *(far right)*. They chose an indigenous species, the bald eagle.

Nuremberg was an imperial town and had two different coats of arms. It developed the heraldic pattern of three shields, the upper one of which contained the imperial eagle to symbolize the fact that the city was directly responsible to the emperor. This system spread to the similarly constituted Swiss cantons, where the shield with the German eagle remained as a symbol of independence long after their final separation from the "empire" in 1648 *(above)*.

129

Right:
Heraldic representations of an ostrich. The horseshoe is so distinctive that the medieval artist has tended to content himself with this and expended little care or even research on the features of the bird itself (first two illustrations at right). The engraving of the seal of the town of Leoben is very different (early and modern versions, far right). Here the ostrich is the symbol of a town which has achieved economic strength through iron, which is the reason for the two horseshoes.

The strong stylization which is found in the figure of the eagle can also be applied to other winged creatures. Insects, with closed or more often with outspread wings, can have a specially decorative effect. Napoleon I made use of this as emperor and also on Elba. The bees on the

coat of arms of the Barberini family of Rome might be said to represent the "honey" brought to them by the nepotism of Pope Urban VIII (1623–1644). Taddeo Barberini, who was given the title of Prince of Palestrina and commander-in-chief of the papal troops, had to flee to France

The phoenix is differentiated from the naturalistic eagle by the flames from which it rises and the crest of feathers usually shown on its head, shown here on a fifteenth-century English standard. The crane *(far right)* is a form of canting arms; the French for crane is *grue* and it is the symbol of the Gruyère region, famous for its cheeses.

In the arms of the Milanese ruling family of the Visconti *(right)*, sinners are swallowed by a snake.

In the seal of Prince Milos Obrenovich of Serbia (murdered in 1868) the snake symbolizes the struggle against the Turks.

before the audit of 1646, and died there in 1647. The symbolism of the *grallatores* or long-legged wading birds is more specific. They are identifiable by subsidiary signs. The ostrich swallows all kinds of indigestible things both in fiction and in reality. This is made clear in heraldry by the addition of some object made of iron. The crane is usually shown with a stone in its raised claw, which would wake a sleeping sentry if it fell.

Opposite:
The Jesuit father Silvester Petra Sancta decorated the title page of his pioneering work *Tesserae Gentilitiae* (1638) with the arms of his patron, Taddeo Barberini. The three bees on the shield are surrounded by personifications of good luck and fame. The French emperor Napoleon III frequently used bees; he saw them as a symbol of the "working classes."

PRÆSIDIVM   ET DVLᶜᵉ   DECVS

The name of the city of Florence refers to a flower, so its heraldic symbol is inevitably a flower also. The Florentine lily is always elaborated with stamens and with subdivisions of its different parts.

There are only two heraldic flowers in the proper sense of the word, the lily and the rose. The lily, far more than the rose, is subject to strong heraldic stylization. In fact the "fleur-de-lis" is represented so differently from its natural original that there is some doubt if it is really a stylization of the lily rather than of the iris. Admittedly, in all languages, the terms used to describe it refer to the lily flower. On the other

been predicted that he would die among flowers. But he did not escape the prophecy, for he died instead in the Castel Fiorentino in Apulia in 1250.

The fleur-de-lis as symbol of the Virgin Mary was the chief emblem of the kings of France. The first to use it on his coat of arms was probably King Louis VII (reigned 1137–1180). The use of

Like the heraldic eagle, the heraldic lily (or fleur-de-lis) is constructed symmetrically; unlike the former, however, the point of the central petal must remain in the vertical axis. As with the eagle, its form became increasingly elaborate with the passage of time until today there is a return to the basic form of the thirteenth century. In the rococo period, the lily had to reflect the curvature of the shield so that the central axis of the flower was itself curved.

hand all heraldic lilies of whatever style show the same horizontal binding with three upper petals protruding above it and a similar but smaller ornament of three tails showing beneath. This has even led to the theory that in the very earliest times the fleur-de-lis had a common ancestor in the *fascine* or bundles of faggots which were used to make marshy ground solid to walk upon. So here we have a distant relationship with the symbol of the fascists. But we can leave such ancient history aside since we know that the fleur-de-lis was regarded as a flower in heraldic times. The emperor Frederick II, being as superstitious as many people of his day, avoided staying in Florence, the town of flowers, since it had

three fleurs-de-lis, since the fourteenth century, had no special meaning. It was merely a suitable number which fitted conveniently into the shape of the shield and stood out well when viewed from a distance. Later in the fourteenth century, the three fleurs-de-lis were identified with the Holy Trinity.

The heraldic rose takes its basis from the dog-rose and hence has five petals. Rose-shaped devices with more petals or fewer are also to be found. Correctly speaking these should be referred to as four-petaled, six-petaled, and so on. One can also speak of a five-petaled "rose" when it is not actually a rose, for instance with a

The form of the fleur-de-lis lends itself ideally to endless repetition in staggered rows. The kings of France, for whom the fleur-de-lis was their chief symbol, made full use of this, even at a time (fourteenth century onwards) when the arms of the kingdom contained no more than three fleurs-de-lis. Lengths of material bearing the fleur-de-lis pattern could be joined onto others in livery colors. Such a graceful motif as the fleur-de-lis also lent itself to execution in precious stones *(left center)*. Legend claims that the clasp shown here was worn by Louis IX (St. Louis).

Altenburg. The rose, moreover, is one of the most popular armorial charges throughout the world.

The motif of a bloom seen from above is by no means restricted to the rose, however; one finds it in Japanese family signs or *mon*, especially since these are constructed almost invariably on the basis of a circle and therefore offer the ideal shape for a flower pattern. The basically circular pattern leads to strong stylization and abstraction. Flowers are rendered with the stamens in the center but the petals shown in profile; whole twigs can be shown bent into a

The use of the rose is widespread in Germany, for instance in the region of Lippe. Here it has a number of distinguishing characteristics. The old Hanseatic town of Lemgo colors the rose of Lippe blue instead of red. It appears twice on a seal of around 1200. On the seal of the new town of 1283–1365, the central roundel is occupied by a man's head, possibly that of Christ with the crown of thorns.

blue flower, which would be taken from hemp, or a yellow one, which would be derived from a medlar flower. But generally a five-petaled flower is a rose and is therefore red or white. An obvious instance is the signs of the competing English royal houses of York and Lancaster, whose adherents wore a white rose and a red rose respectively. The most important roses in Germany are those of Lippe and of the estate of

circular form. The extraordinary graphic gifts of the Japanese artists had a decisive effect on European artists when they became known here around 1900. Their style found many imitators and contributed much to Art Nouveau.

It is sometimes hard for European eyes to tell from these severely stylized versions whether for example the plum, cherry, or hibiscus flower is

In Great Britain, floral emblems play an extremely important part among near-heraldic designs. The Wars of the Roses ended with the white and red roses of the houses of York and Lancaster being combined in a single rose of two colors, the Tudor rose. The thistle is the emblem of Scotland, the shamrock that of Ireland.

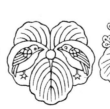

Banner of a Japanese *Daimyo* bearing a *mon* on a plain background.

meant. The frequent use of foreign names – e.g., "Rose of Sharon" for hibiscus – further confuses the issue.

The British custom of using as badges not only flowers but also plants (e.g., the Welsh leek) has spread throughout the English-speaking world, where national or provincial plants often have legal status as heraldic badges.

The plants and flowers shown in the above selection of Japanese *mon* are: 1. Chrysanthemum. 2. Carnation. 3. Plum blossom. 4. Chinese flower. 5. Three mallow leaves in a wreath of wisteria. 6. Trefoil with pendant wisteria branch and swastika. 7. As 6. but with the branch pointing upwards and a butterfly instead of the swastika. 8. Maple leaf. 9. Chrysanthemum flowers with three leaves. 10. Ivy leaf overlaid with small birds. 11. *Paulownia imperialis*. 12. and 13. Cinquefoil with butterflies.

The Japanese have their own terms for these staffs decorated with fluttering pennants which give the effect of a tree. They call them *matoi* or *umajirushi*. Western researchers refer to them as "vexilloids," a word coined from the Latin *vexillum* meaning a Roman banner, or a piece of linen attached to the upper part of a crozier.

rial creations they do appear here and there, and have a good decorative effect. It is a remarkable fact that a frequent motif in folk art, tuliplike flowers growing in a pot, was already widespread before tulips became generally known in Europe around 1551.

Leaves are more frequent in heraldry than flowers, especially those which have distinctive

The Council of Entlebuch in Switzerland once formed an autonomous body and bore its own banner *(above)* with the canting arms of a beech tree *(Buche* in German).

Squirrels help to identify the picture of a Black Forest pine on a banner which the Swiss captured in 1499 in the so-called Swabian War *(above center)*.

The flag from Holstein *(far right)* demonstrates how dangerous it is to rely solely on verbal descriptions. It shows a nettle tree, the German term for which is *Nesselblatt*, or nettle leaf, and this has given rise to fundamental misunderstandings.

Out of the great variety of plants and flowers, in the classical period of heraldry only those were chosen as armorial charges which could be heraldically stylized. This was particularly the case with the rose and the fleur-de-lis, and beside them other plants only play a secondary role. Their appearance can be explained by the circumstances under which the choice of armorial bearings took place. The numerous garden and wild flowers with which the book illustrators of the Middle Ages framed their pictures are almost unknown in classical heraldry. In modern armo-

profiles such as the clover, water-lily, the lime, and the oak. Less frequently, one finds beech or willow leaves, though they are easily identifiable. Generally the trees themselves are shown in stylized form together with some typical leaf-covered twigs. Many trees, such as the pear, are identifiable by their fruit. In recent times there have been repeated attempts to attach an ideological significance to ears of corn. But in fact ears, and particularly sheaves, of corn belong among the earliest armorial charges of specially fertile regions.

Less aristocratic plants are also chosen, but usually only to provide canting arms such as those shown in the penultimate row of the illustration opposite, where we find water-lily *(Seerose)* leaves for Seebach, poppy heads *(Mohnköpfe)* for Maenhaupt *(Haupt* and *Kopf* being synonyms), cabbage (French: *choux)* for Choux, a turnip *(Rübe)* for Ruber, garlic *(Knoblauch)* for Knoblauch, and pea-pods (French: *pois)* for Le Pois.

The selection of escutcheons and banners on the right shows what is meant by the German word *Nesselblatt*. It is the heraldic term for a zig-zag bordure, which already in the late Middle Ages was becoming divorced from its original meaning. As time went by this mysterious charge became increasingly distorted and its triangular points were even regarded as the nails from the cross of Christ.

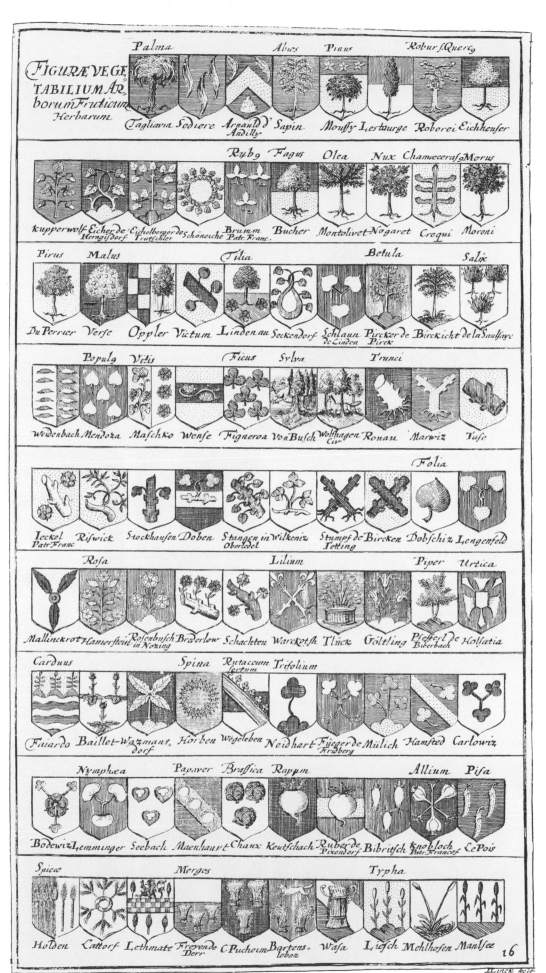

Trees are often associated with the ideas of autonomy and self-determination. The lime tree is a Germanic symbol of justice, and after 1686 the inhabitants of New England confidently set a fir tree alongside the English George Cross.

The English custom of proclaiming adherence to regional factions through plant emblems has spread overseas. In Canada the maple leaf appears both in the country's arms *(above)* and on its flag. The color of the maple leaves on the shield was originally blazoned as "proper" (naturally colored). In 1965 the color was changed to gules to match the leaves on the flag and on the crest. Red (gules) was chosen as a reminder of the blood of Canadian troops shed in the First World War.

From the sixteenth century, publications increasingly made use of the advantages of copper engraving to give résumés of associated groups of charges. Here is a plate from the textbook produced by the influential heraldic expert Philipp Jakob Spener in 1690, in which he successfully endeavored to name at least one family somewhere in the world for every example given.

135

The marklike sign of the dukes of Lithuania was often referred to as the gate with three towers. This led Konrad Grünenberg of Constance to give the knight an incorrectly decorated shield in his version of their arms *(below).*

The famous armorial roll of Zurich is an example of the fact that the arms of distant countries were not always correctly represented. Thus the arms of Spain and Portugal shown here are useful only insofar as they show a "castle" for Castile and a "portal" for Portugal. Many contemporary armorials provided foreign lands or rulers with arms which were totally invented but were nevertheless canting in the language of the artist.

Although buildings do appear in family arms, they are most charac-

teristically found on the seals of towns and the arms developed from them, where they may be direct portraits of particular buildings. To differentiate between similar buildings the ruler's sign of sovereignty is often added.

Right:
An almost unlimited number of artifacts appear in heraldry, and the medieval heraldic artists, particularly the English, seemed to have a boundless imagination. The three swords with a single pommel bring to mind other similar arrangements of three fishes with one head, or three hares with common ears. Next come three musical instruments – "clarions" or "claricords"; three spoons, as canting arms for one John Sponeley; and three stockings.

Human artifacts are governed by the same principle as all other charges on an armorial shield. And this principle is that no subject is too prestigious or too insignificant to be used as an armorial charge. It must only be possible to represent the subject in two dimensions, though a certain amount of sculptural or relief modeling is permissible. In case of difficulty the solution of *pars pro toto* ("the part stands for the whole") is generally adopted, as the illustrations at the bottom of page 138 convincingly show. As in all cases, there are exceptions; thus tables and chairs can hardly be drawn without the help of perspective. Inanimate objects often set difficult or insoluble puzzles for the researcher. This is unfortunate, since arms can be excellent aids to the identification of people and the dating of works of art. And the latter can increase considerably in value once their time and place of origin, patron, and artist are known. For this reason a heraldic expert needs to be thoroughly familiar with all the medieval objects of utility, from weapons of war to the humblest tradesman's sign.

These objects can be divided into those which are used in the course of daily life and those

which serve for the manufacture of products. There are a number of published classifications, but unfortunately none so far is entirely convincing. For curiosity's sake we will look at the best-known list, that of Dielitz, which concentrates particularly on the function of the objects. Dielitz includes a section on "Objects for the satisfaction of spiritual needs." And since, being a Prussian officer, he includes war in this category, he has arranged in it all the buildings of war, including the castle from the arms of Castile. Other lists make insignificant classifications, distinguishing for example between shields with a "semy" and a "sans nombre" ground. These can indeed be seen as two different styles, but the distinction was not considered important in the heyday of heraldry.

Among the articles of everyday use, the different pieces of civilian clothing form a substantial part, most notably the sleeve. And particular

attention is paid to the type with a pocket attached, perhaps for a prayerbook. The English once again are masters in the graphic development of the outline of this sleeve. Because of its curious shape the French call it *manche mal taillée,* the English simply "maunche." Even in pieces of clothing one can find subjects for canting arms. A pair of open breeches is the sign of the Dutch family Abenbroek. Eating utensils are seldom found as charges. In England, however, a surgical instrument known as a "fleam" – an ancient form of lancet – is more frequently

The family of the German painter Albrecht Dürer was originally called Ajto after its place of origin in Hungary. They translated this name into Dürer and created canting arms for it in the shape of a door (*Tür* in German).

of a particular place, so that there were very few general arms of a particular trade or profession. The smiths and the painters are two examples of occupations for which there were special arms.

Naturally, several objects of utility from different sources can be combined in one shield. An example is the table of the guild of tanners of Solothurn, on page 139, where we see both a plow (denoting origin) and a tanner's knife (denoting the profession). Among the rather dim figures is the tile-making form which appears in the arms of families with names like Ziegler (tile is *Ziegel* in German). The shape appears twice on the tanners' table. The ropemaker's hooks, on which ropes are twisted, will be apparent only to the expert. A family with these hooks is represented on the table four times. The tools consisting of shafts have a certain resemblance to the medieval so-called merchant's marks. The fact that these merchant's marks themselves

The four escutcheons with maunches – sleeves with a pocket for a prayer book – belonged to vassals of the elector of Trier and do not show that they were related but that they shared a common feudal status.

found. Being English it is naturally stylized, so that it appears somewhat like a figure seven.

With the spread of heraldry beyond the circle of knights, the number of arms with tools and implements on them increased. The range included everything from agriculture – plowshares and whole plows – to the tools of small-scale handicrafts. These implements did not only appear in the arms of people who plied a particular trade, but also in the arms and banners of guilds. These were often combined with the arms

Implements appear most frequently in the arms of craftsmen and their corporations. For smiths we have the tongs holding a piece of glowing iron and the hammer; the fire-breathing asp is also commonly found *(left)*.

A frequently used charge in heraldry is that of the belt buckle or clasp *(above)*. It appears in a variety of different forms, often with the tongue stuck through the shield.

137

The fetterlock (a type of lock used to hobble horses) is frequently found in British heraldry. A fetterlock enclosing a falcon was the badge of Richard, Duke of York (d. 1460). It was supposedly shown open because the "falcon" who hoped for the throne was not to be locked up. Richard's son Edward IV (d. 1483) and his grandson Edward V (d. 1485) also left the lock open when they came to the throne.

The wards of a key can take numerous forms, one of which has given its name to a form of cross (see page 107). For this reason, when blazoning a key one must describe the wards. The arms of the Franconian Speth family, for instance, are only correct if the rather primitive form of the skeleton keys is shown as illustrated (left).

have a certain formal resemblance to runes led to wild speculation in the years after the First World War that the origin of heraldry itself might be found in the runes. But the similarity between runes and merchant's marks exists only in the technique used, the lines being carved across the grain of the wood. For this reason there are no curved lines in the merchant's marks, only angular corners.

Merchant's marks do not appear in classical arms, and practically none have been granted containing one of these marks. Occasionally, when the person in question has been raised to the nobility, one finds a merchant's mark has been transformed into a true heraldic charge. There is a parallel here with Polish and Lithua-

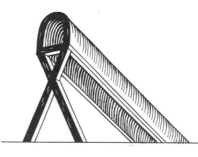

The heraldic documents which have been handed down to us contain many a secret. Many everyday objects remain unidentified. Often the profession or the name of the bearer of the arms holds their explanation. Though obscure, the two figures on these escutcheons are actually front ends of the special benches on which the tanners stretch their hides to clean them.

nian heraldry in which small objects such as horseshoes, arrows, and suchlike are typical. How far there is a connection with the Tatar house signs (tamga) which are still used in central Asia, for instance over the threshold of their tents, has yet to be seriously investigated. Such signs, like the types of merchant's mark, have their own specific meaning and they were often misunderstood in western Europe. An example of this misinterpretation appears in the arms of Lithuania (see page 136).

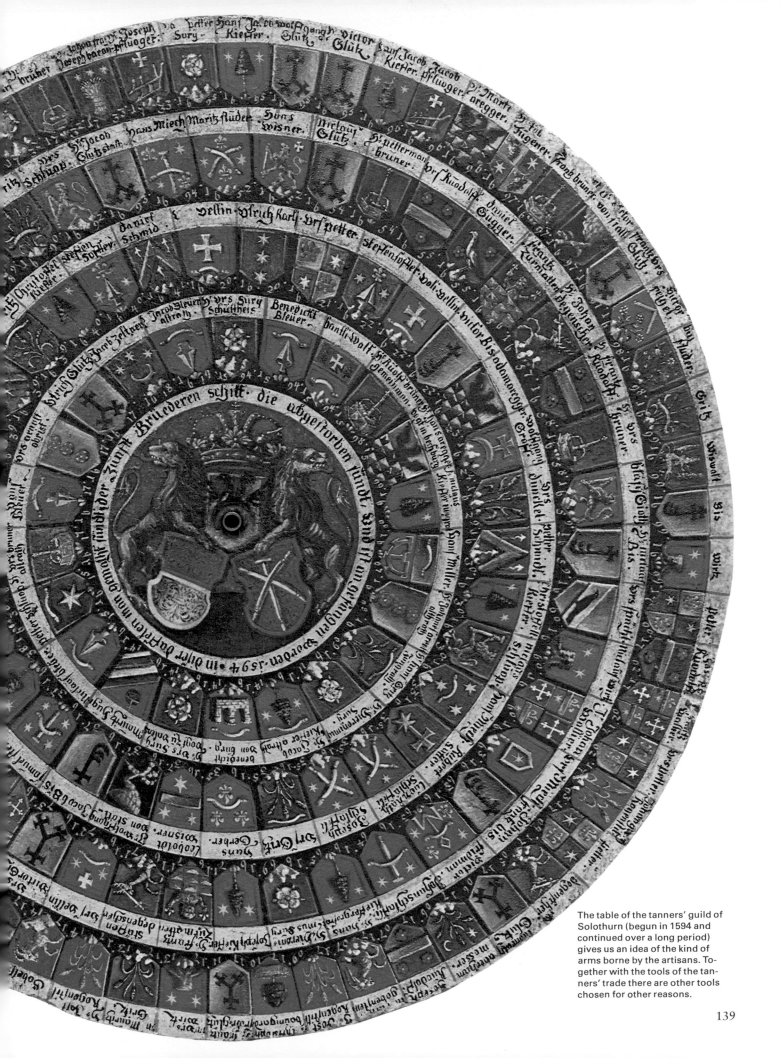

The table of the tanners' guild of Solothurn (begun in 1594 and continued over a long period) gives us an idea of the kind of arms borne by the artisans. Together with the tools of the tanners' trade there are other tools chosen for other reasons.

139

THE TOWN OF MAASTRICHT

THE REGION OF WALDECK

INN SIGN

Arms of the city of Portsmouth, England; the same arms are borne by the town of Portsmouth in the American state of Rhode Island. The star or "estoile" drawn with wavy lines is typical of English heraldry.

The banner of Jean de Luxembourg, the Burgundian governor of Douai, which was lost to the

One of the impressions which moves man most deeply is undoubtedly that of the starlit sky. The realization that all life is governed by a star counts among his highest experiences. The sun, the moon, and the stars have appeared in symbolism from the dawn of time, partly as objects of worship, partly as simple occupants of the heavens. Innumerable town seals show the sun, moon, and stars soaring over their walls, or, in the case of a harbor town, over a ship headed towards the polestar.

Veneration of the sun is not restricted to particular peoples; its course has been observed by all men at all times and used as the basis for far-reaching decisions. The measurement of time and the calendar are but two examples. The calendar with its numerous figures does not feature in heraldry but personifications of the planets do occasionally appear. Constellations of the stars are also rare in early heraldry. In modern arms and flags of states, however, they appear quite frequently, with the Southern Cross coming at the top of the list.

Heraldry has developed several forms for representing the moon. In this set of marriage arms (below), the husband bears two small crescents, while the woman bears a full moon face.

Swiss in 1486. His family was related by marriage to the southern French dynasty which ruled from Les Baux. The proud lords of Les Baux compared themselves with the sun and bore the latter in their arms.

There are many ruling families which have claimed descent from the sun, such as the Tenno of Japan and the kings of the Incas. Others have compared themselves with it, including many Indian maharajahs, the king of Nepal, the lords of Les Baux of Provence, and the Sun King,

Louis XIV. The latter's manner of representing the sun with a human face is derived from classical antiquity and also appears in many ancient arms of the Inca kings. It is undoubtedly the origin for the "May Sun" on the Argentine flag, which is drawn with a woman's face and marks

| VICTORIA (AUSTRALIA) 1910 | REPUBLIC OF THE CONGO 1960–1963 | CANTON OF WALLIS (VALAIS) 1815 | SICILIAN COIN | TOWN OF HALLE ON SAALE | SULTAN OF BAGHDAD | COIN FROM TRIESTE | TOWN OF MONDSEE |

the outbreak of revolution against Spain on 25 May 1810.

The enormous power of the sun is expressed in heraldry sometimes by straight and at others by flaming rays. Only the eastern Asia nations have found strict graphic forms for representing the sun, which are given specific names. Color is also a part of the symbolism. Thus the Japanese sun is "rising," completely red and without rays – in fact, perfectly true to nature. The Chinese sun on the other hand – now only found in the arms and flag of Taiwan – is fully risen, alluding to the twelve daylight hours with "blue sky and

Thus we find it in the arms of the Bahamas, the Ivory Coast, and the Central African republics: Mali, Niger, Chad, and Uganda. When only the upper half is to be seen, the sun is rising in a symbol of freedom and the hope of a better future. It is shown naturalistically in this form in the arms of Cuba. In the arms of Morocco, on the other hand, the sun is setting, since in the native language of the country Morocco is called the *Maghreb,* that is, the West. For Ecuador the sun serves as an indicator of date, when linked with the astrological signs for the months of March to June 1845. A similar but purely naturalistic use is that of the "dawn" of revolu-

The sun, the moon, and the stars make man aware of his mortality. He feels ruled and led by them, and expresses this in arms and on coins. Stars are also used quite simply for counting. The sun is often shown rising, as a symbol of a better future.

English pattern books for engraving show all the different celestial bodies *(left)*. The traditional rule whereby crests must make firm contact with the helmet is largely overlooked.

The number of the United States – originally thirteen and now fifty – has always been expressed by the number of stars on the American flag. Since the origin of this

white sun." The eight tripartite groups of rays on the Philippine flag, on the other hand, signify the eight provinces which were the first to rebel against the Spaniards. The sun is included in the arms of hot countries, perhaps as a kind of exorcism – to ensure that it will not scorch the crops.

tion in Panama, which led to the establishment of a republic.

One must also regard as sun's rays the rays of light radiating from the caps which are a symbol of freedom of some Central American states.

device is still the subject of speculation, it may be worth mentioning that the system of counting by means of stars was customary on military banners as early as the time of the Thirty Years' War (1618–1648).

IMAGE FROM
A DUTCH COIN

KING OF
FRANCE 1547

OTTOMAN
EMPIRE

SAKANKPUR
(INDIA)

UGANDA 1962

REPUBLIC OF
LATVIA 1921

BRITISH
COLUMBIA 1906

REPUBLIC OF
CHINA 1928

The celestial bodies are often used by ruling families as a symbol of godlike status. The Inca kings also used their legendary mountain retreat for the same purpose.

In 1889 Japan introduced a sun-ray pattern on its first naval ensign and on its military colors by adding regularly arranged rays to the simple sun of the national flag.

The sun and the moon are given equal weight in the arms of Nepal, signifying that the kingdom will last as long as these heavenly bodies remain in the sky. When the Republic of Ceylon declared its native name of Sri Lanka to be its sole internationally valid name, it enriched its arms with religious symbols which included the sun and the moon. Such attitudes, based on astrological considerations, do not appear in classical heraldry but probably form the basis of the Iranian sign of royalty, the sun in the constellation of Leo.

The heavenly bodies, then, as we have seen, occur more frequently in signs of royalty and sovereignty than in family arms.

charge; frequently it may be associated with the mysterious influence which the moon has on human lives. But it is often unequivocally a symbol of veneration of the Virgin Mary, with the queen of heaven represented on a horizontal crescent moon. In a blazon, the shape of the moon must always be given. In French and English blazon the moon is described not as *lune* or moon but as *croissant* or crescent, respectively, indicating clearly that it is the crescent moon which is generally used. Besider this, it is necessary to blazon the moon's position. The crescent with the horns pointing dexter is "increscent"; pointing sinister is "decrescent"; pointing up is "crescent"; and pointing down is "crescent reversed."

Stars, either in groups or singly, appear often in arms and on flags. Nations differ in the number of points they prefer, central Europeans usually giving their stars six points, Latins five.

The Hanseatic town of Stralsund bore an arrowhead (or several) as canting arms, for *Strahl* in old German means arrow. When this had been forgotten a radiant sun appeared in their place *(above)*, *Strahl* in modern German meaning a ray of light.

Louis XIV of France, the Sun King, used a radiant sun with a face as his emblem and added the motto *Nec pluribus impar* ("equal to many").

The moon, however, appears in non-Islamic as well as Islamic lands as a favorite motif in family arms and communal heraldry as well. The waxing moon appears as a simple crescent, or with a human face in the sickle, sometimes with flowers in its mouth. The full moon shown on page 140 is unusual; more frequently one finds several moons, usually two placed back to back. A favorite combination in Spain is four moons with the tips of their horns touching, and this even has a specific name – *lunel*. It is often not known why the moon is chosen as an armorial

The identity of the ancient sign of the swastika with the sun's disk is particularly clear in Japanese documents, where they appear side by side. A cross in a circle can also be used instead of the swastika.

Opposite:
Among the numerous *mon* appearing on Japanese war banners, the circle occurs very frequently, often filled out to make a sun's disk or its equivalent, the cross within a circle.

The helmet is the most important of all defensive devices, as it covers the most indispensable part of the body. In this picture an armorer receives attentive service while forging a helmet.

And a helmet well beaten
From steel soft and malleable,
Many markings so beautiful
Thereon were found,
By the smith's masterly hand
Strewn in the metal's sheen.

From the German epic poem
Biterolf und Dietleib (ca. 1250)

the helmet

A battle scene around 1330, from a contemporary illustration. It shows the two basic forms of helmet. The iron hat with its broad brim left the face free. The closed helmet with its traplike visor could be opened during pauses in the battle for the wearer to take breath, as it would get very hot inside.

Though skilled in weaponry the Normans wore a cruder form of helmet. The event shown *(right)* was historically decisive, at least for the English: Duke William of Normandy shows his men, who believed him dead, that he is alive and well. To do this he had to raise his whole helmet and push it onto the back of his head. The use of heraldic emblems as a means of recognizing people was soon to make such situations much easier.

Any device made of stiff material and intended to protect the head against external injury may be described as a helmet. Whether such injury arises through the act of an enemy or merely by accident is immaterial. The kind of protection offered is indicated by the name of the helmet. Thus a crash helmet is intended to prevent or diminish injury in the case of a crash. Of course the kind of crash such helmets are designed to offer protection against did not exist in the Middle Ages. But without the helmets of that time, heraldry would probably never have come into existence.

The helmets which were responsible for the invention of heraldry covered the face either completely or to such an extent that the person inside could not be adequately identified. They were above all intended to ward off arrows, which might come flying from any direction. In the eleventh century, protection of this kind was something new. At the Battle of Hastings (1066), Duke William of Normandy had to raise his helmet to show that he was alive and well. Fortunately for him there happened to be no archers within range at that moment. The English archers and crossbowmen were much feared as

opponents in later wars, having possibly learned their skill from the Saracens. By 1200, people had come to recognize the need for better face protection. In the process, however, they gave up one technical advantage, probably without being aware of it. For the helmets used up to this time were tapered off to a cone at the top, and in this way sword blows aimed at the wearer's head would often slide off. No doubt it was due to the iron-working techniques of the time that this sensible shape was abandoned. The new helmet was quite flat on top and looked like an inverted pot placed over the wearer's head. A slit was left for the eyes, the nose piece was reinforced and sometimes ornamentally decorated. The cheeks were covered by plates running right down to the chin instead of the simple ear flaps used previously. The wearer of such a helmet could only breathe with difficulty through the air holes left in the cheeks. Thus it was a great improvement when the front part could be opened like a cupboard door. For this it was first of all necessary to be able to make hinges. Contemporary poets sang at length of the broad reinforcing bands, which were often covered with gold. But nobody mentioned the fact that a sword blow on

HELMET AND CREST   AN ELEGANT COMBINATION

The so-called prank helmet (ca. 1350) is one of the few well preserved examples of its kind. It comes from Seckau in Austria and has been in the Staatliche Waffensammlung (National Weapons Collection) in Vienna for about the past hundred years.

Technically, this helmet represents an important advance. The five steel plates from which it is

made are brought together into a cone shape at the top, so that sword-blows are likely to slip off. The reinforcing plate on the right cheek suggests that the helmet was used for jousting with lances, in which case the opponent's approach was from the right-hand side. This hypothesis is supported by the crest, which is that of the Styrian family of Pranckh. Such an elaborate crest would only be worn in a tournament and not in a real battle.

It seems unlikely that the buffalo horns with the fringe at the sides were always attached to this helmet. The style of the crest, which weighs 1,409 grams, dates it around the beginning of the fifteenth century. That of the helmet, which weighs 5,357 grams, dates it around the middle of the fourteenth century.

The row of illustrations below shows a collection of different forms of helmet in chronological order. Not all of these helmets have been used in heraldry.

top of the potlike helmet could have fatal consequences for the wearer.

More than a century was to pass before a return to the conical shaping of the top plates of the helmet, providing better protection against sword blows. The increased weight of this new type of helmet, which had something of the shape of an inverted bucket, was made easier to bear by extending the sides downward so that the helmet sat on the wearer's shoulders. Here

"bucket" helmet clearly represents an advance in the techniques of metal working, and further improvements were to follow, connected with changes in the style of combat.

Together with the invention of gunpowder and the possibility of combat over greater distances came the decline in the value of the horse as a means of transport and intimidation. Its lack of effect against the long pikes of the Swiss soldiers proved decisive in the battle between Austria

ITALO-GALLIC HELMET

OSTROGOTHIC-FRANKISH BUCKLE HELMET

"WENDEL" HELMET, UPPSALA

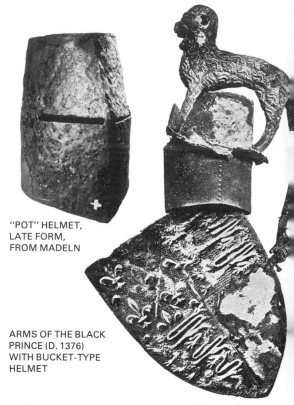

"POT" HELMET, LATE FORM, FROM MADELN

ARMS OF THE BLACK PRINCE (D. 1376) WITH BUCKET-TYPE HELMET

the force of the enemy's sword could do less damage than it could on the top of the head. Considerable changes in the type of crest used resulted from this development. Curiously enough there is no specific name in the study of arms for this form of helmet; an accepted term for it has been and still is the subject of much argument among the experts. Nevertheless, the

Below right:
Count Frederick von Cilli with couched lance outside the walls of Constance on 20 March 1415, ready to joust with Duke Frederick of Austria. Note the "coronel" tip to the lance. His helmet carries the crest of the Cilli family, an ostrich plume in front of a bunch of cock's feathers. Two escutcheons on the horse trapper repeat the motif of the jousting shield on his left arm.

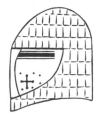

During the first third of the fourteenth century, in northern Europe, a quilted hood was drawn over the helmet to keep out the cold. Some colorful examples are shown on the folding table of Lüneburg (see pages 154–155).

and the Swiss at Sempach in 1386. Thus it was that two separate lines of development appeared. The first was purely military, aiming at the annihilation of the enemy; the second was more sporting, aimed only at victory. Fighting as a sport was carried on in tournaments arranged in the traditional manner. It was more important for the development of heraldry than proper military wars. In war, which increasingly made use of paid soldiers instead of feudal conscripts, the armor used was relatively simple. There was an iron hat which had a broad brim to protect the wearer against sword blows and left the face free, making for easier breathing and general mobility. Breathing seems to have been a great problem in helmets. A further improvement on the "bucket" helmet was the movable visor which raised to open and was easier to use than the flap which opened like a cupboard door. This new visor fitted in with the general develop-

146

The German *Schallern (right)* is an iron hat lengthened to give protection at the back of the neck. This type of helmet could be provided with a horizontal visor, but not with a chin piece, which was either a separate part or else joined onto the armor of the upper part of the body *(right, below)*.

ment of Gothic art, in which pointed forms tended to predominate. For sporting purposes there was created the jousting helmet, which extended into a point at the front and was used for jousting – the form of tourneying in which combattants with lances tried to knock each other from their horses. In order to meet the demands of this type of activity, the connection between the helmet and the rest of the armor was made more secure. On 20 March 1415, according to a contemporary account, an unsuc-

In the trench warfare of the First World War, protection of the head was as important as in the Middle Ages. Thus the suggestion that the German steel helmet *(above)* was derived from the *Schallern* may have some truth in it.

| "BUCKET" HELMET, EARLY FORM | JOUSTING HELMET, FLORENTINE MADE | HELMET FOR MACE TOURNEYING | BARRED HELMET, LATE FORM | CEREMONIAL HELMET, 1558 |

cessful diversionary maneuver was carried out by Duke Frederick of Austria, who wanted to ensure the fugitive Pope John's secret departure from the Council of Constance. The duke, in armor, had already drawn a jousting partner, though they had not yet engaged in battle, when his servant whispered an important piece of news into his ear. We can assume, then, that at that time the helmet was fastened on shortly before a passage of arms with the straps and other things so often mentioned by the minnesingers.

As an improvement on this unreliable type of join, the front part of the helmet was elongated so that what was now the jousting helmet could be firmly screwed into the armor of the upper part of the body. The form of helmet which resulted became the standard model of the heraldic helmet for the next few centuries. The armorial collections of the fifteenth century contributed substantially to this usage. Only two further developments have left their mark on heraldry, one without extensive consequences, the other of far-reaching heraldic importance.

Instead of the helmet being fastened to the body armor by means of its breastplate, it could be arranged that the lower part of the helmet was no longer attached to the helmet itself, but

formed part of the body armor, which was extended upwards. The helmet then only consisted of the upper part, in which case it was known by the French name of *salade*. There was also the basinet, which was worn under the actual fighting helmet. One often sees on gravestones a representation of the buried man wear-

ing a basinet, with his battle or tourneying helmet lying by his head.

The *salade* is difficult to use as a heraldic helmet because without shoulder pieces it cannot rest on an armorial shield. For this reason there are very few examples of a *salade* being used. In existing cases, a chin piece has had to be added.

Part of the ceremonial of a knight's funeral was the bearing of his armor with the body. In heraldic times ceremonial helmets were made for this purpose which could be used over and over again. The ceremonial helmet *(above right)* of the funeral procession of the emperor Charles V (d. 1558) was fitted with a replica of the imperial crown, since the emperor's arms did not include any particular crest.

Hand-to-hand fighters had little time to raise their visors in the heat of battle. This fourteenth-century artillery man, far from the center of the fighting, could however take time out from his exacting task to draw a few deep breaths.

147

In tourneying, the crested helmet was only put on at the last moment. The squire brought the helmet to his knight. With his right hand the knight held his lance with pennant and guided his horse; with his left hand he raised the helmet for all to see.

RANK HELMETS

The abolition of the most dangerous forms of tourneying, and the change from jousting with lances to tourneying with maces, when the object was merely to strike off the opponent's crest, brought further alterations. The field of vision was enlarged and only a few bars were used to protect the face. The use of this "barred" helmet was restricted by the imperial chancellery in Vienna to the nobility as upholders of the tradition of tourneying. This privilege was also shared by certain people who enjoyed the same standing as the nobility, for example those who had a doctor's title in law or theology. In countries not subject to the jurisdiction of the German emperor, other principles were developed based on attitudes which were more favorable to the nobility or more democratic as the case might be. In English heraldry the barred helmet is reserved for peers only and is known as the "peer's helm," while a steel helmet with closed visor and facing dexter is in fact the esquire's and gentleman's helm.

Opposite:
The Restorational trend of German politics after the fall of Napoleon was accompanied by a romantic glorification of the past. Even the old Prussian nobility took part in nostalgic court celebrations. One famous festivity, known as "the spell of the white rose" took place in Potsdam on 13 July 1829.

tion, introduced a king's helmet, either seen from the front with the visor up, or with a crown of the appropriate rank on top and all in gold.

Such helmets appeared in the arms of the kings of Prussia (see page 53) and appear in those of the king of the Belgians today (see page 113). Other coats of arms express royal rank with a barred helmet done in gold; examples are not only Great Britain but also the Bahamas (where it was specially bestowed), Grenada, Guyana, Jamaica, Canada, Trinidad and Tobago, and Malta up to 1975. The number of bars to appear

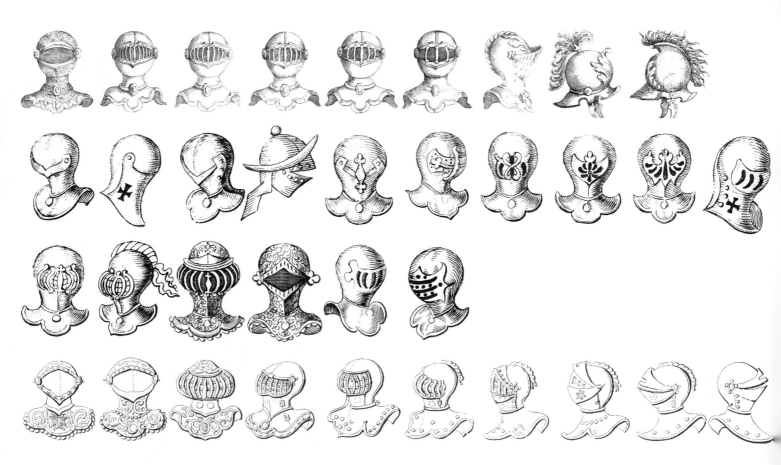

The numerous heraldic textbooks and guides endeavor to classify helmets according to niceties of design which were seldom observed in practice.

The art forms of the Renaissance were not favorable to the depiction of armorial helmets, but they did not disappear from heraldic art. All heraldic textbooks deal with them in detail, and the kings, who had been hesitant in their adop-

on the helmet and the direction in which it points are given a specific significance in many manuals and sets of rules. This is not a convention which dates from the classic period of heraldry, however, and is currently less often observed.

In the heyday of heraldry, crests on helmets played a highly decorative role. In order to understand them, however, we must first of all examine exactly what is really meant by a crest, and above all distinguish between what is worn in battle, and at a tournament, and for burial.

A crest creates various technical problems, related to the weight on the wearer's head and the raising of the latter's center of gravity.

The conical helmets of the twelfth century were real battle helmets designed to provide protection against the blows of enemy swords. If they were riveted together out of several pieces of metal sheet, this left seams which could easily be filled on top with horsehair, feathers, or some stronger material. Many seals show how this was done. Designs could also be painted on the side pieces. The two types of decoration could be combined. When Richard Cœur de Lion had his second seal as king of England engraved around 1195, he was represented on the reverse side as leader of the army on horseback. The titles relating to Normandy, Aquitaine, and Anjou are included as in the former seal but the coat of arms is altered, with, significantly, a different type of helmet. If the available impressions have been correctly interpreted, this is no longer merely conical, but ends at the top in a crest topped with feathers or horsehair, the sides of which are painted with a heraldic lion. Richard's grandfather Geoffrey Plantagenet had merely worn a lion represented on the side of the head covering.

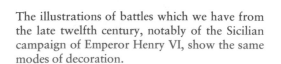

The illustrations of battles which we have from the late twelfth century, notably of the Sicilian campaign of Emperor Henry VI, show the same modes of decoration.

The Praetorian Guard, the bodyguard of the Roman emperors, wore a decorative crest of plumes on their helmets. This served as a prototype for all the elite troops or guards regiments of modern standing armies.

The advantages of reinforcing a helmet along the top seam and fitting it with a crest of horsehair or feathers had already been discovered by the Greeks and put into use by them in the Persian Wars at the beginning of the fourth century B.C. We even know the name of this Greek soldier who volunteered to defend his homeland against the Persians; he was called Chrysippos, which means "gold-horse."

The bronze statuette (right) is presumed to be an Etruscan figure of Minerva.

151

With the conical helmet of the type shown here, practically the only way of recognizing the wearer is through a painting on the side of the head. The illustrations show some of the earliest examples of armorial painting.

The comblike crests were themselves subject to some development; they could be enlarged and decorated with patterns of varying richness, or with a simple color scheme dictated by the armorial shield. It is because of the comblike shape of these early helmet decorations that they are all known in English as crests. The equivalent word in German, *Schirmbrett,* applies only to the fan crest while all the others are known by the name of *Helmzier* – "helmet decoration." The *Schirmbrett* plays an important part in central European heraldry. It can be ribbed as a

upon crests as an artistic form of decoration. In referring to the pictorial sources from the Middle Ages, however, one must always consider whether they represent real or ideal examples. This remains true up to a point even today – one finds illustrations of ceremonial garments which could only theoretically be worn.

One early pictorial source which comes into this category is the Berlin Codex, the *Aeneid.* This can be dated, from the shape of the helmets, around 1220. It shows scenes of opponents fighting one another to the death, scenes which are supposed to have taken place several thousand years later, but are in fact enacted in contemporary costume. The courtly character of von Veldeke's epic is evident among other things from the fact that the warring parties have the kind of crests used in tourneying, though some are symbolic.

Soon after the year 1200 a new form of helmet appeared with a completely flat top. It caused certain problems in fixing the crest, which was designed to fit in with the other armorial signs.

The crest was often so distinctive that it could be used instead of the shield in seals used for the authentication of documents. On the right-hand seal, the knight's

reminder of its original fanlike construction. It can also be decorated with feathers, placed to give the effect of a bird's wing. Such designs give almost unlimited scope to the imagination. Another type of crest which imitates a bird's wing is the *vol-banneret,* which appears almost exclusively in the Netherlands. This is a rectangular bannerlike plumed crest, the top edges of which are shaped like the pinions of a bird's wing (see page 160, the pictures on the bottom two rows).

The flat tops of the helmets used could be adorned with whole figures, also banners, branches, or trees, fixed singly or side by side in pairs, in rings fastened to the top of the helmet. Alternatively the old fan type of crest could be extended to cover the whole helmet. Since there was enough space to arrange cylindrical or tube-shaped structures in pairs, the old German bull's horns reappeared, especially in central Europe (see pages 145–146, 154–155).

The bucket-shaped helmet which became established around 1300, with its more conical form,

spouse places the helmet on his head before a tournament. The knight in the picture *(far right)* is wooing the lady, as is evident from the stylized letter A (= *Amor*) on his armorial coat.

The increasing splendor of helmets and their decorations reflected the tone of the chivalrous way of life, which reached its apogee in courtly tournaments. The people of the time looked

Left:
The supporting framework for the feathered decoration is often playfully embellished. The repetition of the shield design on the helmet is frequently seen.

be seen from all sides. In transferring it to paper, some reflection is required to determine how the most favorable overall effect can be achieved. One factor which has to be borne in mind is that the crest should appear on the same axis as the helmet. This was true for the pot-shaped helmet and remained so for the bucket-shaped helmet. Both helmets are easily represented, from the side as well as from the front. So long as the crest consists of only a single figure, such as a branch, for example, then it does not matter which aspect of the helmet is shown on paper, for a branch can be represented equally well from all sides. This is also true of a peal of bells mounted on a shaft, or similar contrivances which were often misunderstood in later centuries. Thus a hoop with pendant lobes or wattles became a currycomb which was subsequently assumed to symbolize the office of master of the horse.

With time, heraldry extended to one of the most attractive elements of the ensemble, the helmet mantling. At first this covered only the back of the neck, but larger pieces of drapery were later a sign of noble status.

A distinction should be made between these draperies and the quilted hoods which were worn over the helmet in the first third of the fourteenth century in north and northwest Europe. The quilted pattern and seams are often shown on contemporary seals. It is understandable that they have remained almost unnoticed since there is only a single set of colored illustra-

The Vikings made their helmets so steeply pointed that enemy sword blows had little effect. The joins between the different sheets of metal gave an opportunity for decorative embellishment. The nose piece is patterned also.

The armorial of Konrad Grünenberg shows the typical forms of mantling. Here we see *(left to right)*: material in strips; material with scalloped edges; a similar pattern but with the metal side outward as the mantling is joined directly to the crest; strips of material with a decorative pattern of folds.

allowed more elaborate crests to be developed without abandoning the previously established types. Changes of fashion made their contribution. The changing shape of hats matched that of the helmet, and it was the general practice to have a bunch of peacock feathers on top. In fact peacock feathers were a particularly popular feature of crests, either with the whole tail displayed in a fan, or in a bunch. Feathers are also found as a border on the outer edge of the crest (see pages 154–155), not only with the familiar bull's horns but also, particularly in southern Germany and Switzerland, as a special crest along the back of a sculpted animal form. Such animal forms, and also human ones, became more and more popular. Often only the upper part of the body was shown, in which case it was blazoned "naissant," or alternatively without the forelegs or arms. In French blazon, which serves as a model for most other languages, the term used for such beasts without forelegs is *tête et col.*

The form of the crest affects the way it is graphically represented. The real helmet can of course

Along the edges of the Gothic folding table of Lüneburg are the arms of the chief rulers of the time *(left to right):* the German emperor with the crest of Ludwig of Bavaria; the king of France with the crest of Philip Augustus; the king of Bohemia; the king of Denmark; the legendary Prester John or King Sultan; the king of Sweden; not yet identified, but probably a Scandinavian royal administrator or chancellor (the crest is a ring hanging between two halves of a fleur-de-lis); the king of Norway.

tions of such hoods, in the arms on the Gothic folding table from the town hall of Lüneburg. The painted armorials show no knowledge of them.

The Gothic table mentioned also contains a piece of evidence that the shield and helmet (with its crest) were regarded as two separate things. In this case there seemed to be no

objection to placing them side by side instead of one on top of the other in what had become the normally accepted way of representing them.

The mantling, as we have said, was at the beginning only a piece of colored cloth covering the back of the neck and helmet, and it is generally thought to have originated in the hot climate of

1330. The five medallions on the table surface represent scenes from the Bible.

155

The personification of strength holds a helmet of the Viscontis aloft with delicate gestures. The cloth mantling is stylishly scalloped round the edge.

The arms of Nils Erengnislesson of Hammersta from his painted bookplate, 1409–1440. The helmet, a transitional form between the "bucket" helmet and the jousting helmet, carries a mantling which is still seen as a straightforward strip of cloth with arbitrary colors.

the Near East. Whether a piece of cloth really cooled the neck adequately is open to doubt, and it seems more likely that the aim was to provide mechanical protection for the neck as on modern firemen's helmets.

However that may be, the modern German rule is that the mantling has to be colored to fit in with the shield or the crest (in England, the mantling can be of any color). In the classical period of practical heraldry, however, an informative collection of material such as the *Armorial de Gelre* admits all possibilities. The mantling is like a miniature cloak, somewhat longer than the neck of the helmet, and the edges may be scalloped. Only occasionally, on a side-facing helmet, the edge is turned up to show the inside (see the arms of France, page 35); somewhat more frequently it can be seen on either side of a front-facing helmet. Despite its meager size, in Gelre's book the mantling is already used as a graphic element, a possibility which had not hitherto been exploited. In the armorial roll of Zurich the mantlings are little more than neck

Decoration of the mantling can also take the form of small designs on one or even both sides of the material. The motifs can be derived either from the crest (as with the lozenges, *left*), or from the shield (the billets and "water bougets," *right*).

coverings. But on the more naturalistic knight's seals and other small art objects, one finds efforts to render the fluttering of a longer piece of material fixed to the top of the helmet (see page 86, the second arms from the left). Such realistic tendencies appear again and again. When the mantling is shown fastened in a position of rest, the artist has a choice whether to show it hanging down to one side or falling away freely at the back. A front-facing helmet with the mantling tucked up to one side is today considered against the rules, but in the classical period of heraldry it was not unusual (see pages 150–151). The more heraldry shifted from actuality to a graphic plane, the more textile fashions influenced the helmet mantling, which apart from a few "aberrations" was always assumed to be made of cloth. So the helmet mantling gained a graphic function which arose not from its origins but from the artistic currents that so influenced popular fashions from the Renaissance to the Restoration.

Apart from the formal element, the helmet mantling is also to be considered as an element of color. The oldest examples display no more color than a pocket handkerchief. Later, with the Gelre herald for example, any color may be used, but also there is already a connection between the colors of the crest and the mantling. Often the mantling serves to repeat, for some

The arms of alliance of the counts of Görz, who once owned practically the whole of the Tirol, relate not to the marriage mentioned in the text of the picture, but to the fact that two brothers have undertaken to make donations. These arms, like marriage arms, are turned towards one another out of courtesy, and as is heraldically correct the one is a mirror image of the other. When the crest is covered with fur or hide, it is natural for this to be extended into the mantling; note the edges modishly scalloped in the style of the time.

bearing of crests had long since gone out of fashion in that country.

With the growth of national consciousness in Europe, the social structure changed radically,

The full achievement of arms of the kingdom of Aragon with a dragon issuant for a crest *(below)*. In accordance with the exaggeration of the late Gothic style, the mantling is slashed into deep fringes with tassels at the ends.

reason or other, some particular part of the armorial bearings. Such is the case with the fitched cross of Aragon and the arms of the Bruces in Scotland. Very often the entire contents of the escutcheon are repeated on the mantling. This custom persisted on the armorial cloaks of eighteenth century France, when the

along with its exterior manifestations. This was particularly noticeable in the value attached to the crest. In Italy, the country which can be regarded as the birthplace of the Renaissance, until around 1500 crests were particularly impressively designed and executed. Large families vied with one another in the invention

Above left: A version of the arms of the duke of York, later James II of England (1661). The ornamental forms of baroque also influenced heraldry. The mantling is often over-rich and hardly recognizable as strips of material.

157

The physical appearance of the knight on horseback *(left)* shows exactly the arrangement of the diagonally placed shield with the helmet on top which became customary in heraldic representations of arms. He is wearing a typically German crest.

of different crests for different purposes. Thus the Viscontis either bore the same snake on their helmet as they did on their shield, or they bore the snake and a red tree as well (see page 156). Gothic forms not only made possible the bearing of helmets and crests without the addition of a shield, but also created an optical top-heaviness, especially when the three-cornered shield was replaced by the rectangular jousting shield. The architectonic forms of the Renaissance, on the other hand, did not lend themselves to the development of this style.

In France the *cimier*, as the crest was called, was not subjected to the same type of graphic display as in Italy, nor to the same cult as in Germany.

the dukes of Burgundy had no claim on the crest of their fathers, even when they were legitimized and were allowed to bear arms which closely resembled the paternal arms.

With the end of the age of chivalry, the value attached to the helmet declined in Germany as elsewhere. But the helmet with its crest remained an essential part of the full achievement of arms. In the fourteenth century at any rate it played a far greater role in German heraldry than in France or England. In the latter country heraldry developed in a particularly individualistic way.

After about 1230, the helmet and crest were regarded as so important in Germany that they

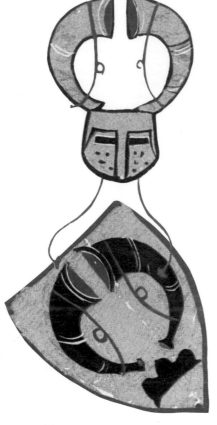

When the shield and helmet were taken off after battle, they were hung on the wall, where they formed a pattern which was adopted in graphic representations of coats of arms.

Some families with many ramifications used different crests to identify the different lines. Among the most inventive were two Alsatian families, the noble von Müllenheims *(right)* with twenty-four variants in the so-called Siebmacher armorial and the Zorn von Bulachs with thirty-three in the same book.

Opposite:
The minnesinger Wachsmut von Künzingen demonstrates how crests consisting of two pieces were fastened to the flat-topped "pot" helmet.

Nor was it treated separately as in England. But at least in the royal family, it was subject to certain restrictive rules.

The sons of the kings of France and the other *princes des fleurs-de-lis* attached small bundles of feathers to the fleurs-de-lis of their crests. The numerous bastards of the kings of France and of

appeared on seals instead of the complete coat of arms. Hitherto there had been few restrictions on changing the crest according to taste. But a seal must have an indisputable legal significance, and the picture on it must represent this significance. Thus it was essential to be able to prove the legitimacy of the picture on the seal, and this purpose could be served by a deed of sale. We do

Opposite:
A review of helmets. A freelance herald hired for the occasion inspects the helmets of the participants in a tournament; their escutcheons are painted on the necks of the helmets.

Right:
It is doubtful whether the minnesinger Wolfram von Eschenbach is shown here with his real arms. It seems unlikely that he would have exchanged what are usually assumed to be his family arms (flowers in a pot with handles) for the battle axes in order to please a lady. Perhaps it was the other way round, and it is the flowers in the pot which were adopted as a symbol of love. In any case the picture shows clearly how a pole-shaped crest could conveniently be attached to the side of the "pot" helmet. Shield, crest, and banner all carry the same design.

in fact know of some deeds for the purchase and sale of helmets and crests. The most important refers to the purchase of a helmet with a crest consisting of the head and shoulder of a hound by Frederick von Hohenzollern, burgrave of Nuremberg, on 10 April 1317 from one Herr Leutold von Regensburg. The price paid was 36 marks of silver, which amounted to some 9 kilograms of the metal. The rights acquired with the purchase are expressed in a helmet seal of 1354.

The value attached to the helmet and crest is most clearly expressed in the review of helmets which took place before a tournament, and which represented a strict process of selection. According to the tournament book of King René, the candidates had to behave impeccably towards the fairer sex, but in Germany, where rougher manners prevailed, such a test was less often applied. Here enquiries were made not as to the candidate's conduct, but as to his ancestry and whether he was descended from men who had taken part in tournaments. And by no means every candidate passed the test. If the herald rejected him, a pursuivant literally threw out his helmet. However, Konrad Grünenberg envisaged a more lenient procedure: "The helmets are inspected in this manner, and whoever is not eligible is ordered to remove his crest, so that he shall not be reviled."

The high esteem in which the rights attached to

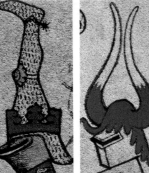

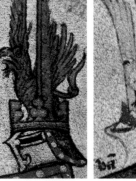

A selection of the most typical crests from the classic period of heraldry: figures of men issuant, torsos without arms, heads of all races, arms, legs, buffalo or bulls' horns, peacock feathers, three-dimensional fleurs-de-lis, bodies of animals and birds, in particular wings of all different shapes.

the helmet were held in Germany explains the fact that it was only here, with a few minor exceptions, that is was considered possible to have more than one helmet on one shield. The crucial point, it was argued, was not that a man had only one head, but that each helmet represented a right, which was also represented on the shield. In the fifteenth century people still hesitated to display all their rights on one shield and preferred to arrange a ring of smaller shields around a relatively simply divided shield (see page 227). At the same time they took the

opportunity to combine two crests on a single helmet when this was technically possible. Since there were limitations to the possible combinations, high-ranking families which had to display their prestige often had recourse to the use of more than one helmet.

find the wreath of strips of twisted material on top of the helmet which was designed to conceal the fixing of the crest. This item never became a sign of class privilege, however.

Also in Gelre's armorial we find a crown or

The arms of the dukes of Mecklenburg in the sixteenth century were surmounted by three helmets which bring together the most typical German crests. The middle crest (Mecklenburg) combines a *Schirmbrett* or fan-crest with a motif repeated from the shield and a plume of peacock feathers; on the left are two buffalo horns in the armorial colors (Schwerin), on the right a pair of wings in the armorial colors (Rostock). All the crests emerge from coronets set on the particularly well drawn barred helmets. The illustration is by one of the best-known German artists of the early sixteenth century, Lukas Cranach the Elder.

Considerations of rank continued to play a significant role into modern times. In heraldry this appears not only in the use of crowns denoting different ranks but also in helmets, even if not in a very clear fashion.

After the last mace tournament in Worms in 1487, a rule became established, though it was often broken, whereby the mace-tourneying or barred helmet could only be used by noble German families. The use of the jousting helmet, on the other hand, was open to anyone. In the *Armorial de Gelre* we also find early forms of jousting helmet which are closed with a single clasp, a type of helmet adopted by the non-noble upper classes in Germany. In the same work we

coronet on the helmet appearing in the arms of families who forty years previously would not have dared to use such a badge. On the folding table of Lüneburg (pages 154–155), only the helmet of the archduke of Austria bears a crown, in accordance with his royal rank. But this interpretation of things seems to have passed away, for in Gelre's book (ca. 1390), while all the kings bear crowns, other far more lowly families do so as well; there are even colored rather than golden crowns.

Barred helmets and crowned helmets can therefore be seen as privileges of the nobility in Germany. Such was not the case in neighboring countries, where a general antipathy for the hel-

Albrecht Dürer strove for realism even in his heraldic drawings. His helmet mantling is always treated so that it appears almost three-dimensional. In the arms of the noble von Rogendorfs, the crests of the Rogendorf arms (buffalo horns with peacock feathers) and the Wildhausen arms (lion issuant crowned) are combined on a single helmet *(left)*.

Even a recognized artist like Albrecht Dürer was plagued by patrons who thought they knew better than he did. Michael Behaim wanted the "foliage on the helmet," by which he meant the mantling, to be swept upwards. Dürer wrote a firm refusal on the back of the wood block *(below)*.

As a young man Dürer labored much over the design of the mantling. He did in fact try drawing it as foliage *(below left)*.

A late baroque ornament from Italy *(below)*. Heraldic art has come a long way from its beginnings.

met took forms which no longer harmonized with classical heraldry. Crests without the helmet, emerging from an oversized crown, and sometimes even facing to sinister, spoiled the heraldic style. Ever more intricately interlaced mantlings were a test of skill for heraldic artists.

There was also the question of the colors of the mantling. In England, from 1580 until 1790, red mantlings lined with silver were normal. Thereafter and until about thirty years ago "livery colors" were the rule, that is, the metal and color first mentioned in the blazon. The same color scheme is used for the wreath around the bottom of the crest, which is very popular in English heraldry. English armorials from the late Middle

The arms borne by European sovereigns such as Duke Bernhard Erich Freund of Saxe-Meiningen presented a problem for English heraldic officials. They created hierarchical crowns unknown on the Continent, and the inherited helmets above these.

The helmets are arranged in the set "jumping" order of rank; i.e. 5, 3, 1, 2, 4, 6.

Ages to the nineteenth century tended merely to show the crest resting on the wreath, and this led to the fashion for using the crest alone instead of the full coat of arms. Today it is considered as more or less outdated. Other rules apply for the colors of the royal family. The sovereign and the heir to the throne have gold mantlings lined with ermine, while the remaining members of the royal family have mantlings lined with silver. Multicolored mantlings such as are customary in

Germany and even more in Hungary, are unknown in England, where the observation of the classical forms of heraldry has taken a particularly firm footing. There is in England however a tradition of using crests as a badge, for example those of England and Scotland (see page 118).

A certain aversion for the heraldic helmet, seen as too militaristic, is found in many private and

public circles. This resulted in some large overseas possessions of Great Britain receiving only a crest without the helmet in their achievement of arms, as was the case with Fiji, Ghana, Nigeria, and Australia and its member states. Indeed, it was quite recently that Western Australia, with British approval, renounced the helmet formally granted to it, on the grounds that the bearing of armorial helmets was not customary in Australia. On the other hand,

Jamaica and South Africa have reintroduced the helmet into their arms.

Other countries have received royal helmets (see page 148) or esquire's helmets (in the case of Barbados, Gambia, Malawi, and Rhodesia), which give scope for elaborate displays of mantling.

The arms of the margraves of Brandenburg-Ansbach from the last period of this principality's existence consist of a shield with twenty-one quarterings, which are also found in the arms of the Prussian cousins of the royal line. The six separate coats of the Sayn inheritance are added underneath. The record number of helmets is again arranged in the "jumping" order characteristic of Continental heraldry: 12, 10, 8, 6, 4, 2, 1, 3, 5, 7, 9, 11, 13.

Portrait of the legendary King Arthur. On his clothing and the pennant of his lance he bears the arms attributed to him by posterity, consisting of three crowns.

We promise faithfully…by our
oath of allegiance
to keep this crown
of the kingdom of Poland
safe and intact and undamaged
and neither to alienate
nor diminish
any districts or parts of the same,
but to increase and reclaim them,
just as we are
and were obliged through our oath
at our coronation.

Coronation oath of King Ludwig the Great of Hungary and Poland, 1370, text according to the patent for the town of Košice.

the crown

Whatever social order man creates for himself, it always has at its summit a supreme representative, whether he is called chief, prime minister, commander-in-chief, king, king of kings, or emperor.

Human nature requires community of thought and action, and needs some manifestation of that community. In each group a more or less exceptional personality emerges, and from here it is only a small step to providing this personality with some external mark or sign which indicates his privileged position. The charisma which often attaches to such a person is not always easily explicable. The high priest and the supreme leader of a group of men may sometimes be interchangeable. The consciousness of

nature of kingship everywhere, at a time when the narrow cloth band had become a gold circle set with precious stones. And this continued to be the case for a long time during the "heraldic" era with which this book is concerned.

The cultural collapse of Europe which accompanied the popular migrations of the post-Roman era was followed in the eighth century by a turning back to the values of antiquity. This process was achieved with difficulty, since it had to be built on facts which had been almost completely forgotten. Nevertheless, princes came to wear a headband again, though it remains uncertain what form this took. In the heyday of heraldry, from the thirteenth to the fifteenth centuries, there was a standard crown

Seal of Queen Margaret of Denmark (d. 1412). She was also queen of Sweden and Norway as a result of the Union of Calmar, and this is expressed in her arms, consisting of three crowns.

Representation of a fourteenth-century herald *(above right)*, wearing a cloak with three crowns on it. It identifies him, not as a Swedish herald, but as a herald pure and simple.

Opposite:
Portrait of the emperor Henry VI in "majesty" with all the emblems of his rank in the *Grosse Heidelberger Liederhandschrift (Great Heidelberg Song Manuscript)*. He sits on the throne, wearing a simple leaf crown and holding the scepter and a length of parchment. Beside him is the sword and above him the shield with the imperial eagle, which also forms the crest of the crowned helmet on the other side.

being chosen can be so strong that a dignified appearance in public can be a sufficient sign in itself. A narrow cloth band worn round the head and hanging down at the back of the neck was considered an adequate sign of status by the kings of the ancient Near East. The Greek word *diadem,* which is used today for a luxurious head ornament, in fact only means "bound together," from διαδέω ("I bind together"). The loose ends of the royal diadems from Asia Minor (see the top of page 168) emphasize the spiritual

consisting of a headband on which four leaves were mounted, one over the forehead, one at the back, and one over each cheek. In heraldic depictions one leaf is completely visible, and two leaves each half visible. Frequently there are no tines in between. In representations such a crown was sufficient to identify a king, and indeed to express the concept of kingship itself. Kings were represented wearing this type of crown even under circumstances where they would not actually be able to wear it, for in-

Egyptian royal couple *(below)* from the throne of Tutankhamen (eighteenth dynasty). The pharaoh wears a crown consisting of several crowns combined, his wife a crown of falcon's feathers, together with the sun's disk.

stance while lying down asleep. A crown of this kind became a symbol of royal dignity to such an extent that many princes, when taking over newly won lands as their kingdoms, simply used one or more crowns as their arms, when there were none already in existence. Such was the

other ways. He sat on a raised seat provided with status symbols which might consist of no more than extended back- or arm-rests. This was his throne, from which he could look down on his subjects. He was a step nearer than the people to the heaven from which he drew his

The tutelary gods of the lands of the Nile are seen wearing their respective crowns *(above right)*. Horus, with the falcon's head, wears the crown of the whole kingdom, while Uto, the goddess of the Nile delta, wears the red crown of lower Egypt.

case with the Union of Calmar, which brought together the three Scandinavian kingdoms in the fourteenth century, also with Toledo and Murcia, the Irish province of Munster, and with the imperial dynasty of the Cantacuzenes in Byzantium.

The nobility of the ruler was also expressed in

mandate to rule. The formula "by the grace of God" was a genuine recognition of God as the source of all order. It was only in the sixteenth century that absolutist kings began to use it as a justification for autocratic arrogance.

All the pre-Christian rulers justified their wielding of power by ascribing it to higher forces. The

168

unification of the two parts of ancient Egypt was expressed by the joining of the two crowns which the two protecting goddesses had previously worn separately. In the Christian world things were not very different. Spiritual authority was held by Christ, or rather by the pope,

sun worship was replaced by idolatry, the sun's disk invariably appeared in the tall feathered constructions which served as crowns.

The closeness between priesthood and kingship is shown by the headgear worn by the kings of

The Eastern character of the Norman kingdoms in southern Italy and Sicily appears here *(below left)* not only in the Greek inscription and King Roger's garments, but also in the construction of the crown with its pendants.

who consecrated the crown. The appearance of the crowns which received the holy blessing depended entirely on local custom. Thus the Byzantine crown which King Roger of Sicily received in 1138 is as distinctive as his ceremonial robes. The crowns of the kings of Asia Minor imitate the rays of the sun (see opposite, top, Ptolemy coin). In ancient Egypt, before

Asia Minor, such as the tiara of King Tigran of Armenia. But the military commander-in-chief and emperor could also be the same person. The emperors of ancient Rome were literally called "commander" – *imperator*. They wore a plain laurel wreath of pure gold and this may be derived from the veneration of victors in sporting events who wore a real laurel wreath as a

Headdresses which increase the height of the human form to godlike proportions have been developed throughout the world. This example is from the Cambodian temple of Angkor Wat.

169

The book illustrators of the ninth century painted the Biblical King David with a crown, as if he were a contemporary of their Carolingian kings.

GERMAN CROWNS

CONRAD I
(911–918)

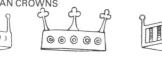

HENRY I
(919–936)

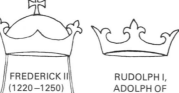

OTTO I
(936–973)

OTTO II
(961–983)

OTTO III
(983–1002)

HENRY II
(1002–1024)

HENRY II
(1002–1024)

CONRAD II
(1024–1039)

Up to the fourteenth century, the royal crowns were too varied in form to show any real development. A look at these German and English crowns taken from seals and book illustrations makes this clear.

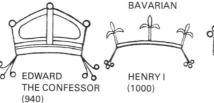

FREDERICK II
(1220–1250)

**RUDOLPH I,
ADOLPH OF
NASSAU,
ALBRECHT I,
HENRY VII
AS KING,
LUDWIG THE
BAVARIAN**

**HENRY VII
AS EMPEROR**
(1312–1313)

emperor was revived by the French in the nineteenth century, its holders adorned their heads with the ancient laurel wreath not only on coins (see page 169) but also at ceremonial appearances. Napoleon I had himself proclaimed emperor in May 1804. At the coronation which took place in December of the same year, he set a golden laurel wreath upon his own head.

ENGLISH CROWNS

ATHELSTAN
(924)

CANUTE
(930)

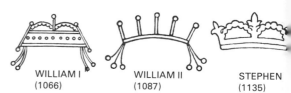

**EDWARD
THE CONFESSOR**
(940)

HENRY I
(1000)

WILLIAM I
(1066)

WILLIAM I
(1066)

WILLIAM II
(1087)

STEPHEN
(1135)

Contemporary picture of the visit of the emperor Charles IV to King Charles V of France in Paris on 4 January 1378. It is said that the French king received and entertained his uncle with all due pomp, but avoided treating him as his superior. Portraits of the two rulers nevertheless recognize their difference in rank by showing the emperor wearing a crown with an arch.

sign of victory. Such simplicity however was not sufficient to protect Julius Caesar from the suspicion that he sought the much detested status of kingship. His name and the title of *imperator* in any case became indications of a status far above that of king. When the title of

The implied connection with ancient Rome was inevitable, for Napoleon's achievement of the status of emperor had developed out of a republic just as in the Rome of the Caesars. Napoleon's empire took very little interest in the medieval past. Only the symbolism of Charlemagne was adopted and this was incorrectly interpreted. It is in any case not so easy to interpret it correctly, for the forms of the royal and imperial crowns, for example, were not systematized until the thirteenth century. A look at the two rows of crowns illustrated shows that one can hardly talk in terms of a "development." Much depends on the reliability of the source of the illustration. Seals and coins are to be preferred for they can be supposed to have been "commissioned" by the wearer of the crown himself.

Book illustrations, on the other hand, tend to be based on accepted stereotypes rather than on reality. Thus the emperor Henry II is shown on coins with a crown which is heraldically correct, while a miniature shows a bow or hoop spanning the top of the head by which Christ holds the crown as he places it on the emperor's head. The jewels which occasionally appear hanging from short chains over the wearer's ears reveal an oriental influence. They almost certainly represent one of the many attempts at emulation of the eastern Roman emperors, though the latter became progressively less worthy of imitation as their standing in the

Portrait of the emperor Charles IV with the imperial crown *(far left)*. Since the reign of King Henry VII of England *(left)*, the basic form of the English monarch's crown has not essentially changed.

HENRY III (1039–1056) **HENRY IV** (1056–1106) **HENRY IV** (1056–1106) **LOTHAR** (1125–1137) **CONRAD III** (1138–1152) **FREDERICK** 1152–1190 **PHILIP** (1198–1208) **OTTO IV** (1198–1218)

Western world declined together with their power. In the fourteenth century a strict heraldic viewpoint prevailed in the Western world and the Byzantines had nothing to compare with this. Different ranks now found expression in the form and adornment of the crown. A hoop over the basic crown became the sign of an emperor, and the holiness of the empire soon came to be expressed by the addition of a bishop's miter, turned through ninety degrees so that the imperial hoop passed between the horns of the miter.

For a long time this form of crown was evidently restricted to the Holy Roman Empire of the Germanic nations – there may perhaps have

HENRY II (1154) **HENRY III** (1216) **EDWARD I** (1272) **HENRY VI** (1422) **EDWARD IV** (1461) **HENRY VII** (1485) **HENRY VII** (1485) **HENRY VII** (1485)

been a parallel form inspired by Charlemagne in France. This type of crown became the pattern for imperial crowns, when other emperors appeared besides the German Roman emperor, in particular the tsars in Moscow.

The imperial crown is perhaps the first crown to show a consistent development, and it is a development in which its spiritual character, expressed in the addition of the bishop's miter, can easily be forgotten. In the nineteenth century, when there was not a single emperor left, emperor's crowns were developed on paper. Starting from a stylized king's crown, the designers enlarged the five arches visible out of eight, or shaped them specially so that they looked rather like the raised wings of an eagle.

The arches rising above the head of the crowned sovereign were regarded as the symbol of sovereignty and became increasingly important in the hierarchy of crowns which developed during the Renaissance. This can be observed in the development of electoral crowns. The German electors had an official costume which they actually wore, part of which was a purple red cap rimmed with ermine. An elector was not himself a sovereign, at least not before 1648, when the treaties of Westphalia gave the German landed princes an international freedom of movement which princes elsewhere did not possess. After that, electoral crowns were closed with arches, and were soon imitated by the prince's coronet

The emperor Frederick III (d. 1493) devoted particular attention to the crowns on his tomb *(left)*. A typical imperial crown appears on the emperor's head and on the shields of the empire and of the Holy Realm. Other crowns of high rank surmount the shields of Lombardy and Old Austria, while the helmets of the other territorial arms carry simple leaf crowns.

Overleaf:
The "Nine Worthies" *(left to right):* the three good heathens – Hector, Julius Caesar, Alexander the Great; the three good Jews – Joshua, David, and Judas Maccabaeus; the three good Christians – King Arthur, Charlemagne, and Godefroi de Bouillon. They are identifiable not only from their arms or banners but also from the type of crown they are wearing. The kings, Alexander, David, and Arthur, have open crowns, the "emperors" Caesar and Charlemagne have closed ones. Godefroi de Bouillon, who refused the crown of Jerusalem, bears the cross of that kingdom, and wears a crown of thorns instead of a royal crown.

171

The crown cap of the empress Constance *(above)*, the wife of the emperor Frederick II. This type of crown, known as a "kamelaukion" is completely eastern Roman, as can be seen from the latticed side pendants.

The municipal banner of Cologne, probably designed by Stephen Lochner in 1450, with the splendidly formed crowns of the municipal arms. These relate to the legend according to which the three kings of the Gospels rest in the Shrine of the Three Kings in Cologne.

(see page 178), which is basically equal in status to a prince's crown. The arches spanning the head were invariably decorated with a closely-set row of pearls and normally topped off by a mound or orb.

From the Renaissance onward, pearls became the most important indicators of rank after the leaf shapes on the headband. At first (i.e., in the fifteenth century) they were mounted directly on the headband, many pearls being used for a high ranking noble such as a count, and a small number for a lower ranking one such as a baron. Chains of pearls wrapped around the headband were also fashionable. Since the eighteenth century, varying rules have been developed according to regional traditions.

The degree of importance attached to the crown as an individual object varied considerably from age to age. Research on this subject is made

IMPERIAL CROWN OF AUSTRIA

STEPHEN'S CROWN OF HUNGARY

CROWN OF THE KINGDOM OF PRUSSIA

CROWN OF THE KINGDOM OF BAVARIA

IMPERIAL CROWN OF RUSSIA

Once the form of the imperial crown had been fully established, all German imperial crowns were made to this pattern. The emperor Rudolph II had one of these crowns made in his court workshops at Prague in 1602. Generally known as the "house" or "family" crown, it was declared the Austrian imperial crown in 1804 *(above)*. It was with this crown that the German emperors rode into the church of their coronation after taking the oath.

considerably more difficult by these varying attitudes. From the point of view of their physical existence, however, we can distinguish three main types:

1. Crowns which have a single "one-time" purpose.
2. Crowns with which some mythical idea is connected and which are therefore carefully preserved and even regarded as holy.
3. Crowns which belonged to the second group but which for some reason or other have been lost.

The crowns of the first group include all those which were created for a single decorative or ceremonial purpose. They are occasionally found as grave ornaments in the tombs of kings and are often remarkably unpretentious, as for example in the imperial tombs of Speyer.

Sometimes these graves include remarkable trinkets which a royal person has worn or greatly valued during his or her life. Examples

The regalia of the kingdom of Scotland *(right)* – sword, scepter, and crown. The crown is very similar to the English one in construction, but has twice as many crosses and fleurs-de-lis on the headband.

THE Regalia of SCOTLAND

are the so-called crown cap of the empress Constance, and even more remarkable, the Castilian royal crown found in Toledo. As crowns have nothing to say about their past, the question of who once wore them may remain uncertain. The crown cap of Constance for example was found in 1781 at the second opening of the empress's grave in the cathedral of Palermo. It would appear that Constance (d. 1222) had not had to conform to Byzantine court ceremonial, according to which only men had the right to wear side pendants. She lived far from the metropolis, which was grown torpid and overrun with Latin influence. Alternatively it may be supposed that her grief-stricken husband, Emperor Frederick II, laid his own crown in her grave.

Such genuine pieces give an idea of the standard of the jeweler's and goldsmith's art which was increasingly applied to the fabrication of

magne, was transported from one repository to another in the Middle Ages; whoever possessed it was the legitimate ruler. The nomadic way of life of the German emperor prevented this crown from having any permanent place of residence until 1424. The emperor Sigismund first created a permanent storage place for it in Nuremberg, whence it had to be brought by special envoys

The head reliquary of Charlemagne *(far left)* in the cathedral treasure at Aix-la-Chapelle bears an imperial sign in the hoop passing from front to back of the head. This matches the so-called imperial crown *(left)*, first commissioned by Otto I the Great for his coronation as emperor in 962. Its construction from eight plates shows eastern Roman influence. The illustrations on four of the plates show Biblical kings. The cross on the frontal plate is like that on all German crowns, but the hoop was added by the emperor Conrad II (reigned 1024–1039) who had his name inlaid on it in pearls.

ST. EDWARD'S CROWN OF ENGLAND

IMPERIAL STATE CROWN OF GREAT BRITAIN

HERALDIC CROWN OF THE KINGDOM OF ITALY

CROWN OF THE CROWN PRINCE OF SWEDEN

STEEL CROWN OF THE KINGDOM OF RUMANIA

crowns. Progress in the techniques of working precious stones also affected their design and decoration. Here again a cultural gap of several hundred years had to be overcome before reaching the level of ancient times when the cloth headbands known as diadems were set with precious stones. Crowns became more and more richly decorated with precious stones of all colors, with gems and cameos and pearls. The pictures on page 176 give some idea of their lavishness. The fact that such crowns are still in existence is due more to their arresting beauty than to any symbolic meaning.

The crowns which were venerated because of the meaning attached to them were not necessarily masterpieces of the goldsmith's art. They could be quite roughly hammered together, like the crown of Stephen of Hungary. But their connection with a much venerated leader made them the embodiment of an idea of the state which rendered them inviolate. The German imperial crown, which up to the nineteenth century was generally believed to have been worn by Charle-

A miniature from around 975 in the cathedral treasure at Aix-la-Chapelle shows the emperor Otto II with his household. He and his sons are wearing crowns. The sons are carrying red pennants to denote that they are dukes.

For the coronations of the German Roman emperor, which took place in Frankfurt-am-Main from 1562 to 1792, all the imperial regalia had to be brought by special embassy from Nuremberg. The coronations had never taken place in Nuremberg – before 1562 they had been in Aix-la-Chapelle. Displayed above we see what was supposedly the crown of Charlemagne, and beside it one the prototype imperial crowns, the originals of which no longer exist. The scepter and orb, two swords, reliquaries, and coronation robes can still be seen for the most part in Vienna.

The crowns shown here are existing originals, all masterpieces of the goldsmith's and jeweler's art.

Left column, top to bottom:
Crown from the head reliquary of the emperor Henry II, possibly made in Bamberg (1260).
Crown of the empress Kunigunde, probably made in Metz (ca. 1020).
Crown of an unknown German princess (ca. 1350).

Right column, top to bottom:
Crown of an English princess, probably Blanche of Lancaster, the daughter of King Henry IV (d. 1437). She must have taken the crown to Germany in 1402 when she was married to the Elector Palatine Ludwig.
The crown of King Christian IV of Denmark, 1596.

for each coronation, which took place first in Aix-la-Chapelle and then in Frankfurt. (In the confusion of Napoleonic times it was taken to safety in Vienna, in 1796, where it remains today after a short interruption from 1938 to 1945.) The Stephen crown of Hungary represented the Hungarian state absolutely, and the locks which guarded it could only be opened by four different key-holders together. In the same category comes the Wenceslas crown at Prague Castle, which is probably the crown which has been subjected to the most careful scientific research. These three crowns are decorated partly with enamel work and partly with precious stones, but the precious stones are still unpolished, reflecting the early date of fabrication.

Once the need had arisen in representative art for realistic portraiture of people, this also had an effect on crowns. They were no longer fashioned without reference to the people who were to wear them. Neither the Stephen nor the Wenceslas crown were "ordered" by the kings after whom they are named, but they were given

individual features, of which the German imperial crown offers an impressive early example. The imperial crown with a hoop between the horns of a miter could be regarded as a norm as

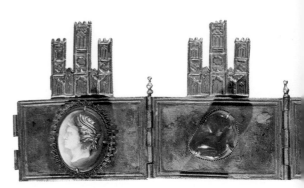

early as the fourteenth and fifteenth centuries. It was left to an artistically minded emperor to have a work of art made from this model according to his personal requirements. In 1602 the emperor Rudolph II had an imperial crown made in his world-famous court workshops at Prague, which represented four scenes from his

In 1525 Charles I of Spain ordered that the crown closed with arches as a symbol of sovereignty should be reserved for the king, and the leaf crown *(far right)* should be assigned to the Spanish grandees.

life on the external sides of the miter. The latter are worked as low reliefs and represent the three coronations of Rudolph as emperor, as king of Hungary, and as king of Bohemia, and finally

urgently required in 1742 when an elector of Bavaria had become emperor and there was no appropriate crown in the jewel house for him or his wife.

Below:
The enameled segments of this crown found in a tomb in Toledo are hinged together and set with real gems. Instead of the usual leaves they bear castles (the arms

show the emperor as conqueror of the Turks. This crown still exists; other similar ones have disappeared, for a variety of reasons.

Many crowns were quite simply melted down for their metal. This was especially the case with overthrown monarchies. There were many losses of this kind in France, where only a few crowns escaped destruction. Among them is the crown of the empress Eugenie, which has been preserved because it was paid for with private means. King Frederick the Great of Prussia (1712–1786) had little respect for his crown; as a substitute for love, he presented his wife with jewels which he had had removed from the royal crown.

The weight of a crown is considerable; we know that before her coronation Queen Elizabeth II had to practice wearing it for days in front of a mirror. For this reason many monarchs have had lighter substitute crowns made, similar to the official crown of their country; indeed the British Queen Victoria was so pleased with her miniature crown that she almost always wore it over her widow's veil.

The crown which the emperor Rudolph II had made in 1602 originally had no purpose other than to enable the emperor to appear "under the crown," as for instance before the formal imperial coronation in Frankfurt where he had already taken the oath as emperor when he rode into the town. The weight of the crown used gave rise to the construction of a lighter, stylistically modified, "substitute" imperial crown, which lacking symbolic value was melted down without protest in 1871. Nor was this the only duplicate, for when an emperor was to be crowned with his wife, a second crown was obviously needed. New crowns were particularly

A coronation is a unique event in the life of a monarch. Multiple coronations were an exception which nevertheless took place; for instance in the case of Richard Cœur de Lion, who had himself crowned a second time after defeating

his treacherous brother, and in that of the German Roman emperors who were also kings of Hungary and Bohemia. In fact there is no particular reason why a ruler should be crowned at all. Up to 800, the Frankish kings were anointed on the hands. It was not until the early ninth

of Castile), influenced by the Moorish building style.

The pope wears the tiara *(left)* not only at his coronation but also on the highest feast days, when he appears as Vicar of Christ. The bishop's miter *(above)* is adequate for liturgical purposes.

177

CROWNS AND CORONETS OF RANK

	KING	PRINCE (CROWN)	PRINCE (CORONET)	DUKE	"ILLUSTRIOUS" COUNT	MARQUIS

FRANCE

Only members of the royal house can wear fleurs-de-lis on the head-band of their crowns.

DENMARK

A hierarchy of crowns and coronets was established in a regulation of 1693.

SWEDEN

The Swedish system is basically the most conservative.

SPAIN

The Spanish system is built up consistently.

ITALY

The Italian rules take into consideration the fact that many families hold titles from the German Roman empire.

GERMANY

Ordinarily there is no difference between the crowns of a duke and a prince. Counts with the title of "illustrious" are a creation of the post-Napoleonic restoration.

RUSSIA

Russian imperial heraldry was based on German usage.

NETHERLANDS

The Dutch hierarchy of crowns shows influences from all the neighboring states.

BELGIUM UP TO 1795

At the time of the "Spanish Netherlands," legislation concerning the nobles in Belgium was very strict.

BELGIUM SINCE 1838

After the creation of the kingdom of Belgium many Dutch rules remained in force.

ENGLAND

The English hierarchy is strictly observed. Princely coronets exist but vary with relationship to the sovereign. The coronet caps are optional.

COUNT, NORMAL	COUNT OR EARL, PERMITTED	VISCOUNT	BARON, NORMAL	BARON, PERMITTED	KNIGHT	UNTITLED NOBLE, NORMAL	UNTITLED NOBLE, PERMITTED

THE CORONATION

Right:
The three sleeping men are represented with crowns to identify them as kings. They are in fact the three kings of the East to whom the angel appeared in a dream and showed the way to Bethlehem.

century that the ceremony developed whereby the crown was bestowed on them by a high-ranking churchman. In the case of the emperors the ceremony remained essentially the same until the eighteenth century, its words as follows:

assistas, Regnique a Deo tibi dati, et per officium nostrae Benedictionis, vice Apostolorum, omniumque Sanctorum suffragio tuo Regimini comissi, utilis Executor, Regnatorque proficuus semper appareas; ut inter gloriosos Athletas virtutum gemmis ornatus, et praemio aeternae felicitatis coronatus, cum Redemtore ac Salvatore Domino nostro Jesu Christo, cujus nomen vicemque gestare credens, fine sine glorieris. Qui vivit et imperat Deus, cum Deo Patre, in unitate Spiritus Sancti, per omnia saecula saeculorum.

Two coronations are shown in the illustrated chronicle of the archbishop of Trier, Baldwin of Luxembourg, one of the brothers of the emperor Henry VII. One is the coronation of the ruler and his wife in Aix-la-Chapelle on 6 January 1309 with open crowns *(above)*. The other *(above right)* is an imperial coronation in Rome on 29 June 1312. Here the imperial crown is closed by an arch.

Accipe coronam Regni, quare licet ab indignis, Episcoporum tamen manibus, capiti tuo imponitur, quamque sanctitatis gloriam et opus fortitudinis expresse significare intelligas, et per hanc te participem Ministerii nostri non ignores, ita ut, sicut nos in interioribus Pastores, Rectoresque animorum intelligamur, ita et tu in exterioribus verus Dei cultor strenuusque contra omnes adversitates Ecclesiae Christi, Defensor

Translated this means:

Accept the imperial crown which is placed on your head by unworthy hands, yet those of a bishop, and know that it expressly represents the glory of sanctification and the work of bravery, and by this you may partake of our holy office, so that just as we in inward matters are the shepherds and rulers of souls, so you in outward

180

matters should be a true servant of God and in the face of all adversity a courageous defender of the Church of Christ and the kingdom given to you by God; and also through the office of our blessing, for we act in place of the Apostles, with the agreement of all the saints, remain at all times ready for the profitable management of the authority entrusted to you and for useful ruling; so that you may be considered among the ranks of well-known fighters and decorated with the precious stones of virtue, and crowned with the reward of eternal happiness, with our savior and beatifier Jesus Christ, whose name and place you represent, and may glorify without ending. For in him God lives and reigns with the Father in unity with the Holy Ghost for ever and ever.

Apart from the setting on of the crown, a complete coronation ceremony also involved the dressing of the monarch in ceremonial robes and the handing over of the insignia of power such as the orb, scepter, and ceremonial sword. All the objects were consecrated during the ceremony by a priest who called down God's grace upon the monarch, though this could become slightly farcical if the monarch himself felt inclined to dispute the authority of the religious representative. At the coronation of Napoleon in Paris, for instance, the emperor took the Pope, who had been summoned to Paris for the occasion, completely by surprise. He first of all seized the laurel wreath from the alter where he had laid it on entering, then held the empress's crown over his head as if to crown himself with it, and finally set it on the head of his wife.

Three pictures of crownings *(left to right):*
A late medieval imaginary picture of the crowning of Charlemagne in Rome in 800.
The crowning of Richard II of England in 1377.
The crowning of King Charles V of France in 1380.

The crowning is not valid, however, if the representative of God is not genuine *(right).*

Napoleon I *(below)* forestalled the pope by himself taking the laurel wreath from the altar, as he had planned. He then set the crown on his wife's head himself.

Since that time, the actual crowning of the monarch has been omitted from the "coronation" (now called *enthroning*) ceremony in Europe. The constitutional monarchs of today bear the title "by the grace of God" only as a matter of tradition, and often add "and through the will of the people." In fact, the dramatic crowning of William I of Prussia on 18 October

Left:
The morning of the last overnight stop before arriving at the Council of Constance (1414). Pope John XXIII, whose status was to be disputed, shows his gratitude to the abbot of Kreuzlingen by investing him with a miter with *infulae* (bands).

181

One of the acts of generosity expected of a prince by his people was the distribution of coins at popular festivals such as coronations. These coins were specially minted for the purpose and bore inscriptions relating to the event. When the husband of the famous Maria Theresa, herself the daughter of an emperor and queen of Hungary, was crowned emperor in 1745, the inscription named him firstly "King of Jerusalem," followed by his titles as duke of Lorraine and grand duke of Tuscany. On the reverse side the shining eye of God watches over the imperial regalia placed on an altar, with the promise to serve "God and the Empire" inscribed above.

The portraits of the eight electors of the time: the archbishops of Mainz, Trier, and Cologne, the duke of Bavaria, the duke of Saxony (king of Poland), the margrave of Brandenburg (king of Prussia), the count palatine on the Rhine and the elector of Hanover (king of Great Britain).

The coronation was accompanied by boisterous popular celebrations *(above)*. The people fought over the coins which were scattered before them, overturning the stalls set up to provide them with food. The municipal guard meanwhile kept their distance in front of the Frankfurt town hall on the other side of the square.

1861 was already the target of violent criticism even from the royalist people of the time.

The development of crowns in modern times has had a far-reaching influence on heraldry. The architectonic forms of the Renaissance were unsuited to the rendering of helmets and crests, but favorable to the symmetrically effective

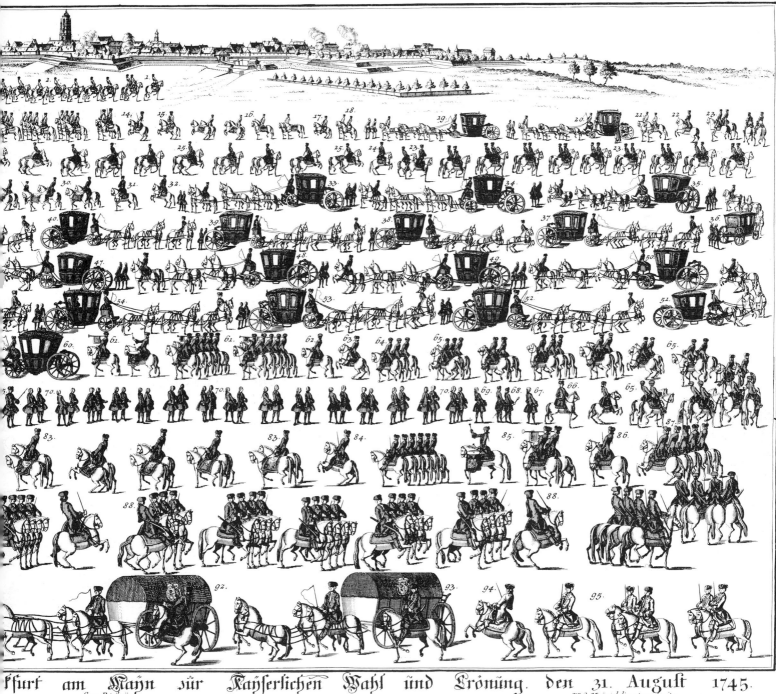

ffurt am Mayn zur Kayserlichen Wahl und Crönung den 31. August 1745.

Cum Privilegiis.

W. C. Mayr delin. et sculpsit.

crowns. In this way a whole hierarchy came into being, expressed by the form and number of ornaments on the crown. The crowns of monarchs appear on their coats of arms, and usually there was some attempt to make these resemble the actual crowns worn.

The elector of Mainz approaches Frankfurt-am-Main with his retinue. The other electors arrived in equal style.

183

In this sloop the royal couple of Sweden, Carl XVI Gustav and Queen Silvia, were carried across the water to the royal castle after their wedding on 19 June 1976. On the ship's bow the three crowns of the state arms are shown beneath the royal crown. On the stern flutters the large split flag and on the bow fly the king's standard with his royal commission pennant on top. These two flags have small additional white rectangles containing the complete royal arms.

Great Britain is the only country in the world where all the splendor of the monarchy is still put on show and draws thousands of

visitors from overseas. Pictures of the coronation of the reigning Queen Elizabeth II not only appeared in the world's press but also reached millions of homes via television. It was the first ime a coronation had been televised. The ceremony took place in London's Westminster Abbey on 2 June 1953. Elizabeth is shown here in the Henry VII chapel, which is flanked by the banners of the "Knights Grand Cross of the Order of the Bath."

184

On the royal French
and Danish seals
and the silver capsules
which belong to them,
you will discover
how the same two kings
bear their royal pavilion.

Note from the
Prussian king
Frederick I, 1701.

SUPPORTERS

Few sovereigns can resist the
impression of splendor
afforded by a pair of heraldic
beasts supporting their coat of
arms. These beasts can be
borrowed from the coat of
arms itself, as in the case of
the kingdom of Bavaria *(left)*,
or they can be one of the
pictorial badges (see page
210) which are displayed by
the ruler in other contexts,
such as the porcupines of
King Louis XII of France
(below).

Arms soon grew out of their role of providing
identification on the battlefield. But the pictorial
arts had picked them up long before they lost
this practical function.

The artists of the twelfth century oriented themselves on reality. The knight bearing his own
shield or the esquire carrying his equipment
offered a frequent and magnificent spectacle
which asked to be recorded graphically, just as
their obvious connection with death and danger
gave food for thought.

This is confirmed by the oldest coat of arms we
know, that of Geoffrey Plantagenet, from the Le
Mans cathedral. It is carried by the bearer himself and appears in magnificent colored enamel
work on a plate from his tomb. This portrait of
an armigerous lord with his shield thus shows
one kind of shield bearer who can be looked on
as a forerunner of the "supporter." The latter
has in the course of time developed into an integral part of the coat of arms, to which certain
definite principles have been applied. These
principles, which have hardly ever been strictly
formulated, are based on social developments
which produced many social divisions even
within the upper class. These divisions are expressed, for example, in the designations of the
different grades of nobility. In most countries the
higher ranking nobility have the right, but not
the obligation, to choose particular supporters
and have these granted to them where such a
procedure is possible. Here again we find confirmation of the opinion, current since the early
days of heraldry, that documentation of the
bearing of arms by some authority is desirable.
This authority can be the lord of the land, the
government, or some office created by the
monarch. The regulations concerning the rank
of those who may bear permanent supporters in
their arms are fairly variable. In England, for
example, counties, cities, towns, boroughs, and
districts may be granted supporters, but other

186

corporate bodies are not necessarily allowed this distinction. The British Crown normally grants supporters to colonies and countries within the Commonwealth.

Of the some 160 sovereign states of the world, almost a third bear arms with supporters in the

mplo fit Augustule Ferdinandi Cæsaris, cum tessera Avstriaca,

strictest sense (i.e., one on either side of the shield). It is increasingly becoming the custom for the supporters to consist of animals of two different species. No animal can compete with the lion, however, which is generally preferred as a supporter, if it does not already appear in the shield itself. The latter is the case with a large number of Dutch municipal arms, including those of Amsterdam, and also with those of Hamburg and Bremen. Just as the lion as a charge appears in different poses, so as a supporter it can appear with different positions of the head, for example "reguardant," looking towards the rear, or "guardant," looking at the observer. The normal position, in which the lion faces forward in profile, is termed "rampant." In the correct English blazon, the position of the head must be stated in each case – rampant, guardant, or reguardant. It may be assumed that the souvenir print published in Bruges in 1468 (see pages 188–189) contributed much to the heraldic lion's becoming such a favorite supporter. It also lends itself naturally to graphic witticisms, as when a single lion holds the shield and the helmet is shown placed on his head, his forepaws projecting round the edge of the shield or gripping it from behind and the tuft on the tail hanging down beneath.

But before such conventions could be established a long and fairly obscure process of development

The Jesuit priest Silvester Petra Sancta is wrongly credited with the invention of heraldic hatching. In fact he only worked for its wider adoption in his classic work *Tesserae gentilitae.* However, he also made fruitful investigations into heraldic subjects, including the ornamental emblems which could be used in conjunction with armorial shields. For the emperor's coat of arms he invented a tent-shaped background which would have the double eagle suspended in front of it, supported by two heralds in Austrian tabards and with Austrian banners *(left).* These did in fact become the most impressive royal ornamental emblems.

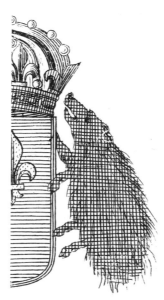

Bertrand du Guesclin *(right)* who appears in French historical legend as an appendage of the Nine Worthies *(Neuf Preux),* is depicted in the book *Le Triomphe des Neuf Preux (The Triumph of the Nine Worthies)* wearing the tabard of the French heralds. He is also holding his shield by the strap as if it belonged to another.

was necessary. This began as early as the thirteenth century and is scarcely documented in the armorials. Any documentation must be sought in single pattern sheets, and chiefly in seals. Seals would in fact provide a fairly exact picture if one could check a sufficiently large number of them.

In a work such as Schedel's *Weltchronik (Chronicle of the World,* 1493), coats of arms are used for illustrative purposes. The escutcheons of the so-called quaternions (see page 128) are presented by elegantly tripping figures or figures growing out of flowers. In the upper row are the four counts: Schwarzburg, Cleves, Cilli, and Savoy; and beneath them the four landgraves: Thuringia, Hessen, Leuchtenberg, and (Lower) Alsace.

The representation of the possessor of the seal on the seal is older than heraldry. As soon as a shield or the complete armorial bearings are looked upon as characterizing the person, then the shield or the armorial bearings will appear in the appropriate place on the seal. For the latter must take its legal validity from all those elements which will support its authenticity. Even an archaic configuration can sometimes contribute to this, as with the Ascanian margraves of Brandenburg or in Scandinavia.

It was not only ruling monarchs who had themselves represented on their seals. Highly placed ladies, acting as regents for their children after

the loss of a royal father, appeared as supporters of their inherited arms and arms by marriage. They are generally shown holding the shield aloft, or raising the helmet above the shield, the thong of which may be hung over their three free fingers.

The supporters of the arms of England gradually ceased to change under Henry VII. During the last three Tudor reigns, the English lion stood on the right and the Welsh dragon of the Tudors on the left (below).

There are also seals of duchesses, who are shown with a free-standing armorial beast stretching out its paw to them.

In view of the concept that the arms or the armorial beast directly represented the armiger, one must expect to find near-heraldic beings appearing on seals, particularly those which are identical to or related to a badge. The space between the shield and the edge of the seal is ideally suited to the insertion of small animal reliefs, which spring not so much from the whim of the engraver as from the intentions of the person who commissioned the seal. Many may be purely ornamental while others relate to facts.

Left:
Spectators of the *Joyeuse Entrée* ("joyful entry") of Mary of York into Bruges on 2 July 1468 as the wife of Duke Charles the Bold were reminded of the magnificent tableau presented to them at the Prinsenhof by this print by the Master W.A. The large lions became the ancestors of numerous supporters.

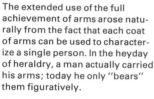
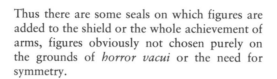

The extended use of the full achievement of arms arose naturally from the fact that each coat of arms can be used to characterize a single person. In the heyday of heraldry, a man actually carried his arms; today he only "bears" them figuratively.

Top row, left to right:

Three seals of ruling women; they contain the arms of their families of origin and those of their current position.

The figure of a lion derived from the arms of Nassau is tethered by a woman.

The horses flanking the arms of the earls of Arundel serve to distinguish the different lines of this family.

The hound in the seal of the Hohenzollerns is derived from their crest.

Supporters in the true sense of the word, these two ladies, recognizable by their richly folded garments, are found as early as 1292 on the seal of Heinrich von Scharfeneck. They flank the shield and hold it with outstretched arms, each gracefully decorating its upper edge with a noble flower.

Thus there are some seals on which figures are added to the shield or the whole achievement of arms, figures obviously not chosen purely on the grounds of *horror vacui* or the need for symmetry.

The *horror vacui* (abhorrence of empty space) plays a not inconsiderable role in seal engraving, since a plain, unengraved surface does not imprint well in sealing wax or wax. An empty background can be damasked just like the field on a coat of arms and filled out with a lattice or scroll pattern. If figures of men or beasts are chosen instead of this, a particular significance can be attached to them, though such seals are admittedly rare. Almost every seal on which the space between the shield and the edge is filled with figures must therefore be looked at individually in order to establish what motive may have led to the choice of these accompanying figures.

It is not always just a question of filling the space between the edge of the armorial shield and the inscription running round the circular seal. There are also trefoils and quatrefoils and similar multiform shapes, the angles and arches of which are occupied by small figures.

On the seal of Catherine of Savoy-Vaud, Countess of Namur (1352), there are the symbols of the four evangelists. On that of Isabel of Chalon-Arlay, mistress of Vaud (1338), we find music-playing melusines, a reference to the blood-relationship with the Cypriot royal house of Lusignan, together with eagles and lions from Savoyard heraldry.

Without venturing to establish a chronological order, we will now take a look at some groups of supporters established by the study of seals.

The simplest method of depositing a shield somewhere in a more or less decorative fashion

is to hang it from a hook on the wall or on a tree – there is technically no difference between the two. Ladies who used not to bear a helmet and crest frequently showed their unaccompanied shield hung from a tree fork or branch, and this arrangement was emphasized by the clear representation of the shield strap. English queens and widows of kings have their arms represented on their seals in this way, the earliest being Queen Eleanor between 1189 and 1204. The same device was used by the similarly named wife of Edward I, a princess of Castile and León, between 1254 and 1290, and also Edward's second wife, a princess of France, after 1299. Men too used the tree in this way, including Thomas Earl of Lancaster around 1300 and John Holland, Earl of Huntingdon and Duke of Exeter (beheaded in 1400).

In Germany shields sitting in the tops of trees are a typical feature of old municipal arms. In many of them the shield is clearly hung from a branch by its strap. An example is the Mecklenburg shield with a bull's head at Neu-Buckow (thirteenth century).

The already mentioned earl of Lancaster provides an example of the well-thought-out choice of accompanying figures. He and his brother Henry (1281–1345) were the only members of the English royal family who did not bear a lion as their crest. Instead they used a dragon, which appeared in miniature on their seals as a crest or large and clear on either side of the shield. The dragon was the crest of the arms of Brabant at that time and the mother of the two brothers was the daughter of Mathilda of Brabant by her marriage with Robert I, Count of Artois, a brother of St. Louis, the king of France.

These dragons cannot however be regarded as supporters in the strictest sense. They certainly touch the shield but do not support it any more than the bears in the great seal of Berlin of 1280.

Bottom row, left to right:

A comfortably seated man supports helmet and shield on his legs.

The shield can be hung by its strap in the top of a tree.

Supporters often hold the helmet instead of the shield in the full achievement of arms.

An animal used as a badge can have the shield hung around its neck.

Count Otto of Nassau stands over his castle, and a wild man of the woods comes out of the Harz mountains.

The minnesinger "Winli" swears to his mother by the edge of his shield to behave in a chivalrous fashion.

Right:
Human figures contribute admirably to the effectiveness of room decorations. An example is this candle holder, intended to be hung from the ceiling in the middle of a large room. The armorial shield the woman is holding indicates who is the master of the house.

191

Opposite:
In historic galleries of ancestors, the figures act as supporters for their own arms. On the fourteenth century stained glass windows of St. Stephen's cathedral in Vienna, the eagle of the youthful-looking Rudolph (d. 1291) is turned politely towards that of his bearded son Albrecht I (d. 1308).

An angel watches over the tomb of the elector and archbishop Theodoric of Cologne, holding in its hands the arms of his diocese.

This richly figured pastry mold *(right)* is decorated with the arms of the southern German town of Villingen. Above the escutcheon are not only the helmet with its crest which is derived from the Austrian arms, but also two shields, each bearing an eagle, that of the emperor Charles V and that of his brother, the Roman king Ferdinand I. The supporters are those of the arms of the arch-dukes of Austria at the time, for it was an archduke of Austria who had granted the new municipal arms.

Opposite:
Barred helmets can be placed on the heads of the supporters so that they look out through the bars. This even became the rule in many arms, such as those of Pomerania and Brandenburg.

Equally incapable of offering support were the ostrich feathers of the Black Prince (d. 1376) and the English dukes Edward of Somerset (1406–1455), Henry of Lancaster (1399), and Thomas of Gloucester (ca. 1385) or the flaming swords of Louis de Bourbon of 1487 (see page 211).

and not beasts. From this it would appear that the representation of the armiger himself was an iconographic forerunner of the supporter, which extends far back into the prehistoric past. In the time of the Roman empire and Carolingian times it was the custom to reproduce the head of the seal bearer only. Until the tenth century no one except the king was allowed to ratify a document with a seal. Then began a whole series of bishop's seals, which gradually progressed from a rendering of the head to the bust and finally the whole figure, with the spiritual insignia being ever more strongly emphasized.

The oldest seal of a non-royal ruler in Germany is that of Duke Henry VII of Bavaria, dated 1045. He appears in full figure with a pointed

The gigantic lion supporters press the helmets down onto the shield with their forepaws – an unusual form of design. They grimace at one another, showing their enormous tongues. They are supporting the arms of a princely family and specifically of Duke Bogislaw XIII of Pomerania-Barth, who had married Clara of Brunswick in 1592.

However, the living figures appearing on many badges proved ideal as supporters for the shield so long as they did not appear with their back turned to the latter and once their decorative effect was recognized. The fact that this was the case no later than around 1290 is illustrated by the seal of Heinrich von Scharfeneck (see page 190).

The first true shield bearers were human figures

oval battle shield and a lance with a pennant. A hundred years later a coat of arms might appear on the shield, but this did not happen immediately everywhere if there was no necessity for changing the type of seal in customary use. (The Ascanian margraves of Brandenburg were still using such seals in 1200.)

The representation of the ruler with his shield, either with or without a coat of arms, whether

The almost naturalistic "Marzocco" lion with the arms of Florence under its right forepaw is a masterpiece by Donatello and was originally intended for the papal apartments in the monastery of Maria Novella (ca. 1416).

standing, on horseback, or seated on a throne (see page 43) formed the most important type of seal. The image of the standing ruler eventually went out of fashion, but as late as 1393 the seal of Count Otto of Nassau-Dillenburg showed him standing threateningly over the battlements of his castle with raised sword and holding an armorial shield.

More attractive is "Beautiful Else" of Bavaria as she appears in the topmost field of the trefoil into which her seal is divided. She stands holding the armorial shield with a magnificent coiffure, while the two hounds from the crest of her husband, the burgrave of Nuremberg, Frederick I of Hohenzollern, turn their backs to the shield. The counts Konrad and Berthold of Freiburg (in Breisgau) appear on their seal of 1239 holding their shield in front of their bodies. This is typical of a case in which the bearers, being still minors, have not as yet established any control over the eventual conditions of their inheritance.

The animal figures accompanying an armorial shield can be in three different poses: in a pair turned away from the shield; in a pair turned towards the shield and usually actually holding the shield or the helmet of the achievement of arms; or singly, holding the shield, helmet, and banner. The latter type is closely related to the human figures, if one starts from the premise that the coat of arms legally represents its owner. Then by extension it will be seen that one of the armorial charges used as a supporter will represent the person of the owner of the seal. Several seals of the counts of Savoy can be interpreted in this manner.

The choice of animal depends largely on the prior choice of armorial charges and above all of the crest or badge. Examples are the white lions of the English earls of March from the house of Mortimer, which begin as mere accompanying figures (1301) and later become helmet bearers and finally proper supporters of the full achievement of arms. The wild men riding on deer in the seal of the chamberlain of France, Louis de Bourbon (1367), may be seen in the same way. Many bearers of seals dressed the supporters in their own tabards, as for instance Girard de Gramont, in 1336. One of the very oldest examples of a beast acting as a supporter is the lion found on the seal of the Brabantine Gilles de Trazegnies of 1195. This is also an example of the transfer of a single supporter to the shield itself, where it appears in adumbration, which is a reminder that the lion was originally a supporter. Such single figures, carrying the shield hung round their necks, are in fact quite common. We might mention the eagle of the earl

Two Brunswick thalers with wild men *(right)*, one with a burning light and the other, which was issued jointly by two dukes, with two men of the Harz.

Above:
Arms of the artistically minded king of Hungary, Matthew Hunyadi, known as Corvinus, at the Görlitz town hall. They are supported by a woman, representing peace and culture, and a knight, representing power and military might. The shield contains the fields of Hungary, Bohemia, Lower Lusatia, and Silesia and is carried on the back of a lion.

Right:
An unusual representation of the Swedish royal arms with a wild man and woman as supporters. The woman has an excessive covering of hair, while the man is armed with a club. The customary garlands of leaves are greatly reduced.

Far right:
A wild man guarding the arms of the aristocratic Frankfurt family of Holzhausen. He is conventionally represented with garlands of leaves round his head and loins.

The colonizer of Maryland, Lord Baltimore, bequeathed his arms to the naissant state. The feudal-style leopard supporters, however, were replaced by local inhabitants, a ploughman and a fisherman. The "male chauvinist" Italian motto – "Deeds are a man's, words a woman's affair" – was allowed to remain.

of Cornwall, which was used in memory of his father Richard, the king of the Romans around 1290 (see page 126). The banner-bearing lion of the house of Savoy often wears the helmet on its head (e.g., in 1375 and 1383), as often happens later with paired supporters (see page 195).

If the normal desire for a symmetrical impression is abandoned, an animal couchant can also carry a shield with the strap around its neck. Such is the case with the doe which the earl of Kent, Thomas Holland, incorporated into his seal in 1380, evidently to please his brother King Richard II of England. Richard's badge was a deer.

After supporters became an established part of the achievement of arms, their choice was no longer dictated by the requirements of a seal. They could appear under any guise and become an important part of the whole. And from about 1400 onward people did not hesitate to introduce two different supporters into heraldry, first of all in England. Examples are the falcon and

the antelope used by John Beaufort, Duke of Somerset (d. 1444), the king's grandson who did not inherit the throne.

The use of two different supporters was to some extent necessitated by the growing tendency to distinguish between the different lines of a family by unchanging supporters. Examples are the lions (1375), griffins (1397), and horses (ca. 1400) used by the English earls of Arundel. The griffins correspond to the crest.

Notable supporters from a particular coat of arms can also be transferred to another coat of

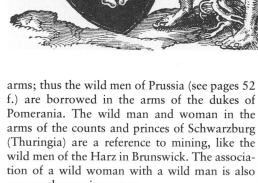

arms; thus the wild men of Prussia (see pages 52 f.) are borrowed in the arms of the dukes of Pomerania. The wild man and woman in the arms of the counts and princes of Schwarzburg (Thuringia) are a reference to mining, like the wild men of the Harz in Brunswick. The association of a wild woman with a wild man is also seen on the previous page.

Opposite:
A pattern sheet for wild men and attractive ladies as supporters. Emil Doepler the Younger contributed this sheet to the *Heraldic Atlas* published by Hugo Gerard Ströhl in 1897.

Human beings as supporters

1   Married couple with arms of alliance.

2   A couple as accompanying figures, the man paying the woman the wages of love.

3   A servant with the escutcheons of his masters.

4   The mistress herself with the family banner.

5   A young bride.

6   A Nuremberg servant girl with her employer's achievement of arms.

7   The knight with the badge of an order round his neck is the armiger himself.

8–9   Aboriginal inhabitants: An Indian for an Englishman and a Varangian for a Russian.

Imaginary figures as supporters

10   Neptune for a sea lord.

11   A Melusine for the kings of Naples.

12   Minerva with a Medusa shield.

13–16   Angels are most suitable for religious arms.

17   The double-headed German imperial eagle as supporter.

18   The printers' griffin as a publisher's mark.

Winged beings and other legendary beasts

19   This grouping, which was popular in the rococo period, is called *en baroque*.

20   An English basilisk.

21   The winged bull of Luke the evangelist, with the arms of artists.

22–23   The winged deer is French, the Wyvern was meant to be the Welsh dragon.

24   A dragon draped round the edge of the shield recalls a Hungarian order.

25   The lion carrying the pillar personified the strength of Samson.

26–27   Individual lions show their extremities round the edge of the shield; the lion's heads biting the shield are unique.

28   Any four-legged animal makes a suitable supporter in some pose or other, like this elephant for one of the lines of the Fugger family.

29   The supporting animal can also be crouching.

30–31   In England, the covering of an animal supporter with a pattern is a popular convention.

32–33   Shields hanging by their straps from forked branches.

34–36   Garlands of banners were used by the Spaniards as a reminder of their victories over the Moors.

1

2

3

10

11

12

13

19

20

21

22

28

29

30

31

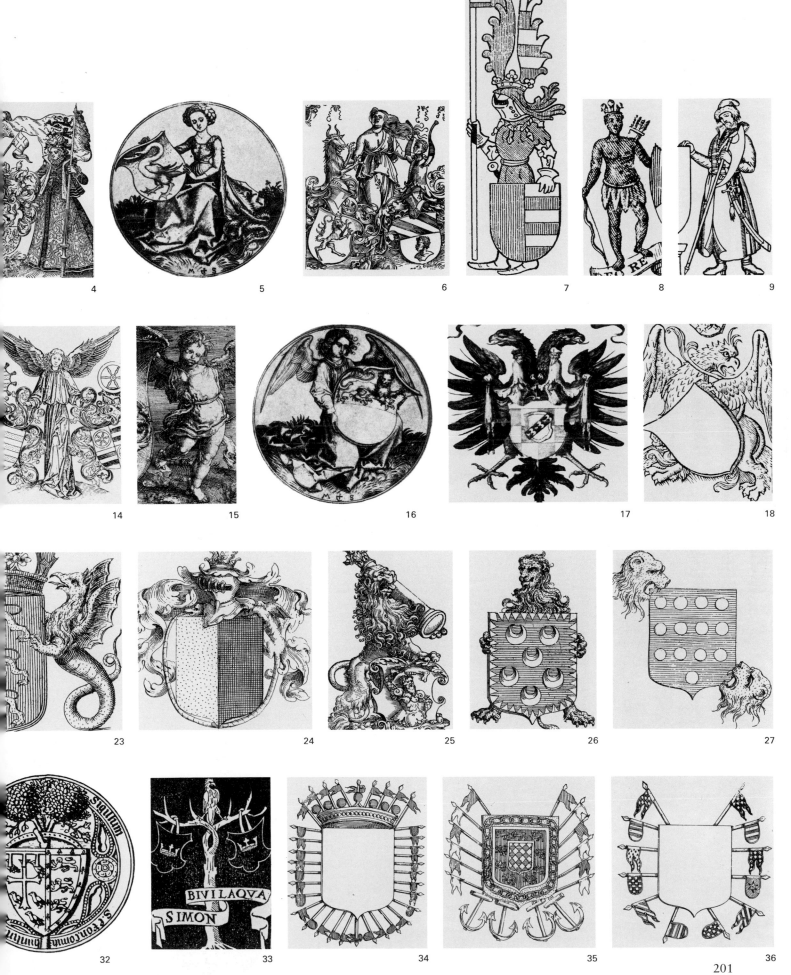

4

5

6

7

8

9

14

15

16

17

18

23

24

25

26

27

32

33

34

35

36

201

A shield is held while standing or sitting, in the latter case on a throne or on a horse. The attitude taken up while doing this influenced the way of combining the shield and helmet so decisively that the slanting position of the shield has remained the normal one to this day. The sight of an armed soldier was so familiar in the Middle Ages that the reclining figure of a dead man was depicted as though he were standing. At his feet he trampled a lion or a hound while his head was framed by a pediment or even a fully sculpted baldachin.

Once the restricting frame of the seal was removed from the representation of the human figure, the supporter could be placed on a ground which was only restricted by the space available. The solution then offered itself,

The tomb of an English knight with a recumbent lion serving as a footrest.

202

Right:
The badge of the dukes of Burgundy consisted of two branches crossed in saltire and fire-steels with flints showering sparks. To this Charles the Bold added his personal motto *Je l'ay emprins* ("I have undertaken it"), which appeared on all his banners.

Below:
In recent decades, new states have shown a tendency to use real landscapes as bases for their arms – for example the Thaba Bosiu in Lesotho *(left)* and Mt. Kilimanjaro in Tanzania *(center).* A much earlier example is found in the arms of the city of Southampton, granted in 1575 *(right).*

governed not by heraldic but by ornamental considerations, of placing the arms and their supporters on an architecturally constructed pedestal, called a compartment. In blazons such compartments are usually mentioned but not described, their design being left to the imagination of the heraldic artist. In periods of overflowing artistic forms such as the Renaissance, baroque, and rococo, an often excessive use was made of the possibilities provided by this freedom. This was particularly true of situations in which heraldry was only one component of the whole, such as tombs, title pages of books, and bookplates.

Against this there were always the armorials with their purely informative intention, in which ornaments are only briefly mentioned. The placing of supporters on a compartment can add to the impression of pomp given by a badge or coat of arms. The Prussian kings in the eighteenth century inscribed their motto *Gott mit uns* ("God with us") on a plinth richly decorated with royal eagles. Their princes on the other hand had to be content with a simple shelf, on which the two wild men supporting the coat of arms give an impression of equilibrium. The

wild men on the Danish coat of arms, by contrast, seem to be standing on cliffs. In this they resemble the French angels of the French royal

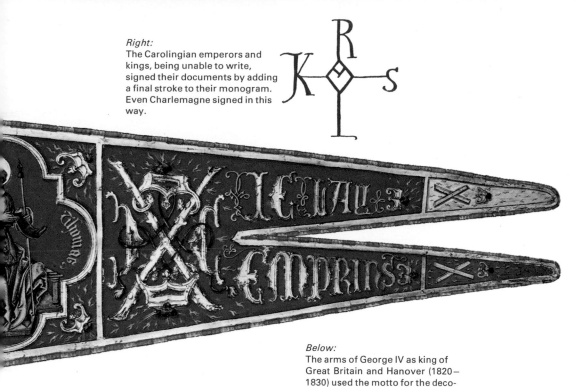

Right:
The Carolingian emperors and kings, being unable to write, signed their documents by adding a final stroke to their monogram. Even Charlemagne signed in this way.

Below:
The arms of George IV as king of Great Britain and Hanover (1820–1830) used the motto for the decoration of the foliage.

The royal arms of France which Philippe Moreau designed in 1609, incorporating all the armorial insignia for the first time, was regarded as correct throughout the world. Only the kings themselves did not bear them in this way. Their battle cry was indeed *Montjoie St. Denis,* however, and it is correctly placed above everything else.

arms, which were dressed as heralds and could not use their wings to support the shield in the air as did the angels of Hungary or the dragons of Portugal. Some mottoes become an integral part of the coat of arms, such as the *Dieu et mon droit* ("God and my right") of the English king Henry V (reigned 1413–1422) and his successors. This became an integral part of the coat of arms with Henry VIII (reigned 1509–1547). When this is the case, the motto appears beneath the coat of arms on a fluttering banderole, which serves as a basis for the supporters. Alternatively it is inscribed on a plinth. The custom of bearing mottoes, rather like a present-day political slogan, was widespread among the ruling houses of the late Middle Ages. Many of these mottoes, such as *Dieu et mon droit,* were retained by the person's successors. Most of them, however, remained attached to the person who had chosen them, such as the motto *Je l'ay emprins* (in modern French, *Je l'ai entrepris* – "I have undertaken it") which Charles the Bold (d. 1477) had inscribed on all his banners. He did not recognize it as an actual part of his coat of arms, yet the motto appears on the version of the arms drawn in Bruges as early as 1468, inscribed on the frame as if on a pedestal (see page 189).

Admittedly the use of letters is forbidden in heraldry as the sign should speak for itself without elucidation, but the ornamental possibilities of the shape of letters are not altogether lost. The kings of the Middle Ages devised their monograms out of skillfully combined letters, and artistically designed words such as the *Libertas* of the Italian city states (see page 240) are another illustration of this.

In the past few centuries, despite their personal character, mottoes have found their way into the heraldry of families. This has happened because, at least since the eighteenth century, the offices of particular orders, when asking a newly created knight for a proposal of arms to be inserted in the order's register have also asked for details of his motto. In modern state arms, especially those which are influenced by British

George IV.

heraldry, pedestals and bases gain a new expressive value; e.g., the mountain lake of Grenada, between an armadillo and a wood pigeon.

A distinction should be made between mottoes and battle cries such as the French *Montjoie St. Denis* or *Flandre au lion* ("Flanders of the lion"). These should appear if at all above the coat of arms. In Scotland the motto is almost invariably treated as a battle cry and placed above the crest. Although in England mottoes seldom form part of a grant of arms, in Scotland they are formally and legally assigned.

In the bookplate of the Austrian monastery of Raigern *(above),* the front edge of the pedestal serves as a label indicating the book owner's name.

Right:
The war tent of a victorious English king in France is recognizable by the red St. George's crosses round the edge of the roof. The defeated opponent kneels submissively in front of the king.

The state arms of a modern monarchy of European stamp appear in their most luxurious manifestation equipped with an armorial cloak or tent. Exceptions here confirm the rule. This was possible in the form in which we understand it only since the seventeenth century. At the beginning of that century, in 1609, a Bordeaux lawyer by the name of Philippe Moreau was compiling his *Tableau des armoiries de France*. He had the idea of using the throne seals of kings, on which they were realistically represented, as a model for sumptuously presented coats of arms. For this he replaced the figure of the king by his shield, which now appeared under a canopy of billowing material. The symbol of sovereignty which Moreau represented over the shield of France with its fleurs-de-lis was not in fact accepted as a part of the coat of arms by the French kings themselves. However as a result of widespread distribution in printed works of many different kinds, it found much approval among admirers of French customs. This was particularly the case in Savoy (see page 47), in Denmark, and in Prussia, where

High-ranking lords did not renounce their customary comforts even on the battlefield. In the fourteenth century a French book illustrator represented a negotia-

tion between the emperor of Byzantium and the king of Jerusalem on one side and the sultan on the other as if it had taken place in his own time, although it would only have been possible in the twelfth century. On the brow of each tent we see the coat of arms of its occupant, while the latter's armorial banner flies from the top.

a distinction was established between the armorial tent (with a dome) and the armorial cloak (without a dome). The dome of the armorial tent became a privilege of the ruler of the state, while the cloak was attributed to princes and princesses. Today, this difference only survives in the Netherlands. In 1972 the newly constituted arms of the king of Denmark abandoned the distinc-

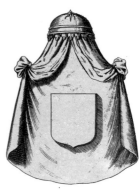

In his standard work on heraldry in 1638, the Jesuit father Silvester Petra Sancta uttered the opinion that the arms of dukes and sovereign princes should be embellished with a cloak-shaped piece of drapery, which would fall away from the top of the helmet like the classical mantling, and would resemble the latter in its multiple colors. For the lining he envisaged not natural but heraldically stylized ermine.
Draperies falling away from a cupola and hitched up at the sides *(above right)* were only to be attributed to monarchs (i.e., an emperor or king).

The historic meeting between King Francis I of France and Henry VIII of England, which took place in the Field of the Cloth of Gold *(Camp du Drap d'Or)* on 7 June 1520. It was held in a gigantic tent of gold brocade decorated on the inside with fleurs-de-lis.

graphic possibilities discovered by Moreau and his engraver L. Gaultier.

The proper armorial cloak developed out of the armorial surcoats which princes wore themselves and also had their heralds wear in the form of tabards. These cloaks are characterized by the fact that they bear the complete image of the armorial shield, but only reveal those parts which are at the edge of the cloak, and even these are seen in reverse. Royal armorial cloaks and tents are generally purple on the outside. They can be decorated with small motifs, including charges such as the French fleur-de-lis (on a blue cloak), the cross of Savoy, the Prussian eagle, the lion of Zähringen and Nassau, and the triple crowns of Sweden. Alternatively they may be decorated with crowns indicating the bearer's rank or badges not derived from the coat of arms itself such as the bees of Napoleon.

Such badges have existed since the fourteenth century and carry almost as much significance as the coat of arms itself. They evade the systematization which is a part of heraldry, but are among those elements of graphic art which can be very useful in establishing an object's date and provenance.

Above: In central European heraldry the lining of the armorial cloak was nearly always naturalistically represented, as in the real cloak or cape *(left)*. In the Latin nations however it was often shown in a heraldically stylized form, with the contents of the armorial shield repeated on the outside of the cloak. As women did not bear helmets, one often finds these cloaks spread over a crowned shield.

One of the pope's signs of status was the red and yellow striped umbrella which was carried over

tion and introduced an armorial cloak which has the character of a coronation robe and not of the drapery from which it was originally developed.

In fact the prototype of the tent and cloak is not the robe worn by the monarch to his coronation, but the movable canopy of oriental potentates and of the pope as well as the fixed canopy over the throne of worldly and spiritual rulers, shown in chronicles and on seals. The princes of the Middle Ages frequently lived in tents while engaged in sport or military campaigns. Large quantities of tents were also required for their

him during the Middle Ages, at least from the twelfth century. In the same category were the throne canopy or baldachin – either fixed or portable – the overhanging edge of which was trimmed with fringes in particular colors.

numerous retinue and these were graded in size and luxury according to the status of the occupant. Negotiations were held either in the tent or in the open air. The picture of the prince posing in front of his tent became the prototype of the armorial tent after 1638, when the heraldic writer Silvester Petra Sancta eagerly adopted the

Graphically, badges often cannot be distinguished from armorial charges, indeed the two are often identical. Badges have the advantage that they can be used in unlimited numbers, somewhat like a fabric pattern, as is the case with the French fleur-de-lis. For his coronation in 1483, Richard III of England is said to have

206

In 1890 two ducal lines were founded, those of Savoy-Aosta and Savoy-Genoa. The dukes' crown is derived from the royal crown. An armorial drape is borne; the complete pavilion is the privilege of the king.

A ruling of 1 January 1890 laid down differences between the arms of the Italian royal family and those of the Italian state. After the unification of Italy, the arms of the ducal family of Savoy in fact became the state arms of Italy, but numerous individual questions remained unresolved. The ornamental emblems borne by the dukes of Savoy before they were kings of Sardinia (see page 47) were confirmed as royal arms of Italy in 1890.

Opposite:
Bronze doors of the funeral chapel
of King Henry VII in Westminster
Abbey (1509) with the armorial
charges of the royal house (fleurs-
de-lis and lions) and its badges.
These are a sunburst, a portcullis,
a falcon and fetterlock, a crown
with tendrils of roses and daisies,
and a monogram consisting of the
intertwined letters R and H.

ordered 13,000 white boars. These were to be
distributed at the ceremony over the clothes of
the doorkeepers and the king's retinue, who
were dressed in "livery colors" decorated with
badges.

Some very well known badges have even given
their names to political factions, the best-known
being the white rose of York, which represented the side of King Richard III in the Wars of
the Roses. The conclusion of this war still finds
expression today in the Tudor rose (see
page 210). In England the badges of prominent,
politically influential personalities were at times
so popular that Shakespeare could presuppose a
knowledge of them in his historical plays.

The eighteen different badges of
the "illustrious family of Stafford"
were certified by Garter King of
Arms in 1720. Half are on a half-
black, half-red ground; i.e., in the
livery colors of the family.

Originally the livery colors in which a lord
dressed his servants were a matter of free choice,
but they then tended to be maintained within a
family. The dynasty of Lancaster used blue and
white, the house of York blue and murrey (a
mulberry color), the Tudors white and green,
and the Stuarts gold and scarlet. In accordance
with the now established heraldic rules, the
ruling English dynasty uses red and yellow.

The strictness of heraldic rules led again and again to currents or whole eras in which additional badges appeared, won popularity, and then disappeared again. Many nations have proved highly inventive in this field, in particular Japan.

JAPAN
Flags of coastal lords *(daimyo)*, each bearing a *mon* in particular colors. Nineteenth century.

ASANO, DAIMYO AT HIROSHIMA

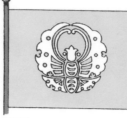
IKEDA, DAIMYO AT OKAYAMA

IKEDA, DAIMYO AT OKAYAMA, VARIANT

UESUGI, DAIMYO AT YONEZAWA

ENGLAND
In England and its overseas possessions, the use of badges has persisted to the present day. Many of them have lasted over several generations.

HEIR APPARENT TO THRONE

EDWARD III

EDWARD III

EDWARD IV

TUDOR ROSE

JANE SEYMOUR, 3RD WIFE OF HENRY VII

FRANCE
Relating to a single person only, the pictorial badges *(corps de devise)* in French heraldry are usually accompanied by a descriptive motto (the *âme de devise*), which often reflects attributions of the badge.

PORCUPINE LOUIS XII

ERMINE, ANNE OF BRITTANY, QUEEN OF FRANCE

SALAMANDER FRANCIS I

SWAN, CLAUDE OF BRITTANY WIFE OF FRANCIS I

ITALY
Italy was rich in pictorial badges during the Gothic period; shown here is a series of badges belonging to the count of Pavia of the Visconti family in Milan (1495).

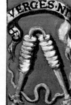

THE BADGES FROM THE BANNER OF THE COUNT OF PAVIA, OF THE VISCONTI FAMILY. THE MOTTOES ARE PARTLY LATIN *(MERITO ET*

SPAIN
Unframed images, partly taken from the coat of arms, have been used as near-heraldic badges in Spain from the twelfth century right up to the present.

CASTLE OF CASTILE

LION OF LEÓN

YOKE (YUGO) OF FERDINAND I

ARROWS (FLECHAS) OF QUEEN ISABELLA

ST. JOHN'S EAGLE OF ARAGON

PRUSSIA
The naturalistic eagles, accompanied by mottoes which the Hohenzollerns derived from the black eagle of the dukedom of Prussia, varied little from 1740 onwards.

FREDERICK I: SUUM CUIQUE (TO EACH HIS OWN)

FREDERICK WILLIAM I: NON SOLI CEDIT (HE DOES NOT YIELD TO THE SUN)

FREDERICK II: PRO GLORIA ET PATRIA (FOR FAME AND FATHERLAND)

FREDERICK WILLIAM II: SAME MOTTO

WILLIAM II: SAME MOTTO

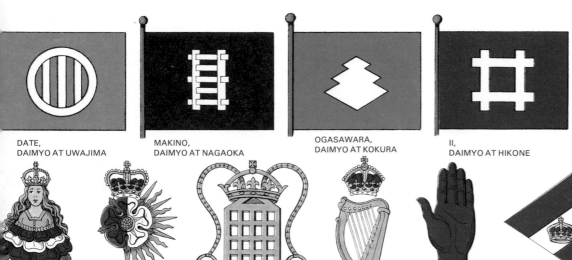

DATE,
DAIMYO AT UWAJIMA

MAKINO,
DAIMYO AT NAGAOKA

OGASAWARA,
DAIMYO AT KOKURA

II,
DAIMYO AT HIKONE

TOKUGAWA,
DAIMYO AT MITO

CATHERINE PARR,
6TH WIFE OF HENRY VIII

RICHMOND
HERALD

PORTCULLIS

HARP
OF IRELAND

HAND OF ULSTER

STRAITS SETTLEMENTS

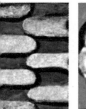 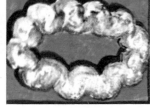   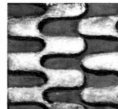 

THREE CROWNS
HENRY III

LOUIS XIV, THE SUN KING,
FORTRESS GATE AT LANDAU

FLAMING SWORD
CARDINAL LOUIS DE BOURBON

TEMPORE), PARTLY FRENCH *(A BON DROIT)* AND PARTLY GERMAN *(VERGESS NIT).* THE FIELDS ARE DIVIDED BY A TYPICAL ITALIAN WAVE PATTERN.

POMEGRANATE AND
ENGLISH ROSE

CATHERINE OF ARAGON
MARRIED HENRY VIII
IN 1509

FLINT AND STEEL

TWO BRANCHES
IN SALTIRE, ADOPTED
FROM THE FORMER
DUKEDOM OF BURGUNDY

PILLARS OF HERCULES
OF CHARLES I OF SPAIN
(EMPEROR CHARLES V)

The Italians produced the most obscure *imprese.* They treated everyday objects in the most esoteric way, while Spanish badges were based on armorial charges or other easily understood elements. In the union of Ferdinand I and Isabella (Ysabel), the allusion to the yoke of marriage, and to its strength in the bundle of arrows bound with a ribbon, was linked with the initials of the partners. This particular marriage had far-reaching historical consequences.

Left:
The first splendor-loving king in a series to last over 200 years, Frederick I raised his armorial eagle to the level of animal myth by attributing to it the motto "To each his own" – be it the praise symbolized by the laurel wreath or the blame symbolized by the thunderbolt. His son, the later soldier king, had found another property for the eagle while still a prince. For him, it would not yield before the sun (i.e., France). His own son, Frederick II, would not hear of such resentment against a nation of culture. Henceforth the motto was to be "Fame and fatherland" until the bitter end in 1918.

In 1395 the most powerful and most important of all the dukes of Milan, John Galeazzo of the house of Visconti, had received the title of duke from the German emperor Wenceslas, together with the right to bear the German imperial eagle on his coat of arms. He surrounded his arms with his favorite *impresa,* consisting of two fire buckets attached to a burning gnarled branch. These branches normally appear alone or in groups of three but always with two fire buckets hanging from the end of a rope, which are never found in the act of putting out the fire. The *biscia* (serpent) swallowing the child is the armorial charge of the ancestral arms of the Visconti; it also forms the normal crest and is not customarily used as an *impresa.* However, another Visconti crest, the tree (see page 156) often occurs as the major motif in *imprese.*

The arms granted to Australia in 1912 are formed not from the arms but from the badges of the six component states. After South Australia had been granted a coat of arms with a rising sun in 1935, the latter was erroneously inserted in the fourth quartering on newly minted florin coins, replacing the attractive Australian piping shrike. However this only happened on the florins (1936).

England and Italy are the countries in which the custom of using emblems other than the coat of arms itself has flourished most vigorously. Indeed it is still alive in England and its sphere of cultural influence. Above all in humanist circles during the Renaissance, people vied with one another in the invention of impressive puzzle pictures which can seldom be solved at the first attempt. An example is the two pillars of Hercules of the emperor Charles V, which bear the motto *Plus ultra* (see page 211). It was evident that this was a reference to the expansion of Spanish power beyond the Strait of Gibraltar. However, the fact that one pillar is topped with a higher ranking crown than the other is often overlooked. And until the twentieth century no one took exception to the grammatical error of interpreting the French *Plus outre* simply as *Plus ultra.*

Italian badges or *imprese* are of two kinds. In the first the picture is accompanied as above by a not always very informative motto on a fluttering band. In the second, the picture remains unexplained, and must have caused almost as much head-scratching among contemporary observers as among those of the present day, who seldom find an explanation. The scientific approach to *imprese* and other badges is still in its infancy, but at least there are some historically arranged collections now in existence. In order to interpret the images, one requires an intimate knowledge of the world of fables and fairy tales and the proverbs of many ages. In the

first of the Milanese *imprese* reproduced on the right, an arm holding a bag obviously crammed with money emerges from clouds and rays of light indicating the "weather." The message is that the right time for giving money is *Qu(a)ndo sarà tempo* – when the time is right, or when the weather is right. The dove also is

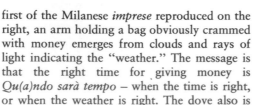

shown the right time to settle on the edge of the plate by the presence of the sun and the words *Ades(s)o el tempo* ("now is the time").

In the illustration upper right, raindrops are not enough to wash in – *Tu lavi indarno* ("you wash in vain").

Many pictures will appear quite obvious to a modern observer. A few examples will make this clear.

A mountain torrent is walled in at the sides. Motto: *Per più sigurez(z)a* ("for greater safety").

A man sits wailing on a small hill; a snake crawls out of his clothing and bites him on the right cheek. Motto: *Io levato la bis(ci)a in sene* ("I nourished the viper in my bosom").

A beehive aswarm with bees. Motto: *Per mel merito* ("for well-deserved honey").

A lamb lying on its back is bitten in the neck by a wolf standing over it. Motto: *Che per gra se fa* ("what happens through mercy").

A bush with knotted branches. Motto: *Per non fallire* ("so as not to grow awry").

A fruit tree with grafting places. Motto: *Seg(v)ndo el tempo* ("at the appropriate time").

A horse lashing out backwards. Motto: *Ven-det(t)a de tre(n)ta an(n)i* ("vengeance for thirty years").

A jousting shield leans against a boulder, with several smashed lances tipped with coronels lying in front of it. Motto: *Tu perde el tempo* ("you are wasting your time").

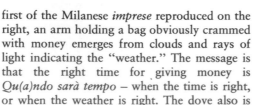

QVNDO SARA TEMPO

TV LAVI IN DARNO

ADESO EL TEMPO

in uso da Barinba Veceon

213

Wearers of the insignia of three representative orders from the three main classes of orders of chivalry *(from left to right):*

AN ORDER OF CRUSADING KNIGHTS
A member of the Order of the Knights of St. John wearing the tunic of the order.

A COURT ORDER
Duke Charles the Bold of Burgundy as grand master of his Order of the Golden Fleece, an order of knights based on feudal loyalty.

AN ORDER OF MERIT
Sir Winston Churchill with the British Order of Merit around his neck.

When the term "order" is mentioned today, people immediately think of the crosses and medallions which are pinned to the chests of the survivors of wars as a mark of public gratitude for their services. This association of ideas shows just how much the meaning of the word has become distorted from its original sense, when it was closely linked with heraldry.

Order initially meant rule, statute, regulation – a regulation to which a man freely submits and may carry some sign of on his clothing as a token of that submission. Those who "took the cross" in the wave of enthusiasm which gripped the Western world after the Council of Clermont in 1095 had to find some form of organization to make their lofty task possible. It went without saying that the Crusaders, in the hostile surroundings in which they found themselves, drew closer together and fought if possible beside those to whom they could make themselves understood. The situation was comparable to

because of the military power incorporated in them. There were three possible solutions to this problem. First, the king could make himself the head one of these orders, as happened in Spain and Portugal. Second, the king could attempt to more or less totally eliminate an order which had become too powerful, as did Philip the Fair of France in the years 1307–1314. Third, the king could himself set up an order into which he could draft reliable supporters. This was the origin of the courtly orders based on feudal loyalty, some of which have survived to this day, above all the English Order of the Garter. The number of members in this order, which is still constituted according to its original specification, is so small that admission is only open to the highest classes of society. In the Middle Ages this difficulty in winning loyal supporters was remedied by the creation of "companions," who wore badges similar in type to the insignia of the real order, and often brought them back as marks of favor and travel souvenirs from far

Communal meal of the French Order of the Star. John II of France founded this order on 6 November 1351 in answer to the founding of the English Order of the Star. The order was to consist of 500 knights, forming the backbone of the national army. Charles V let the order die out again.

that which had developed in the Iberian Peninsula, where a rugged, centuries-long struggle to drive out the Muslims had also led to the formation of groups among the Christian knights.

These groupings were oriented toward the church by reason of their motivation, and could present a threat to the struggling kingdoms

distant lands. It should not be forgotten that a journey in those days was a dangerous and exhausting undertaking.

This development was part of a progression toward a system of rewards relatively free of obligation, instead of the loyalty demanded by the original system. Under this system decora-

A carpet background *(far left)* and memorial plaque *(left)* showing Nicholas von Diesbach, lord of Signau, and his various orders, including the Order of the Sword of Cyprus, the Collar of SS of England, the Order of St. Catherine of Sinai (the toothed wheel), the Tankard Order of Aragon, the Order of the Swan of Cleves and the Order of the Holy Ghost or the Dove of Castile. His family arms appear on the shield and the horse blanket.

tions were bestowed as a reward for merit; they were also called orders and accompanied by certain requirements, but even in the beginning they established only superficial relationships between the holders, and finally none at all. These are what are generally understood by the term order today, and their number has grown steadily since the eighteenth century.

There is scarcely a country which has not taken part in this development since the French Republic abolished all royal orders and established that of the *Légion d'honneur*, thereby removing many objections to the existence of orders in a non monarchic state. Moreover, the combined action of several allied nations against Napoleon removed the incompatibility of two or more

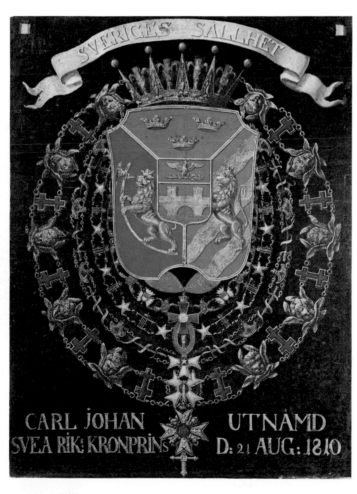

Five Soviet generals stepping up to the Soviet war memorial in Berlin-Treptow in June 1960. Their long rows of decorations are due to the fact that the most important Russian orders can be awarded more than once. In addition they are wearing medals awarded for the military successes of their divisions.

Armorial panel of Prince Henrik of Denmark as a knight and chancellor of the Danish Order of the Elephant in Frederiksborg Castle, 1967 *(below).*

Left:
Armorial panel of Carl Johan Bernadotte as crown prince of Sweden (later King Charles XIV) as a knight of the Swedish Order of Seraphim, with the chain of this order and of all the other Swedish orders (1810).

215

The archdukes of Austria from the line of Tuscany continued the traditions of the Grand Duchy of Tuscany when it was abolished in 1866, and with them the grandmastership of the Order of St. Stephen (red cross). Archduke Albrecht was decorated on a personal basis as a knight of the first class of the Military Order of Maria Theresa (white cross).

Above, far right:
A print commemorating the death in 1519 of Emperor Maximilian I, the "last knight," assembles the shields of all the religious orders of the time.

The inner sides of both doors of the church of St. Elizabeth in Marburg are painted with the arms of the grand master of the Teutonic Order of knights.

orders of different countries being worn by a single man.

A man who had taken the cross and, if his social standing permitted it, entered an order of knights, not only wore the cross on his clothing but also used it for his personal emblem, on his seal and on his shield.

The number of orders of knights which arose in the Holy Land and on the Iberian Peninsula is considerable. Three of them in particular gained outstanding significance:

1. The Order of the Knights of St. John traced its origin to a hospital for the care of pilgrims which had already existed in Jerusalem some thirty years before the first Crusade. It was here that the crusading knights founded a brotherhood after the taking of Jerusalem in 1099. The duties of the order, originally restricted to the care of sick soldiers, expanded under Muslim pressure to those of an order of knights. This first became clear long after the loss of the Holy Land in 1291. In 1530 the order was invested with the island of Malta as a base, and from there it battled against the North African pirates, becoming known as the "police of the Mediterranean." Like all the other chivalrous orders which had started in Jerusalem, the Order of Malta, as it was generally known after 1530, recognized the pope as its highest authority. One of the provinces of the order, the bailiwick of Brandenburg, removed itself from this authority during the Reformation. And the autonomous Scandinavian orders of the Knights of St. John, also of Lutheran persuasion, split away from this after the Second World War, chiefly for reasons of financial security. The original Order of Malta surrendered Malta to Napoleon in 1798

and eventually settled in Rome, where the Grand Magistry still controls the fortunes of the order, which is accepted by many nations as an international, sovereign entity devoted to charitable works.

2. The Teutonic Order only accepted "Germanic" members, though this term covered any

Left:
Heraldry of the Teutonic Order *(from left to right):* seal of the land master, 1244–1255; escutcheon of a landgrave of Hesse as a knight of the order; arms of the grand master; seal of the last grand master in Prussia, Albrecht of Brandenburg (until 1525).

Above:
On the Iberian Peninsula the religious orders of knights contributed significantly to the expulsion of the Muslims. In Portugal the king was grand master of the Avis Order, whose green cross fleuretty he incorporated in his arms in such a way that only the fleurs-de-lis at the tips appear round the edge of the shield.

The Order of the Knights Templar, destroyed between 1307 and 1314, was eventually very rich. In the

beginning, however, it was apparently so poor that there was only one horse between every two knights, as is shown on many of the order's seals.

The tasks of the orders of knights included not only military protection but also humanitarian care of the pilgrims. A pilgrim who had been to the Holy Sepulcher bore a cross on his knapsack; the shell was the sign of a pilgrimage to Santiago de Compostela *(left)*.

of the countries belonging to the German Roman empire. Its year of foundation is generally regarded as 1190, for that is when the crusading knights besieged the fortress of Akkon. The knights of different orders distinguished themselves from one another by the color of their cloaks and the crosses sewn onto them. The cloaks of the knights of St. John were

Above:
The Sovereign Order of St. John of Jerusalem at Malta, named after its patron saint, John the Baptist, is a religious order of knights generally known as the Order of Malta, after being given the island of Malta as a fief by the kingdom of Naples in 1530. Shown here are *(left to right):* seal of a commander from the year 1355; two examples of the regulations for combining family arms with the arms of the order (grand master, left, and bailiff); and seal of the English Order of St. John, established as a royal British Hospitaller Order in 1888. The actual arms were granted on 1 February 1926.

Left:
The bailiwick of Brandenburg of the Order of St. John separated from the main order on becoming Protestant. This factor, together with its close connection with the Hohenzollern dynasty, ruling at first in Brandenburg and then in Prussia, produced divergences in the design of the badge of the order and its linking with the family arms of the knights. A history of the Protestant Order of St. John brought out in 1728 gave an authoritative ruling in the matter.

1 Badge of the order
2 Scheme for commanders
3 Scheme for arms of one quarter
4 Scheme for quartered arms
5 Scheme for arms parted per fess
6 Scheme for quatered arms with inescutcheon
7 Scheme for arms parted per fess and in chief per pale with an inescutcheon

Memorial plaque of the Nuremberg patrician Ulrich Ketzel, who in 1462 made a pilgrimage to the Holy Sepulcher via the sea route and is supposed to have acquired the membership of seventeen different orders in the process. At least eight members of the Ketzel family went to the Holy Sepulcher and brought back the Cross of Jerusalem, as well as the Order of the Sword of Cyprus.
On two pilgrimages between 1389 and 1462 the dangerous detour was supposedly made to the

monastery of St. Catherine on Sinai (the corresponding order is the Catherine Wheel). This travel-loving family is also supposed to have received the Aragonese Order of the Tankard six times; that they twice received the Order of St. Anthony (represented by the small bell hanging from a tau cross) also seems probable, but the remaining orders are probably mere ostentation.

black with white crosses, those of the Teutonic knights the reverse. As a result the black cross potent which they wore has been considered the "Teutonic cross" right up to the present. From 1234 to 1525 a state created by this order existed on the Baltic; Prussia's claim to sovereignty can be traced back to this time.

3. The mainly French-oriented Order of the Knights Templar was named after the temple of Solomon near its seat in Jerusalem, a picture of which appears on several seals of the order (see page 66). The Templars were originally more intent on fighting the heathen than on the care of the sick. Their order was founded approximately twenty years after the taking of Jerusalem and was distinguished by a white cloak with a red cross. The confusion with the white cloaks of the Teutonic knights led to complaints being made to the Holy See, which was for both orders the highest authority. But the pope could not protect them against Philip the Fair of France.

The loss of the Holy Land to the Muslims did not affect the urge to ensure one's salvation by means of a pilgrimage, be it to Santiago de Compostela in Spain or to Palestine. The holy places remained accessible to pilgrims, who could be dubbed knights of the Holy Sepulcher at the tomb of Christ and then bear the cross of Jerusalem on their garments. On these pilgrimages, high-ranking lords would visit the royal courts they passed on the way, in Cyprus for example, and receive other ceremonial orders. The status attached to these orders depended on the status of the person who conferred them.

The example of the kings of Cyprus was followed by many smaller potentates whose foundations could hardly compete in status with the Order of the Garter of the kings of England

TEUTONIC ORDER OF KNIGHTS

AVIS ORDER (Portugal)

(founded around 1348), the Order of the Golden Fleece of the powerful duke of Burgundy (founded around 1430), and the Order of the Annunciata of the dukes of Savoy (founded around 1360). Thus the margrave of Brandenburg created an Order of the Swan, which he dedicated to the Virgin Mary. A duke of Bourbon, although he was not a sovereign, created the Order of the Camail, the dukes of Austria an Eagle and a Dragon order, and Emperor Sigismund the Dragon Order of Hungary, which was so popular there that its badge became transferable by inheritance. Many of these orders were destroyed by political developments or by the Reformation; also it became too difficult for the knights to make the expensive journeys to the capital seats. The statutes of a genuine order relate mainly to its internal life, and this could not be maintained without constant contact

Florian Waldauf of Waldenstein placed the chain of his most distinguished order, the Brandenburg Order of the Swan, around the shield on his bookplate. Others hung from the sides. It was unusual to combine so many orders.

The Austrian Order of the Salamander is placed beside the

helmet *(above)* in the same way as many badges of orders in the books of the Arlberg Brotherhood.

between the members. Even the highly regarded Order of the Golden Fleece held its last chapter – which means a meeting to discuss the affairs of the order – in Bruges in 1555.

With the Renaissance, the development of orders took on a new and unfamiliar direction. They became increasingly a tool for political propaganda. The number of knights of the French Order of St. Michael (founded in 1569) had so increased by the end of the sixteenth century that its status had sunk considerably. As a result, King Henry III founded in 1578 a second, higher order whose membership was to be restricted to a hundred knights; this was the Order of the Holy Ghost. It was the first politically planned order which had a cross as its badge and not just the emblematic figure chosen in previous cases.

ORDER OF THE GARTER (England) | **ORDER OF THE GOLDEN FLEECE** (Burgundy) | **ORDER OF ST. STEPHEN** (Tuscany) | **ORDER OF THE ELEPHANT** (Denmark) | **ORDER OF ST. CATHERINE** (Russia)

The number of orders grew constantly, until finally the word "order" could only be applied to the cross-shaped badge.

The possibility of a sovereign's maintaining several different orders for different purposes was thoroughly exploited in France. In 1693 Louis XIV founded a military order of merit which was named after the French king St. Louis (reigned 1221–1270). It comprised the three grades which had also been maintained by the religious orders of knights: grand cross, commander, and knight. In 1759 it was complemented by a neutral order known simply as the Military Order of Merit, since the protestant officers – including many Swiss – could not be expected to pay homage to St. Louis.

The concept of chivalrous cooperation was not

Left:
James of Savoy, Count of Romont, was lord of the Vaud from 1460 to 1486, and his arms are framed not by the Savoyard Order of the Annunciata, but by the French Order of the Camail, which had existed from 1394 to 1498 and is also called "The Porcupine" (see page 210). The letters c and e stand for *cominus* and *eminus* ("close to" and "at a distance").

Opposite:
The Soviet Marshal Zhukov is shown here wearing a maximum number of decorations, including two Soviet Victory orders and several Grand Crosses of the Allies from the Second World War.

Right:
Portrait of Heinrich Blarer from St. Gallen in 1460 wearing the sash of the Tankard Order of Aragon. The ornamental emblem with a griffin hanging on the wall also belongs to this order.

Right center:
In this portrait of the widely traveled Tirolean minnesinger Oswald von Wolkenstein (1377?–1445), he wears the chain of the Tankard Order of Aragon and also its sash, to which he has added the Hungarian Order of the Dragon.

Far right:
The portrait bust of Louis XIII of France solved the problem of how to wear the chains of two orders simultaneously. Here they are arranged concentrically. The superior order, that of the Holy Ghost, hangs deeper, while the other, that of St. Michael, has the shorter chain.

Below:
The knight Florian Waldauf of Waldenstein hangs the chain of his order on a ledge next to his armorial shield.

entirely extinguished, but it was hardly effective any longer. Plans to perpetuate the bodyguard of Emperor Constantine the Great (d. A.D. 337) in an Order of St. George under the grand mastership of a Byzantine prince in exile, and even to set up a company of soldiers to fight the Turks in

order from enemy ships hangs in the church of St. Stephen in Pisa.

The absolutist concept of the state produced some curious consequences. The foundation of new orders was painstakingly explained as a renewal of ancient communities of knights, in order to give them a higher status. This was true especially of the Danish Danebrog Order, which in 1671 shifted its year of foundation back to 1219. Similarly the English Order of the Bath in 1725 traced its origin back to a foundation of 1399, the Danish Order of the Elephant in 1693 to a predecessor of 1462, and the Swedish Order of Seraphim in 1748 at least to the sixteenth century.

To distinguish them from the military orders, whose badge was and in some cases still is a large fabric cross borne on a cloak, the insignia of the courtly orders consisted of a symbolic figure which hung on a chain composed of several symbolically significant links. These orders on chains, some of which still exist, such as the Garter and the Golden Fleece, are the prototype of the numerous "chain" orders which are customarily used for the highest ranks of orders containing several grades. The division of an order into several classes is the result of the abolition of the French military orders of merit with their maximum of three classes and their replacement by the *Légion d'honneur* in 1802. Its division into five classes became a model for most of the orders of merit awarded today.

The reaction against this, which is to divide an order into classes as little as possible or not at all, can be seen most clearly in the orders of the Soviet Union. There were no classes there until the Second World War, when exceptions arose.

Above right:
The orders of Duke Frederick William of Brunswick *(from left to right):* the Prussian Order of the Black Eagle, the Danish Union Parfaite, two capitular crosses from Magdeburg, the cross of St. Sebastian, and that of the cathedral.

Dalmatia, were never brought to fruition. Rather more successful was the founding of the Tuscan Order of St. Stephen in 1562, charged with the protection of Tuscan merchant shipping, as a result of which the battle flag of Tuscany showed a red cross on a white ground. The extensive collection of flags taken by the

the right of arms

And the Lord spake
unto Moses and unto Aaron, saying,
Every man of the children of Israel
shall pitch by his own standard
with the ensign of their father's house:
far off about the tabernacle
of the congregation
shall they pitch.

4 Moses 2: 1–2

Classical representation of the Holy Trinity as the arms of the bishop of York *(above)* and as symbolic arms of God himself *(below)*.

During the classical period of heraldry, which can be considered to last into the early sixteenth century, a coat of arms formed part of the life style of the ruling classes. This was true to such an extent that arms were even attributed to the unseen forces of the spirit. The pictorial language of heraldry was ideally suited to making the abstract powers manifest. The Biblical prohibition against making images of God could

arms. Different types of this representation emerged among the various Christian nations, which could be largely independent of one another even within a single country.

Just as in central Europe Christ was regarded as the ruler of the world and the supreme holder of all worldly and spiritual power, so a similar role might fall to saints, most notably in times when

Symbolic arms of Death *(above center)*, an etching by Albrecht Dürer.

Implements of the passion of Christ as a papal sign of favor in a quarter of the banner of Schwyz, Switzerland, 1512 *(above right)*, and in the arms of Christ, the feudal lord of all other powers *(opposite)*.

easily be circumvented by representing the elusive concept of the Holy Trinity symbolically.

More frequently the instruments of the passion of Christ are represented either individually on several memorial shields, together as a single escutcheon, or even distributed between the shield and crest in the form of an achievement of

a throne had become vacant. The saints were then treated as the actual lords of the land, from whom the human sovereign had to hold his estates as it were in feudal tenure. This is demonstrated by a whole series of state seals from Scotland, from Sweden, and from Hungary, to name only the most notable among the old monarchies.

222

The arms of exotic kingdoms as represented by central European compilers of arms collections in the fifteenth century.

Left to right:
The arms attributed to the sultan of the sect of the Essenes (the S's are canting on the German form of *Essen*), to the king of Armenia (two variants which come close to reality), the kingdom of Saba (also Sava, the place of pilgrimage in Bosnia), and Ruthenia (using the charges from the real arms of Chernigov).

If saints could have arms attributed to them, then so even more could people who were real or considered to be so. Learned arms collectors of the seventeenth century tended to be restrained in their acceptance of this attitude. In the fourteenth and fifteenth centuries, however, people ascribed arms to every ancient prince or exotic

Konrad Grünenberg, who had himself been to the Holy Land. From there he brought all kinds of fairy tales, including the belief that the great khan of the Tatars had a dog's head, since the name for dog is *canis* – unfortunately a Latin and not a Tatar word.

Many of the imaginary arms in Grünenberg's work are in fact partially explained by modern oriental research. Thus the typical stonework pattern in the arms of the king of Java can be traced back to Javanese coin symbols of the fifteenth century.

Discoveries related to whole kingdoms can of course be matched by discoveries relating to single prominent historical figures. This applies not only to such venerated figures as Charlemagne (see page 30) and others of the Nine Worthies (see pages 172–173), but also as far back as the founding of Rome. The Capitoline she-wolf (see page 118) is easily explained as the alleged arms of the twins Romulus and Remus,

Juda Isaschar Sebulon Ruben Simeon Gad

Ephraim Manasse Benjamin Dan Asser Naphthali

Above:
The badges of the twelve tribes of Israel mentioned in the Bible were looked upon by the seventeenth-century heraldic experts as the forerunners of the coat of arms and depicted by them not on shields but on curtains. At present these badges are once again playing a role in the public heraldry of the State of Israel.

kingdom which had been heard of. This was often done on the basis of a report by a world traveler such as Marco Polo, though often through a misinterpretation of such reports, and in most cases, unfortunately, we are now unable to discover the intention which lay behind the choice of these imaginary arms.

In some cases a meaning is nevertheless clear. The arms of the king of Morocco consist of three chess pieces – they are rooks, which makes them canting in German (Morocco – *Maroch*; rook – *Roche*) – though Spanish sources show the whole chessboard instead of the single figures. The lions of Armenia with their small cross are based on genuine images on coins, and may have become the arms of the Ethiopian empire as the symbol of the legendary Prester John.

Philological interpretations of the constructions given by amateur blazons can often provide the solution for particular arms. This is true not only for armorials but also for ancestral arms on tombs which refer to generations far in the past. A lot of material on this subject is provided by

appadoces Chaldæi Corinthus Græci

Sicyonii Syri Juda Ruben

Vexilla Equestria Rom. Adrastus Agememnon Antiochus

Right:
The heraldic textbooks of the seventeenth century contain whole pages of coats of arms illustrating the prehistory of heraldry. These give the supposed emblems of ancient races, families, towns, and people, though their origin is often unclear.

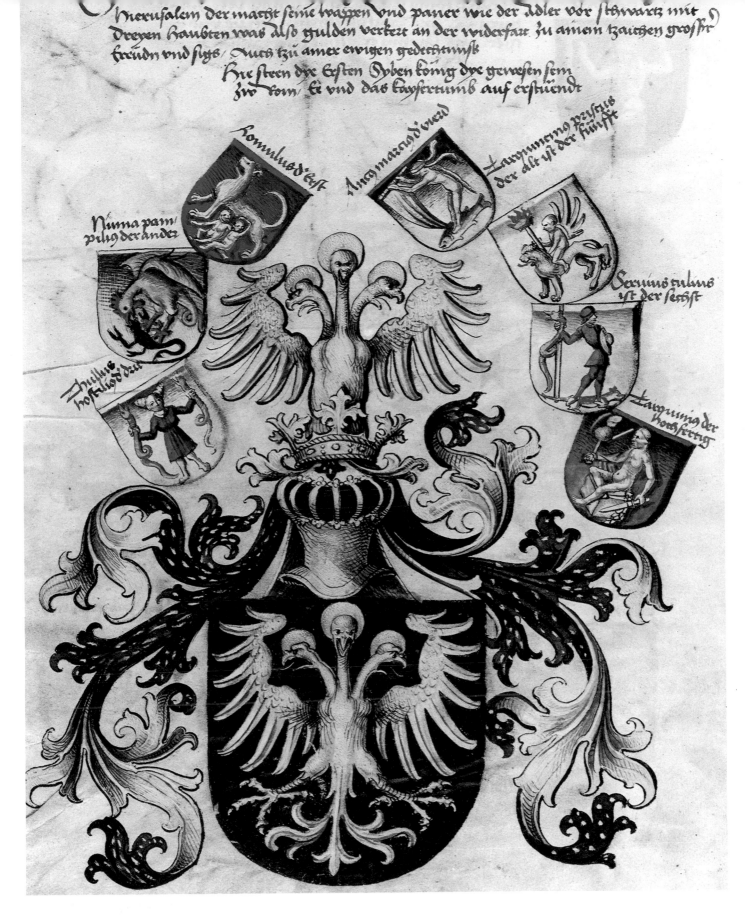

Jerusalem der macht seine wappen und paner wie der Adler vor schwartz mit dreyen haubten was als gulden verkert an der widerfar zu ainem zaichen grosser freudn und syg / Auch zu ainer ewigen gedechtnuss

Hie steen die Ersten Syben könig die gewesen sein zu rom / und das kaysertumb auf erstuendt

Romulus d' erst

Ancy marcy d' vierd

Tarqumus pryscus der alt ist der fünft

Numa pam pilg der ander

Seruius tulius ist der sechst

Thullus hostilius d' drit

Tarquinus der hochfertig

although the shields of the remaining six kings are more enigmatic.

In the same way as arms were ascribed to the Nine Worthies, they were also given to pre-heraldic and pre-Christian kings. The best known are the three toads attributed to the Frankish king Chlodwig, from which the three fleurs-de-lis of France are supposed to have developed. Napoleon looked upon the small figures found in Chlodwig's grave as bees (see page 130) rather than toads.

Imaginary arms of the seven kings of Rome from the years 753 to 510 B.C., invented in the fifteenth century, with the three-headed eagle of the German Roman empire introduced after the reconquest of the Holy Land.

People in the Middle Ages required visible proof of legal realities. The hierarchy of ruler and ruled, essential for building up an ordered system of government, had been developed out of the feudal system from Carolingian times and lasted into the sixteenth century. It was an arrangement whereby the king was lord of all the land and leased parts of it to individuals bound to him by duty.

The Latin word for feudal tenure is *feudum,* a Germanic word with a Latin ending. It is probably formed from a Frankish word combination, *fehu-* and *od,* derived in turn from the root word *faihu* (in modern German *Vieh,* which means livestock) and the word *Ôd* meaning movable possessions, property (still found in the German word *Kleinod*). This expresses the basic concept of feudal life, that the fief holder serves his feudal lord by means of his husbandry.

idea of the inheritability of arms was only practicable after the feudal tenant had succeeded by constant effort in making the possessions entrusted to him during his lifetime transferable to his descendants. In this way a permanency could be developed which extended both to directly related heirs and to other successive proprietors. In this way we can understand how, even in very early times, arms could come into being for official positions such as that of count palatine, whose possession could not be regarded inevitably as a matter of inheritance.

Feudalism provided the basis of political development in the succession states of the Carolingian empire, and was the source of the feudal arguments with which the kings of France gradually gained the upper hand over their vassals. But in Germany this development took place in exactly the opposite manner. In 1180 the arrogant duke of Bavaria and Saxony, Henry the Lion, was dispossessed of his imperial fief because of an offense against the duties of a vassal, although he retained the Guelphic family estates. The emperor Frederick II made efforts to reorganize the German state on a feudal basis, in which a hierarchy of loyalties, known as *Heer-*

The historically important collection of medieval German legal principles known as the *Sachsenspiegel* (Saxon mirror) was written down around 1240. Some copies are enriched with vigorous illustrations. The basis of feudal law is elucidated by the illustration above with its seven *Heerschilde* (army shields). These are the king (eagle), princes of the church (bishop with miter, Bible, and crozier), temporal princes (lion), free lords (two fishes), free vassals (two bars), and feudatory knights (barry of four). The seventh shield is empty and has no foot, signifying incapacity for feudal service. In our illustration the bearded teacher is with unmistakable gestures drawing the crosslegged pupil's attention to the text which reads, in present-day language: "Whoever would learn feudal law, should follow the teaching of this book. First of all we should note that the *Heerschild* begins with the king and ends with the seventh." Beneath this we see the recipient of a fief standing before the crowned king and paying homage; i.e., he lays his hands together, as in prayer, and between the hands of his feudal lord.

The seals of the landgrave Conrad II of Thuringia around 1234; on the left-hand seal enthroned as ruler of his lands, on the other on horseback as leader of his army, in both cases bearing his armorial shield. As ruler, he shows the banner bestowed on him by his feudal lord; as leader of his troops he only required at the time a flag without an image on it – a gonfanon.

The fact that the fief holder is bound to the land by his duty to serve the feudal lord does not exhaust the character of feudal life, which from an economic point of view was both primitive and exclusive in nature. Because of the importance of feudal life the hierarchy of social relationships in the Middle Ages is often classified as "feudalism," and even dismissed as such by an economically determined view of history. The economic aspect emerges clearly in another Latin word for feudal tenure, namely *beneficium.* The loyalty inherent in feudal life was thus based on two elements, one personal and one derived from necessity.

In the light of these two components, the early forms of heraldry become understandable. The

schilde ("army shields") reached from the king through the princes to the knights and even those in bondage. These efforts culminated in 1231 in the Statute in Favor of the Princes (*statutum in favorem principum*). Its result was the division of Germany into innumerable territories, and eventually the federal composition of the republics of Germany and Austria.

The unification of Italy was also long delayed by the consequences of a hierarchical policy based on feudalism. A comparison can be made with the acquisition of lands by the conquering Normans in England in 1066. This was characterized by a total dispossession of the subjects and the transference of all land to the ownership of the new king, which with the help of feudal-

Two pages from the armorial of Jörg Rugenn (1495). In the middle of each is the achievement of arms of a sovereign (above, the elector of Saxony; below, the king of Sicily and duke of Lorraine). The subject lands and titles possessed by these rulers are represented by the shields surrounding the central coat of arms. As yet there was some hesitation at dividing up the shield into a large number of quarters.

ism led to the formation of a complete new upper stratum of society. It was a rehearsal, all but an unconscious one, of a similar process in Palestine after the victory over the Saracens, although this was not so long lasting.

Arms were already customary in the time between the first and the second Crusades, and as the strict feudal conditions in the Crusader states demonstrate, as far as arms were concerned

Below:
Charlemagne installs Roland as his representative in Spain and presents him with a gonfanon as a sign of sovereignty. He then takes his leave with a wave of the hand while Roland vainly tries to ram the staff of the banner into the rocky ground.

personal ties were decisive, and territorial ones only so when they were based on feudal law. As shown by the first bestowal of arms in England (see page 54), a knight's ties with his sponsor were closer than those with his own father.

With the strengthening of sovereign power in the German empire, which was expressed in the collection of several territories in one man's hands, the number of arms a single person was entitled to bear also increased. This was the origin of the German princely arms with many quarterings (see pages 90–91). In England, on the other hand, and in France, genealogical motives were the prime factor behind the amalgamation of different arms (see pages 64, 95, and 235).

Overleaf:

Eighteen pages from the *Armorial equestre* of the Bibliothèque de l'Arsenal, Paris. The knights are *(from left to right):*

1st row: the dukes of Normandy, Brittany, and Luxembourg, the king of France, bishop of Langres, king of England.

2nd row: the dukes of Geldern and of Brieg (in Silesia), kings of Sicily, Castile, and Aragon, count of Toulouse.

3rd row: kings of Portugal, Sweden and Norway, count of Champagne, kings of Scotland and Navarra.

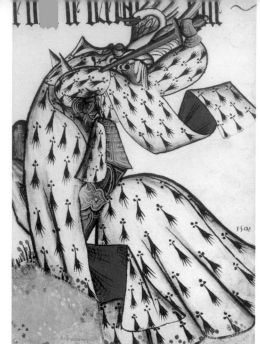

le conte de toulouse

conte de champaigne

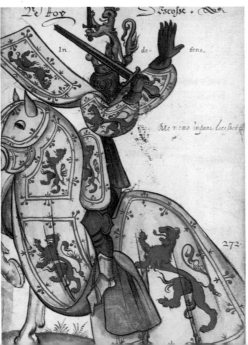

ROV LE NAUANE

Below and far right:
The present-day arms of the cathedral city of Aix-la-Chapelle were thought to be those of Charlemagne throughout the Middle Ages. They consist of the arms of the Holy Roman Empire impaled with those of France.

Left:
Women took part in the knightly lifestyle of their husbands. They approved their military service and would even make them gifts of costly pieces of armament such as a richly decorated scabbard.

The four coats of arms *(below)* represent two married couples. A bearer of the arms with the cross and scallop shells, Guy de Montmorency, lord of Laval, had married Philippe, the mistress of Vitré (with the lion arms) in 1239. Jeanne, a daughter of King Charles VI of France, had married Duke John VI of Brittany in 1386. The latter's mother was a French princess from the line of Evreux (Navarra).

Among the most interesting forms of heraldic research is that into the relationships which have produced an escutcheon of several different fields. In the beginning, that is to say from the first third of the twelfth century and for about a century afterward, the aim was to be as unequivocal as possible, so that there was no combining of several quarterings on one escutcheon. At the most, shields were halved or "impaled," giving rise to such curious figures as half eagles with lions butting onto them or bears with lions, back to back. Many examples of this

are to be found in western Poland and also in Switzerland (for example the red lion with the blue eagle which the counts of Toggenburg bore until about 1250). The arms ascribed to Charlemagne are also formed in this way, though occasionally they show a whole or a double-headed eagle in the first quartering instead of a half eagle. Whole quarterings could be superimposed on one another; thus the arms of Brittany were created out of a single quartering containing different charges.

A significant event in the development of heraldry occurred in Spain. Not only had the heartland of Castile, together with the kingdom of León to the northwest, carried the main burden of the *Reconquista* but its kings had repeatedly ruled one or the other land or both at the same time. Around 1230, the idea had arisen there of showing each coat of arms twice on a quartered shield. In this way the graphic presentation of the castle and the lion was hardly affected, and that only in the two lower quarterings. The example set a precedent and was probably taken up for the first time a century later in England. In 1337 King Edward III unleashed the so-called Hundred Years' War and adopted the title of "king of France," giving it precedence over his own title as the king of England. On his arms he imitated the Spanish method of combining the arms of two states on a quartered shield, with France taking precedence over England. It seems probable that in so doing he was following the example of the arms of his grandmother Eleanor of Castile (d. 1290), the first wife of Edward I.

Edward III's mother, Elizabeth (Isabelle) of France (d. 1357), after she had had her husband murdered in 1327, even bore a shield with quarterings of England and France in the upper half and Navarra and Champagne in the lower half. On one of her seals, the royal widow also bore two impaled shields, the one English and the other divided between France and Navarra in the manner customary at the time. From then on quartered arms grew increasingly in popular-

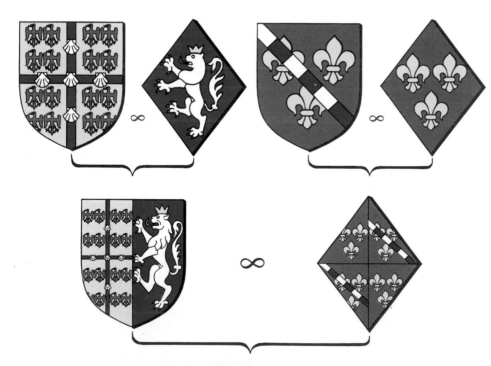

When the patron of the arts Jean de Malestroit, lord of Derval, married Helène de Laval, the latter would have been able to bring with her the ermine field of Brittany from the side of her mother Isabelle, as well as the Montmorency arms with the five scallop shells of the line of Laval. How-

ever, this was not done. Reference was instead made to the ancestral arms of previous generations, which included the French fleur-de-lis, and as the royal arms always take pride of place, the impression is given that a king of France had married a princess of Evreux (France differenced).

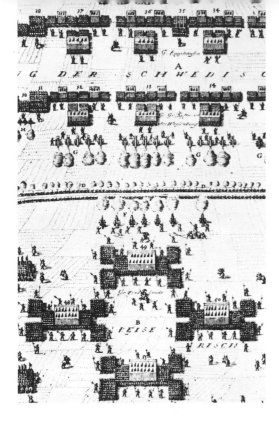

The death of the "Lion from the North" (King Gustavus Adolphus) in the Battle of Lützen in 1632 (depicted *left*) decisively influenced the course of world history but had no heraldic consequences. Instead it was internal political events which found expression in the arms of the kingdom of Sweden.

COMMAND FLAG OF THE KING OF SWEDEN

1523

1654–1720   1720–1751   1751–1818

After the abdication of Queen Christine, the royal dynasty changed several times. The Palatine dynasty was followed in 1720 by that of Hessen. In 1751 the different territories again elected a German prince, from the house of Gottorp, whose successor adopted Marshal Bernadotte (King Charles XIV) in 1818. Since then the arms of Wasa have once again risen to a position of honor.

 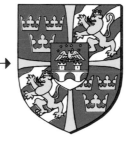

Since 1818

ity. In the *Armorial de Gelre* there are almost exactly a hundred, among 1707 entries, with Spain having the most.

Up to the fifteenth century arms with more than four quarterings were avoided; people preferred to quarter one of the fields again. In 1430 the powerful duke of Burgundy could incorporate only two of his numerous territories in his armorial shield without disturbing the quartering.

The decisive steps away from quartering in the arrangement of fields seems to have been taken in the fifteenth century by King René le Bon, who made a study of court ceremonial (see the illustrations from his tournament book on pages 13 ff., and the Capetian family pedigree, page 101), and by the archduke of Austria. The arms of both contain more than four quarters, and instead of the conventional repetition the single arms of their territories or titles appear next to one another on a large shield.

The technically possible combinations of arms are, then, as follows:

1. The two shields of a married couple, on which an inheritance is based, are placed side by side, particularly during their lifetime.
2. The two armorial bearings are placed side by side on a divided shield without alteration of their contents, but in such a way as to fit the altered shape of the background.
3. Half of each of the two armorial bearings is combined on a divided shield (impalement).
4. One of the two armorial bearings suited to it is halved, while the other remains unchanged.
5. The two armorial bearings are combined on a quartered shield so that the senior coat appears

in the first and fourth quarters, and the less important in the second and third quarters. Thus in the arms of Spain, the arms of Castile-León appear before those of Aragon-Sicily, although they were introduced by a woman, Queen Isabella of Castile. This precedence was established in the marriage contract in 1469. In the Spanish sphere of cultural influence, diagonal quartering instead of the normal type is not unusual (see page 233, number 4).

6. If further armorial bearings are to be introduced, they can be given a place in an inescutcheon shield which may be regarded as the best or the least significant position according to circumstances.

The oldest arms of the Swedish state are simultaneously those of the Folkunger dynasty (the lion on a wavy field). The three crowns have been accepted as the actual arms of the country since the fourteenth century. From the fifteenth century it was the custom to bear the arms of the ruling dynasty inescutcheon. After Gustavus Wasa, the leader of a national uprising, was chosen as Gustavus I, King of Sweden, in 1523, this system was continued. The arms of his family, a sheaf (Swedish: *Vase*), remained in use until Queen Christine became Catholic and abdicated in 1654.

Shown on the left are the arms of the kingdom of the Two Sicilies, the most complicated of the Capetian arms ever devised. The basis is provided by the combination of the arms of Spain (quarters 1–5 in the diagram below) and Austria-Burgundy (6–11), to which the arms of the house of Bourbon-Anjou (14) were added in 1701.

After the Spanish *infante* Charles (b. 1716) had succeeded his great-uncle Anthony as duke of Parma and Piacenza in 1731, he conquered Naples in 1734 and was recognized there as King Charles VII. Having renounced the dukedom of Parma, he was then invested by the pope with Sicily and the kingdom of Jerusalem in 1738.

He retained all the quarters inherited from his father (1–11 and 14) and added beneath them quarters 12 and 13 for the kingdom won in

In the diagram shown on the left, the different quarters are numbered in accordance with the nineteen shields on page 233, to facilitate reference. Quarters 1 to 11 had already been borne by the emperor Charles V (King Charles I of Spain). The inescutcheon was added when a grandson of the French king Louis XIV (see the Capetian family tree on page 98) became king of Spain. The addition of all the remaining quarters created the arms of a kingdom which existed until 1867. Quarters 15 to 19 persisted until 1931 in the arms of the Spanish state.

The map below indicates the areas whose arms were incorporated in the arms of the kingdom of the Two Sicilies. The numbers relate to the diagram on the right.

1735. At the sides were added the arms of Parma (15–18) and Medici (19) derived from his mother Elizabeth (Isabel Farnese, see page 233).

When he unexpectedly inherited the throne of Spain from his half-brother Ferdinand VI in 1759, quarters 12 and 13 were removed, but 15 and 19 were included in the arms of succession (see the illustration on page 232).

As second wife of Philip V, the first Bourbon king of Spain, Queen Elizabeth (Isabel) had no hope of her children succeeding to the throne of Spain, but had successfully managed to provide them with other states. She brought with her the claim not only to Parma but also to Tuscany.

As a result of the marriage of Duke Octavio with a daughter of the emperor Charles V, the arms of the dukedom of Parma had consisted since 1556 of a combination of the arms of the house of

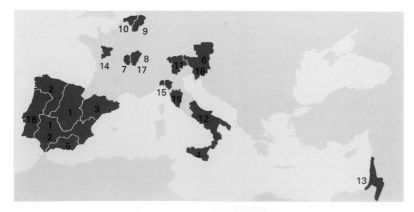

Right:
The coins of the kingdom of Naples in the fourteenth and fifteenth centuries emphasized its claim to the kingdom of Jerusalem. Thus the cross of Jerusalem takes precedence over "Old Anjou."

1 CASTILE

Gules, a castle or with gate and windows azure (canting arms).

2 LEÓN

Argent, a lion gules (originally purpure) crowned or (also canting arms).

3 ARAGON

Paly of nine or and gules, really the arms of the county of Barcelona (= Catalonia).

4 SICILY

Quartered per saltire of Aragon and Hohenstaufen (argent, an eagle sable).

5 GRANDA

Argentz, a pomegranate with leaves, proper (canting arms).

6 AUSTRIA

Gules, a fess argent (see number 16).

7 NEW BURGUNDY

Azure, semy-de-lis or, within a bordure compony gules and argent (see pages 50–51).

8 OLD BURGUNDY

Bendy of six or and azure within a bordure gules (see pages 50–51).

9 BRABANT

Sable, a lion or; the present-day arms of Belgium.

10 FLANDERS

Or, a lion sable; today the arms of the Belgian province of Eastern Flanders.

11 TYROL

Argent, eagle gules crowned or, wings surmounted with trefoils on stems or.

12 OLD ANJOU (the kingdom of Naples)

Azure, semy-de-lis or, with a label of five points gules.

13 KINGDOM OF JERUSALEM

Argent, a cross potent or, cantoned of four crosses or.

14 NEW ANJOU

Azure, within a bordure gules, three fleurs-de-lis or.

15 PARMA (FARNESE)

Or, six fleurs-de-lis azure (3, 2, 1); really the family arms of the house of Farnese.

16 AUSTRIA

See number 6. Often the coat of arms for Hapsburg districts before 1477.

17 OLD BURGUNDY

Bendy of six or and azure (see number 8).

18 PORTUGAL

With a bordure gules surmounted by seven castles or, the so-called quinas.

19 TUSCANY (MEDICI)

Or, six balls (1, 2, 3, 1), the five lower ones gules, the uppermost azure surmounted with three fleurs-de-lis or.

Farnese with the Austrian-Burgundian arms and the attribute of the papal standard-bearer. The son of this marriage, Alexander (d. 1592) had married Maria, a daughter of the pretender to the vacant throne of Portugal, and could therefore hold out some hope of his son Ranuncio I becoming king of Portugal. For this reason the latter incorporated the Portuguese shield as inescutcheon in the arms of Parma. The office of papal standard-bearer lapsed with the excommunication of Odoardo in 1641 and the corresponding badge of office had to be removed. The quarters of Farnese and Austria-Burgundy, previously kept apart in the quartering, were now

rearranged into six quarters of the same size. The claim to Tuscany was based on an agreement made in 1731 because Duke Odoardo I, the great-grandfather of Queen Elizabeth, had married Margaret the daughter of the grand duke of Tuscany, Cosimo II (d. 1621). The succession became due in 1737, but the powers that be had decided otherwise. Tuscany went to the former duke of Lorraine, later the husband of Maria Theresa and also German emperor from 1745. Thus the princess Farnese retained only the title to pass on to her children. This title, which was only real from 1731 to 1735 or at the most to 1759, was revived at the restoration of the united kingdom of the Two Sicilies in 1816.

The armorial quarters of Farnese and Medici still remain today in the arms of the heads of the royal houses of Spain and the Two Sicilies, who are known as the count of Barcelona and the duke of Calabria, respectively.

Instead of the complicated arms of the kingdom of the Two Sicilies, a simplified version *(left)* could be used in which only the essential quarters appeared. These were Castile (1) and León (2) for Spain, with Old Anjou (12) beneath for Naples, surmounted in the middle with the family arms of the dynasty of Anjou, known in Spain as "Borbón." To dexter are the Farnese arms (15) for Parma, and those of Portugal (18); to sinister are the Medici arms (19) for Tuscany.

Left, below:
Prince Charles of Spain, who had inherited the dukedoms of Parma and Piacenza in 1731, provisionally placed next to his ancestral arms as infante of Spain the two coats of arms which he laid claim to as his mother's son. These were the shield of the grand dukes of Tuscany with the six balls of the house of Medici, and the multiple quarters of the arms of Parma.

Below:
In 1545 Pope Paul III (d. 1549) of the house of Farnese appointed his illegitimate son Peter Louis duke of Parma and "Standard bearer of the Church" *(Gonfaloniere della Chiesa)*. In his coat of arms the badge of the Gonfaloniere, the papal umbrella (see page 238), appeared between the six fleurs-de-lis of Parma. In 1538 Peter Louis's son married an illegitimate daughter of the emperor Charles V, Margaret (1522–1586), who like the other imperial children bore a simple coat of arms consisting of the shield of Austria (16) impaled with that of Old Burgundy (17). She became known historically as the unfortunate governor general of the

Spanish Netherlands, installed in 1559.
Her husband, Duke Octavio, received the badge of the Gonfaloniere and quartered the background with the Farnese arms in quarters 1 and 4 and Margaret's contribution in quarters 2 and 3.

Opposite:
These figures are on the side panels of a triptych by Lucas van Leyden, the center of which represents *The Healing of the Blind Man.* The young woman carries the lozenge shield customary for her sex in the Netherlands.

Right:
Lozenge arms of the future English Queen Catherine of Aragon as widow of Prince Arthur of England (d. 1502), with her ancestral arms, instead of the English ones, in the third quarter.

Adopted arms of the minnesinger Heinrich Frauenlob, who not only abandoned his real name of Margrave Frederick von Meissen, but also gave up his real arms (a lion) in favor of the lady's head.

One of the most significant marriages in world history was that in 1477 between Archduke Maximilian of Austria and Marie, the heiress of the dukedom of Burgundy. In one of Maximilian's old seals *(above right)* the achievements of arms of Austria and Steiermark are accompanied by the shields of Kärnten, Tyrol, and Hapsburg. In the "counterseal" of the bride *(above, far right)* an angel holds the much quartered shield of the dukedom of Burgundy between the shields of Franche-Comté, Holland, and Artois. In the new seal of the ruling couple *(center)* most of the arms are combined in a compatible way; however, in the arms of Maximilian the central shields are brought together and their order changed, so that the Tyrol appears in the Burgundian quarter and Flanders in the Austrian quarter.

Bookplate of the abbot of St. Gallen, Ulrich VIII Rösch (1463–1491). The personal shield of the abbot, surmounted by a miter, is supported by the armorial beasts of the abbacy. The same beasts appear in heraldic colors in the inclined shields held by angels. These are the arms of the abbacy of St. Gallen (the bear) and the county of Toggenburg (the dog).

Bella gerant alii; tu, felix Austria, nube ("Others may wage war; you, fortunate Austria, marry"). Such was the surprised or envious reaction to the persistent policy of marriage which turned a minor family of Swiss counts into a major dynasty whose empire lasted for many centuries. Such a policy produced constant changes in the family's armorial bearings, owing to the custom of combining the arms of married couples. These arms were made the basis of new combinations by the couple's offspring, when the mother was the heiress to a territory or at least a title.

Women were only reluctantly regarded as fit to bear arms, for under feudalism a woman was freed from the duties of a vassal because of the weakness of her sex *(ob imbecillitatem sexus).*

However this situation became untenable because the high mortality rate among the feuding nobility, especially in the thirteenth century, led to an increasing number of inheritances falling to women. In countries where the French Salic law restricting the succession to the male line did not apply and women were allowed to succeed to the throne, as in England and Castile, the bearing of arms by women was naturally more frequent than elsewhere. Thus in England complicated rules were developed for the combination of marriage arms and arms of widowhood, from which the status of widowers also can be established. According to these rules, a woman's arms are borne not on a shield but on a lozenge, a convention which did not establish itself in central Europe and which makes the rendering of somewhat complicated armorial bearings very difficult.

The heraldically expressed alliance need not necessarily be a marriage. A business partnership, such as that of the printers of incunabula Fust and Schöffer, can equally well be expressed by shields turned towards one another, as can a combination of several territorial or official arms. Whether the shields are free standing and tilted towards one another or merged into a single shield often depends on how binding the combination is to be considered.

Basically, the arms to dexter, which are normally those of the higher ranking partner – in marriages, therefore, those of the man – should be inclined towards the arms of the other partner out of courtesy, though this is often not the case for a variety of reasons.

Two armorial shields may also be placed side by side in the case of city-states, especially those which for some reason have two different sets of arms. Such was the popularity of this type of arrangement in Switzerland that we even find two similar escutcheons being grouped together like arms of alliance (see page 129).

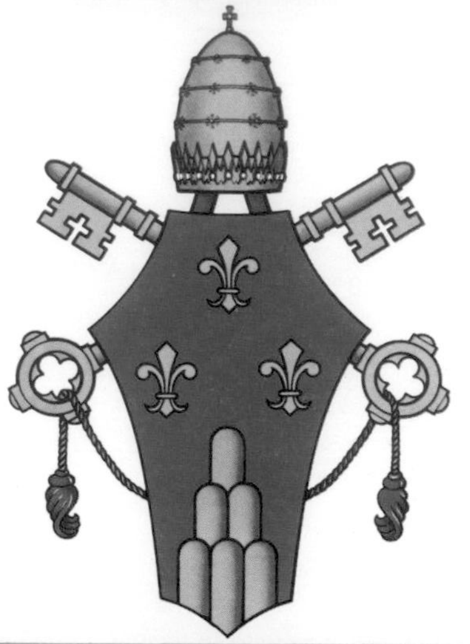

The arms borne by the popes are either their real or probable family arms or, particularly in recent decades, they consist of symbols chosen at the latest on the occasion of their installation as archbishop. This applies in particular to Pius X, Pius XII, and Paul VI. The only recent pope to use an old and unadulterated coat of arms, which is also canting, is Benedict XV of the della Chiesa family. Pius X and John XXIII made reference in their arms to offices they held in Venice.

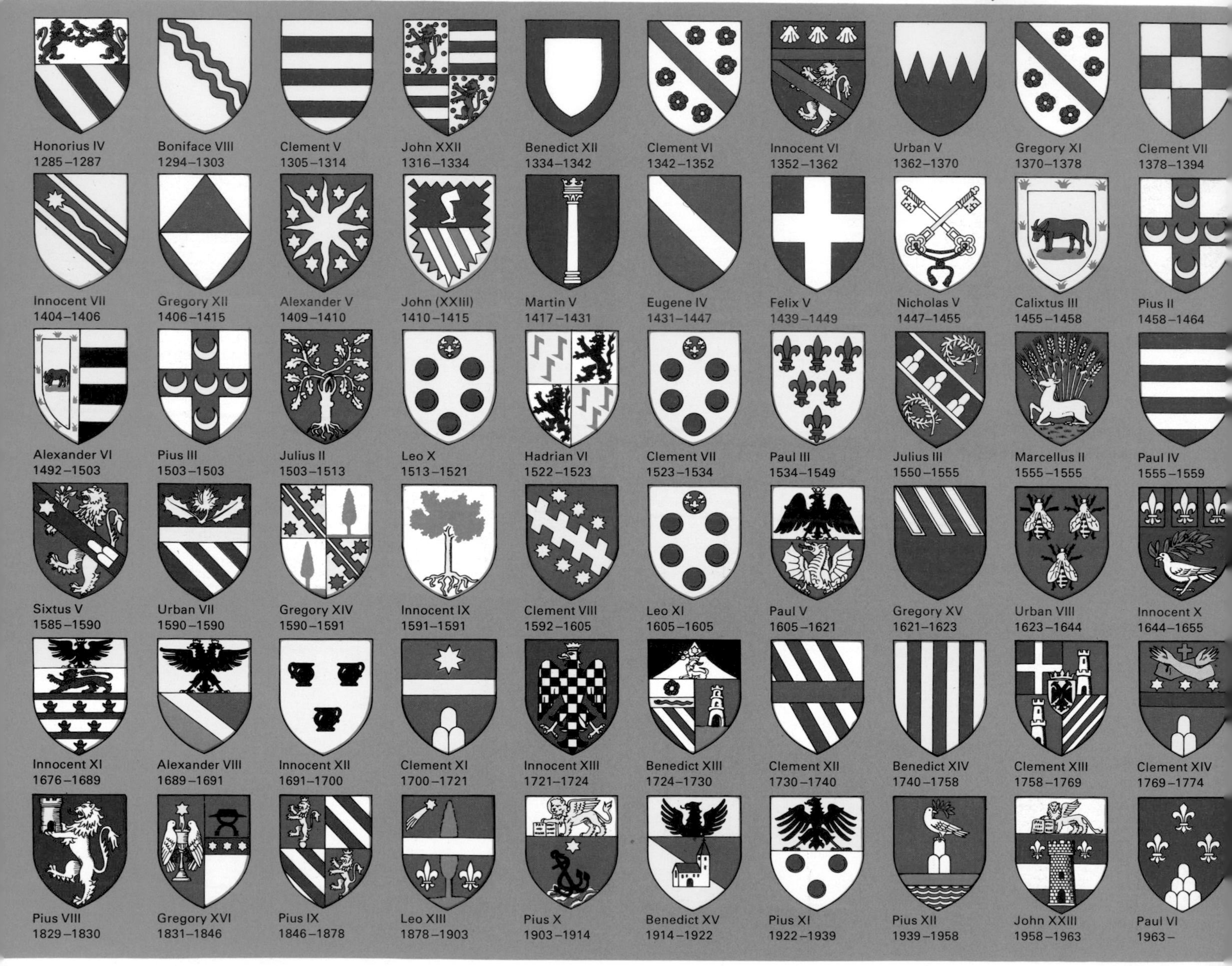
Honorius IV 1285–1287
Boniface VIII 1294–1303
Clement V 1305–1314
John XXII 1316–1334
Benedict XII 1334–1342
Clement VI 1342–1352
Innocent VI 1352–1362
Urban V 1362–1370
Gregory XI 1370–1378
Clement VII 1378–1394
Innocent VII 1404–1406
Gregory XII 1406–1415
Alexander V 1409–1410
John (XXIII) 1410–1415
Martin V 1417–1431
Eugene IV 1431–1447
Felix V 1439–1449
Nicholas V 1447–1455
Calixtus III 1455–1458
Pius II 1458–1464
Alexander VI 1492–1503
Pius III 1503–1503
Julius II 1503–1513
Leo X 1513–1521
Hadrian VI 1522–1523
Clement VII 1523–1534
Paul III 1534–1549
Julius III 1550–1555
Marcellus II 1555–1555
Paul IV 1555–1559
Sixtus V 1585–1590
Urban VII 1590–1590
Gregory XIV 1590–1591
Innocent IX 1591–1591
Clement VIII 1592–1605
Leo XI 1605–1605
Paul V 1605–1621
Gregory XV 1621–1623
Urban VIII 1623–1644
Innocent X 1644–1655
Innocent XI 1676–1689
Alexander VIII 1689–1691
Innocent XII 1691–1700
Clement XI 1700–1721
Innocent XIII 1721–1724
Benedict XIII 1724–1730
Clement XII 1730–1740
Benedict XIV 1740–1758
Clement XIII 1758–1769
Clement XIV 1769–1774
Pius VIII 1829–1830
Gregory XVI 1831–1846
Pius IX 1846–1878
Leo XIII 1878–1903
Pius X 1903–1914
Benedict XV 1914–1922
Pius XI 1922–1939
Pius XII 1939–1958
John XXIII 1958–1963
Paul VI 1963–

Church heraldry has two individual characteristics. Most notable is the omission of the helmet, with its military associations. On the other hand, the shield, also derived from military equipment, remains uncontested as the basis of the arms of ecclesiastical dignitaries. Instead of the helmet and crest, ecclesiastical insignia are used. These include the broadbrimmed pilgrim's hat, with different colors and arrangements of tasseled cords to denote rank, also the shepherd's crook, with or without a sudarium, and the processional cross, sometimes with two or even three crosspieces. A striving for greater simplicity in the last few decades has led to the less frequent use of insignia, especially the miter, by some prelates of the Roman Catholic faith. The miter (see page 239) was once much used by archbishops, bishops, and abbots to ensign their arms.

The pope is the only church dignitary who bears

In 1954, Pope Paul chose canting arms *(left);* the sextuple mount is a play on his family name of Montini. Above the escutcheon is the tiara which was presented to him at his coronation, and which he then sold for the benefit of the poor.

The hierarchy of the Church is expressed heraldically in the gradations of head coverings in ecclesiatical arms. Recently an effort has been made to show only one type of headgear, preferably the broadbrimmed hat with tassels *(fiocchi)* denoting rank by their number and color.

Left, top to bottom:

CARDINAL (30 red tassels).

PATRIARCH (30 green tassels), also bailiff of the Maltese Order of the Knights of St. John.

ARCHBISHOP (20 green tassels), also knight grand cross of the Order of the Holy Sepulcher.

BISHOP (12 green tassels).

ABBESS. Family arms in the German style surmounting the arms of the convent (a Cistercian one), with a crozier behind the shield.

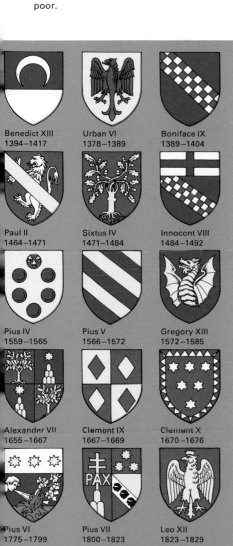

Benedict XIII 1394–1417	Urban VI 1378–1389	Boniface IX 1389–1404
Paul II 1464–1471	Sixtus IV 1471–1484	Innocent VIII 1484–1492
Pius IV 1559–1565	Pius V 1566–1572	Gregory XIII 1572–1585
Alexander VII 1655–1667	Clement IX 1667–1669	Clement X 1670–1676
Pius VI 1775–1799	Pius VII 1800–1823	Leo XII 1823–1829
John-Paul I 1978	John-Paul II 1978–	

EXEMPT ABBEY. The bishop's insignia are accompanied by the crozier with sudarium and the sword *(right).*

Top right:
Religious seals are generally in the form of a pointed oval.
Shown here is the papal seal of dispensation for travelers to the Holy Land around 1490.

Above:
Papal sign of favor; a corner segment of the "Julius banner" of Zurich, 1512.

237

Arms of the contemporary primate of Poland, Cardinal Wyszinski, with a representation of the black Madonna of Tschenstochau, the fleurs-de-lis of the bishopric of Gnesen, and the head of John the Baptist (for Breslau).

Opposite:
An armorial sheet of 1712 commemorating the bishop of Bristol's role as negotiator for the treaty of Utrecht. The sheet shows the arms of all the bishoprics of England (including Wales).

Cardinals entering Constance for the council of 1410, after a wood engraving of 1483. Servants carry the cardinals' hats on poles.

a crown, the so-called tiara – also known as the *triregnum;* he places it on or above his armorial shield. Behind the latter lie the two keys of the apostle Peter, one gold and one silver, with which according to tradition the apostle is authorized to bind and to set free.

The papal arms shown here illustrate the other peculiarity of church heraldry, namely that the bearing of arms depends upon the status of the dignitary. When a certain step is reached in the hierarchy, which is as soon as the dignitary is entitled to the use of a documentary seal, he must also choose a coat of arms. And as the highest offices in the church are open to the sons of poor and unknown parents as well as to the offspring of great families, it often happens that a priest achieves such a status without having a personal, traditional coat of arms. Thus the series of papal arms offers examples both of

(1513), with its six balls (or six pills of a *medicus*). Clement VII was retrospectively declared to be nobly born. Pius IV came from a Milanese family and not from the Florentine one. Only Leo XI was again a true Florentine Medici. Among the last seven popes are four with old coats of arms (Pius IX, Leo XIII, Benedict XV, and Pius XI, though it is possible that the latter's are not genuine). Pius XII modified his inherited arms. Pius X chose a new coat of arms as bishop of Mantua.

A few popes added their arms to those of the religious order to which they had originally belonged; for example, Benedict XIII (the Dominicans), Clement XIV (the Franciscans), Pius VII (the Benedictines) and Gregory XVI (the Camaldolites). This procedure has a certain similarity with the Anglican method of impaling the arms of an English bishopric with the

Above:
In the time between the death of a pope and the installation of his successor, the business of the Vatican was carried out by one of the cardinals, the so-called camarlingo. The badges of his worldly status were the *ombrellino* with the two keys of St. Peter (with which to bind and to set free) combined with the emblem of his cardinal's status.

The bishopric of Innsbruck, newly created in 1968, based its arms *(right)* partly on those of the former bishopric of Brixen. Passau *(far right)* has recently incorporated its emblems of ecclesiastical rank (the crozier and cross on a field) into its shield.

tradition and of newly chosen arms. In the Renaissance, the popes often came from well-known families, but on many occasions they also came from families which only bore a great name without being actually related to the famous house. This explains, for example, the frequency of the arms of the Medici after Leo X

personal arms of the incumbent bishop (see page 230). In central Europe, however, the quartering of the two arms is the customary combination. Examples of this arrangement can be found in the German Roman empire under Charles IV (as in the armorial hall at Lauf, ca. 1370).

Arms of Cardinal Felice di Peretto Ricci (*above center*), later Pope Sixtus V (reigned 1585–1590), with a lion holding a pear twig (*pero*). In the arms of the monastery of Seuben (*above*), in the German style, the family arms of the abbot stand next to the escutcheon of the monastery, which bears the apocryphal arms of the founder.

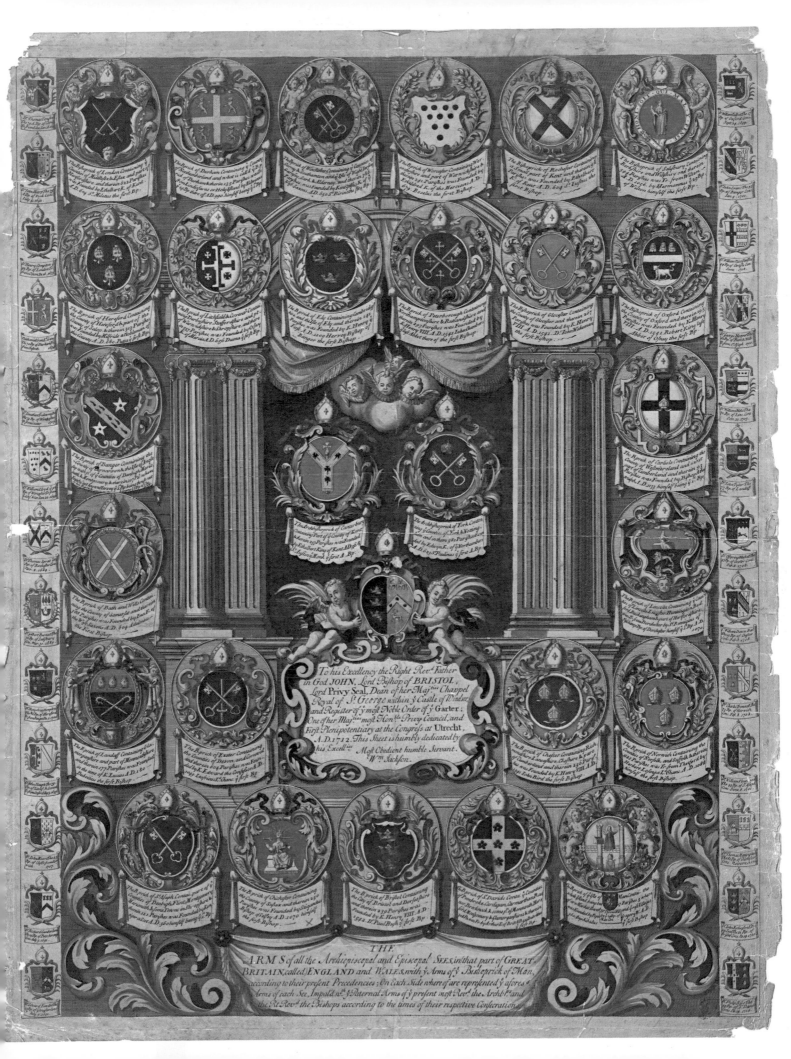

The oldest assembly of university arms is to be found in the book of the Council of Constance (*right*); many of these arms may have been invented by the collector.

UNIVERSITY
OF VIENNA

UNIVERSITY
OF HEIDELBERG

UNIVERSITY
OF LONDON

UNIVERSITY
OF BOLOGNA

UNIVERSITY
OF PARIS

UNIVERSITY
OF ALEXANDRIA
(EGYPT)

ST. ANDREW'S
UNIVERSITY
(SCOTLAND)

UNIVERSITY
OF BOLOGNA

UNIVERSITY
OF DILLINGEN

UNIVERSITY
OF FRANKFURT
AN DER ODER

UNIVERSITY
OF LEIPZIG

Martin Schrot considerably extended the range of university arms in his armorial which appeared in 1576. Combinations of the appropriate regional or municipal arms remained the customary form, but additional motifs were now included, such as the patron saint in the case of St. Andrew's, or the dove of the Holy Ghost.

The word university is a contraction of *Universitas litterarum,* which means generality of knowledge. Obviously, in order to be able to organize this generality, a univerity must be institutionalized, and as such it will need to bear a genuine seal.

Since there is nowhere in the world where universities serve directly military ends, at the most assisting them by scientific research, their relationship with heraldry depends on external, intellectual considerations. The picture on the

combination of the regional arms with the symbol of learning, a book (usually closed). The existence of such arms seems probable enough as they would have been required as badges on the placards used by academic deputations to congresses such as the Council of Constance. The extent to which these were transferred to seals depended on individual circumstances. As was the case with many towns, the seals developed independently of the arms – a late example being that of the University of Pennsylvania. Combinations such as that of Salzburg are very frequent.

Academic life in the Middle Ages: These ladies of Italian society, listening to the lecturer or taking notes, are a proof of female participation in Renaissance culture.

seal can be a heraldic or a non-heraldic motif, or both together.

The armorials of the Middle Ages, and their imitators at the beginning of modern times, contain many university arms which are based on a

DOMI MINA
NVS TIO
ILLV MEA

UNIVERSITY
OF OXFORD

UNIVERSITY
OF PENNSYLVANIA

UNIVERSITY
OF AVIGNON

UNIVERSITY
OF PRAGUE

UNIVERSITY
OF COLOGNE

HUNGARIAN
UNIVERSITY

Whereas the armorial collections of the fifteenth and sixteenth centuries contained arms for universities in numerous different countries, the picture in recent centuries has been somewhat differ-

UNIVERSITY
OF PADUA

UNIVERSITY
OF ROME

UNIVERSITY
OF SEVILLE

UNIVERSITY
OF TÜBINGEN

UNIVERSITY
OF WITTENBERG

UNIVERSITY
OF ZURICH

ent. The world of learning has tended to reject heraldry. As a result many universities have only the seal essential for the ratification of documents, usually with some kind of symbolic image. In the present day an interest in heraldry has revived in this context.

In 1932 the Philip's University of Marburg (*far left*) revived its arms according to the data given in the armorial of Martin Schrot.

On the two central seals are the arms of the prince-bishop of Salzburg, Paris Count von Lodron (reigned 1619–1653).

UNIVERSITY
OF MARBURG

UNIVERSITY
OF SALZBURG
UNTIL 1962

UNIVERSITY
OF SALZBURG
SINCE 1972

FREE UNIVERSITY
OF BERLIN

UNIVERSITY
OF CAMBRIDGE

EDINBURGH
UNIVERSITY

TRINITY
COLLEGE (IRELAND)

HARVARD
UNIVERSITY

YALE
UNIVERSITY

UNIVERSITY
OF HONG KONG

British culture created academic institutions in all areas of British influence, as for example in Grahamstown, Natal, South Africa (*far left*). The arms contain, in the chief, references to the family arms of the heirs of Cecil Rhodes; beneath are scallop shells from the arms of the town's founder, Colonel Graham.

A tendency to express modern scientific discoveries in heraldic terms can be found among the younger universities. An example is offered by the wave forms and the symbol of an atomic nucleus in the arms of the University of Warwick (*left*).

The seal of the University of Pennsylvania (*left*) shows a pile of books with the motto: "Without morals, in vain."

The ceremonial of academic appearances in public was underlined by the scepters which the beadles carried in processions in front of the professors. *Left*: the scepter of the University of Basel from the sixteenth century.

241

The magic word *Libertas* ("freedom") accompanied the Italian city-states through the centuries, and in the case of San Marino has even maintained its value to the present day. Both the arms of Ragusa (Dubrovnik) and of Bologna express the old will to independence.

The use of the distinction between a monarchy and a republic to describe the constitution of a state has largely been replaced in the present day by the distinction between democracy and dictatorship. But until the end of the eighteenth century it remained fully valid. As a result of the feudally-based policies of the Hohenstaufen emperors, the towns known as republics up to

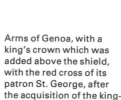

Arms of Genoa, with a king's crown which was added above the shield, with the red cross of its patron St. George, after the acquisition of the kingdom of Corsica.

Arms of the town of Lucca, 1838. The form is that in which they were borne by the town during the time of its independence, with the addition of the ducal medal of merit.

The arms of San Marino – named after its founder, the hermit Marinus – contain stylized representations of the position of the republic on Monte Titano, a massive peak in the Apennines. The three feathers (in Italian *penne*) are a play on this name. The crown expresses the sovereignty of the state.

The desire for independence from the power of the local sovereign was accompanied by the belief in the protective power of a patron saint. In Ragusa (Dubrovnik), St. Blaise was venerated for this reason. A flag bearing his image flew from a high mast in the market square. The unusually large merchant fleet of Ragusa bore his picture or initials or the word *Libertas* on their white flags.

that time had acquired an autonomy unimaginable to communities lying outside the German Roman empire. This autonomy had little to do with democracy, since it was exercised by "families capable of ruling" which in many places had to defend themselves against the up-and-coming tradesmen's guilds. The city-states in Italy, Switzerland, and to a certain extent Germany, created subject territories for themselves and justified their status by reference to feudal lords whose titles had ceased to have any significance. Their arms seldom go back to the images on seals, being more often derived from military banners. This is the case with the Swiss cantons of Zurich, Lucerne, Fribourg, and Solothurn, whose arms consist of simple ordi-

The state of Andorra in the Pyrenees has maintained its hybrid status until the present day. Its "co-princes," the bishop of Urgel and the count of Foix (the latter represented by his heir the French head of state), are both featured on the coat of arms.

The independent status of the Swiss cantons was expressed by a crown of sovereignty on their coats of arms. An example is Bern, whose state seal, engraved in 1768, is shown here; as with Lucerne and Solothurn, the use of the crown establishes a clear distinction between the state arms and those of the capital town of the same name.

naries, and Lucca and Siena in Italy. The cross of Genoa and the figure of St. Blaise of Ragusa (Dubrovnik) demonstrate the subjection of these places to a local spiritual figure.

The arms of the former sovereigns are recalled by the pales of Foix and Catalonia and the cows of Béarn, as well as the bend in the canting arms of Bern, since the founder of the latter city was an ancestor of the margraves of Baden (whose arms were: or, a bend gules).

An example of genuine arms of sovereignty is offered by those of the Republic of Venice,

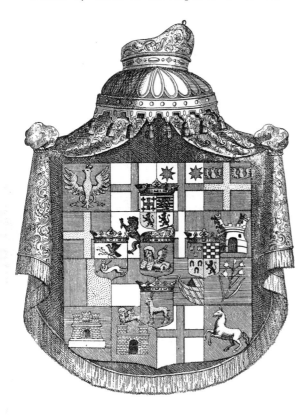

which are formed from quarters of Venetia and the Adriatic coastal territories of Istria and Croatia, with Dalmatia and Rascia and the islands of Zante and Cyprus.

How deeply rooted was their control of the Adriatic coastal district is shown by the lion of the seven Ionic islands (see page 112, number 42), the so-called heptarchy, which was still a recognized national insignia several centuries after the end of the Venetian Republic. The coat of arms of the kingdom of Cyprus with all its dynastic quarters is also found in the arms of the kingdom of Sardinia (see page 47), and the arms containing the goat of Istria were borne as well by the Austrian emperors (see page 91).

The Republic of Venice was not alone in representing her territorial sovereignty with a series of arms. The armorial stained glass roundels of the Swiss cantons are of great interest from an historical and artistic point of view, especially those of Bern, Fribourg, Zurich, and Lucerne. On these roundels the shields of the former local lords are assembled and used as the arms of the governed districts (see page 266).

St. Ambrose was venerated as the patron saint of Milan, which during a temporary period of independence received the name "Ambrosian Republic" (1407 and 1447–1450).

The banners strewn with the crowned word LIBERTAS and the Milanese arms in the form of a cross are a testament to the short life of this republic. The Swiss succeeded in capturing them in 1512 and made careful copies of them.

In the last decades of the eighteenth century the tree, a symbol of self-government, became the emblem of republican freedom in Europe and of the rejection of English tutelage in America.

As early as 1754, Benjamin Franklin used the symbol of a divided snake *(below)* in urging the so-called New England colonies to unite or face the fatal alternative.

JOIN, or DIE.

The central government (1797) in Padua (seal *below*) was in January

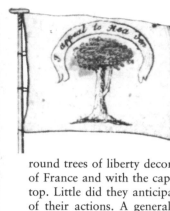

round trees of liberty decorated with the colors of France and with the cap of liberty placed on top. Little did they anticipate the consequences of their actions. A general enthusiasm for the model of the republic of ancient Rome led to the adoption of its symbolism as well – women in flowing garments with the fasces of the lictors, bound sheaves of arrows, cornucopias, and Phrygian caps. Switzerland, which was then called the Helvetian Republic following the French model, reached rather less far back into its own store of traditions. In William Tell and his successful shooting of the apple from his son's head with a crossbow, the Swiss found their own indigenous symbol of defiance.

The American and French revolutions had shown the world that whole nations could be

To the innovator the rules of heraldry are irrelevant, even if he cannot do without the symbolism which even a revolutionary needs for the articulation of his literary or verbal appeals. The separation of the American colonies from Great Britain was symbolized by the tree which free peoples used as a place of assembly and judg-

1798 united with the Cispadane Republic (banner *right*). The Swiss chose a scene from the saga of William Tell *(far right)*. In South America *(below)*, republican hopes were represented by native women, symbols of prosperity, and an oath of fidelity under the cap of liberty.

RÉPUBLIQUE HELVÉTIQUE
UNE ET INDIVISIBLE
CANTON DE BÂLE

ment even in ancient times, as the Basques do today at Guernica. The spruce appeared on the flag of New England as early as 1686 (see page 135), and it appears today in that of Massachusetts.

The tree was also the symbol of the French Revolution, and men who had "freed" themselves from the aristocratic oppressors danced

ruled democratically and not just city-states or unions such as the States-General of Holland. Can one regard the Commonwealth of the Lord Protector Oliver Cromwell from 1649 to 1658 and of his son Richard, bearing the same title from 1658 to 1660, as a politically authentic republic? If so then it is the prototype of those non-monarchic states which in their choice of symbols cling as closely to history as their republican constitution allows them. In this process, traditional armorial figures are preserved as far as possible and only openly monarchic emblems are brought into question. If these are unmistakable emblems of rank, such as imperial crowns, then their days are clearly numbered. Ornamental crowns, declared to be "people's crowns" and a sign of the sovereignty of component states, have often overcome understandable prejudices against them, as in the case of Bavaria (see page 8),

Up to 1848, the autonomy of the Swiss cantons was expressed by the fact that each canton had its own citizens' army with its own banner. Here are the "standard bearers" of Uri (black and yellow) and Schwyz.

red regional colors added to them. The solution was generally felt to be unsatisfactory, and had in the meantime been made redundant by the creation of the "southwestern state" of Baden-Württemberg. Some years ago Baden-Württemberg even revived the old arms of the dukedom of Swabia, while in Lower Saxony the war horse of the Guelphs still survives. The people's or socialist republics, with their more all-embracing republican attitude, have rather more difficulty in maintaining traditions.

What was true of the Old World and particularly of Europe cannot be applied without reservation

The Czechoslovak Republic has retained the Bohemian lion under all its forms of government *(left)* and the Republic of Finland the arms from the tomb of the king of Sweden, Gustavus Wasa.

Hessen, Baden-Württemberg, the Rhineland Palatinate, and, with modifications, West Berlin. One of the oldest republics of the nineteenth century, the Spanish republic of 1868, adopted the mural crown in its meaning as a citizens' crown (see page 246), an example followed by the republic of Austria.

The republican form of state, which in nineteenth-century Europe was as yet an exception, became widely established after the end of the First World War. The downfall of small and large monarchies in Germany everywhere created the problem of how the insignia of the new states were to be constituted. In general, the coats of arms borne by the local rulers were retained, even though these were nearly all their family arms. Only in Württemberg was there an attempt not to offend the deposed king. His arms with their three sets of deer's antlers (see page 121) were retained, with only the black and

to the younger nations. Despite the weight of tradition there are some stretches of territory devoid of a heraldic tradition even in Europe. In the Middle Ages, a simple king's crown or several such crowns were chosen for a newly created kingdom (e.g., Galicia, see page 91). This is hardly to be contemplated for a new republic, for which indigenous motifs must be used instead. Thus a bear was chosen by Finland for East Carelia and by Czechoslovakia for Carpatho-Ruthenia when heraldic symbols were required for these newly created political entities.

When in 1918 the crown was removed from German coats of arms, the arms themselves were spared where possible *(far left,* Oldenburg; *center left,* Württemberg); also in Portugal in 1910 *(above left).* In 1920 Hungary *(above)* revived its arms of 1848, which it retained until 1957.

The inclusion of the arms of Navarra in the fourth quarter by the Spanish Republic of 1868 has survived all later changes of regime. However, the red, yellow, and violet banner *(far left)* remained linked with the republican idea.

In the New World the procedure is much the same; emblems are created from the reservoir of motifs provided by revolutionary symbolism and indigenous natural forms. Heraldic rules and style not infrequently get left behind in the process. Any connection with Spanish colonial times tends to be restricted to the towns, although nowadays it is consciously cultivated there.

Despite its imperial origins the heraldic eagle was nevertheless made use of in the arms of the republic of Austria *(far left),* of the republican German empire of 1918, and of the present-day Federal Republic of Germany *(center left);* also as the national symbol of Poland (the white eagle) and in the Byzantine double eagle (see page 124) by the People's Republic of Albania *(above).*

Since the eighteenth century the mural crown has become the heraldic symbol of the self-governing town; in many countries there are even systems whereby the rank and size of the town can be deciphered. Other places combine the symbol with historical references, as in the case of Bar-le-Duc *(right)*, where it is merged with a ducal crown.

Town air makes free, says an old German proverb. But for this to be possible the town itself must be free, and free from royal sovereignty.

Some of the old town centers left by the Romans had survived the popular migrations and served as a focus for traders and craftsmen. These people organized a form of self-government for their communal existence which was closely

cially in Italy and Germany, the towns could achieve considerable independence, a result of the feudal constitution of the state in which the towns could to a large extent pursue their own interests. Only in the area of the old German empire were there "imperial towns" which were directly subject to the emperor.

From the middle of the twelfth century, the big towns on the Rhine used seals of a considerable size.

These seals are not, however, the forerunners of the municipal arms, although in later centuries there were many such arms which could be traced back to the images of saints, as for example those of Bingen (see page 121).

The municipal seals which can be regarded as the forerunners of municipal arms are those

The seals above show a selection of municipal motifs.

Reverse of a gold seal of the emperor Ludwig of Bavaria with a bird's eye view of Rome, 1328.

Back of a seal of King Baldwin I of Jerusalem (1118–1131) with the representation of the three most important buildings in this "city of the king of kings."

Great seal of Hamburg, 1254, model for the official seal of 1864.

Municipal seal of Emmerich (Lower Rhine) with the stylized representation of a town and above it shields with the canting arms of the town (pails = *Eimer*), 1237.

Back of the seal of the town of Arles (southern France) with the image of the town's patron saint and representatives of the guilds forming the municipal government.

linked with the constitution of the church. The connection appears clearly in the community seals of the large medieval towns on which the patron saints are represented, sometimes in scenes of martyrdom, and sometimes characterized by their attributes and framed by buildings which may form a portrait of the town. Espe-

Below, left to right:
The oldest colored representation of the arms of Berlin.
Arms of the West Berlin district of Charlottenburg, a combination of the arms of the former town of Charlottenburg with the special mural crown of the twelve districts of West Berlin.

 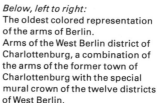 

Seal of the town of Hamelin with the representation of a characteristic building instead of a mural crown.

Right:
Complete arms of the town of Carlisle in England. The shield is the main element (or, a cross formy cantoned between four roses gules and surmounted by a single rose or), with a mural crown resting on top. The supporters are two red dragons, their wings spattered with gold roses, standing on a grassy mount. The motto bears the inscription BE JUST AND FEAR NOT.

which only contain the attributes of saints and are therefore easily transferable to an armorial shield. These seals are formally similar to those on which the insignia of the sovereign appear either alone or with a distinguishing mark, as in the case of the German imperial towns (see page 126). If the sovereign possesses the territory as well as the title, as in the case of the Hanseatic town of Lemgo (see page 133), his emblem can also be framed architecturally.

The possibilities are unlimited. But it must be emphasized that the images on municipal seals are not automatically placed on a shield and turned into municipal arms.

The choice of armorial charges depends to a considerable degree on how closely the town is attached to some superior authority, or how independent it feels itself to be. Despite its status

with a helmet and crest. Others add crowns of one kind or another, including Amsterdam (an imperial crown) and Berlin (an electoral crown, later a king's crown). By far the most common are mural crowns going back to antiquity which the three most important German imperial towns, Nuremberg, Augsburg, and Frankfurt, placed on their shield on seals and coins at the beginning of the eighteenth century. These

Development of the municipal arms of Mainz *(from left to right):*
Seal of 1392.
Initial from around 1440.
Napoleonic armorial letter, 1811.
Arms after the fall of Napoleon.
Arms granted in 1915.

Medal of the "good towns," commemorating the birth of the king of Rome, 1811 *(above right).*

as a Hanseatic town, Hamburg for some time bore the "nettle leaf" bordure of Holstein (see page 134) on its gates.

The recognition that seals, despite their relationship with coats of arms, are not identical to the latter has established itself in the last few decades. At the same time there is no unanimous view as to whether a municipal coat of arms should consist of ornamental emblems in addition to the shield. Many old and important towns, such as Oxford in England (see page 121), Prague in Bohemia, and Hanover and Göttingen in Lower Saxony complete the arms

crowns have become widespread since the nineteenth century, although in Germany they have been falsely suspected of being an inheritance of the despised Napoleonic heraldry (see page 150).

Apart from this minor question, it should be pointed out that there has been a widespread tendency in Europe over the last few decades to create arms for every community and not only for those which carry the title of a town. Thus even in democratically governed countries, such as Switzerland or Finland, there is scarcely a community which does not have its own arms.

Document by which the emperor Frederick III on 12 August 1461 granted his capital of Vienna an augmentation of its arms – the right to bear the imperial double eagle in reversed colors. The city of Vienna made special use of this augmentation by superimposing the traditional coat of arms (gules, a cross argent) on the breast of the double eagle. Today only the shield with the cross is used, although a single-headed eagle appears on the seal.

This gallery of the arms of such capitals as have them, supplemented by a few further major towns, will give us a rapid survey of the kind of elements used to make up municipal arms.

Since Reykjavik created a coat of arms for itself in 1957, Athens is the sole European capital which has only a seal, showing the goddess Athene from which it takes its name. Moscow is left out of consideration because its historical arms go against the current political attitude, and a provisional coat of arms dating from 1925 has fallen out of use. Moreover the current movement in the Soviet Union to provide new arms which conform with the system has achieved results in towns such as Kiev, Odessa, Sochi, Saporoshje, Riga, Stalingrad, and others, but has not yet affected Moscow. Historic arms such as those of Novgorod are still occasionally to be found.

Ancient tradition lives on in the letters SPQR (*Senatus Populus Que Romanus* – the Roman senate and people), which are found on arms dating back to the Middle Ages. Also of medieval origin are the armorial cross of the Crusader port of Marseilles, the Guelphic cross of Milan, and the German armorial cross of Vienna.

The canting arms with bears of Berlin and Bern are very old, as is the city of London's cross of St. George with the sword of St. Paul. The castles in the arms of Bratislava (Pressburg) and Hamburg can be traced back to old municipal seals; today they are drawn in a more modern fashion, whereas the castle of Prague sticks closely to Hussite prototypes.

The arms of Naples are probably based on figures from medieval banners, those of Zurich definitely so. Examples of coats of arms based on local mythology are the very old arms of Warsaw showing a mermaid, and the newly constituted arms of Reykjavik showing the traditional throne supports of the Vikings immersed in water.

Almost all the arms of capitals of former colonies are newly created, and in the English-speaking area most have been granted by the English kings of arms.

This is a continuation of an old Spanish tradition, for in the sixteenth century this former colonial power bestowed a coat of arms in the Spanish style on many overseas towns. Many of these have persisted into the present or been recreated in recent times.

248

ABIDJAN   ADDIS ABABA   ALGIERS   AMSTERDAM   ASUNCIÓN

BOGOTÁ   BONN   BRATISLAVA   BRAZZAVILLE   BRUSSELS

DELHI   DEN HAAG (THE HAGUE)   DUBLIN   EDINGBURGH   FRANKFURT-AM-MAIN

KINGSTON   KINSHASA   COPENHAGEN   KYOTO   LAGOS

LUANDA   LUXEMBOURG   LYON   MADRID   MANILA

NAPLES   N'DJAMENA   NEW YORK   OSAKA   OSLO

RANGOON   REIMS   REYKJAVIK   ROME   SALISBURY

SOFIA   STOCKHOLM   TANANARIVE   TOKYO   TORONTO

| ATHENS | BAMAKO | BANJUL | BELFAST | BELGRADE | BERLIN | BERN | BISSAU |

| BUCHAREST | BUDAPEST | BUENOS AIRES | CANBERRA | CARACAS | CASABLANCA | CHICAGO | DAKAR |

| FREETOWN | GENEVA | GUANABARA | GUATEMALA | HAMBURG | HELSINKI | JERUSALEM | KAMPALA |

| LA HABANA (HAVANA) | LA PAZ | LIBREVILLE | LIMA | LISBON | LONDON | LOS ANGELES | LOURENÇO MARQUES |

| MARSEILLES | MEXICO CITY | MILAN | MONACO | MONTEVIDEO | MONTREAL | MOSCOW | NAIROBI |

| OTTAWA | PANAMA | PARIS | PORT-AU-PRINCE | PRAGUE | PRETORIA | QUEBEC | QUITO |

 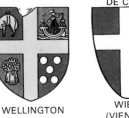  

| SAN FRANCISCO | SAN JOSÉ DE COSTA RICA | SAN MARINO | SANTA ISABEL | SANTIAGO DE CHILE | SANTO DOMINGO | SEOUL | SINGAPORE |

    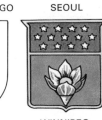

| VADUZ | WARSAW | WASHINGTON | WELLINGTON | WIEN (VIENNA) | WINDHOEK | WINNIPEG | ZURICH |

Philippe Pot, Grand Seneschal of Burgundy, chamberlain to King Louis XI of France and governor of Burgundy, commissioned his own tomb in 1493, shortly before his death. The mourners carry the escutcheons of seven of his great-grandparents; the mother of the mother of his father being unknown, he placed his family arms (or, a fess azure) in the eighth position to fill the gap. The mourner at the head end (on the right) bears the augmentation in a canton added by Philippe's grandfather Regnier, in memory of the fact that during a campaign against the heathenish Prussians in 1389 he was awarded the heroic name of "Palamades."

Below:
The siege of the Siennese by the Florentines at San Romano in 1432 formed the subject of an epoch-making painting by Paolo Uccello around 1455–60. The banners attached to the trumpets bear heraldic designs which have the effect of an optical signal working in conjunction with the sound of the trumpets. Also notable is the distinction between ordinary and jousting shields on the saltire, and the red Guelphic crosses which appear on them.

The Chariott drawne by foure Horses vpon whic[h] stood the Coffin couered wth purple Veluett and that the representation. The Canapy borne by six [...]

Death and burial have been the occasion for solemn ceremonies and have been recorded in pictorial form since time immemorial. The higher a man's rank in the world, the greater his need to leave evidence of his importance for posterity. Powerful men order their tombs far in advance of their death. As a result their heirs then frequently forget to add the date of death when the time comes.

Many have confined the decoration of their tombs to a portrayal of themselves in full figure, dressed in clothing or in armor. Where possible they had this figure accompanied by the arms of their parents and grandparents and even other more distant generations (see page 252). It was fairly unusual, however, to show the mourners on one's tomb, even as supporters for the ancestral arms.

still known as funeral banners in memory of the material they replaced.

Contemporary artists have often left very exact illustrated records of the solemn processions which accompanied highly placed persons to the grave. They provide valuable historical documentation both of the costumes worn and of the arms and banners used at the time. The banners which accompanied Queen Elizabeth I of England to the grave bore the arms of her forefathers over twelve generations, nine of which had taken their place on the throne. The male line of descent was broken with Henry VII's wife in favor of a female line of descent. Although the

Below:

Funeral procession of Queen Elizabeth I of England, 1603. The dead queen or her likeness lies in state on the sarcophagus, surrounded by the twelve banners of her forebears. The first is that of Henry II, married in 1152 to Eleanor of Aquitaine; beneath it John (of no estates), married in 1200 to Isabel of Angoulême. The next pair, Henry III, 1236 married to Eleanor of Provence; Edward I, 1254 to Eleanor of Castile. Edward II, 1308 to Isabel of France; Edward III, 1328 to Philippa of Hainault. Edmund Langley, Duke of York, 1372 to

Among the higher nobility, those in the funeral procession often acted as bearers of the ancestral or other arms. The funeral banners, usually black and painted with the ancestral arms, were then hung up in the church where the corpse was buried, and here, eaten away by the black coloring, they slowly disintegrated. This could be avoided by the use of more durable material such as wooden boards, which in Sweden are

daughter of a king, she only contributed his original arms of the earls of March.

Elizabeth's funeral procession was further decorated with the dead queen's arms on the horse trappers, surrounded by the emblem of the Order of the Garter. On their heads and cruppers the horses also carried pennants with the initials and the badges of Elizabeth I.

Isabel of Castile; Richard, Earl of Cambridge, to Anne Mortimer from the house of the earls of March. Richard, Duke of York, 1438 to Cecily Neville; Edward IV, 1464 to Elizabeth Woodville. Elizabeth, a daughter of this royal mariage, 1468 to Henry VII; and finally Henry VIII to Anne Boleyn, the marriage which produced Queen Elizabeth I.

251

Coats of arms incorporated into architecture are among the most important and significant from a historical, artistic, and heraldic point of view. All nations where heraldry is known have produced beautiful examples of this phenomenon. Unfortunately many of them were irrevocably destroyed, as reminders of the feudal past, in the revolutionary frenzy around 1800.

Below, center:
Italian sculptors carved in marble such noble forms as the fleur-de-lis, executed here in full relief on an armorial slab in the church of St. Giovanni in Laterano in Rome. The shield is "semy-de-lys" (i.e., with the flowers covering it in a carpetlike pattern).

The knight Hans von Bischofswerder appears on his fifteenth century gravestone, in the church at Ebersbach near Görlitz, framed by the eight coats of arms of his ancestors.

And we have given them
this coat of arms and give it with
the present document,
to use it in all places
and amongst all people,
as they may think fit,
both in time of peace and in time of war,
without any hindrance being placed
before or prepared for them
in any way or at any time
either now or in the future,
but rather the opposite.

From the document in which King Louis XI of France
granted Peter de Medici the right to bear
the three fleurs-de-lis of France in his arms.
Issued at Montlucon in May 1465.

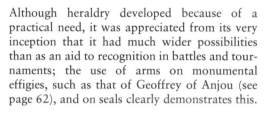

armorial display

Although heraldry developed because of a practical need, it was appreciated from its very inception that it had much wider possibilities than as an aid to recognition in battles and tournaments; the use of arms on monumental effigies, such as that of Geoffrey of Anjou (see page 62), and on seals clearly demonstrates this.

A person was symbolized, represented, and identified by his armorial bearings, either in

infante Fernando de La Cerda (d. 1275) at Burgos, the rationale of the arms depicted has defeated armorists and historians. On other occasions, such as on the tower at Innsbruck (see page 253) the pattern of the armorial decoration is easily understood.

One of the joys of heraldry, from the point of view of the artist and craftsman, is that it is three-dimensional, thus lending itself to sculp-

Above, far right:
In the internal courtyards of Italian town halls one can find whole walls decorated with sculpted heraldic panels, incorporating images created when the late Gothic was at its height. This wall from Florence shows the Florentine fleur-de-lis and the arms of some powerful families.

addition to his name, monogram, or portrait, or in lieu of one or all of these. Arms were an attractive, simple, and unequivocal way of referring to an individual or, after the fourteenth century when corporate bodies began to use arms, to an institution.

Sometimes, as in the case of the sword belt decorated with arms, discovered in the tomb of the

ture; but because it is simply an arrangement of symbols and because the shield is, in any case, almost two-dimensional, it can equally effectively be represented in two dimensions.

This gives it a versatility which many other forms of symbolism, such as the Japanese *mon* and the modern logo, do not possess to anything like the same degree.

252

It is not surprising therefore to find arms sculptured in the round in stone and equally attractively rendered in stained glass from the very early days of heraldry (see pages 264 ff.). In fact this particular form of armorial display has persisted over the centuries and has never lost its popularity. Although few can afford complete windows of stained and painted glass, craftsmen still do a brisk trade in panels of glass, which can be hung in windows or mounted for use as freestanding ornaments.

The uses to which heraldry can be put are only limited by one's ingenuity and imagination but, because arms are ensigns of honor, the tendency has been to use them principally in the adornment of personal treasures rather than of common objects. Unwritten conventions, which vary from country to country, dictate what forms of armorial display are acceptable. It is a fair generalization to say that the principal criterion is aesthetic but that there is also a fine line between ostentation and inverted snobbery. Thus a full achievement of arms carved in stone over the entrance to a castle is an ancient and acceptable way of displaying arms; and presumably, as

The serpent of the Visconti family is also found outside Milan, for example in the castle at Passau (above), and also on the monuments of the Polish queen Bona Sforza (1518–1558).

Demolished in 1766, the armorial tower in Innsbruck (left) was painted in 1497 with the arms of all the Hapsburg subject territories, right down to the very smallest in Flanders (e.g., Aalst) and the Grisons (e.g., Rhäzüns).

every man's home is his castle, a less obvious and ostentatious rendering of the arms could equally acceptably adorn a bungalow, but when it comes to an armorial saucepan the natural tendency would be to use nothing, or at the most the relatively humble badge.

In the days when platters were made of pewter or silver, they were sometimes marked with

In 1784 the Austrian imperial eagle was laid out in colored tiles on the roof of St. Stephen's cathedral in Vienna. In accordance with the custom of the time, the initial of the emperor Francis I appears in the middle of the shield on the eagle's breast. On the other side of the roof, two modern eagles, those of Austria and Vienna, were added in 1950.

253

Swiss motor vehicles carry the coat of arms of their canton of origin on the number plate, next to the canton's identifying letters. The principality of Liechtenstein, which is allied to Switzerland by a customs agreement, also subscribes to this tradition.

arms, but armorial tableware became really popular in the early eighteenth century when armorial porcelain was imported from China. This porcelain was mostly manufactured at Chin-Te-Chen and then decorated at Canton, whence it was exported to Europe. That which came to England was called Armorial Lowestoft, but in fact it has no connection with the soft-paste porcelain factory established at Lowestoft in Suffolk, England, in 1757.

What happened was that firms in Europe sent

The publicity value of graphic signs was quickly recognized by airlines. The rudder assemblies of modern aircraft are decorated to

take advantage of this, even in the case of the Islamic societies which on religious grounds are against the use of figurative images.

The fondness of the Swiss for armorial images is also seen on the livery of the Swiss railways. The front of each locomotive bears the federal cross, while on the side is an accurate representation of the arms of a particular town or community, surmounted by its name (e.g., Flüelen, *above*).

representations of their clients' arms to China; these were copied onto the porcelain which was then exported. The use of porcelain instead of metal was at first considered a luxury and was very much à la mode. Frequently the designs sent to China were those which had been engraved

Many museums of applied arts contain pieces of china and porcelain whose arms still await identification, and in some cases also dating. The examples shown are *(above, left to right)* a German box of 1674, the beaker of a married couple from Enkhuizen (Netherlands) around 1630, and a silver gilt ornamental dish from the workshop of Edward Farell, 1824. Definite attributions have been made for the silver gilt tankard *(far right)* from Augsburg, 1743, a chocolate jug from Boston, U.S.A., 1755, the Swedish porcelain plate of 1709, and the plate from the still active Wedgwood porcelain factory in England, dating from 1796.

Below, left to right:
A pendant with a reversible stone, engraved on all three sides; a seal ring with arms of alliance engraved in a mirror image, and next to it the impression with the arms shown the right way round. Unfortunately rings have recently appeared with arms formed in relief, or even imitation arms,

on the metal utensils previously used, so that the arms on early armorial porcelain often resemble engraved designs. Later other designs emerge, but invariably these are copies of existing representations of the arms and were not especially designed for the purpose to which they were to be put. For this reason Chinese porcelain may be intrinsically exquisite but the armorial decoration usually ranges from the pedestrian to the meretricious.

As the eighteenth century proceeded, English firms – notably Wedgwood – started to produce

the sixteenth century it was fashionable to replace metal drinking receptacles with fine Venetian glasses. The vogue swept Europe, and before the close of the sixteenth century Venetian glass-workers were setting up glasshouses all over the Continent. Indeed it is often difficult to determine the provenance of an early seventeenth-century glass *à la Venise*, so strong was the Venetian influence. As metal cups and

which cannot even be used to seal a registered letter.

A well-established use of arms is in the embossing or "blind-embossing" (without ink) of visiting cards or letterheads. Shown here *(far right)* is the letterhead of engineer Ingemar Sjöblad of Linköping.

armorial porcelain. Some is no better, armorially, than the Chinese, but there is much which is of the highest quality. It is encouraging to note that Wedgwood is still very much in business and, along with one or two other firms, is still producing exceedingly fine armorial porcelain.

What is true of porcelain is also true of glass. In

Bookplate of a member of the Order of St. John (Knights of Malta). Design by Rudolf Niedballa, 1976.

Left:
Hand-painted bookplate of the judge of Upland in 1440, the knight Benedikt Jensson Oxenstierne, with his arms in the middle and the shields of his grandparents and the mother of his paternal grandfather in the corners.

Bookplate of a German officer in 1942, in the style of the armorials of the Arlberg brotherhood. Design by Ottfried Neubecker.

tankards had been engraved with arms, the custom persisted with drinking glasses which, as early as the late sixteenth century, are to be found with arms engraved on them. Later, especially in Germany and the Low Countries, painted glass also became popular. Fortunately the art of engraving on glass is not dead, and while new sets of armorial glass are rare, individual examples are frequently used as presentation pieces.

Arms are still frequently used on seals by corporate bodies but personal seals are currently not much in evidence, although seal rings are as popular as ever. Here the custom has varied. In the eighteenth and early nineteenth centuries,

The silver casket made in 1438 to house the imperial regalia, after their transfer to Nuremberg in 1424, is covered on all sides with the two coats of arms of Nuremberg on lozenge fields *(right)*.

rings and fobs usually contained a stone onto which the arms were engraved, sometimes with crest and motto. In the nineteenth century the crest, or crest and motto, replaced the arms; but in recent years there has been a return to the use of the shield alone.

On the continent of Europe the full achievement is much used; but it is a sign of the times that, because seal rings are for the most part no longer functional, the arms on them are often a positive scratch engraving rather than the deep, negative engraving required for sealing.

Surrounded by four small shields engraved with the bull's head of Mecklenburg, this sculpturally formed head forms an impressive doorknocker to the sacristy of the church of St. Peter at Lübeck.

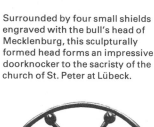

The nine quarterings in the shield of an English Jones family *(below)* represent a summary of their

There was a great vogue for armorial stationery in the last century, and this is still popular. Even the old snobbery that arms must never be printed but always embossed in monochrome or "blind-embossed" (without ink) is still very much alive. However, colored representations of arms, whether embossed or printed, may properly adorn the writing paper of corporations but never that of individuals. This social stricture applies in Great Britain to a much greater extent than elsewhere in Europe, just as the use of armorial insignia on a visiting card, though acceptable in most European countries, is anathema in Britain, where an armorial card at once proclaims the bearer a commercial representative.

Among the most prized possessions of a cultured

using arms. Fashions in bookplates, like fashions in art, have varied from age to age, giving the bookplate an interest far beyond the narrow confines of armory. People collect bookplates in the same way as they collect prints or postage stamps. There are bookplate societies, facilities for exchanging specimens, bookplate magazines, and a wealth of literature on the subject.

In past centuries the use of arms in the embellishment and decoration of buildings, furniture, silver, tapestry, and other valued personal possessions is eloquently illustrated on pages 258–260. Today such expensive and exotic displays of arms are rarer than they used to be, but there are still artists and craftsmen who are able to render a coat of arms in any medium and to any specifications and there are still people

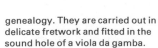

genealogy. They are carried out in delicate fretwork and fitted in the sound hole of a viola da gamba.

The four armorial shields on the wooden chest enable us to place it fairly accurately as coming from Pisa in the second half of the thirteenth century.

person are books, so it is not surprising to indicate ownership in a manner both attractive and unequivocal, namely by using an armorial bookplate. From the time of Albrecht Dürer – an early and famous designer of bookplates – to the present day, the bookplate or *ex libris* sign has been one of the most popular and useful ways of

who want their arms carved in stone or wood, engraved on metal, enameled on brass, painted on wood, canvas or vellum, worked in tapestry (armorial hassocks in churches are increasingly popular), rendered in precious stones and metals, and transferred onto the doors of automobiles.

This chandelier with the bust of a king mounted on a deer's antler probably represents the emperor Maximilian I; it is attributed to Jörg Lederer around 1516–1519. However, the shield on the breast shows the single-headed eagle which Maximilian bore as king of Romans only until 1508, when as emperor elect he exchanged it for the double eagle.

Left:
The double doors of this late fourteenth century cupboard from Lower Saxony are decorated above with the arms of the four grandparents of a married man and below with those of his wife.

On this bed frame by the famous woodcarver Peter Flötner, decorated with inlays, the arms of death hang over the head of the sleeper, serving as a constant *memento mori*.

King James III of Scotland and his wife Margaret of Denmark, whom he married in 1460, in late sixteenth century costume in a Scottish armorial produced in 1591. The queen's dress bears the Danish arms of the period around 1572.

Below center:
The arms of Great Britain against a background of drapery consisting of the French Tricolor and the British Union Jack on the occasion of a recent state visit of the British queen to Paris.

Arms of the Duke of Burgundy, Charles the Bold, as the centerpiece of a *mille-fleurs* tapestry, one of the oldest examples of this type, manufactured in Brussels in 1466 and taken as booty by the Swiss at the battle of Grandson ten years later.

Opposite:
A *mille-fleurs* tapestry in its present restored condition, with the likeness of Jean de Dillon (d. 1481–1482) as a knight bearing a standard. The tapestry was probably made in Arras in 1477, when de Dillon was the king's representative there.

are the new patrons and it is their arms which are becoming increasingly prevalent.

A corporate body can be much more blatant than an individual in its display of arms, because its arms are only partly a symbol of its excellence; they are also the symbol of its corporate unity, an aspect of its "public image" and even, in some cases, its trademark. It is therefore accepted that the arms of a corporation shall adorn its stationery in full color; mark even the most humble of its possessions, such as bookmatches, menus, table napkins, and disposable cups, and generally proclaim the corporation in every way and in all its aspects.

Arms, quite rightly, adorn the freedom certificates of towns and the caskets in which these are sometimes contained; they decorate diplomas and testimonials issued by professional and academic institutions and, on a lower level, the blazers, ties, and stationery of the members of such bodies, and they add luster and identity to the jewels of chairmen, mayors, chancellors, and other heads of corporate bodies. On bunting they fly above offices and town halls; engraved

Individuals, then, are still patrons of heraldic artists and craftsmen, but their patronage is limited by the economic exigencies of the day. In the past the very wealthy were the nobility who,

Above, far right:
Tammany Hall in New York on the occasion of the national convention of 4 July 1868, decorated with the seal designs of the component states of the U.S.A. and gathered federal flags. This use of national flags as bunting is no longer allowed today. Instead only the colors and graphic motifs of the flags may be used.

being proud of their armorial achievements, displayed them whenever possible, thus patronizing every form of heraldic art. Today the new rich tend not to have arms, and since there are very few official armorial authorities left in Europe, they cannot acquire them and so extend their patronage in other directions. The old aristocracy has not, therefore, been replaced by the new plutocracy as patrons of heraldry, but rather by rich, armorial, corporate bodies; they

in metal they proclaim the common seal to the illiterate; cast in fiber glass or a more traditional medium they add a splash of color and a link with the past when boldly displayed on the severe, epicene façades of modern edifices.

Although in the nature of things few commercial firms have arms of their own, many use designs which give the impression of being armorial so as to give a cachet to their products; for this

The luxury goods industry often makes use of the arms of the countries of origin of its products as a motif in its packaging and publicity. In the tobacco industry the most popular arms are those of Spain, to which Cuba once belonged, but the arms of Havana,

reason this type of heraldry may conveniently be referred to as "cachet heraldry."

Arms suggest excellence, permanence, and reliability and there is no doubt in the advertising trade that certain products, if adorned with arms

crowns, and supporters, which usually take the form of lions since it is believed, and quite rightly, that the rampant lion is the very essence of ancient heraldic design.

The use of cachet heraldry annoys purists and, in

of Cuba, and of Brazil are also used as a basis for graphic designs. The smith and the personification of liberty in the arms of the Brazilian state of Bahia became two wild men carrying cigars on the labels of its principal cigar manufacturer *(top row, far right)*.

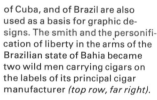

Many packages show existing coats of arms, with the permission of the person concerned. For example, the pack for St. Moritz filter cigarettes carries the personal arms of Prince Bernhard of the Netherlands, since the manufacturer is a supplier to the prince By Appointment.

The lion is the typical heraldic beast and for this reason plays a leading part in the heraldry of publicity and packaging.

In his graphically polished designs for the firm of Neuerburg, O.H.W. Hadank broke new ground, taking his inspiration not from the classical forms of heraldry but from those of the late nineteenth century.

The use of heraldic designs on sports shirts, especially those of national teams, has contributed to the popularity of heraldry. Armorial shields on the left breast represent the arms of the players' native country or a variation of them. In our picture the Dutch national football team are wearing a shield with a lion on it, derived from the Dutch national arms.

Similar shields are also worn by riders *(far right)* and form part of the uniform of many private schools, especially in the English-speaking world.

or colorable imitations of arms, will appeal to certain people. That is why automobiles, cigarettes, and a host of other goods are embellished with cachet heraldry. Sometimes, as on wine

Scotland, can lead to protests to which the Procurator Fiscal to Lyon Court must lend an ear and possibly institute legal proceedings. Even the most dilettante armorist may consider that

labels, the arms used are genuine and are those of the owner or eponym of the vineyard, but usually they represent what a commercial artist imagines noble heraldry should look like. There is an abundance of barred helms, plumes,

those taken in by popular and cachet heraldry have only themselves to blame. This is true to some extent, but it must be remembered that the users of these types of heraldry are taking advantage of the ignorance of the public to create a

false impression. In the final analysis, then, they may be said to be obtaining money by false pretenses.

Another form of heraldic display relates to the use of symbols that are also not real heraldry, but are not intended to deceive and which, to a great extent, are accepted by everyone. This may be called "para-heraldry." It relates to the use of badges, often looking like arms, by sporting clubs, schools, masonic lodges, military corps, divisions and regiments, and certain logos and symbols frequently found spattered over the ties and stationery of clubs and societies. A purist may take exception to such emblems, in that they too closely resemble arms; particularly where the body using the badge is of such status or stature that it might reasonably be expected

The heraldic style has had a lasting effect on the graphics of publicity. Beasts of all kinds are common – the lion of the Diederich Press, formerly of Jena, the lion's head of Monarch Machinery in Canada, AGIP's fire-breathing dog with many legs, the shell of the Shell company, and the serpent of Aesculapius of the Stroschein chemical factory. Elsewhere we find ingeniously formed human figures such as the rubber tire Michelin man, the St. George of the Reynolds aluminium firm or the figure composed of letters of the Bolle dairy in Berlin, one of the oldest of its kind. Letters form the basis of the logograms of the Swedish firm of Huskvarna, the Volkswagen concern, and the Takashivaya silk factory in Japan.

to be properly armigerous. But usually para-heraldry is tolerated.

In the monarchies of Europe it has been the custom, at least since the early nineteenth century, for the ruler, and sometimes certain members of his family, to allow those who provide them with goods or services of a certain excellence to state that they are "By Appointment" and to display their arms. Obviously the display of royal arms cannot but give a cachet to the products or services of those lucky enough to be so appointed. But this is not cachet heraldry, for this armorial cachet has been properly acquired as an acknowledgment of excellence and can only be enjoyed as long as the firm entitled to it conforms to the rules and limitations laid down by the donor. It is not a homemade, self-awarded cachet but a rare and much sought-after privilege; so much so in fact that in an age of leveling out it is beginning to incite envy, a development militating against its continuance in certain countries. For the time being, however, colorful and dignified royal arms may be seen embellishing a wide variety of products.

Like tobacco manufacturers, producers of alcohol make extensive use of armorial designs. The arms of French provinces and cities, such as Bordeaux, are frequently used, as are those of Portugal, Spain, and Savoy. Automobile manufacturers also tend to rely closely on local arms. The badge of Alfa Romeo combines the arms of the city and the dukedom of Milan; that of Porsche the arms of the free state of Württemberg with the arms of Stuttgart inescutcheon; the arms of Cologne are also made use of. The crown on the American Cadillac badge *(above center)* gives the impression that the firm originated in some European baronial family, while the shield suggests English associations.

263

Circular glass window painted with the arms of the abbot of Kreuzlingen (Switzerland), Peter I von Bubenberg, from Kempten. According to the inscription the window was endowed by the abbot himself in 1513. On the shield, the arms of the imperial foundation of Augustine canons at Kreuzlingen (the cross and crozier) are quartered with the family arms of the abbot (the four-spoked wheel).

A typical armorial window of a Swiss Canton is that of Glarus dating from 1608. The region's patron saint, St. Fridolin, is shown

Below:
One of a series of twelve windows endowed by the Zurich guilds in the "zur Linde" inn in 1605. Executed by the Zurich glass painter Josias Murer, they are each devoted to a particular month (in this case October). At the bottom of each window is the coat of arms of the guild which endowed it, and round the edge are the shields of the members of the guild.

The custom of attributing arms at a later date to historical, Biblical, and mythical persons, whose existence or notional existence antedates heraldry, goes back to the thirteenth century. Arms have been attributed to Adam, the archangels, Christ, the apostles and other saints, Charlemagne, King Arthur and his knights, the pre-Norman monarchs of England, and a host of others too numerous to mention. Arms are still attributed today, but the principal, practical application of newly attributed arms is in connection with churches. The custom of using arms attributed to the saint or religious conception to which a church is dedicated is of reasonable antiquity. Such arms appear on the notice board outside the church, on the parish magazine, parochial seal, and other places where it seems sensible and reasonable to symbolize the parish. It is true that most of the major saints have long ago had arms attributed to them, but sometimes a variant from a well-known coat is required, or else the incumbent of a new church does not know where to discover what arms have been attributed to the saints and so decides to start *de novo*. In other cases the dedication may be a quite new one, such as to St. Joseph the Worker or Christ the King; although there are now many churches dedicated to the latter, no attributed arms have yet appeared in books of reference, which leaves the field open.

The proper use of attributed arms has never been

not only on the shield and banner, but also in the top right-hand corner, leading Ursus, who has been woken from the grave, before the judge so he can prove his innocence.

questioned. It was already a part of the heraldic scene in the late fourteenth century, when King Richard II of England showed his royal arms impaled by the attributed arms of St. Edward the Confessor.

Paradoxically, the widespread interest in heraldry today has to a great extent been stimulated, and unhappily sometimes also satisfied, by the suppliers of heraldic plaques. Firms who trade in popular heraldry supply a reproduction of arms, usually taken from a reference book, which has at some point in history been used by a family having the same or similar surname to that of the purchaser. But without establishing a definite pedigree, it is not possible to determine whether one is rightfully entitled to bear existing arms.

There is no harm, on the other hand, in individuals and corporations creating anew distinctive arms, for no identifying mark has yet emerged which contains all the properties of a well-designed armorial achievement.

B.-L.

* * *

Heraldry is a living art. The general growing interest in heraldic phenomena follows on an interest in genealogy. Newly gained knowledge demands aesthetic satisfaction. Ever increasing is the number of those armed with cameras who record pictures of heraldic motifs and present them to a specialist for identification. In this manner they may often be dated and so put into their proper historical context; this book contains many such examples, published here for the first time.

It is now generally accepted that the art of any generation is largely dependent on the patronage of wealthy individuals and organizations. This was true in the past, and it is no less so today. And since art influences as well as reflects a particular historical period, this means that civilization as we know it is not only the result of impersonal "historic currents" but depends in great measure on the activities of individuals deeply involved in their immediate environment. For centuries there have been many among them whose way of life included – and in some cases necessitated – the bearing of arms.

The color pictures on these last few pages make it clear that the ancient art of heraldry not only continues to live but has become an integral part of everyday life. It will continue to survive, both a mirror and an instrument of historical events.

O. N.

The custom of presenting armorial windows is still very much alive in Switzerland. In the past it was the custom to present a fellow citizen who moved into a new house with an armorial window as a sign of friendship. Today it is usually civic communities which endow a window bearing their arms in a community building.

The Lucerne stained glass artist Eduard Renggli is adept at transforming conventional models into modern terms, as is demonstrated by the window with the red lion of the town of Willisau *(left),* and another showing St. Martin with the goose customarily slaughtered at a popular festival at Sursee *(below).*

The armorial windows of the baroque period demonstrate all the consciousness of their own superiority which characterized the patrician rulers of the city states. In the example below, designed by Jacob Brunner, 1557, two golden lions support the achievement of Bern, Switzerland, with the arms of districts under Bernese dominion round the edge. It makes a striking contrast to the simplicity of the Eduard Renggli window from Lucerne, 1973, with its strong, modern shapes and large areas of color.

266

EARLY ARMORIALS

The following list is as complete as possible. Many armorial rolls only exist in copies. Locations are usually given only where the originals exist. Details of their contents are indicated when not clear from the title. Publications are listed when they reproduce a substantial portion of the original. The order is chronological within each category.

Abbreviations:

AHS – Swiss Heraldic Archives.
BGH – Berchem, Galbreath, and Hupp. "Die Wappenbücher des deutschen Mittelalters," in *S.A.H.* 1925, 1926, 1928 (also as off-prints).
ZWR – *Die Wappenrolle von Zürich (Zurich Roll of Arms).* Walther Merz and Friedrich Hegi (eds.). Zurich, 1930.

OCCASIONAL ROLLS

Rôle d'armes Bigot, 1254

Descriptions in Picardy dialect of 295 blazons. Contents: The knights of both sides involved in a campaign in Flanders or the subsequent truce. Original lost, copy from the seventeenth century: Paris, Bibliothèque Nationale, ms. fr. 18648, fol. 32–39. Published: AHS 63, 1949, pp. 15–22, 68–75, 115–121.

Tournoi de Compiègne, 1278

Contents: Description of the arms of the participants in the tournament, probably 1278. Original lost, several copies from the fifteenth century. Only published in extracts.

Rôle d'armes de l'ost de Flandre (Rôle d'Armes Chifflet-Prinet), 1297

Blazons from the fifteenth century and 156 colored drawings of shields. Contents: Participants in the campaign of Philip the Fair, King of France, against the counts of Flanders. Original lost, several copies of the text and illustrations, in particular: Besançon, The Library, ms. 186. Published: *Le Moyen Age,* 2nd series, Vol. 22, 1920; and AHS 1959, pp. 2–7.

Falkirk Roll, 1298

Descriptions in French of 111 blazons. Contents: English knights taking part in the Battle of Falkirk in Scotland, 22 July 1298. Published: Henry Gough, *Scotland in 1298,* pp. 129–159.

Caerlaverock Poem or Roll, ca. 1300

Contents: Description of 106 coats of arms of the conquerors of Caerlaverock Castle in Dumfriesshire, July 1300, in French and in verse. Original: London, British Museum, ms. Cotton Caligula A. AVIII, fol. 26b.

Galloway Roll, 1300

Contents: Descriptions of the arms of 259 knights taking part in the battle of Galloway on the side of King Edward I in the campaign against Scotland.

Nativity Roll, ca. 1300

Contents: In French, descriptions of the arms of seventy-nine knights who assembled at an unknown place in an unknown year on the day of birth of the Virgin Mary (8 September).

Stirling Roll, 1304

Contents: Description of the shields of 102 participants in the siege of Stirling by King Edward I of England on 30 May 1304.

Armorial shields in the "Zum Loch" house in Zurich, 1306

Erected for the visit of the German king. Remains of the roof beams decorated with armorial shields in Zurich, Swiss National Museum; reconstruction in the same place (see above, page 36). Published in ZWR, color plates 28–32.

First Dunstable Roll, 1308

Contents: Arms of the participants in a tournament at Dunstable in 1308, about 240 shields, some drawn, some with English and French descriptions.

Series of arms from the tower in Erstfeld (Canton of Uri), 1309

Connected with the Imperial Diet in Speyer. Only known from drawings (cf. BGH, p. 9).

Tournoi de Mons, July 1310

Contents: Arms of the participants. Original lost, copies from the fifteenth century in Brussels, Royal Library, ms. 14.935; and Vienna, National Library, No. 3297. Published: *Annuaire du Cercle Archéologique,* Vol. 19, Mons 1886, Vol. 38, 1909.

Arms of Rivoli, 1310 (?)

Probably connected with an imperial visit in the year 1310. Original: Paintings in the demolished castle of Rivoli near Turin. Description from the fifteenth century: Turin, State Archives, sez. I protocolli, serie di carte no. 2, protocolli Tribù no. 1, fol. 134–136.

Turin Armorial, 1312

In French, 119 blazons. Contents: Armigers present at the coronation of Henry VII as emperor in Rome on 29 June 1312. Original: Turin, State Archives, Diplomi Imperiali, Mazzo 4, No. 12.

Noms des nobles de Flandres du temps du comte Louys de Nevers, qui commença sa principauté l'an 1322.

Seventeenth century ms. on paper, Lille, Public Library, fol. 103–118.

Boroughbridge Roll, 1322

Contents: Descriptions of the arms of 214 knights on the side of the defeated King Edward II of England at the Battle of Boroughbridge on 27 March 1322. Original: London, British Museum, ms. Egerton 2850.

Folding table from Lüneburg Town Hall, ca. 1328

Eight colored achievements of arms

of kings and princes. Thirty colored shields with helmets and crests beside them (see above, pages 154–155) of the duke of Brunswick and Lüneburg, his relatives and supporters. Original: Lüneburg, Museum Lüneburg. Published: *Lüneburger Blätter,* Vol. 2, 1951.

Armorial shields of Mainz families, after 1332

Sketches of 129 armorial shields, twenty-two left empty. Contents: The patrician families of Mainz, outlawed in 1322 and then rehabilitated. Original: Darmstadt State Archives, No. 207/5. Lost in the Second World War (cf. BGH, p. 30).

Rôle d'armes des rois et princes confédérés pour faire la guerre au duc Jean III de Brabant – vassau du part du duc, ca. 1332

Seventy armorial shields of the opponents of Duke John III of Brabant, 1332. Seventeenth-century line drawings. Paris, Bibliothèque de l'Arsenal, ms. 5014, fol. 150.

Carlisle Roll, 1334

Contents: 277 painted shields of the retinue of King Edward III of England during his visit to Carlisle on 12 July 1334. Original: Cambridge, Fitzwilliam Museum, ms. 324.

Second Dunstable Roll, 1334

Contents: In French, 135 descriptions of the arms of the participants in the tournament at Dunstable.

(Third) Calais Roll, ca. 1348

Contents: Twenty-four roughly painted shields of lords and prominent persons who perished in the siege of Calais (1345–1348). Original: London, British Museum, ms. Additional 29502.

Armorial hall at Lauf (near Nuremberg), 1360

Descriptions of 114 carved and colored armorial shields in the castle built in 1357–60. Contents: The territories and followers of the emperor Charles IV who stayed in Lauf on numerous occasions. Numerous publications, the most recent: Wilhelm Kraft and Wilhelm Schwemmer, *Kaiser Karls IV. Burg und Wappensaal zu Lauf,* Nuremberg 1960; a new edition in preparation, Passau.

Armorial documents of German knights in Italy, 1361

Descriptions of 106 colored armorial shields in two documents of 12 November and 29 December 1361. Contents: German knights released from captivity on parole, after taking part in the family feud of the Gonzagas. Original: Mantua, Archives of the Gonzagas, Esterni B 27, No. 1, busta 48. Published: *Der Deutsche Herold,* Vol. 42, 1911, pp. 27–32, 59–66, 86–92, 109–111, 170, 244; also independently, Paderborn 1911.

Rôle d'armes du traité de Guérande, ca. 1381

Descriptions of 253 painted armorial

shields of Breton nobles who promised to observe the treaty agreed between Brittany and France at Guérande in 1381. Copy from the seventeenth century, Paris, Bibliothèque Nationale, ms. fr. 22361, fol. 11 ff.

Chi sont li duc li conte li visconte li banereche et li chévaler qui furent sur le Kuunre en Frise lan nre Singnr. m. ccc. xcvi., ca. 1396

Descriptions of 333 coats of arms of the participants in the campaign of Albrecht of Bavaria against Friesland, 1396. Original: The Hague, Royal Archives. Published: J.-M. Lion, 1889, 2°, 14 plates.

Folding table in the Musée Cluny, Paris, ca. 1400

Four panels with eight achievements of arms, only two of which are identified; forty-four armorial shields from a variety of sources running round the edge, of which eleven are no longer recognizable. Probably from the monastery of Wienhausen near Celle. Discussed by Neitzert, Gabriele: "Der Peter-und-Pauls-Altar der St.-Lamberti-Kirche in Hildesheim," in *Niederdeutsche Beiträge zur Kunstgeschichte,* Vol. VI, Berlin 1967.

Chi so li duc li conte et li chevalier qui furent devant Gorinchen l'an notre seigneur mcccc et deux, 1402

Coats of arms of the participants in the siege of Gorinchem (Seeland). Original lost, old copies include that by the Gelre herald "Beyeren," Vienne, Public Library, 3297.

Ulrich Richental's Chronicle of the Council of Constance, 1414–1418

Original lost, nine almost contemporary copies exist. Published numerous times (see above, pages 34, 181, 206, 224, 238, 240; cf. BGH, pp. 33 f.).

Nobles de Flandres, accompaignans le duc Philippe II, a la journée première qu'il feit en France, pour la vengeance de son père, 1421

Armorial roll of the participants in the campaign of revenge against France, 1421, by Philip II, Duke of Burgundy. Paper ms. from the seventeenth century, 2°, Lille, Public Library, 486.

Armorial des chevaliers dauphinois tués à la bataille de Verneuil, 1424

Armorial roll of the knights from the Dauphiné who perished in the Battle of Verneuil, 1424. Published: In *Revue nobiliaire, héraldique et biographique,* Vol. V (VII in the series), Paris 1869, pp. 37–47.

Barnard's Roll of Badges, 1475

Contents: Sketches and descriptions of the badges of the participants in the campaign against France. Original: London, College of Arms.

Writhe's Book of Knights, ca. 1500

Contents: Arms and banners of knights created since 1460. Original: London, British Museum, ms. Additional 46354.

ILLUSTRATED CHRONICLES AND MANUSCRIPTS

Eneît (Aeneid), 1174–1188

Author: Heinrich von Veldeke. Basically imaginary arms (see above, pages 26, 152) of preheraldic persons, but partially derived from contemporary arms and partially based on the opposition between imperial and royal power. Original: Berlin, State Library, Cod. germ., fol. 282. Published: Heinrich von Veldeke, Eneide. Die Bilder der Berliner Handschrift, ed. Albert Boecklar, Leipzig 1939.

Carmen de bello Siculo inter Henricum VI. Imperatorem et Tancredum, 1195–1196

Author: Petrus de Ebulo. The arms and emblems are contemporary (see above, pages 118, 152). Original: Bern, Civic Library, Cod. 120, Bibl. Bongarsiana; cf. BGH pp. 1 f.

Historia Anglorum, Chronica Majora, Abbrevatio Chronicarum, Liber Additamentorum, before 1260

Compilation by Matthew Paris (d. 1259). Contents: Altogether about 100 shields. Originals: London, British Museum, ms. Royal 14 C VII, or ms. Cotton Claudius D VI (f 17). Frequently dealt with in literature, especially Dr. Vaughan, Matthew Paris, Cambridge 1958.

Chansonnier du roi (Song Book of the King) 1253–1270

Contains eleven representations of the song composers in knightly attire. Original: Paris, Bibliothèque Nationale, ms. fr. 844. Published: In Mélanges Linguistiques, Littéraires offerts à A. Jeanroy, Paris 1928, pp. 521–537, plates.

Grosse Heidelberger Liederhandschrift (Great Heidelberg Song Manuscript), ca. 1300

The so-called Manesse Codex. Original: Heidelberg, University Library, Cod. palat. germ. No. 848. Frequently appears in literature, particularly in Karl Zangenmeister, Die Wappen, Helmzierden und Standarten der Grossen Heidelberger Liederhandschrift (Manesse Codex), Görlitz and Heidelberg 1892, XII, 30 pp., LXII color plates, Lge. 2°. Facsimile edition: Berlin 1930.

Weingartener Liederhandschrift (Weingarten Song Manuscript), early fourteenth century

Closely related in content to the Grosse Heidelberger Liederhandschrift but less comprehensive. Original: Stuttgart, Public Library, Poet. germ. I. Heraldically evaluated in Zangemeister, op. cit., plates 20 and 21.

Sachsenspiegel, ca. 1300

Codification of legal maxims of Saxon (North German) law, several versions heraldically illustrated (see above, page 226). Several original manuscripts. Frequently mentioned in the literature of legal history. Facsimile edition: Karl von Amira, Die Dresdener Bilderhandschrift des Sachsenspiegels, Leipzig 1892.

Balduineum or Die Romfahrt Kaiser Heinrichs VII., (The Emperor Henry VII's Journey to Rome), ca. 1345

Continuous series of pictures; those of the participants who were knights are represented with their arms and banners. On the versos are the arms of the burghers of the archbishopric of Trier (see above, pages 144, 180). Original: Coblenz, State Archives. Published: Die Romfahrt Kaiser Heinrichs VII. im Bilderzyklus des Codex Balduini Trevirensis, ed. Georg Irmer, Berlin 1881.

Harleian Roll, ca. 1314

Contents: 191 colored coats of arms in the upper margin of the poem "Manuel des Pechez" by William of Waddington. Original: London, British Museum, ms. Harley 337.

Peterborough Roll, ca. 1321–1329

Contents: Seventeen colored coats of arms of the abbey and abbots of Peterborough in the margin of the Chronicle and Cartulary of Peterborough. Original: London, British Museum, ms. Additional 39758.

Georg Hagen's Austrian Chronicle, 1394–1398

Contents: Fourteen beautifully stylized colored coats of arms of legendary rulers, together with the arms of the dukes of Austria. Original: Innsbruck, University Library, ms. 255.

Sherborne Missal Shields, ca. 1400

Contents: Sixty-six painted coats of arms. Original: Alnwick Castle, duke of Northumberland.

Beijeren's Dutch Chronicle, ca. 1409

The work of the Gelre herald "Beyeren" (Bavaria), whose real name was Claes Heijnenszoon or Heijnen; the illustrations include the arms of twenty-five bishops of Utrecht and Dutch grandees, with blazons in Dutch verse. Original: Brussels, Royal Liberary, ms. 17914.

The Great Coucher Book of the Duchy of Lancaster, ca. 1410

Contents: Sixteen armorial banners belonging to the duchy of Lancaster. Original: London, Public Record Office, D of L/42.

Furness Coucher Book, ca. 1412

Contents: Eighty-four arms of benefactors. The book consists of two parts. Originals: 1. Public Record Office, duchy of Lancaster Records; 2. British Museum, ms. Additional 33244.

Salisbury Roll, ca. 1460

Contents: Heraldically dressed married couples tracing a royal line of descent. Original: Duke of Buccleuch.

Gebhard Dacher's Chronicle of Constance, ca. 1465

Contents: 646 arms relating to Constance and its near surroundings. Original: St. Gallen, Monastery Library, Cod. 646.

Warwick or Rous Roll, 1477–1491

Contents: Richly illustrated history of the house of Rous. The illustrations are partly figurative and decorated with shields, banners, and badges. Originals: Latin version, London, College of Arms; English version, London, British Museum, ms. Additional 48976.

Clemens Specker's Austrian Chronicle, 1479

Contents: Eighty-two colored coats of arms of imaginary rulers. Original: Bern, Civic Library, ms. A 43.

Georg Edlibach, Zurich Chronicle, 1485

Contents: Thirty-three arms of the subject districts of Zurich and heraldically embellished scenes of battle (see above, page 31). Original: Zurich, Central Library, ms. A 75.

GENERAL ARMORIALS

1) PREPARED BY OR AT THE INSTIGATION OF HERALDS.

Wijnbergen Armorial, 1265–1288

Contents: 1,302 colored coats of arms with names above, mostly with Christian names, imaginary kings at the end. In French. Original: The Hague, Koninklijk Nederlandsche Genootschap voor Geslacht- en Wapenkunde. Published: In AHS 1951–1954, and independently (see above, page 29).

Walford's Roll, ca. 1273

Contents: 185 blazons in French. Original lost, several copies. Published: Aspilogia II, pp. 167–204.

Herald's Roll, ca. 1270–80

Contents: 892 painted coats of arms, some of them duplicated. Originals: London, College of Arms, ms. B 29, pp. 20–27; and Cambridge, Fitzwilliam Museum, ms. 297.

Camden Roll, ca. 1280

Contents: 270 painted coats of arms, with 185 corresponding descriptions in French on the versos. Original: London, British Museum, Cotton Roll XV, 8.

Segar's Roll, ca. 1282

Contents: 212 painted coats of arms. Evacuated in: The Genealogist, Vol. IV, London 1880.

Smallpece's Roll, ca. 1300

Contents: 168 painted shields.

Sir William le Neve's Roll, ca. 1300

Contents: 167 painted shields.

The Lord Marshal's Roll, ca. 1300

Contents: 588 painted shields.

The Lord Marshal's Roll Old, Part II, ca. 1300

Contents: Sixty-five shields of sovereigns.

Sir William le Neve's Second Roll, ca. 1320

Contents: 118 painted shields.

Cooke's Book, ca. 1320

Contents: Eighty-nine painted shields.

Ashmolean Roll, ca. 1334

Contents: 498 descriptions of arms, in French. Original: Oxford, Bodleian Library, ms. Ashmole 15 A.

Grimaldi's Roll, ca. 1350

Contents: 167 painted coats of arms with blazons in French. Original: Manchester, John Rylands Library, Western (French and Italian) ms. 88.

Bellenville Armorial, ca. 1364–1386

Contents: 1,722 armorial shields, 478 with helmets and crests relating to sovereigns (from the "tournament" section). Reports in the Recueil du IIe Congrès international des sciences généalogique et héraldique, Liège, 29 May – 2 June 1972.

Armorial de Gelre, 1370–1386

Contents: 1,755 achievements of arms in color (see above, pages 11, 26 f., 35, 121, 160). Original: Brussels, Royal Library, ms. 15652–56. Published: AHS 1961–1968, and independently.

Basygnes's Book, ca. 1395

Contents: 407 roughly painted shields. The part devoted to the English nobility arranged to some extent according to the charges. Original: London, College of Arms, ms. B 22, fol. 62–85 b.

Beijeren's Armorial, ca. 1400

Contents: 1,098 armorial shields accompanied by small banners indicating the armigers' military rank. Original: The Hague, Koninklijk Nederlandsche Genootschap voor Geslacht-en Wapenkunde. Quoted on numerous occaions, not treated at length.

Armorial de la Toison d'Or et de l'Europe, early fifteenth century

Original: Paris, Bibliothèque de l'Arsenal. Published: In facsimile, Paris 1890.

Armoriaux d'Urfé, ca. 1420

Original: Paris, Bibliothèque Nationale, ms. fr. 32.753. Publication in preparation.

The Lord Marshal's Roll Old, Part I, ca. 1420

Contents: Forty-seven painted armorial shields.

Ulster's Roll, ca. 1420

Contents: 672 painted shields. Original: Dublin, Genealogical Office, ms. 41, fol. 45–86.

Fenwick's Roll, ca. 1422

Contents: 1,035 painted shields including those of the Biblical three kings.

Armorial du héraut Sicile, 1425

Armorial of the Sicily herald. Contents: 1,976 armorial shields. Original lost, several old copies including: 1. Paris, Bibliothèque Nationale, ms. fr. 4366; 2. Paris, Bibliothèque de l'Arsenal, ms. 4910.

Bergshammar Armorial, ca. 1435

Contents: 3,388 arms with or without helmet and crest. Original: Stockholm, Riksarkivet, Bergshammarsamlingen. Published: Jan Raneke, "Bergshammarvapenboken," in *Medeltidsheraldisk studie,* Lund 1975.

Portcullis's Book, ca. 1440

Contents: Didactic sections as well as the usual illustrations. Original: British Museum, ms. Harley 521.

Gymnich Armorial, ca. 1445

Original: Brussels, Royal Library, ms. II, 6567 (Fonds Houwaert).

Bradfer-Lawrence's Roll, ca. 1450

Contents: Very comprehensive, including didactic sections. The arms are accompanied by helmets and crests. Original: In private hands.

Kings of Britain Roll, ca. 1450

Contents: 342 shields.

Dublin Roll, ca. 1450

Contents: 324 shields. Original: Dublin, Genealogical Office, ms. 7, fol. 28–324.

Hans Burggraf's Armorial, ca. 1450

Contents: Approximately 600 coats of arms. Original: London, British Museum, ms. Additional 15681.

Armorial No. 8769 in the National Library in Vienna, 1450–1460

Original: Vienna, National Library.

Armorial du Héraut Berry, 1454–1458

Armorial of Gilles le Bouvier, known as Berry, herald of King Charles VII of France. Contents: 1,953 painted shields. Original: Paris, Bibliothèque Nationale, ms. fr. 4985. Partially published.

Hans Ingeram's Armorial, 1459

Contents: Approximately 1,100 coats of arms. This armorial of the pursuivant Hans Ingeram served as a prototype for several later ones. Original: In private hands.

Armorial du héraut Hongrie, 1460–1466

Appendix to a heraldic treatise by the Hungary herald. Contents: several hundred blazons with war cries. Paper ms., Paris, Bibliothèque Nationale, ms. fr. 5242.

Mandeville Roll, ca. 1460

133 painted shields.

Miltenberg Armorial, late fifteenth century

Original: Paris, in private hands.

Randle Holme's Book, ca. 1470

Contents: A very comprehensive collection by an official heraldic artist; contains figures with crowns, helmets, and horses, also imaginary arms and arms of guilds. Original: British Museum, ms. Harley 2169.

London Roll, ca. 1470

Contents: 104 crudely painted shields including arms of London and of London corporations. Original: British Museum, ms. Additional 29502.

Ballard's Book, ca. 1465–90

Contents: Comprehensive collection by William Ballard, who became king-at-arms for the march of West England, Wales, and Cornwall. Original: London, College of Arms, ms. M.3. "Tiltinge."

Whrithe's Book, ca. 1480

Contents: Comprehensive. Original: London, College of Arms, ms. M.10 ("Coats in Colors"), fol. 71–190.

Peter le Neve's Book, ca. 1480–1500

Contents: 2,070 painted arms, including 296 in the form of a banner and 109 with helmet and crest. Original: British Museum, ms. Harl. 6163.

Ansbach Armorial, 1485–1490

Contents: The arms of exotic princes taken from the Book of the Council of Constance, otherwise largely of the southern German nobility. Original: Ansbach, Historical Association for Central Franconia.

Wernigerod (Schaffhausen) Armorial, ca. 1490

This is probably the best preserved armorial manuscript from the fifteenth century. The depictions of coats of arms are among the best of their time. Original: Munich, Otto Hupp Bequest.

Jörg Rugenn's Armorial, ca. 1492

Contents: Over 3,600 arms, including a large number of municipal ones (see above, page 227). Original: Innsbruck, University Library, ms. 545.

Sir William le Neve's Book, ca. 1500

Contents: 936 shields, the last six being municipal arms.

Livro Grande or *Armeiro-mor,* fifteenth century

Original: Lisbon, National Archives of Torre do Tombo. Published: In facsimile, Lisbon 1956. Historical and cultural analysis by Francisco de Simas Alves de Azevedo, Lisbon 1966.

Shirley's Roll, fifteenth century

Contents: 469 painted shields, an elaborately conceived achievement of

arms for the king of England. Original: In private hands.

Devereux Roll, fifteenth century

Contents: 180 painted coats of arms with descriptions in English. Original: Dublin, Trinity College, ms. E 5.30, fol. 87–95.

Rawlinson Roll, fifteenth century

Contents: Seventy-nine crude but powerfully painted shields. Original: Oxford, Bodleian Library, ms. Rawlinson B 107, fol. 26–35 b.

Gorrevod Armorial, late fifteenth century

Original: Brussels, Royal Library, ms. 6563.

Armorial No. 2936 in the National Library in Vienna, late fifteenth century

Contents: 445 coats of arms; the first armorial arranged alphabetically. Original: Vienna, National library.

2) PRIVATE COLLECTIONS.

Clipearius Teutonicorum, 1242–1249

Author: Conrad von Mure. Contents: Seventy-three blazons in Latin verse. Original lost, copies included in *Dialogus de nobilitate et rusticitate,* ed. Sebastian Brant, 1497; since then, frequently covered in the literature.

The Matthew Paris Shields, ca. 1244

Contents: Excerpts from the chronicles of Matthew (see above, pages 19, 63). Original: British Museum, ms. Cotton, Nero D 1, fol. 170–170 b.

Zurich Roll of Arms, ca. 1340

Contents: 450 coats of arms and twenty-eight banners (see above, pages 27, 116, 120, 136). Original: Zurich, Central Library, deposited in the Swiss National Museum. Published: In facsimile with commentaries, Zurich 1930.

The "Van den Ersten" Armorial, ca. 1380

Sketchbook. Contents: 450 coats of arms. Original lost in the Second World War, the last owner was the Heralds' Association in Berlin. Copy of 1578: Brussels, Arenberg Ducal Archives.

Uffenbach Armorial, late fourteenth century

Contents: 640 armorial shields. Original: Hamburg, State Library, ms. in scrinio 90 b.

Donaueschingen Armorial, 1433

Contents: Approximately 1,100 achievements of arms. Original: Donaueschingen, Library of the Prince of Fürstenberg.

Redinghoven's Armorial, 1440

Contents: 425 achievements of arms. Original: Munich, State Library, Cod. germ. 2214.

Stuttgart Armorial, 1430–1446

Original: Stuttgart, Main State Archive.

Scheibler Armorial, around 1450

Original: Munich, Bavarian State Library, Cod. icon. 312 c.

Gabelentz Armorial, ca. 1460

Contents: Mostly southern German nobility. Original: In private hands.

Palatinate Armorial, around 1460

Contents: 1,080 coats of arms. Original: Innsbruck, Tyrolean Society for the Registration of the Nobility.

Innsbruck Armorial, 1460–1470

Contents: 480 coats of arms. Original: Innsbruck, Tyrolean Society for the Registration of the Nobility.

Berlin Armorial, ca. 1460

Contents: Approximately 900 coats of arms. Original: Berlin, State Library, ms. geneal., fol. 271.

Armorial of St. Gallen (Haggenberg's Armorial), 1466–1470

Contents: Approximately 2,000 coats of arms. Original: St. Gallen, Monastery Library, Pap. cod., fol. 1084.

Grünwald Armorial, ca. 1470

Contents: Forty-eight achievements of arms and 467 armorial shields. Original: Munich, Bavarian National Museum, No. 3605.

Leipzig Compendium, ca. 1470

Original: Leipzig, University Library.

Armorial de Clément Prinsault, ca. 1470

An expansion by Clément Prinsault of the armorial of the Sicily herald, 1425 (see above). Original: Paris, Bibliothèque Nationale, ms. n. acq. fr. 1075 (36).

Eichstätt Armorial, 1474–1478

Contents: Approximately 2,000 coats of arms. Original: Eichstätt, State Library, cod. 704.

Conrad Grünenbergs, Ritters and Bürgers zu Konstanz, Wappenbuch, 1483

The armorial of Conrad Grünenberg, "knight and citizen of Constance." Contents: Approximately 2,000 coats of arms (see above, pages 128, 153, 161, 225). Original: Berlin, Private State Archives, Berlin-Dahlem. Contemporary copy: Munich, State Library. Published: In facsimile, Görlitz 1875.

REGIONAL ARMORIALS

Glover's Roll, ca. 1253–1258

Contents: 218 blazons in French, relating to England only, with sketchily drawn shields. Original lost, several copies. Published: *Aspilogia* II, pp. 89–159.

Dering Roll, ca. 1275

Contents: Shields of knights, mostly from Kent and Sussex, assembled on panels. Original: Private collection of Sir Anthony Wagner, Garter King of Arms, London.

Armorial du héraut Vermandois, 1280–1300

Contents: 130 blazons of high-ranking nobles and counts, 856 of ordinary lords, divided into marches. Original missing, copy of around 1400: Paris, Bibliothèque Nationale, ms. fr. 2249.

St. George's Roll, ca. 1285

Contents: 677 British coats of arms with blazons in French.

Charles's Roll, ca. 1285

Contents: 486 British coats of arms with blazons in French.

Collins's Roll, ca. 1295

Contents: 720 British coats of arms with blazons in French. Original: London, Society of Antiquaries, ms. 517.

Guillim's Roll, ca. 1295–1305

Contents: 148 British coats of arms with blazons in French.

Rôle d'Armes Chifflet-Prinet, 1297

Known since 1949 as the *Rôle d'armes de l'ost de Flandre* (see above, OCCASIONAL ROLLS).

Fife Roll, ca. 1300

Contents: Thirty-one painted shields of English families. Original: London, College of Arms, Muniment Room, Box 15, Roll 28.

Holland's Roll, ca. 1310

Contents: Ninety-four painted shields of English families.

The Great Parlamentary (Bannerets' Roll), ca. 1312

Contents: 1,100 blazons in French of the arms of the high nobility of England and the bannerets, arranged by counties. Original: British Museum, ms. Cotton, Caligula A XVIII, fol. 3–21b. Published on various occasions, including *The Genealogist,* New Series, Vols. XI, 1885, and XII, 1886.

Povey's Roll, ca. 1320

Contents: Eighty-two armorial shields of English nobles. Original: London, College of Arms, ms. B 29, fol. 29–38.

Balliol Roll, ca. 1332

Contents: The oldest collection of Scottish arms, painted. Original: Private collection of Sir Anthony Wagner.

Cooke's Ordinary, ca. 1340

The oldest register of armorial charges in the world. Contents: 646 shields bearing English family arms, with a banner inserted at each change of category. Original: Private collection of Sir Anthony Wagner.

Cosgrave's Ordinary, ca. 1340

Contents: 556 blazons in French with 219 explanations and illustrations, mottled edges.

Sixth Nobility Roll, ca. 1340

Contents: Seventy-one painted armorial shields of English lords. Original: British Museum, ms. Additional 29505.

Powell's Roll, ca. 1350

Contents: 672 painted shields. Original: Oxford, Bodleian Library, ms. Ashmole 804. IV.

Antiquaries' Roll, ca. 1360

Contents: 352 painted shields of English nobles. Original: Society of Antiquaries, ms. 136, Part I.

Sir George Calverley's Book, ca. 1350–1450

Contents: 350 painted shields of English nobles.

Bruce Roll, ca. 1370

Contents: Scottish arms and banners. Original: London, College of Arms, ms. 2nd L. 12, last fol.

Armorial du héraut Navarre, ca. 1370

By Martin Carbonnel, king-at-arms of King Charles the Bad of Navarra, 1368–1375. Armorial of the French nobility, divided into marches. Fifteenth-century copy, Paris, Bibliothèque Nationale, ms. fr. 14356. Published: Louis Douët d'Arcq, Paris 1859, 8°, 56 pp.

Armorial du Baillage de Senlis, ca. 1370

Arms of twenty-one vassals of the bailiwick of Senlis. Original: Paris, National Archives (P. 146). Published: *Bibliothèque de l'Ecole des Chartes,* Vol. XC, 1929, pp. 316–336.

Terrier des vassaux de comté de Clermont en Beauvaisis, 1373–1374

Contents: Approximately 1,700 painted coats of arms, divided according to feudal retinues. The bannerets have rectangular shields, the high-born esquires a shield and pennant, the ordinary nobility only a shield, and the gentry heart-shaped shields. Original: Paris, Bibliothèque Nationale, ms. fr. 20082. Partially published.

William Jenyns' Ordinary, ca. 1380

Contents: 1,161 painted shields including some banners of English families. Original: London, College of Arms, ms. Jenyns' Ordinary.

County Roll, ca. 1385

Contents: 696 mostly colored armorial shields of English families, arranged by counties.

Willement's Roll, ca. 1395

See below, ARMORIAL ROLLS OF CORPORATIONS.

Norfolk and Suffolk Roll, ca. 1400

Contents: 150 painted shields.

Thomas Jenyns' Book, ca. 1410

Shields arranged by ordinaries, with French blazons (see above, pages 30–31). Original: Queen Margaret's Version: London, British Museum, ms. Additional 40851.

"Rouen" Roll, ca. 1410

Incorrectly supposed to be the arms roll of the participants in the siege of Rouen. French blazons. Published: *Notes and Queries,* 6th series, Vol. II, 1880, Vol. III, 1881.

Visitation héraldique du pays de Caux, ca. 1415

Armorial of the lords of the region of Caux in Normandy, with family trees. Original: London, College of Arms, ms. M 19.

Bowyer's Book, ca. 1440

Contents: The arms of English families, including preheraldic ones, in three columns with English text, picture, and name. Original: London, College of Arms, ms. B 22, fol. 3–22.

Talbot Banners, ca. 1442

Contents: Fifteen armorial banners, quartered; the family of Talbot and others related by marriage to John Talbot, the first earl of Shrewsbury. Original: London, College of Arms, ms. B 29, fol. 8–17 b and 18.

Military Roll, before 1448

Contents: Pictures of jousting with each pair of riders heraldically fully equipped, with lance or sword, but only a wreath on the helmet. Original: London, British Museum, ms. Harley 4205.

Armorial de Guillaume Revel, ca. 1450

By Guillaume Revel, Auvergne herald in the service of Duke Charles I of Bourbon (d. 1456). Contents: 750 achievements of arms. Frequently made use of in literature. Fifteenth century original, 506 pages: Paris, Bibliothèque Nationale, ms. fr. 22297.

Armorial of the Austrian Dukes, ca. 1446

Contents: 141 achievements of arms, twenty-one armorial shields, four double coats of arms. Original: Vienna, State Archives, No. 157.

Red Book Roll, ca. 1450

Contents: 548 armorial shields of the English aristocracy. Original: London, College of Arms, ms. Vincent 164, fol. 176–93 b.

Lucy's Roll, ca. 1450

Contents: 282 painted shields of English families.

Clarence Roll, ca. 1450

Contents: 102 painted shields of the English upper nobility.

Atkinson's Roll, ca. 1450

Contents: Eighty-eight descriptions of arms of the English upper nobility, English blazons. Original: London, British Museum, ms. Harley 1408, fol. 107–108b, 105–106b, 109.

Portington's Roll, ca. 1450

The connection between the three parts remains unclear; almost entirely arms of English families, but also of the City of London.

Noms et armes des seigneurs et gentilshommes présents aux montres générales du Duché de Bretagne, 1455–1458

Armorial of the participants in the general reviews of Brittany. Original: Paris, Bibliothèque Nationale, ms. fr. 5506.

Clare Roll, ca. 1456

Contents: Eleven coats of arms painted partly with gold; the members of the Clare family and their wives, 1248–1456. Original: London, College of Arms, Box 21, No. 16.

Ditiers faits et armoriés pour des noces de nobles bourgeois et pour la confrérie des Damoiseaux de cette ville, ca. 1460

Marriage poem composed by Engherant le France, herald of Valenciennes between 1459 and 1468, illustrated with coats of arms. Published: Society of Belgian Bibliophiles, No. 18, Mons 1856, 8°, 87 pp.

Second Segar Roll, ca. 1460

Contents: 150 painted arms of English families.

Friar Brackley's Book, ca. 1440–1460

Contents: Seventy-three painted shields from the kinship of the Paston family. Original: In private hands.

Starkey's Roll, ca. 1460

Known from three copies, contains at least 1,124 sketched shields of English families.

Gossenbrot Family Book, ca. 1469

Contents: Eighty-five well drawn armorial shields of Augsburg families and the relations of the Gossenbrot family. Original: Munich, State Library, Cod. mon. germ. 98.

Tregoz Roll, late fifteenth century

Contents: Painted half-round shields without blazons, relating to the Tregoz and Grandison families. Original: London, College of Arms, Muniment Room, Box 21, No. 11.

Domville Roll, ca. 1470

Contents: 284 arms of English families, including some with "color on color." Original: In private hands.

Sir John Fenn's Book of Badges, ca. 1470

Contents: Fifty-seven painted

badges. Original: London, British Museum, ms. Additional 40742.

Gentry Roll, ca. 1480

Contents: Thirty-six shields of English families. Published: *Walford's Antiquarian Magazine and Bibliographer,* Vol. II, London 1882.

Conrad Grünenberg's Austrian Chronicle, ca. 1480

Contents: Eleven achievements of arms, seventy arms of alliance and fourteen triple groups; arms of the Austrian rulers from approximately 850 to 1484, the oldest being imaginary arms. Original: Vienna, State Archives.

Nassau-Vianden Codex, ca. 1480

Contents: Dynastic arms of the Middle and Lower Rhine. Original: Munich, estate of Otto Hupp.

Basel Armorial, ca. 1480

Contents: Twenty-eight achievements of arms from the Lake Constance area. Original: Basel, University Library, ms. O. III 47.

Genealogy of the Counts and Dukes of Cleves, 1467–1481

Contents: Arms of the members of the house of Cleves. Original: Cleves, Municipal Archives.

Koch Armorial, ca. 1490

Contents: 320 leaves with four achievements of arms or six shields on each side. In the middle of the page stands a herald. Original: Basel, University Library, ms. O.I. 13.

Gerold Edlibach's Armorial, ca. 1493

Arms of families from Zurich and environs. Original: Zurich, Antiquarian Society, deposited in State Archives.

Armorial of Gallus Öhem, ca. 1496

Contents: Arms relating to the monastery of Reichenau. Original: Freiburg im Breisgau, University Library.

Cottonian Roll, fifteenth century

Contents: 461 armorial shields, of dubious value as sources in view of the uncertain dating. Original: London, British Museum, ms. Cotton, Tiberius E VIII, fol. 104–108.

Leipzig Armorial, late fifteenth century.

Contents: Chiefly noble participants in tournaments from the Upper Rhine district. Original: Leipzig, Municipal Library, Sig. 11, 12ᵉ, 164.

Netherlandish Armorial, late fifteenth century

Contents: Chiefly arms from the region around Delft. Original: Münster, Municipal Archives.

Painted Armorial of the Munich State Library, ca. 1500

Contents: Chiefly arms from the region around Passau. Original: Munich, Bavarian State Library, Cod. icon. 309.

Collingborne's Book, late fifteenth century

Contents: A large number of painted arms explicable in contemporary terms. Source: London, College of Arms, ms. B 22, fol. 50–60 and 26–49.

Le Neve's Equestrian Book, late fifteenth century

Contents: Eighty-eight figures of knights on horseback, described in English. Original: In private hands.

Armorial from Breisgau, late fifteenth century

Contents: Arms from the Upper Rhine district. Original: In private hands.

St. Gallen Roll, late fifteenth century

Contents: Chiefly arms from the general district of Lake Constance. Original: St. Gallen, State Archives.

Armorial d'Assignies, ca. 1500

Contents: Arms and *cris de guerre* of thirty-one knights of Flanders, Hainault, Artois, and Cambrésis. Published: A. Dinaux, in *Archives historiques et littéraires du Nord de la France et du Midi de la Belgique,* Vol. IV (Vol. VIII of the collection), 1842, pp. 5–26.

Livro da Nobreza, 1541

Contents: Achievements of arms of Portuguese nobles. Original: Lisbon, National Archives of Torre do Tombo.

ARMORIAL ROLLS OF CORPORATIONS

Register of arms of the burghers of the electorate of Trier, ca. 1345

Contents: 258 armorial shields arranged by boroughs, painted on the back of the *Chronicle of the Emperor Henry VII's Journey to Rome* (the so-called *Balduineum*). Original: Coblenz, State Archives.

Fief Book of the Monastery of Murbach, ca. 1350

Contents: Arms of feudal tenants, mostly from Alsace. Original: Colmar, Archives Départementales.

Willement's Roll, ca. 1395

Contents: Twenty-five shields of the founding knights of the Order of the Garter, surrounded by the sash of the order; followed by 576 shields of English aristocrats.

Necrology of the Viennese Minorites (Requesta Sepulchrorum), late fourteenth century

Contents: Chiefly the arms of benefactors of the monastery. Original: Vienna, Municipal Collection.

Cofraria dos Cavaleiros de Santiago, Burgos, from the fourteenth century

Contents: Representations of the members of the brotherhood of knights of Santiago on horseback, in full heraldic array. Original: Burgos, State Archives.

Books of the Brotherhood of St. Christopher on the Arlberg, early fifteeth century

Contents: Arms of members scattered throughout the German-speaking area. Main original: Vienna, Österreichisches Haus-, Hof- und Staatsarchiv.

Necrology of the Franciscans in Landshut, from 1400

Contents: Arms of the founders of the monastery. Original: Munich, Main State Archives, Ref. Franziskaner-Orden A. 3, Landshut.

Erfurter University Register, from 1420

Contents: Outstanding painted arms of the rector, with four ancestors' arms, and enrolled students from all social levels. Original: Erfurt, Municipal Archives, Cod. Erfurt, fol. 104. Some of the sheets published separately on numerous occasions.

Necrology of the Franciscan Monastery in Munich, from 1424

Contents: Portraits of the donors of requiem masses with their arms (see above, page 28). Original: Munich, Franciscan Monastery.

Wappenbüchlein E.(iner) E.(hrbaren) Zunft zu Pfistern in Luzern, 1428

Arms booklet of an honorable guild at Pfistern in Lucerne. Contents: Arms of the members of the guild. Original: Lucerne, Civic Library.

Bruges' Garter Book, ca. 1430

Contents: Twenty-six colored representations of the founding knights of the Order of the Garter. The author, William Bruges (d. 1450), was the first king-at-arms of the Order of the Garter (see above, page 21). The first British armorial of which the author is known by name. Original: London, British Museum, Stowe 594.

Anniversary Book of Elgg, ca. 1439–1465

Contents: Twenty-one unpretentiously drawn armorial shields, mostly of bourgeois families of Elgg. Original: Elgg, Zivilgemeinde, Archiv III, 39 or 72.

Fief Book of the Bishopric of Basel, 1441

Contents: Arms of the feudal tenants of the bishopric. Original: Karlsruhe, Family archive of the grand-ducal house of Baden.

Armorial de l'ordre du Croissant, ca. 1450

Armorial of the members of the Order of the Crescent, founded by René of Anjou in 1448. sixteenth century manuscript: Paris, Bibliothèque Nationale, ms. fr. 5225.

Fief Book of the Bishopric of Speyer, 1465

Contents: Arms of the feudal tenants of the bishopric. Original: Karlsruhe, General Regional Archives, Kopialbücher, 300.
Published: By Karl Freiherr von Neuenstein, *Wappenkunde,* 4th year, 1896.

Basel University Register, Vol. I, from 1460

Contents: Outstanding drawings of arms of the rectors of the university. Original: Basel, University Library, MSA N II 3–4a.

Fief Book of Elector Frederick I of the Palatinate, 1471

Contents: Arms of the Elector's vassals, not very skilfully drawn. Original: Karlsruhe, General Regional Archives, Kopialbuch 1057. The arms were traced and published in lithographic reproductions by Karl Freiherr von Neuenstein, Karlsruhe 1892.

Anniversary Book of Uster, 1469–1473

Contents: Approximately sixty briskly drawn arms from the kinship of the Landenberg-Greifensee and Bonstetten families, also shields of bourgeois and peasant families. Original: Zurich, Central Library, ms. I 703.

Heralds Book of the Jülich Order of St. Hubert, 1480

Contents: Over 1,000 achievements of arms and more than 100 shields, mostly ancestral arms of the knights of the order. Original: Berlin, State Library, ms. germ., Quart 1479.

Fief Book of Count Kraft VI of Hohenlohe, 1476–1503

Contents: Ancestral arms from the kinship of Count Kraft VI. Original: Waldenburg, Princely Hohenlohe Archives.

Necrology of the Franciscans in Bamberg, from 1486

Contents: Approximately 210 colored arms of the benefactors of the monastery. Original: Bamberg, Historical Society for Upper Franconia.

Armorial de l'ordre de Notre-Dame de la Table ronde de Bourges, 1486–1508

Armorial of the civic "round table" at Bourges. Seventeenth-century copy: Bourges, Carpentras Library, ms. 1793, fol. 627–629.
Published: Bourges 1837, 8°, 20 pp.

Writhe's Garter Book, ca. 1488

Constituted similarly to *Willement's Roll* (see above). Original: Private collection of the duke of Buccleuch.

Basel Grave Book, ca. 1490

Contents: Arms of the founders of seasonal masses. Original: Karlsruhe, General Regional Archives, Anniversa 4.

Brotherhood Book of the Order of St. Hubert, late fifteenth century

Contents: Arms of the knights of the order with their ancestral arms. Original: Munich, Bavarian State Library, Cod. icon. 318.

Armorial of the "Zur Katze" society, Constance, 1547

Published: Karl Freiherr von Neuenstein, Karlsruhe 1904. Republished: One color plate with 159 coats of arms, Constance 1904.

BIBLIOGRAPHY

The order is chronological within sections unless otherwise indicated.

GENERAL

Bernd, Christian Samuel Theodor. *Allgemeine Schriftenkunde der gesamten Wappenwissenschaft,* 4 vols. Bonn, 1830–41.

Classed Catalogue of books on Heraldry. London, 1912.

Berchem, Egon Frhr. v. *Heraldische Bibliographie (Familiengeschichtliche Bibliographie,* Vol. V). Leipzig, 1937; reprint Neustadt, 1972.

Saffroy, Gaston. *Bibliographie généalogique, héraldique et nobiliaire de la France,* 3 vols. Paris, 1968–74.

Achen, Sven Tito, and Ole Rostock. *Bibliografi over heraldisk litteratur i Danmark og om Danmark 1589–1969.* Christiansfeld, 1971.

MANUALS AND GUIDES TO HERALDRY

Bara, Hierosme de. *Le Blason des Armoiries.* Lyon, 1581; reprint Paris, 1975.

Böckler, Georg Andreas. *Ars Heraldica.* Nuremberg, 1688; reprint Graz, 1971.

Spener, Philipp Jakob. *Insignium theoria (Opus heraldicum, pars generalis).* Frankfurt, 1690.

Rudolphi, J.A. *Heraldica curiosa.* Nuremberg, 1698.

Rietstap, J.B. *Handboek der Wapenkunde.* Leyden, 1856; 3rd ed. (Cornelis Pama, ed.) 1943.

Sacken, Eduard Frhr. v. *Katechismus der Heraldik.* Leipzig, 1862; 8th ed. 1920.

Hildebrandt, Adolf Matthias. *Wappenfibel.* Berlin, 1887; 14th ed. 1943; 15th and 16th ed., as *Wappenfibel, Handbuch der Heraldik,* Neustadt, 1967 and 1970.

Seyler, Gustav Adelbert. *Geschichte der Heraldik (J. Siebmacher's Grosses Wappenbuch,* Vol. A). Nuremberg, 1890; reprint Neustadt, 1970.

Keller, Alfred von. *Leitfaden der Heraldik.* Berlin, 1891; 2nd ed. 1908.

Hauptmann, Felix. *Das Wappenrecht.* Bonn, 1896.

Ströhl, Hugo Gerard. *Heraldischer Atlas.* Stuttgart, 1899.

Gritzner, Maximilian. *Heraldik (Grundriss der Geschichtswissenschaft,* ed. Aloys Meister, Vol. I, Part 4). Leipzig, 1906; 2nd ed. 1912.

Hauptmann, Felix. "Wappenkunde," in *Handbuch der Mittelalterlichen und Neueren Geschichte,* ed. G. von Below and F. Meinecke. Munich and Berlin, 1914.

Fox-Davies, Arthur Charles. *A Complete Guide to Heraldry.* London, 1909; revised and annotated by J.P. Brooke-Little, *1969.*

Galbreath, Donald Lindsay, and H. de Vevey. *Manuel d'Héraldique.* Lausanne, 1922.

Philippi, Friedrich. *Wappen, Versuch einer gemeinfasslichen Wappenlehre.* Dortmund, 1922.

Gevaert, Émile. *L'héraldique, son esprit, son language et ses applications.* Brussels, 1923.

Beck, Edward. *Grundfragen der Wappenlehre und des Wappenrechts.* Speyer, 1931.

Galbreath, Donald Lindsay. *Handbüchlein der Heraldik.* Lausanne, 1931; 2nd ed. 1948.

Le Juge de Segrais. *Resumo da Ciência do Brasão.* Lisbon, 1951.

Moncreiffe, Iain, and Don Pottinger. *Simple Heraldry, Cheerfully Illustrated.* London and Edinburgh, 1953; 10th impr. 1963.

Neubecker, Ottfried. *Wie finde ich ein Familienwappen.* Berlin, 1956.

Pama, Cornelis. *Handboek der Wapenkunde – J.B. Rietstap.* 2nd ed. Leyden, 1961.

Almeida Langhans, Franz Paul de. *Heráldica – ciência de temas vivos.* Lisbon, 1966.

Neubecker, Ottfried. *Kleine Wappenfibel.* Constance, 1969.

Zmajić, Bartol. *Heraldika, sfragistika, genealogia.* Zagreb, 1971.

Zenger, Zdeněk M. *Heraldika.* Prague, 1971.

Volborth, Carl Alexander von. *Heraldik aus aller Welt in Farben.* Berlin, 1972.

Sturdza-Săucesti, Marcel. *Heraldica, Tratat tehnic.* Bucharest, 1974.

Galbreath, Donald Lindsay. *Manuel du Blason.* Lausanne, 1942; revised by Léon Jéquier, 1976.

REGIONAL GUIDES

Zieber, Eugene. *Heraldry in America.* Philadelphia, 1895.

Arendt, Léon, and Alfred de Ridder. *Législation héraldique de la Belgique 1595–1895, Jurisprudence du Conseil Héraldique 1844–1895.* Brussels, 1896.

Ströhl, Hugo Gerard. *Japanisches Wappenbuch "Nihon Moncho."* Vienna, 1906.

Lukomskii, W.K., and Baron N.A. Tiepolt. *Russkaja geraldika.* Petrograd, 1915.

Grandjean, Poul Bredo. *Dansk Heraldik,* Copenhagen, 1919.

Fourez, Lucien. *Le droit héraldique dans les Pays-Bas catholiques.* Brussels, 1932.

Ewald, Walter. *Rheinische Heraldik.* Düsseldorf, 1934.

Waltz, Jean-Jacques. *L'art héraldique en Alsace.* Nancy, 1937, 1938, and 1949; reprint 1975.

Lindgren, Uno. *Heraldik i svenska författningar.* Lund, 1951.

Wagner, Anthony R. *Historic Heraldry of Britain.* London, New York, and Toronto, 1939; reprint London and Chichester, 1972.

—— *Heraldry in England.* London, 1946; reprint 1949.

Mathieu, Rémi. *Le système héraldique français.* Paris, 1946.

Innes, Thomas. *Scots Heraldry.* Edinburgh, 1956.

Kamentseva, E.I. and N.V. Ustjugov. *Russkaja sfragistika i geral'dika.* Moscow, 1963; 2nd ed. 1974.

Gumowski, Marian. *Handbuch der polnischen Heraldik.* Graz, 1969.

SOCIOLOGICAL THEMES

Knötel, Paul. *Bürgerliche Heraldik.* Tarnowitz, 1902; 3rd ed. Breslau, 1922.

Freier, Walter. *Der Rechtsschutz des bürgerlichen Familienwappens.* Greifswald, 1920.

Franklyn, Charles A. *Heraldry Simplified, with Especial Reference to the Bearing of Arms by Women.* Baltimore, 1973 (reprint of *The Bearing of Coat Armour by Ladies,* London, 1923).

Bauer, Konrad Friedrich. *Das Bürgerwappen.* Frankfurt, 1935.

Reise, Heinz. *Vom Wappenwesen und Wappenschwindel.* Göttingen, 1948.

Heim, Bruno Bernard. *Wappenbrauch und Wappenrecht in der Kirche.* Olten, 1947.

—— *Coutumes et Droit héraldiques de l'Eglise.* Paris, 1949.

Rabbow, Arnold. *dtv-Lexikon politischer Symbole A-Z.* Munich, 1970.

Herman, Leonard. *Die Heraldik der Wirtschaft.* Düsseldorf and Vienna, 1971.

Wagner, Anthony R. *Pedigree and Progress.* London, 1975.

MONOGRAPHS ON THE EARLIEST HISTORY OF HERALDRY

Ganz, Paul. *Geschichte der heraldischen Kunst in der Schweiz im XII. und XIII. Jhdt.* Frauenfeld, 1899.

Berchem, Egon Frhr. von, Donald Lindsay Galbreath, and Otto Hupp. "Die Wappenbücher des deutschen Mittelalters," in *S.A.H.* 1925, 1926, 1928 (also as off-prints).

——, and Kurt Mayer. *Beiträge zur Geschichte der* Heraldik. Berlin, 1939; reprint, as *J. Siebmacher's Grosses Wappenbuch,* Vol. D, Neustadt, 1972.

Ulmenstein, Christian Ulrich Frhr. von. *Über Ursprung und Entstehung des Wappenwesens.* Weimar, 1935; reprint 1941.

Wagner, Sir Anthony (ed.). *Aspilogia, Being Materials of Heraldry: I. A Catalogue of English Mediaeval Rolls of Arms; II. Rolls of Arms of Henry III.* London, 1950 and 1957.

Alves de Azevedo, Francisco de Sivas. *Uma Interpretação históricocultural do Libro do Armeiro-mor.* Lisbon, 1966.

Raneke, Jan. *Bergshammar Vapenboken – en medeltidsheraldisk studie.* Lund, 1975.

Centre national de la recherche scientifique. *Cahiers d'Heraldique,* Vols. I and II. Paris, 1975 et seq.

TERMINOLOGY

Querfurth, Curt O. von. *Kritisches Wörterbuch der heraldischen Terminologie.* Nördlingen, 1872; reprint, as *Heraldische Terminologie,* Wiesbaden, 1969.

Elvin, Charles Norton. *A Dictionary of Heraldry.* London, 1889; reprint 1969.

Gritzner, Maximilian. *Handbuch der heraldischen Terminologie in zwölf Zungen (Sb.Wb. Einleitungsband,* Part B). Nuremberg, 1890.

Neubecker, Ottfried. *Deutsch und Französisch für Heraldiker.* Berlin, 1934.

Stalins, Gaston. *Vocabulaire-Atlas héraldique en six langues.* Paris, 1952.

Brault, Gerard J. *Early Blazon: Heraldic Terminology in the Twelfth and Thirteenth Centuries.* London, 1971.

SPECIAL MONOGRAPHS

Michelsen, A.L.J. *Über die Ehrenstücke und den Rautenkranz als historische Probleme der Heraldik.* Jena, 1854.

Homeyer, Karl Gustav. *Die Haus- und Hofmarken.* Berlin, 1870; 2nd ed. 1890; reprint Aalen, 1967.

Hohenlohe-Waldenburg, Friedrich-Karl Fürst zu. *Das heraldische Pelzwerk.* Stuttgart, 1876.

Warnecke, Friedrich. *Die mittelalterlichen heraldischen Kampfschilde in der St.-Elisabeth-Kirche zu Marburg.* Berlin, 1884.

Dielitz, J. *Die Wahl- und Denksprüche…* Frankfurt, 1884.

Leist, F. *Notariatssignete.* Leipzig and Berlin, 1896.

Ströhl, Hugo Gerard. "Beiträge zur Geschichte der Badges," in *Jb. der K. K. heraldischen Gesellschaft "Adler" N.F.,* Vol. XII. Vienna, 1902, pp. 75–113.

273

Fox-Davies, Arthur Charles. *Heraldic Badges*. London, 1906.

Hupp, Otto. *Wider die Schwarmgeister*. Munich, 1918; many editions.

Arntz, Helmut. *Die Runenschrift: Ihre Geschichte und ihre Denkmäler*. Halle, 1938.

Ruppel, Karl Konrad A. *Die Hausmarke, Das Symbol der germanischen Sippe*. Berlin, 1939.

Stalins, Gaston. *Histoire, généalogie et alliances des Stalins de Flandre... et quelques considérations sur le briquet héraldique*, 2 vols. Privately printed, 1939 and 1945.

Nickel, Helmut. *Der mittelalterliche Reiterschild des Abendlandes*. Berlin, 1958.

Spruth, Herbert. *Die Hausmarke, Wesen und Bibliographie*. Neustadt, 1960.

Wulff, Aage. "Vaser, Liljer og Kroner i heraldiken," offprint from *Vaabenhistoriske Aarbøger XIII*. Copenhagen, 1966.

Henkel, A., and A. Schöne. *Emblemata, Handbuch zur Sinnbildkunde des 16. und 17. Jahrhunderts*. Stuttgart, 1967.

Dennys, Rodney. *The Heraldic Imagination*. London, 1975.

HERALDIC ART

Amman, Jost: *Stamm- und Wappenbuch*. Frankfurt, 1579; reprint ed. Friedrich Warnecke, Görlitz, 1872.

Hildebrandt, Ad. Matthias. *Heraldisches Musterbuch*. Berlin, 1872; 3rd ed. 1897; reprint Neustadt, 1975.

Warnecke, Friedrich. *Heraldische Kunstblätter*, 4 parts. Görlitz, 1876–1898; 2nd ed. 1890 et seq.

Doepler, Emil d.J. *Heraldischer Formenschatz, Kunstblätter vom 15. Jahrhundert bis zur neuesten Zeit*. Berlin, 1898 (cf. Warnecke, Friedrich, *Heraldische Kunstblätter*, Part 4).

Stückelberger, Ernst Alfred. *Das Wappen in Kunst und Gewerbe*. Zurich, 1901.

Hope, W.H. *Heraldry for Craftsmen and Designers*. London, 1913.

Kretschmar, H.A. von. *Anleitung zur Darstellung von Wappen*. Dresden, 1913.

Hupp, Otto. "Wappenkunst und Wappenkunde," in *Geschichte der Heraldik*. Munich, 1927.

Hussmann, Heinrich. *Über deutsche Wappenkunst, Aufzeichnungen aus meinen Vorlesungen*. Wiesbaden, 1973.

Leonhard, Walter. *Das grosse Buch der Wappenkunst*. Munich, 1976.

COLLECTIONS OF PUBLIC HERALDRY

Order is chronological within geographical areas (listed alphabetically).

General

Germany:

Solis, Virgil. *Wappenbüchlein*. Nuremberg, 1556; facsimile Munich, 1886.

Schrot Martin. *Wappenbuch des Heiligen Römischen Reichs und allgemeiner Christenheit...* Munich, 1581; reprint Unterschneidheim, 1975.

Siebmacher, Johann. *Grosses und allgemeines Wappenbuch (S.W.)*, Vol. I Nuremberg, 1854–1961; reprint Neustadt, from 1970.

Jäger-Sunstenau, Hanns. *General-Index, Zu den Siebmacherschen Wappenbüchern 1905–1961*. Graz, 1964.

Great Britain:

Fox-Davies, Arthur Charles. *The Book of Public Arms*. London and Edinburgh, 1915.

World:

Rentzmann, Walter, and Ottfried Neubecker. *Wappen-Bilder-Lexikon*. Munich, 1974.

Arms of States

Austria:

Ströhl, Hugo Gerard. *Österreichisch-ungarische Wappenrolle*. Vienna, 1894; 2nd ed. 1899.

Germany:

Ströhl, Hugo Gerard. *Deutsche Wappenrolle*. Stuttgart, 1897.

Posse, Otto. *Die Siegel der deutschen Kaiser und Könige, 759–1913*. Dresden, 1909–1913.

Great Britain:

Willement, Thomas. *Regal Heraldry*. London, 1821.

Wyon, A.B. *The Great Seals of England*. London, 1887.

Pinches, J.H. and R.V. *The Royal Heraldry of England*. London, 1974.

De Gray Birch, Walter. *History of Scottish Seals*, 2 vols. Stirling and London, 1905.

Netherlands:

Laars, T. van der. *Wapens, Vlaggen en Zegels van Nederland*. Amsterdam, 1913.

Papal:

Galbreath, Donald Lindsay. *Papal Heraldry*. Cambridge, 1930; 2nd ed. revised by Geoffrey Briggs, London, 1972.

South Africa:

Pama, Cornelis. *Lions and Virgins. Heraldic State Symbolism in South Africa 1487–1962*, Cape Town and Pretoria, 1965.

World:

Heyer von Rosenfeld, Friedrich. *Die Staatswappen der bekanntesten Länder der Erde*. 10th ed. Frankfurt, 1895.

Ruhl, Jul. M., and Alfred Starke. *Die Wappen aller souveränen Länder der Erde*. 10th ed. Leipzig, 1928.

Smith, Whitney. *Flags Through the Ages and Across the World*. Maidenhead, 1975.

Civic Heraldry

Austria:

Ströhl, Hugo Gerard. *Städtewappen von Österreich-Ungarn*. Vienna, 1904.

Belgium:

Servais, Max. *Armorial des provinces et des communes de Belgique*. Brussels, 1955.

Czechoslovakia:

Novák, Jozef. *Slovenské mestské a obecné erby*. Pressburg, 1967; 2nd ed. 1972.

Ruda, Vladimír, et al. *Znaky severočeských měst*. Most, 1970.

Finland:

Municipal Coats of Arms of Finland. Helsinki and Helsingfors, 1970.

Germany:

Hupp, Otto. *Wappen und Siegel der deutschen Städte, Flecken und Dörfer*. Frankfurt, 1895–1912; Speier, 1930.

Neubecker, Ottfried. *Deutsche Städtewappen aus Ost und West*. Memmingen (1955).

Demandt, Karl E. and Otto Renkhoff. *Hessisches Ortswappenbuch*. Glücksburg, 1956.

Stadler, Klemens. *Deutsche Wappen*, 8 vols. Bremen, 1964–1971.

Great Britain:

Scott-Giles, C. Wilfried. *Civic Heraldry of England and Wales*. London, 1933; 2nd ed. 1953.

Hungary:

Széll, Sándor. *Városaink neve címere és lobogója*. Budapest, 1941.

Italy:

Prünster, Hans. *Die Wappen der Gemeinden Südtirols*. Bozen, 1972.

Netherlands:

Rünckel, A. *Nederlandsche Wapens van het Rijk, de Provinciën en de Gemeenten...* 2 vols. De Bilt, 1941 and 1943.

Druif, C. *Nederlandse Gemeentewapens*. Leeuwarden, 1965.

Poland:

Gumowski, Marian. *Najstarsze pieczecie miast polskich XIII i XIV wieku*. Toruń, 1960.

Portugal:

Almeida Langhans, Franz Paul de. *Armorial do Ultramar Português* Lisbon, 1966 et seq.

Rumania:

Cernovodeanu, Dan, and Ioan N. Manescu. "Noile steme ale judeţelor şi municipiilor din Republica Socialistă România, studia asupra dezvoltării istorice a heraldicii districtuale şi municipale Românesti" – "Les nouvelles armoiries des districts et des villes (municipes) de la République Socialiste de Roumanie, Étude sur le développement historique de l'héraldique de district et municipale Roumaine," in *Revista Arhivelor*, Anul 51, Vol. 36, Nos. 1–2. Two languages. Bucharest, 1974.

Sweden:

Scheffer, C. Gunnar U. *Svensk vapenbok för landskap, län och städer*. Stockholm, 1967.

U.S.A.:

Chapin, Howard M. *Civic Heraldry, a Roll of Arms of Cities and Towns in the United States*. Providence, R.I., 1935.

U.S.S.R.:

Winkler, P.P. von. *Gerby gorodov, gubernii, oblastei i posadov Rossiiskoi Imperii... s 1649 po 1900 god*. St. Petersburg, 1900.

Speransov, N.N. *Zemel'nye Gerby Rossii XII–XIX vv. Coats of Arms of Russian Principalities. Les armoiries des villes de la Russie, Russische Länder-Wappen*. Four languages. Moscow, 1974.

World:

Armorial Vignettes. Kaffee HAG (ed.). Bremen and subsidiary companies in Austria, Belgium, Czechoslovakia, Denmark, France, Germany, Great Britain, Netherlands, Norway, Poland, Sweden, Yugoslavia, 1913 et seq.

Corporate Heraldry

Germany:

Gritzner, Maximilian. *Die Siegel der deutschen Universitäten (S.W.,* Vol. I, Part 8). Nuremberg, 1904.

Gaisberg-Schöckingen, Friedrich Frhr. von. *Die Wappen der deutschen Korporationen des In- und Auslandes (Das Akademische Deutschland,* Vol. IV). Berlin, 1931.

Seyler, G.A. *Berufswappen (S.W.,* Vol. I, Part 7). Nuremberg, 1895 et seq.

Ströhl, Hugo Gerard. *Die Wappen der Buchgewerbe.* Vienna, 1891.

Portugal:

Brasonário corporativo. Lisbon, 1955.

Almeida Langhans, F.P. de. *Manual de heráldica corporativa.* Lisbon, 1956.

Ecclesiastical Heraldry

France:

Saint Sand, Comte de. *Armorial des Prélats français du XIXe siècle.* Paris, 1906–08.

Meurgey de Tupigny, Jacques. *Armorial de l'Eglise de France.* Mâcon, 1938.

Germany:

Seyler, G.A. *Bistümer, Klöster (S.W.,* Vol. I, Part 5, Nos. 1 and 2). Nuremberg, 1881–82; reprint Neustadt, 1976 as S.W., Vol. 8, *Die Wappen der Bistümer und Klöster.*

Kissel, Clemens. *Wappen-Buch des deutschen Episcopates.* Frankfurt, 1891.

Zimmermann, Eduard. *Bayerische Klosterheraldik.* Munich, 1930.

Schröder, Brigitte. *Mainfränkische Klosterheraldik.* Würzburg, 1971.

Kolb, Peter. *Die Wappen der Würzburger Fürstbischöfe.* Würzburg, 1974.

Arms of Families

Austria:

Fischnaler, Konrad. *Tirolisch-Vorarlberg'scher Wappenschlüssel.* Innsbruck, 1938–1951.

Denmark:

Achen, Sven Tito. *Danske adelsvåbener, En heraldiske nøgle.* Copenhagen, 1973.

France:

Jouglas de Morénas. *Grand Armorial de France.* Paris, 1934–1952.

Germany:

Siebmacher, Johann. *Wappenbuch (S.W.).* Nuremberg, 1854–1976.

Hupp, Otto. *Münchener Kalender, 1885–1932, 1934–36.*

Wappensammlung in Buntdruck des Verlages J. Perthes. Gotha, 1913 et seq.

Closs, Gustav Adolf. *Deutscher Wappenkalender 1920–1936.* Görlitz, 1919–1935.

Kuodt, Hermann. *Hessisches Wappenbuch,* Part 1. Görlitz, 1934.

Hübner, Otto. *Mühlhäuser Wappenbuch.* Görlitz, 1934.

Deutsche Wappenrolle. Vols. I–V and VIII, Leipzig, 1935–1939; Vols, VI, VII, IX et seq. Neustadt, 1956 et seq.

Kenfenheuer, Johann Josef. *Alphabetisches Namensregister bürgerlicher deutscher Wappenvorkommen.* Cologne, 1937.

Schellenberg, Alfred. *Schlesisches Wappenbuch,* Vol. I. Görlitz, 1938.

Kuschbert, Paul. *Haus- und Hofmarken, Handwerkerzeichen.* Cologne, 1941.

Zimmermann, Eduard. *Augsburger Zeichen und Wappen.* Augsburg, 1970.

Allgemeine Deutsche Wappenrolle, Vol. 1. Berlin, 1971.

Great Britain:

Papworth, John W. *Ordinary of British Armorials.* London, 1874; reprint London, 1961.

Burke, Bernard. *The General Armory of England, Scotland, Ireland, and Wales.* London, 1880.

Fox-Davies, Arthur-Charles. *Armorial Families,* 2 vols. London, 1929.

Luxembourg:

Loutsch, Jean-Claude. *Armorial du Pays de Luxembourg.* Luxembourg, 1974.

Netherlands:

Raadt, J.-Th. de. *Sceaux armoriés des Pays-Bas et des pays avoisinants.* Brussels, 1898–1903.

Norway:

Cappelen, Hans A.K.T. *Norske slektsvapen.* Oslo, 1969.

Scandinavia:

Skandinavisk vapenrulla. Malmö, 1963 et seq.

South Africa:

Pama, Cornelis. *Heraldry of South African Families.* Cape Town, 1972.

Spain:

Nobiliario de Conquistadores de India. Madrid, 1892.

Colección de Documentos inéditos para la histora de Hispano-América. Vol. II: Nobiliario Hispano-Americano del siglo XVI, por Santiago Montoto; Nobiliario de Reinos, Ciudades y Villas de la América Española, por Santiago Montoto. Madrid, 1928.

Sweden:

Klingspor, Carl Arcid. *Sveriges Ridderskaps och Adels Vapenbok.* Stockholm, 1897.

Switzerland:

Nearly all cantons have a special armory of their own.

U.S.A.:

A Roll of Arms Registered by the Committee on Heraldry of the New England Historic Genealogical Society. Boston, 1928–1958.

Hartwell, Rodney Eugene. *The Augustan Society Roll of Arms 1967.* Torrance, Calif., 1968 et seq.

U.S.S.R.:

Obstsii Gerbovnik Dvoryanskich Rodov Vserossiiskaya Imperii, 10 vols. St. Petersburg, 1797–1836.

World:

Spener, Philipp Jakob. *Opus heraldicum, pars specialis.* Frankfurt, 1680.

Renesse, Comte Théodore de. *Dictionnaire des figures héraldiques,* Brussels, 1894–1905.

Rietstap, Jean-Baptiste. *Armorial général.* 2nd ed. Gouda, 1884; many reprints, first in Berlin, 1934 (many only with plates); many textual supplements.

ORDERS AND DECORATIONS

Schulz, H. *Chronik sämtlicher bekannten Ritter-Orden und Ehrenzeichen.* Berlin, 1835; 1st supplement, Berlin, 1870; 2nd supplement, Berlin, 1878.

Ackermann, Gustav Adolph. *Ordenskunde.* Annaberg, 1855.

Trost, L.J. *Die Ritter- und Verdienstorden, Ehrenzeichen und Medaillen aller Souveräne und Staaten.* Vienna and Leipzig, 1915.

Neubecker, Ottfried. "Ordensritterleihe Heraldik," in *Der Herold für Geschlechter-, Wappen- und Siegelkunde,* Vol. I. Görlitz, 1940, pages 17–48, 83–176, 220–245.

Klietmann, Kurt-Gerhard, and Ottfried Neubecker. *Ordenslexikon,* 3 parts. Berlin, 1958 et seq.

Měřička, Vaclav. *Orden und Auszeichnungen.* Prague, 1960.

Hieronymussen, Poul Ohm. *Handbuch europäischer Orden in Farben.* Berlin, 1961; 2nd ed. 1975.

Ganz, Paul. "Die Abzeichen der Ritterorden im Mittelalter," in *S.A.H.* 1905, pages 28–37, 52–67, 134–140; 1906, page 16.

Gritzner, Maximilian. *Handbuch der Ritter- und Verdienstorden aller Kulturstaaten der Welt innerhalb des XIX. Jahrhunderts.* Leipzig, 1893; reprint Graz, 1962.

SEALS

Melly, Eduard. *Beiträge zur Siegelkunde des Mittelalters.* Vienna, 1846; reprint Graz, 1972.

Seyler, Gustav Ad. *Geschichte der Siegel.* Leipzig, 1894.

Ilgen Th. "Sphragistik," in *Grundriss der Geschichtswissenschaft,* Vol. I, Part 1, ed. Aloys Meister. Leipzig, 1906; 2nd ed. 1912.

Ewald, Wilhelm. "Siegelkunde," in *Handbuch der Mittelalterlichen und Neueren Geschichte,* Part 4, ed. G. von Below and F. Meinecke. München and Berlin, 1914.

Berchem, Egon Frhr. von. *Siegel (Bibliothek für Kunst- und Antiquitätensammler,* Vol. II). Berlin, 1918; 2nd ed. 1923.

Kittel, Erich. *Siegel (Bibliothek für Kunst- und Antiquitätenfreunde,* Vol. XI). Braunschweig, 1970.

CROWNS

Biehn, Heinz. *Die Kronen Europas und ihre Schicksale.* Wiesbaden, 1957.

Twining, E.F. *A History of the Crown Jewels of Europe.* London, 1960.

Twining, E.F. *European Regalia.* London, 1967.

Abeler, Jürgen. *Kronen, Herrschaftszeichen der Welt.* Düsseldorf, 1972; 3rd ed. Wuppertal, 1976.

Biehn, Heinz. *Alle Kronen dieser Welt.* Munich, 1974.

LIST OF ILLUSTRATIONS

the *Rous Roll,* 1477–1491.
London, B.M.; ms. Add. 48976.

p. 30 b.r. Arms of Charlemagne and the bishopric of Utrecht.
Beijeren's Dutch Chronicle, around 1409.
Brussels, B.R.A., Manuscripts room; ms. 17914, fol. 12r.

p. 31. Edlibach Chronicle.
Zurich, Central Library; ms. A 75, p. 420.

pp. 32 and 33. Tristan Tapestry.
Wienhausen convent.
Photo: Walsrode AG.
Pub: Doris Fouquet, "Wort und Bild in der mittelalterlichen Tristantradition – Der älteste Tristanteppich von Kloster Wienhausen und die textile Tristanüberlieferung des Mittelalters," in *Philologische Studien und Quellen.* Ed. Wolfgang Binder, Hugo Moser, Karl Stackmann, Vol. 62. Berlin, 1971.

p. 34 a. Mons of Japanese families (*l.* to *r.*: Mori, Hirohashi, Fushihara, and Hino).
Illus. from *J.W.,* pp. 47–50.

p. 34 b. Arms of bishops.
Illus. from *C.C.C.*

pp. 34 and 35. Gelre.
Brussels, B.R.A.; ms. 15652–56, fol. 62v., fol. 46r., fol. 52v., fol. 64r.

p. 36 a. Confirmation of arms of the Garde de l'Armorial général de France, Paris, 1698, for Gilles des Plasses.
Illus. from *Armorial de la généralité de Paris,* Jacques Meurgey de Tupigny. Vol. IV. Mâcon, 1967.

p. 36 c. Armorial frieze in the palace at Lauf an der Pegnitz.
Photo: Oriold, Lauf.

p. 36 b.l. The "Zum Loch" house, replica.
Zurich, S.L.

p. 37. Stemmario del Carpani. Como, 1593, pp. 82 and 99.
Como, Civic Museum, ms. No. 406 c.
Photo: Gastone Cambin, Lugano.

p. 37 c.r. Armorial général, Paris II.
Paris, B.N.; ms. français 32217, fol. 795.

p. 37 b. Obshtshii Gerbovnik Dvoryanskich Rodow Vserossiiskaya Imperii, Part 2. St. Petersburg, 1797, p. 14.

p. 38. Cover of a Prussian patent of nobility from the year 1896, leather with silver fittings.
Marburg, German Archive of the Nobility.
Photo: Konrad Lange, Marburg.

p. 39. Patent of arms for Imperial Tobacco Ltd., London.
London, College of Arms.

p. 40 a. King Juan Carlos I of Spain taking the oath.
Photo: Centifoto, Servicio de Prensa Gráfica, Madrid.

p. 40 b. The *Landsgemeinde* of Nidwalden.
Photo: Leonard von Matt, Buochs.

p. 41 l. Procession at the coronation of Elizabeth II.
Illus. from *H.E.*

p. 41 a. The opening of Parliament by King Edward VIII.

Illus. from *Winston S. Churchill.* Jean Améry. Lucern, 1965, p. 119.

p. 41 b. Ceremony of the Order of the Thistle.
Photo: *The Glasgow Herald.*

p. 42 Man with ram emblem.
Paris, M.L.
Photo: M.N.P.

p. 43 a. M.C.; J.P.Z.

p. 43 b. Three seals.
Stockholm.
Photo: Bengt Lundberg, Stockholm.

p. 44 a. Chroniques de France. Jean Froissart.
London, B.M.; ms. Harl. 4379, fol. 23v.

p. 44 l. Lance tip.
Publisher.

p. 44 b.r. King Edward III of England and St. George.
Liber de Officilis Regum. Walter de Milimete.
Oxford, Christ Church Library, ms. Ch.Ch. 92, fol. 3r.

p. 45 a. Mace tournament.
Copy from manuscript of Konrad von Würzburg, *Trojanischer Krieg,* 1441, pen drawing.
Nuremberg, G.N.M., No. 998, Pap. 79.

p. 45 b. Tournament with lances.
Lucas Cranach the Elder, 1509.
M.G. 621.

p. 46 a. Ms. Harl. 1319, fol. 18
London, B.L.

p. 46 b. Maltese galleys.
Valletta, Malta Library.

p. 47. Author.

pp. 48 and 49. Genealogy of the house of Bourbon.
Généalogie de la Maison Royale de Bourbon. Charles Bernard. Paris, 1645.
Photo: Cine Brunel, Lugano, from copy in Gastone Cambin Heraldic and Genealogical Institute, Lugano.

p. 49 a. Pedigree of four brothers and sisters of the von Erlach family.
Illus. from *S.A.H.,* 1906, pl. II.

p. 50 a. Napoleonic eagle.
Vignette in *Nouveau manuel complet du blason....* J.-F. Jules Paulet du Parcis.
Paris, 1854, p. 152.

pp. 50 and 51 b. Specimens of Napoleonic heraldry.
Ibid., pl. 4, Nos. 186–197 and 177.
Drawings: Werner Luzi, Lucerne.

p. 51 c. Ibid., No. 144.

p. 51 l. and r. Arms of Talleyrand.
Illus. from *S.W.,* I, 3, III, B, pl. 87.

p. 52. Small and medium-sized arms of the kingdom of Prussia.
Illus. from *Type specimens of the imperial printing works, initials, ornaments, eagles and arms.* Berlin, n.d. (between 1900 and 1918).

p. 53. Large arms of the kingdom of Prussia.
Illus. from *Deutsche Wappenrolle.* Hugo Gerard Ströhl. Stuttgart, 1897, pl. II.

pp. 54 and 55 a. Author.

p. 54 l. Publisher.

p. 54 c. Illus. from *Shakespeare's*

Heraldry. C.W. Scott-Giles, London, 1950, p. 3.

p. 55 c. Two seals and a sketch of arms.
Author.

p. 55 b.l. Two seals of King Richard I.
London B.L.

p. 55 b.r. St. Michael from the Abraham's tapestry.
Halberstadt, cathedral choir.
Illus. from *Die deutschen Bildteppiche des Mittelalters.* Betty Kurth.
Vienna, 1926, Vol. 2, pl. 6.

p. 56 a. Seal of Johann von Steglitz, 1272.
Berlin, B.P.K.

p. 56 b. Smithy scene.
Rome, Museo nuovo del Palazzo dei Conservatori.
Photo: Alinari-Giraudon.

p. 57. Shield from Seedorf.
Zurich, S.L.

p. 58 a. Model of Viking ship.
Smithsonian Institution, Washington, D.C.

p. 58 b., l. to r.
– Two warriors.
Stockholm, State Historical Museum Antikvarisk-Topografiska Arkivet, Stockholm.
Photo: Claes Claesson.

– Cadmus kills the snake.
Detail from painting on a Laconian beaker.
Paris, M.L.
Photo: Roger-Viollet, Paris

– Persian warrior.
Paris, B.N.; ms. Suppl. Persan 1280, fol. 500v.

– Roman warrior.
Rome, marble relief on the plinth of the column of Trajan.
Publisher's archives.

– Warrior from a font, found in Gündestrup, Jutland.
Copenhagen, National Museum.

p. 59 l. Publisher.

p. 59 a.r. Japanese standing shields.
Illus. from *J.W.,* pl. XI.

p. 59 c. and r. Two seals of Duke Rudolf IV, the founder of Austria.
Vienna, Ö.St.A.
l. 6 February 1360 (with titles of sovereignty laid claim to).
r. 12 March 1364 (after relinquishment of usurped titles vetoed by the emperor).

p. 60 a.l. Painted face of a Nuba youth.
Photo: Leni Riefenstahl-Film, Munich.

p. 60 a.c. Masai shield.
Publisher.

p. 60 a.r. Arms of Kenya.
Publisher.

p. 60 b. Normans.
Paris, B.N.; N.A.L. 1390, fol. 7.

p. 60 r. Masai warriors.
Photo: Picturepoint Ltd., London.

p. 61 l. Zurich police.
Photo: Comet, Zurich.

p. 61 r. Publisher.

p. 62. Panel on the tomb of Geoffrey Plantagenet.
Le Mans, Musée Tessé.

Photo: Lauros-Giraudon, Paris.

pp. 62 and 63 a. Publisher.
Three drawings: Franz Coray, Lucerne.

p. 63 l. Publisher.
Four drawings: Franz Coray, Lucerne.

p. 63 r. Shield with cross.
London, B.L.; ms. Cott. Nero D I, fol. 171.

pp. 64 and 65. Standard of Queen Mary of Great Britain.
Drawing: Franz Coray, Lucerne, from official design.

In the standard, the arms of Great Britain are combined with the arms arranged on a square field which belong to the queen from birth as princess of Teck. The arms of Great Britain consist of the quarterings of England, Scotland, Ireland, and England a second time.

In the first and fourth large quarters, the arms of the dukes of Teck show the arms of Great Britain in the arrangement which was valid from 1801 to 1837, with the inescutcheon of the Hanoverian arms. The latter consists of the arms of Brunswick (two lions passant guardant), Lüneburg (lion and hearts) and Lower Saxony (horse), but does not carry the central shield with the German imperial crown, which only belonged to the head of the house of Hanover.

This coat of arms in Great Britain has the label of the dukes of Cambridge. As the arms had been granted to Adolphus Frederick, the brother of King George IV who died in 1850, they were passed on to his daughter Mary Adelaide, who brought them with her when she married Francis Paul, Duke of Teck; their children combined the arms of the line of Cambridge with the arms of the dukes of Teck in the second and third quarters (see page 65). In 1917 the dukes of Teck are those of the kings of Württemberg (the arms of Württemberg – or, three deers' antlers sable – impaled with those of Swabia – or, three lions sable) with a black and gold lozengy inescutcheon (the arms of Teck). The title of duke of Teck was granted by the king of Württemberg in 1871 to Francis Paul (created Prince of Teck in 1863), son of Duke Alexander of Württemberg by his morganatic marriage with Claudine Countess Rhédey in 1835.

In this version of the arms of Württemberg, the three black lions have red forepaws, in memory of the death of Duke Konradin of Swabia (1268).

pp. 66 and 67 a. Eight seals.
Paris, A.N.

p. 66 c. Christ leading the Christian knights.
Foto Picture Library, Marburg.

p. 66 b. Illustration in the margin of *Secreta fidelium crucis.* Venice, 1321.
Ms. Tanner 190, fol. 22r.
Photo: Editions Robert Laffont, Paris.

p. 67. Praying knight.
Basel, St. Leonard's Church.
Photo: Historical Museum, Basel, Maurice Babey.

pp. 68 and 69 a. Decorated lodgings of tournament guests.
Cf. *p. 13 b*, fol. 39v.–40r.

p. 68. Knight from the so-called *Lutrell Psalter.*
London, B.N.; ms. Add. 42130, fol. 202v.
Reproduced by courtesy of the Library Board.

pp. 68 and 69 b. Four illus. from M.C.; J.P.Z.

p. 69 c.l. Dubbing ceremony from *Life of King Offa.*
London, B.M.; ms. Nero D I, fol. 3a.
Foto Picture Library, Marburg.

p. 69 c.r. Putting on the spurs.
Paris, B.N.; ms. français 99, fol. 561.

p. 70 a. Medusa shield, made by Filippo and Francesco Negroli, Milan 1541.
Vienna, K.M.; Arms collection A. 693 a.

pp. 70 and 71 b. Four drawings of shield shapes.
Publisher.
Drawings: Franz Coray, Lucerne.

p. 71 a., l. to r.
– Deggendorf jousting shield.
Munich, B.N.M.

– Jousting shield of the Chigi family.
Munich, B.N.M.

– Jousting shield from Hesse.
Marburg, University Museum.
Foto Picture Library, Marburg.

pp. 72 and 73 a., l. to r.
– Viking shield, early 10th century.
Copenhagen, National Museum.

– Tierstein funeral shield, 15th century.
From the monastery church of Rüti.
Photo: S.L., Zurich.

– Raron burial shield.
From the monastery church of Rüti.
Photo: S.L., Zurich.

– Venetian round shield.
B.H.M.; Ref. No. 102 b.

– Jousting shield of Wolf Dieter von Raitenau, Prince Bishop of Salzburg, around 1600.
Offenbach, German Leather Museum.

– Funeral shield of the emperor Charles V.
Augsburg, Municipal Art Collections, Diocesan Museum.
Property of the cathedral chapter of the bishopric of Augsburg.

– Venetian ornamental shield, Arabic work.
Florence, Bargello.
Photo: Scala, Antella (Florence).

– Abyssinian round shield.
Offenbach, German Leather Museum.

pp. 72 and 73 b., l. to r.
– Detail from the tapestry of Queen Mathilda.
Bayeux, Musée de l'Evêché.
By special permission of the town of Bayeux.
Photo: Giraudon, Paris.

– Shield with the arms of the von Nordecks of Rabenau.
Marburg, University Museum.
Foto Picture Library, Marburg.

– Shield of the landgrave Henry.
Ibid.

– Standing shield from the town of Erfurt
Erfurt, Museum.

– Pavis, made by Taddeo di Bartolo with the arms of the Buonamici.
Florence, Museo Bardini.
Photo: Scala, Antella (Florence).

– Jousting shield of Matthew Corvinus.
Paris, Musée de l'Armée, I. 7.

– Burgundian shield.
B.H.M.; ref. No. 271.

– Kuttenberg standing shield with St. Wenceslas.
With agreement of the National Museum, Prague.
Photo: Voitech Obereigner, Prague.

– Horse's head armor.
Paris, Musée de l'Armée, G. 563.

p. 73 a.r. Arms of Christopher Beham.
Illus. from *S.W.*, V 5, pl. 4.

p. 74 l. Knight standing watch, from *Tractatus de ludo scacorum;* fol. 22r.
Photo: Biblioteca Nacional, Madrid.

p. 74 r. Ornamental jousting shield from Winterthur.
Zurich, S.L.

p. 75. Jousting shield with courting couple, Flemish, 15th century.
London, B.M.

pp. 76 and 77. Table of shields.
Publisher.
Drawings: Werner Luzi, Lucerne.
Layout: Michael Stoll, Lucerne.

p. 78 l. Tlingit totem pole, southern Alaska.
Ottawa, National Museum of Canada.
Photo: Richard Inglis.

p. 78 r. Rock drawing.
Photo: Marie E.P. König, Güdingen.

p. 79 l. Cylinder seal.
London, B.M.

p. 79 r. Publisher.
Drawing: Franz Coray, Lucerne.

p. 80 a. Altar of Mithras in Heddernheim.
Wiesbaden, Museum.

p. 80 l. Inn sign.
Publisher.
Photo: Robert Tobler, Lucerne.

p. 80 r. Trading sign of the business associates of Hieronymus Koler, 1495–1527.
Nuremberg, G.N.M.; bibl. Hs 2908, p. 1r.

p. 81 l. and a. Symbols crowning churches.
Publisher.

p. 81 r. Traffic signs.
C.J. Bucher, Lucerne.

p. 82 a. Fire sign.
Publisher.

p. 82 b. Water sign.
Publisher.

p. 83 a.l. Watch order of the guilds of Basel with their arms, 1415.
State archive of the canton of Basel-Stadt.

p. 83 a.r. Shakespeare arms.
Illus. from *Shakespeare's Heraldry.*
C.W. Scott-Giles. London, 1950, pl. I.

p. 83 b. Funeral banner of Count Frederick VII of Toggenburg.
Zurich, S.L., KZ 5720.

pp. 84 and 85 c., p. 85 a. F.A. Brockhaus, Wiesbaden.
Drawing: Author.

pp. 84 and 85 a. Publisher.

p. 84 b. Author.

p. 86 l. Arms of the von Rathsamhausen family.
Drawing by Baron Karl von Neuenstein.

p. 86 r. Publisher.

p. 87 a. Publisher.

p. 87 b. Armorial tiles in the monastery of St. Urban.
Zurich, S.L.

pp. 88 and 89 a. Publisher.

p. 88 b.r. Redinghoven's Armorial.
Munich, B.S.; Cgm 2213/38, fol. 304r.

pp. 90 and 91. Arms of Austria, 1915–1918.
Illus. from official design.
Author.

p. 92. Illus. from *Opus*, pl. 5.

p. 93. Illus. from *Armorial Général.*
J.B. Rietstap. Gouda, 1884.

p. 94. Spanish imperial banner around 1500.
Publisher.
Drawing: Franz Coray, Lucerne, after author.

p. 95. Arms of the Lloyds of Stockton.
London, College of Arms.

p. 96 a. Portrait of Queen Victoria.
London, National Portrait Gallery.

pp. 96 and 97 c. System of labels of the English royal family.
Publisher.
Drawing: Franz Coray, Lucerne.

p. 96 b. Author.

p. 97 a. Arms of the crown princes of Hanover until 1837.
Photo: *Heraldry Today*, London.

p. 97 l. Four Belgian coats of arms.
Publisher.
Drawing: Werner Luzi, Lucerne, after Roger Harmignies, Brussels.

p. 97 r. Arms of the city of Rome, official design.
Author.

p. 97 b. Scottish system of marks of difference.
Publisher.

pp. 98–103. Capetian family tree.
Due to limitations of space, not all the subsidiary lines have been followed without interruption, or to their very end.
Publisher.
Drafted by: Hervé Pinoteau, Versailles, and Ottfried Neubecker.
Design: Emil M. Buhrer, Lucerne.
Drawings: Werner Luzi, Lucerne.

pp. 104 and 105. Publisher.
Drawing: Franz Coray, Lucerne.

p. 106 a.l. The Resurrection of Christ, psalter around 1335.
Engelberg, Monastery library.

p. 106 a.r. Piero della Francesca, *The Resurrection of Christ.*
Sansepolcro, Pinacoteca Comunale, No. 19.
Photo: Fratelli Alinari (Florence).

p. 106 l. Byzantine flag.
Publisher.
Drawing: Franz Coray, Lucerne.

p. 106 b. School of Raphael, *Battle at the Milvian Bridge.*
Vatican, Stanze di Raffaello.
Photo: Scala, Antella (Florence).

p. 107. Publisher.
Drawing: Werner Luzi, Lucerne.

p. 108. Gonfanon of the lords of Blonay.
Blonay château, Canton de Vaud.
Photo: Stamm & Saxod, Lausanne.

p. 109. Banner of the town of Frauenfeld.
Frauenfeld, Thurgau Museum.
Photo: James Perret, Lucerne.

p. 110 a.l. Stone sculpture from the monastery of Steingaden.
Munich, B.N.M.

p. 110 a.c. Seal of Albert III, Count of Gleichen, 12 March 1272.
Illus. from *A.W.L.*, Vol. 3, pl. 28, no. 2.

p. 110 a.r. Lion shield from the grave of King Ottokar I.
Prague, St. Vitus's Cathedral.
Photo: Jan Neubert, Dobrichovice, CSSR.

p. 110 l. Greek coin.
Illus. from *Münzen der Griechen*, Office du Livre, S.A., Fribourg.

p. 110 b. Burgundian armorial tapestry.
B.H.M., ref. No. 15a.

pp. 111 and 112. Models for engraving heraldic lions.
Illus. from *A Dictionary of Heraldry.*
Charles Norton Elvin. London, 1889 and 1969.
Photo: *Heraldy Today*, London.

p. 112 b. Venetian flag from the 17th century.
Venice, Museo Correr.
Photo: Taso, Venice.

p. 113. Official design for the large coat of arms of the kingdom of Belgium accoding to a royal decree of 17 May 1837.

p. 114 a. H.L. Schäuffelein, *Alexander as Air Traveler*, woodcut.
M.G. 1063.

p. 114 b.l. Basilisk from an English bestiary.
Leningrad, National Library.
Novosti Press Agency, Geneva.

p. 114 b.r. Arms of Basel, original impression, 16th century.
Author.

p. 115 l. Personifications of humility and chastity.
Munich, B.S.; ms. Germ. 514, fol. 138r.and 141r.

p. 115 a.r. Garuda from Thailand.
Publisher.

p. 115 r. Two English imaginary coats of arms.
London, B.L.; ms. Harl. 2169, fol. 4v. and 66v.

p. 116 a. Arms of J. Chr. Gottsched.
Illus. from S.W. V, 4, pl. 64.

p. 116 b.l. First great seal of Queen Mary Stuart.
Illus. from *History of Scottish Seals*, Vol. I. Walter de Gray Birch.
Stirling and London, 1905, No. 43.

p. 116 b.r. Two coats of arms with unicorns.
Z.W.R.

p. 117. Tapestry of *The Lady with the Unicorn.*
Paris, Musée de Cluny.
Photo: M.N.P.

p. 118 a. Capitoline she-wolf.
Photo: Leonard von Matt, Buochs.

p. 118 2nd row l. Battle scene from *Carmen de bello Siculo.*
Bern, Civic Library; Cod. 120, fol. 130.

p. 118, 2nd row r. Two badges of King Richard III.
Illus. from *Sir Wriothesley's Armorial;* cf. H.G. Ströhl in *Jahrbuch Adler.* Vienna, 1902, p. 100.
Drawing: Franz Coray, Lucerne.

p. 118, 3rd row l. to r.
– Berlin municipal seal, 14th century.
Photo: Landesbildstelle Berlin.

– Two seals of the town of Bern: small seal 1365, large seal 1717.
Bern, State Archives of the canton.
Photo: Hugo Frutig, Bern.

– Knight's standard from the town of St. Gallen, 2nd half of 16th century.
Museums of the town of St. Gallen.

p. 118 b.l. Arms of Carpathian Russia, 1920.
Illus. from *Staats-, Landes- und*

Städtewappen der Tschechoslovaki-schen Republik. Kaffee Hag AG (ed.). Marienbad.

p. 118 b.r. Arms of East Karelia, official design.
Author.

p. 119 a.l. Seal of the Planta family.
Original stamp in private hands.
Photo: Rhätisches Museum, Chur.

p. 119 a.r. Arms of the rural district of the county of Hoya.
Publisher.

p. 119 b.l. Oldest seal of the town of St. Gallen, 1312.
St. Gallen, Municipal Archives.
Photo: Museums of the Town of St. Gallen.

p. 119 r. St. Julius banner of the valley community of Ursern, 1512.
Andermatt, Town Hall.
Photo: Wyler, Andermatt.

p. 120 a. Arms of the sultan of Baroda.
Author.

p. 120 a.l. Helfenstein arms.
Z.W.R.

p. 120 b., l. to r.
– Urn national banner, borne in the Battles of Morgarten (1315) and Laupen (1339).
Altdorf, Town Hall.
Photo: James Perret, Lucerne.

– Two medieval seals from Mecklen-burg.
Author.

p. 121 c., l. to r.
– Arms of Lower Lusatia, after K.G.A.

– Arms of the town of Turin, official design.
Author.

– Arms of the counts of Foix.
Brussels, B.R.A.; *Gelre*, fol. 122v.

p. 121 a.r. Royal standard from Württemberg.
Publisher.
Drawing: Franz Coray, Lucerne, after author.

p. 121 rem. Six coats of arms.
Illus. from *Brockhaus Enzyklopädie.*
Wiesbaden.
Drawings: Author.

p. 122 a. Gold seal of the emperor Charles VI as king of Spain.
Electrotype from the original, now lost, used 12 August 1707.
Nuremberg, G.N.M.

p. 122 b. Two family coats of arms from *Arl.*; *l.* Peter Tungast zum Klett-stein, *r.* Philipp der Muschrat.

p. 123 l. Glarus national banner, 15th century.
Näfels, Freulerpalast.
Photo: Schönwetter, Glarus.

p. 123 c. Municipal arms in the 3rd Oath Book of the town of Munich, 1686.
Munich, Municipal Archives, parch-ment manuscript.

p. 123 c.b. Italian coat of arms.
Illus. from *H.A.*

p. 123 r. Pattern sheet with human body parts.
Illus. from *A Dictionary of Heraldry* (cf. *p. 111*).

p. 124 l. Seal of Georg Kastriota, known as Skanderbeg.
Author.

p. 124 l., top to bottom.
– Hawk from the royal neck orna-ment.
Cairo, Egyptian Museum, treasure from the tomb of Tutankhamen.
Photo: Giraudon, Paris.

– Breast plate from a royal tomb in Byblos.
Paris, M.L.
Photo: Giraudon, Paris.

– Neck ornament with portrait of the goddess Nekhebit.
Photo: Editions Rencontre, Lau-sanne.

p. 124 r. Sphinx.
Aleppo, Museum.
Photo: Rolf Ammon, Stuattgart.

p. 125 a. Arms of the republics of Columbia and Bolivia.
Illus. from *Die Staatswappen der bekanntesten Länder der Erde.* Fried-rich Heyer von Rosenfeld. 10th enlgd. ed., Frankfurt, 1895, pl. XII.

p. 125 l. Two virgin eagles.
l. Main seal of the town of Nurem-berg, 1253.
Nuremberg, Municipal Archives.
r. Official design.

p. 125 c. Roman *signum.*
Illus. from *Die Weltgeschichte in Bil-dern,* Vol. 4. Lausanne, 1969, p. 33.

p. 125 r. Napoleonic banners.
Illus. from *Die Trophäen des Preussi-schen Heeres in der Kgl. Hof- und Garnisonskirche zu Potsdam.* Gustav Lehman. Berlin, 1898, pl. II.

p. 126 a. M.C., fol. 323r.
Heidelberg, University Library; Cod. Pal. Germ. 848.

p. 126 c.a. Five heraldic eagles.
Publisher.

p. 126 c.b., l. to r.
– Shield with "burning" eagle from the tomb of King Ottokar I.
Prague, St. Vitus's Cathedral.
Photo: Jan Neubert, Dobrichovice, CSSR.

– Pavis of the town of Wimpfen.
Darmstadt, Hesse Regional Museum.

– Pavis of the town of Schongau.
Munich, B.N.M.

p. 126 b.l. Russian double eagle on the golden seal of the treaty of alliance between the grand duke of Moscow, Vassiliy III Ivanovich, and the emperor Maximilian I.
Vienna, Ö.St.A., 1514 (Feb.–March 7).

p. 126 b.r. Publisher.

p. 127. Front and side aspects of the knight's shield with the arms of Raron.
Sion, Musée de Valère.
Photo: Heinz Preisig, Sitten.

pp. 128 and 129. Row of eagles.
Royal Book of Crests of Great Bri-tain and Ireland. London n.d., pls. 96 and 97.

p. 128 a.b. Publisher.

p. 128 b.l. Three eagle coats of arms.
K.G.A.; B.S., Cgm. 145, p. 6a.

p. 128 b.r. Quaternion eagle.
Author.

p. 129 l. Funereal slab of Uwe Tetens, Witzwort.
Photo: F. Sparck & Co., Husum.

p. 129 r. Bernese armorial window.
Zurich, S.L.

p. 129 b.l. Napoleon I's seal for patents of nobility.
Author.

p. 129 b.r. U.S. dollar of 1799.
Courtesy of the American Numisma-tic Society, New York.

p. 130 a. Four ostrich arms.
Author.

p. 130 l. Standard with phoenix.
Publisher.
Drawings: Franz Coray, Lucerne.

p. 130 r. Standard of Greyerz.
Freiburg, Historical Museum.
Photo: Leo Hilber, Freiburg.

p. 130 b.l. Seal.
Photo: Imperial Archives, Copenha-gen.

p. 130 b.r. Banner of the count of Pavia.
Illus. from *Freiburg Book of Colors.*
Freiburg, State Archives.
Photo: Rast, Freiburg.

p. 131. Barberini arms.
Tesserae Gentilitiae. Silvestre Petra Sancta. Rome, 1638.
Author's library.

p. 132 a.l. Florentine lily from the Palazzao Ferroni.
Author.

p. 132 a.c. Royal French cloak clasp.
Paris, M.N.P.

p. 132 a.r. Chroniques de France.
Jean Froissart.
London, B.M.; ms. 14 D IV.
Photo: Editions Robert Laffont, Paris.

p. 133 a. Two seals of the town of Lemgo.
Official design.
Author.

pp. 132 and 133 others. Publisher.

p. 134 c., l. to r.
– Banner of the Council of Entlebuch.
Lucerne, Historic Town Hall Collec-tion, No. 588.
Photo: James Perret, Lucerne.

– A banner of the Swabian Federa-tion, captured in the Swabian War.
Illus. from *Lucerne Book of Colors* copy in S.L.
– Probable flag of Holstein.
John Graydon, ms. *Insignia Navalia,* 1686.
By permission of the Master and Fel-lows of Magdelene College, Cam-bridge, England.

p. 134 b. Nesselblatt forms.
Publisher.

p. 135 l. Pattern sheet with plant motifs.
Illus. from *Opus,* pl. 16.

p. 135 a.r. Flag of New England.
John Graydon, ms. *Insignia Navalia,* 1686.
By permission of the Master and Fellows of Magdelene College, Cam-bridge, England.

p. 135 r. Arms of Canada.
Official design.
Publisher.

p. 136 a. Arms attributed to Spain and Portugal.
Z.W.R.

p. 136 l. Seal of the town of Stadt-hagen, 1324.
Stadthagen, Town Hall.

p. 136 r. Two Lithuanian emblems.
l. Arms from K.G.A.
r. Triple-tower sign from the state flag, 1918.
Official design.
Author.

p. 136 b. Four English coats of arms, 15th century.
Publisher.
Drawings: Werner Luzi, Lucerne.

p. 137 a.l. Albrecht Dürer: the major arms of his family, woodcut.
Nuremberg, G.N.M.; no. St.Nbg. 12859.

p. 137 a.r. Arms of vassals of the elec-tor of Trier on the Neuerburg.
Coblenz, Main Regional Archives; *Balduineum,* fol. 6.

p. 137 b.l. Urs Graf, arms of the guild of smiths of Solothurn, engraving.
Solothurn, Municipal Museum.

p. 137 b.r. Trumpet banner of the company of J.F. Schenk of Schmidt-burg.
Painting by Gabriel Geiger, Heidel-berg, 1620.
Codex in possession of the author.

p. 138 a.l. Fetterlock with falcon.
Publisher.

p. 138 a.r. Arms of the Speth family.
Illus. from *Münchener Kalender.*
Otto Hupp. Munich, 1920.

p. 138 b. Tanner's emblems.
Publisher.

p. 138. Guild table of the guild of tanners.
Solothurn, Blumenstein Historical Museum.
Photo: James Perret, Lucerne.

p. 140 a.l. Arms of the city of Ports-mouth.
Publisher.
Drawing: Franz Coray, Lucerne, from official design.

p. 140 b.l. Banner of Jacques de Luxembourg.
Illus. from *Solothurn Book of Colors.*
Solothurn, State Archives.
Photo: James Perret, Lucerne.

p. 140 b.r. – Moon arms *(Arl.)* of Jakob Grün, a painter in Vienna, and Margarete, his wife.

pp. 140–142 a. Arms with heavenly bodies.
Illus. from *Wappen-Bilder-Lexikon.*
Wilhelm Rentzmann and Ottfried Neubecker.
Munich, 1974.

pp. 140–142 c. Crests with heavenly bodies.
Illus. from. *Royal Book of Crests.*
London, pls. 7 and 8.

pp. 140–142 b. Flag of the U.S.A. carried in the Battle of Yorktown, 1781.
New York, Historical Society.

p. 142 l. Arms of the Inca kings.
London, The Hamlyn Group.

p. 142 b., l. to r.
– Flag of Stralsund with sun.
Publisher.

– French cavalry standard.
Publisher.

– Japanese vexilloid. Publisher.

p. 143. Japanese war sign.
Publisher.

p. 144 a. M.C.; J.P.Z.

p. 144 c. Battle of knights.
Coblenz, Main Regional Archives; *Balduineum.*

p. 144 b. Detail from the tapestry of Queen Mathilda.
Bayeux, Musée de l'Evêché.
With the special authorization of the town of Bayeux.
Photo: Giraudon, Paris.

p. 145. "Prank" helmet.
Frontal and side aspects.
Vienna, K.M.

p. 146 b.l. Two aspects of a helmet with quilted hood.
Drawing by the author from the Lüneburg folding table (cf. *pp. 154 and 155*).

p. 146 b.l. Knight outside town walls.
Illus. from C.C.C.

pp. 146 and 147 l. to r.
– Italo-Gallic helmet.
London, B.M.

– Baldenheim helmet.
Strassburg, Château des Rohan.

– So-called *Wendelhelm.*
Photo: Stockholm, Riksantikvarie-ämbetet.

– "Pot helmet" from the ruins of Madeln castle near Pratteln BL.

pp. 182 and 183. Illus. from the *Krönungsdiarium,* 1745.
Author.

p. 184 l. Queen Elizabeth II.
Photo: Cecil Beaton, London.

pp. 184 and 185. Swedish royal sloop.
Royal wedding, 19 June 1976.
Photo: Presse-Agentur Dukas, Zurich.

pp. 186 l. and 187 r. Lion supporters from the arms of Bavaria.
Illus. from *Deutsche Wappenrolle.* H.G. Ströhl. Stuttgart, 1897, pl. VIII.

pp. 186 and 187, the others. Porcupine supporters and armorial tent.
Illus. cf. *p. 131.*

p. 188 a. Bertrand du Guesclin.
Illus. from *Triomphe des Neuf Preux.* Abbeville, 1481, frontispiece.
Paris, B.N.

p. 188 l. Weltchronik. Hartmann Schedel. 1493.
Illus. from copy of the facsimile edition in the Central Library, Lucerne.

pp. 189 and 190 l. Master W.A., Arms of Charles the Bold, 1468.
Brussels, B.R.A., Print Room.

pp. 189 and 190 r. Arms of King Henry VIII of England.
Illus. from *Regal Heraldry.* Thomas Willement. London, 1821.
Photo: L. Bührer, Lucerne.

p. 190. Two rows with eleven seals.
1st row, l. to r.
– Margaret Bruce, Lady de Ros, 1280.
Illus. from *Boutell's Heraldry.* London, 1970, no. 343.
    Beatrix von Görz, around 1350.
Illus. from *G.H.,* no. 394.
– Duchess Agnes of Brunswick (d. 1341).
Wolfenbüttel, State Archives of Lower Saxony.
– Henry Count of Nassau-Dillenburg, 1444.
Wiesbaden, Main State Archives of Hesse.
– John, Earl of Arundel.
Illus. from *Boutell's Heraldry* (cf. above), no. 346.
– Margrave Sigismund of Brandenburg, 1495.
Illus. from *G.H.,* no. 485.

2nd row, l. to r.
– Winemar von dem Birnbaum, Consul at Cologne, 1425.
Publisher.
Drawing: Franz Coray, Lucerne, from Seyler, *G.H.,* no. 482.
– Front and back, Margaret, wife of King Edward I of England.
Illus. from *Boutell's Heraldry* (cf. above), no. 296.
– Edward Mortimer, Earl of March, 1400.
Ibid., no. 344.
– Thomas Holland, Earl of Kent, 1380.
Ibid., no. 342.

p. 190 b.l. Heinrich von Scharfeneck, 1292.
Waldenburg/Württemberg, Hohenlohe-Waldenburg Royal Treasurer's Office.

p. 190 a.l. John I, Count of Nassau-Dillenburg, 1393.
Wiesbaden, Main State Archives of Hesse.

p. 191 a.c. Coin of Brunswick.
Brunswick, Municipal Museum.
Photo: Otto Hopp.

p. 191 b.l. M.C.; J.P.Z.

p. 191 r. Lascivious woman with the municipal arms of Ochsenfurt.
Original in Munich, art trade, attributed to Tielemann Riemenschneider.
Copy in Ochsenfurt, Town Hall.
Photo: Knittel, Ochsenfurt.

– *p. 192.* Stone sculpture from the tomb of Archbishop Theodoric, around 1460.
Cologne, Cathedral.
Photo: Rheinisches Bildarchiv, Cologne.

p. 193. Glass painting from St. Stephen's Cathedral, Vienna, representing Rudolph I of Hapsburg and his son Albert I.
Vienna, Historical Museum of the Town.

p. 194 a. Pastry mold from Villingen, 16th century.
Author.
Photo: Fred Hugel, Villingen.

p. 194 b. Stone sculpture at Bückeburg Castle, Schaumburg, where it was probably brought by the niece of Clara of Brunswick, Katharina (b. 1577), who had married an inhabitant of Schaumburg in 1609.
Illus. from *Der Deutsche Herold.* Berlin, 1913, supplement to No. 12.

p. 195. Ex libris sign of Duke Wolfgang of Pfalz-Zweibrücken.
Woodcut by Virgil Solis, 1559.
Illus. from *Ex libris.* Walter von Zur Westen. Bielefeld and Leipzig, 1901, from a copy now lost in the Court (now Regional and University) Library in Darmstadt.
Coloring: Franz Coray, Lucerne.

p. 196. Donatello, *The Marzocco.* Florence, Bargello.
Photo: Scala, Antella (Florence).

p. 197. Arms of Jean de Malestroit.
Paris, Bibliothèque de l'Arsenal; *Chroniques de France,* Gaguin manuscript, 1477, p. 1.
Photo: Lalance, Paris.

p. 198 a.l. So-called Light thaler, imperial thaler of 1578.
Brunswick, Municipal Museum.
Photo: Otto Hoppe.

p. 198 a.r. Imperial thaler, 1691, ibid.

p. 198 l. Arms of King Matthew Corvinus of Hungary, made king of Bohemia in 1469.
Görlitz, Town Hall.
Illus. from *Der Deutsche Herold.* Berlin, 1907, No. 2.

p. 198 c. Woodcut on the verso of the title page of the Vasal Bible, Uppsala, 1541.
Stockholm, Royal Library.

p. 198 r. Arms of the Holzhausen family.
Illus. from *Stamm- und Wappenbuch.* Jost Amman. Frankfurt, *1579.*

p. 198 b.l. Arms of Lord Baltimore.
Illus. from a map, attached to a report of 1635.
Pub.: Justin Winsor, *Narrative and Critical History of America,* Vol. III. 1886, p. 520.

p. 198 b.r. Seal of the State of Maryland, U.S.A.
Publisher.

p. 199. Pattern sheet with humans as supporters.
Illus. from *H.A.*

pp. 200 and 201. Various supporters.
– Nos. 1, 3, 5, 6, 14, 15, 16, 17, 25 from *Heraldische Kunstblätter.* Friedrich Warnecke. Görlitz, 1877 et seq.
– Nos. 2, 4, 12, 21, 28 from *Stamm- und Wappenbuch.* Jost Amman. Frankfurt, *1579;* reprinted (ed. Friedrich Warnecke) Görlitz, 1877.
– No. 7 from Seyler, *G.H.,* No. 481.

– Nos. 8, 10, 20, 30, 31 from *Heraldry in Miniature.* London n.d. (1783).
– No. 9 from *Russkaya Geraldika.* W.K. Lukomskii and Baron N.A. Tiepolt.
Petrograd, 1915, pl. XV.
– Nos. 11, 22–24, 26, 27, 34–36, cf. *p. 131.*
– No. 13, A.H.S., 1910–11.
– No. 18, signet of Jacob Bellaert, Haarlem, 1484.
B.S.; Inc. c.a. 365d.
– Nos. 19 and 29 from *Manuel du Blason.* D.L. Galbreath. Lausanne, 1942, pp. 266 and 49.
– No. 32 from *The Royal Heraldry of England.* J.H. & R.V. Pinches. London, 1974, p. 46.
– No. 33, signet of Simon Bevilacqua, Venice, 1495.
B.S.; Inc. c.a. 1185.

p. 202. Publisher.

p. 202 c., l. to r.
– State arms of Lesotho.
Publisher.
– State arms of Tanzania.
Publisher.
– Arms of the town of Southampton.
Illus. from *A Complete Guide to Heraldry.* A.C. Fox-Davis. London, 1969, pl. X.

p. 202 b. Title page of the *Kurmainzer Landrecht,* original impression, 1755.
Author.

p. 203 a. Monogram of Charlemagne.
Publisher.

p. 203 a.l. Burgundian standard with St. Thomas.
Glarus, Regional Archive; *Glarus Book of Colors.*
Photo: Schönwetter, Glarus.

p. 203 a.r. Royal arms of France.
Illus. from D.W.W., pl. 6.

p. 203 b.l. Arms of George IV of Great Britain.
Cf. *p. 189,* pl. XXXIV.
Photo: *Heraldry Today,* London.

p. 203 b.r. Bookplate.
Author.

p. 204 Negotiations in tents.
Paris, B.N.; ms. français 12559, fol. 162.

p. 205 l. Scene of surrender in front of a tent.
Paris, B.N.; ms. français 2675, fol. 189v.

p. 205 a. Cloaklike mantle and armorial tent.
Cf. *p. 131,* pp. 640 and 642.

p. 205 b. Meeting of kings in the Field of the Cloth of Gold, 1520.
Versailles, Museum.
Photo: M.N.P.

p. 206 a.r. Shield with war tent.
Author.

p. 206 a.l. Collar section of the cloak of the Austrian imperial robes.
Vienna, K.M.

p. 206 a.c. Arms of Marie de la Trémouille, 17th century.
Illus. from *H.A.*

p. 206 a., l. to r.
– The emperor Constantine on foot leads the horse on which Pope Sylvester is seated.
Fresco, 12th century, Rome, Church of Santi Quattro Coronati.
Photo: Leonard von Matt, Buochs.
– Page riding before the pope bearing the *ombrellino.*
Illus. from *C.C.C.*
– The emperor Sigismund under a

baldachin; ibid.
– Pope Pius II at his installation in the basilica of San Giovanni, the episcopal church of Rome.
Siena, Cathedral, 1502, fresco by Pinturicchio.
Photo: Scala, Antella (Florence).

p. 207. Arms of the king of Italy and the duke of Savoy-Aosta, official illustrations.
Photo: Laboratorio Fotografico Chomon-Perino, Turin, from a copy in the Royal Library, Turin.

p. 208. Certificate of the English king-at-arms, John Anstis, concerning the badges of the Stafford family, 1720, copy around 1800.
Owner: Paul L. Csank, Cleveland, Ohio, U.S.A.

p. 209. Door of the King Henry VII Chapel, London, Westminster Abbey.
Photo: By courtesy of the Dean and Chapter of Westminster.

pp. 210 and 211. Badges.
– Japan: J.W.
– England: Drawings by Franz Coray, Lucerne.
– France: 1st four pictures, Château de Blois.
Photo: Archives Photographiques, Paris.
– French banner.
Nancy, Musée Lorrain.
Drawing: Franz Coray, Lucerne, from original photograph.
– Sun emblem.
Photo: Author.
– Tailpiece of a missal from Lyons, 1487.
Illus. from *Manuel du Blason.* D.L. Galbreath. Lausanne, 1942, p. 250.
– Italy: cf. *p. 130 b.r.*
– Spain: Drawings by Franz Coray, Lucerne.
– Prussia: Drawings by Joachim von Roebel, Bonn.

p. 212 l. Arms of the Viscontis.
Milan, Biblioteca Trivulziana, Cod. 1390, p. l.

p. 212 l. Arms of the Viscontis.
Milan, Biblioteca Trivulziana, Cod. 1390, p. l.

p. 212 b.l. Author.

p. 212 b.r. State arms of Australia, 19 September 1912.
Publisher.

p. 213. Four *imprese* from the house of Visconti.
Milan, Biblioteca Trivulziana; Cod. 2168.

p. 214 a.l. A knight of the Order of St. John.
Paris, B.N.; ms. français 854, fol. 113v.

p. 214 c. Duke Charles the Bold of Burgundy.
From the statute book of the Order of the Golden Fleece.
Vienna, Ö.N.; Cod. 2606, fol. 70v.

p. 214 a.r. Sir Winston Churchill.
Photo: Keystone Press, London.

p. 214 b.l. Knights of the Order of the Star at table.
Grandes chroniques de France.
Paris, B.N.; ms. français 2313, fol. 394.

p. 214 b.r. Five Soviet generals.
Illus. from *Frankfurter Illustrierte,* No. 24, 11 June 1946.
Author.

p. 215 a. Heraldry of Nicholas von Diesbach.
l. B.H.M.
r. Ibid., ref. No. 11814.

p. 215 b.l. Armorial panel of King Carl XIII Johan of Sweden as crown prince, 1810.
Stockholm, Kungl. Livrustkammaren.

p. 215 b.r. Armorial shield of Prince Henrik of Denmark as knight and chancellor of the Order of the Elephant.
Frederiksborg Castle.
Photo: Poul Ainow, Copenhagen.

p. 216 a.l. Two coats of arms of Austrian archdukes.
Illus. from *Österreichisch-Ungarisch Wappenrolle*. H.G. Ströhl. Vienna, 1894, pls. II and III.

p. 216 a.r. Hans Weiditz, print commemorating the death of the emperor Maximilian.
M.G., No. 1525.

p. 216 b.l. Doors with the cross of the Grand Master of the Teutonic Order.
Marburg, Church of St. Elisabeth, west portal.
Foto Picture Library, Marburg.

p. 216 b.r. Detail from the surround of the pediment on the portal of Autun Cathedral. Two pilgrims rise from their graves at the Last Judgment; the one with the cross on his knapsack went to Jerusalem, the one with the shell to Santiago de Compostella.
Photo: Musée des Monuments Français, Paris.

p. 217 a., l. to r.
– Seal of the land master with the flight to Egypt.
Illus. from *Geschichte der Preussischen Münzen und Siegel*. F.A. Vossberg. Berlin, 1842, pl. I, no. 6.

– Shield of the landgrave Conrad.
Foto Picture Library, Marburg.

– Arms of the grand master.
Author's tracing from *Gelre*.

– Seal of the last grand master in Prussia.
Illus. from F.A. Vossberg (cf. above), pl. XI.

p. 217 c., l. to r.
– Arms of Portugal.
Author's tracing from *Gelre*.

– the others. Publisher.

p. 217 b.l. A seal of the Order of the Knights Templar, no. 9863.
Photographic service of the Archives Nationales, Paris.

p. 217 b.r. Table of armorial schemes for the bailiwick of Brandenburg of the Order of St. John.
Illus. from *Geschichte des ritterlichen Johanniter-Orden*. Justus Christoph Dithmar. Frankfurt a.O., 1728.

p. 218 l. Detail from the pilgrim's memorial of Ulrich Ketzel.
Nuremberg, G.N.M.; Gm. 581.

pp. 218 and 219. Costume of orders of chivalry.
Illus. from *Abbildungen und Beschreibung aller Hohen Ritter-Orden in Europa*. G. Eichler, Augsburg, 1759.

p. 219 a.l. Bookplate of Florian Waldauf of Waldenstein.
Publisher.

p. 219 a.r. Arms of Conrad von Krieg, around 1436.
Illus. from Arl.

p. 219 b. Arms on the back of the portrait of James of Savoy, Count of Romont.
Basel, Art Museum.

p. 220 a.l. Heinrich Blarer.
Constance, Rosgarten Museum.

p. 220 a.c. Oswald von Wolkenstein.
Innsbruck, Univerity Library, Song Manuscript B.

p. 220 a.r. Jean Warin, Bronze bust of King Louis XIII.
Paris, M.L.

p. 220 b.l. Marx Reichlich (active 1480–1520); altar painting depicting the knight Florian Waldauf (detail).
Municipal museum of Solbad Hall. Now stored in Innsbruck, Tyrolean Regional Museum, Ferdinandeum.

p. 220 b.r. Detail from portrait of Duke Frederick William of Brunswick.
Ministry of Works, London.

p. 221. Korin, portrait of Marshal Georgii Constantinovich Zhukov.
Photo: Novosti Press Agency. Geneva.

p. 222 a. Arms of the bishop of York.
London, B.L.; ms. Harl. 2169, fol. 9v.

p. 222 b.l. Arms of the Trinity from the so-called *Wernigerod Armorial*.
Original lost.
Drawing: Otto Hupp, from copy in Maria Hupp collection, Oberschleissheim near Munich.

p. 222 b.c. Albrecht Dürer, arms of Death.
Schweinfurt, Otto Schäfer collection, D-98.

p. 222 b.r. Quarter of the St. Julius banner of Schwyz.
Schwyz, Federal Document Archives.
Photo: James Perret, Lucerne.

p. 223. Miniature from the Lüneburg manuscript of the *Sachsenspiegel*, 1442–1448.
Lüneburg, Municipal Library.
Photo: Wilhelm Kreuzien, Lüneburg.

p. 224 a. Exotic arms.
Illus. from *C.C.C.*

p. 224 b. Emblems of the tribes of Israel and preheraldic emblems.
Illus. from *Opus*.

p. 255. Imaginary arms of the seven kings of Rome and the Roman emperor.
Illus. from *K.G.A.*, p. 30.

p. 226 a. Illustration of feudal law. Heidelberg manuscript of the *Sachsenspiegel*.
Heidelberg, University Library; Cod. Pal. Germ. 164, fol. 1r.

p. 226 b. Two seals of the landgrave Conrad II of Thuringia, 1233 and 1234.
Wolfenbüttel, State Archives of Lower Saxony.

p. 227 l. Two pages from the armorial of Jörg Rugenn.
Innsbruck, University Library; Codex 545, fol. 34v. and 36r.

p. 227 r. Enfeoffment of Roland.
Der Stricker, *Vita Caroli*.
St. Gallen, Municipal Library (Vadiana); ms. 302, fol. 26v.

pp. 228 and 229, l. to r. Paris, Bibliothèque de l'Arsenal; ms. Ars. 4790, fol. 64, 69, 40v., 47v., 48v., 78, 42v., 22v., 100, 82, 108, 53v., 105, 121v., 87, 53, 130, 115.

p. 230 a. Ivory mirror-back.
Brussels, Musées Royaux d'Art et d'Histoire, Sculpture and Furniture section.

pp. 230 and 231. Marshaling.
Publisher.
Drawings: Franz Coray, Lucerne.

p. 231 a. Battle of Lützen, 1632.
Ullstein Picture Service, Berlin.

p. 232 b. Coins of King Louis of Sicily (b. 1362).
Photo: State Coin Collection, Munich.

p. 233. Simplified form of the arms of the Two Sicilies.
Illus. from D.W.W., pl. 15.

pp. 232 and 233, the others. Publisher.
Drawings: Author and Franz Coray, Lucerne.

p. 234 a. Lozenge shield of an English queen.
Illus. from *Regal Heraldry* (cf. *p. 189*).

p. 234 l. M.C.; Publisher.

p. 234 c. Three seals.
Illus. from *Sigilla Comitum Flandriae*. Olivarius Vredius. Brussels, 1639, pp. 103, 104, 101.

p. 234 b. Bookplate from the Abbey of St. Gallen.
St. Gallen, Abbey Archives, Vol. B. 436.
Photo: Carsten Seltrecht, St. Gallen.

p. 235 Lucas van Leyden, side panels of the triptych *The Healing of the Blind Man*.
Leningrad, Hermitage.
Photo: Novosti Press Agency, Geneva.

p. 236 a. Arms of the reigning Pope Paul VI.
Official design.
Author.

pp. 236 and 237. Arms of the popes.
Publisher.
Drawings: Joachim von Roebel, Bonn.

p. 237 b.l. Bookplate of Dr. theol. Nicolaus Lang, professor in Ettiswyl, 17th century.
Photo: S.L., Zürich.

p. 237 a.r. Papal seal of dispensation.
Illus. from *Papal Heraldry*. D.L. Galbreath. London, 1972, p. 45.

p. 237 c. Corner segment of the Zurich banner of St. Julius.
Photo: S.L., Zurich.

– *The others.* The church hierarchy.
Illus. from *Wappenbrauch und Wappenreihn in der Kirche*. Olten, 1947.
Drawings: B.B. Heim.

p. 238 a. Arms of the primate of Poland.
Official design.
Author.

p. 238 a.l. The cardinals' entry into Constance.
Illus. from *C.C.C.*

p. 238 c.l. Arms during papal vacancy. Illus. from *H.A.*

p. 238 c. Arms of Cardinal Felice Peretto, 1585.
Illus. from *Der Deutsche Herold*. 1901, No. 4.

p. 238 c.r. Arms of the monastery of Suben. Austria.
Original impression.
Author.

p. 238 b. Arms of two modern bishoprics.
Official design.
Author.

p. 239. The English episcopate.
Original sheet, 1712.
Author.

pp. 240 and 241 a. University arms.
Illus. from *C.C.C.*

pp. 240 and 241, second row. University arms.
Illus. from *Wappenbuch des Heiligen Römischen Reichs*. Martin Schrott. Munich, 1581, Sheets 124–156.

p. 240 b.l. Academic lecture.
Relief by Pier Paolo dalle Masegne. Bologna, Medieval Civic Museum.

p. 240 b.r. University scepter, 1461.
Basel, Historical Museum, ref. No. 1942.533.
Photo: Museum.

p. 241. Different university arms.
Official designs.
Publisher.

p. 242 a. Crowned *Libertas*.
Drawing: Franz Coray, Lucerne.

p. 242 l. Nicola Bozidarevic, Dalmatian school, 16th century, left-hand panel of the triptych of the altar in the Bundic family chapel.
Dubrovnik, Dominican Church; St. Blaise showing a model of the town of Dubrovnik, and the apostle Paul.
Photo: André Held, Ecublens, Canton of Vaud, Switzerland.

p. 242 r., top to bottom.
– Arms of Genoa.
Illus. from *Illustrazione Storica dello stemma di Genova*. Angelo Boscassi, Genoa, 1919, pl. VIII.

– Arms of Lucca.
Official design 1835.
Author.
Photo: Cortopassi, Lucca.

– Arms of San Marino, steel engraving.
Author.

– Arms of Andorra.
Author's drawing.

– Seal of the republic of Bern, 1768.
Bern, State Archives.
Photot: Hugo Frutig, Bern.

p. 243 l. Arms of the republic of Venice.
Illus. from D.W.W., pl. 21.

p. 243 r. Banner of the city of Milan.
Freiburg, State Archives; *Freiburg Book of Colors*.
Photo: Benedikt Rast, Freiburg.

p. 244 a.l. Divided snake, *Pennsylvania Gazette*, 9 May 1754.
Photo: Publishers.

p. 244 c. "Dance around the Tree of Freedom."
Photo: Benziger Verlag, Zurich.

p. 244 a.r. New England flag.
Publisher.

p. 244 c.l. Seal.
Padua, Museo Bottacin.

p. 244 c.c. Tricolor flag.
Photo: Author.

p. 244 c.r. Heading of the legal ordinance of the Helvetian government of 26 July 1798.
Bern, Swiss National Library.

p. 244 b.l. Two coats of arms of Columbia, 1819 and 1821.
Illus. from *Heraldica Nacional*. E.O. Ricuarte. Bogota, 1954, pp. 63 and 79.

p. 244 b.r. Arms of Argentina.
Publisher.

p. 245 a.l. Swiss soldiers.
Zurich, S.L.

p. 245 a.r. Arms of Czechoslovakia and Finland.
Publisher.

p. 245 l. Infantry banner of the Spanish Republic, 1931.
Official design.
Author.

p. 245 c., l. to r.
– Arms of Oldenburg and Württemberg.
Illus. from *Die Wappen und Flaggen des Deutschen Reichs und der deutschen Länder*. Berlin, 1928, pls. VII, IV.

– Arms of Portugal.
Publisher.

– Hungarian coin. *Weltmünzkatalog*. Günther Schön. No. 48.
Photo: Battenberg Verlag, Munich.

p. 245 b.r. Arms of Austria, Federal Republic of Germany, Poland, and

Albania.
Publisher.

p. 246 a. Crown of the town of Bar-le-Duc.
Official design.

p. 246 c., l. to r.
– Imperial gold seal of Ludwig of Bavaria, 1328, from impression of the stamp.
Munich, State Coin Collection.

– Seal depicting Jerusalem.
Publisher.

– Great seal of Hamburg, around 1300–1800.
Hamburg, State Archives.

– Seal of the town of Emmerich, 1237.
Düsseldorf, Main State Archives.

– Seal of Arles.
Author.

p. 246 b.c., l. to r.
– Arms with bear.
Author.

– Arms of Charlottenburg and Hamelin.
Official designs.
Author's drawing.

p. 246 b. Arms of the town of Carlisle.
Official design.

p. 247 a., l. to r.
– Bronze casting of the medieval town seal on which the symbol of the double wheel first appears.
Mainz, Municipal Archives.

– Initial with the municipal arms from the town's treaty book of 1435.
Ibid. Sect. 4, No. 50.

– Arms from a document of Napoleon of 13 June 1811 (granting the status of a "Bonne Ville de l'Empire").
Ibid., Picture and Chart Collection, VI D 3.

– Water color drawing of the municipal arms from the 19th century.
Ibid., VI D 5.

– Representation of the arms valid since 1915.
Ibid., VI D 6.
Photos of all the above: Pilko, Mainz.

– Medal of the "Bonnes Villes," 1811.
Photo: Musée Monétaire, Paris.

p. 247 b. Armorial letter for the city of Vienna, 1461.
Original in Viennese Municipal and Regional Archives, Pat. No. 46.

pp. 248 and 249. Arms of capitals and major cities.
Publisher.
Drawings by the author for the Brockhaus Encyclopädie, colored by Joachim von Roebel, Bonn.

pp. 250 and 251 a. Eight mourners.
Paris, M.L.
Details in "Les Armoiries de Regnier Pot et de Palamède," Jean Bernard de Vaivre. In Cahiers d'Héraldique, II. Paris, 1975, pp. 179–212.
Photo: M.N.P.

pp. 250 and 251 b. Funeral procession of Queen Elizabeth I of England.
London, B.L.; ms. Add. 35324, fol. 37v.

p. 250 b.l. Paolo Uccello, The Battle of San Romano, detail, Counter-attack by the Florentines.
Paris, M.L.
Photo: M.N.P.

p. 252. Three stone sculptures.
– Tombstone.
Ebersbach bei Görlitz.
Illus. from Der Deutsche Herold, 1927.

– Shield with fleurs-de-lis.
Rome, San Giovanni in Laterano.
Illus. from Der Deutsche Herold, 1900.

– Florentine armorial wall.
Florence, bridge.
Photo: Author.

p. 253 l. Innsbruck armorial tower.
Printed sheet, 19th century.
Author.

p. 253 a.r. Arms of the Viscontis.
Illus. from H.A.

p. 251 Imperial roof of St. Stephen's Cathedral, Vienna.
Pub.: "Über den Wappenschmuck am Chordach von St. Stephan," Hanns Jäger-Sustenau. In Wiener Geschichtsblätter, Vol. 6 (66), 1951, No. 1.
Photo: Franz Hubmann, Vienna.

p. 254 a. Liechtenstein automobile badge.
Publisher.
Photo: Robert Tobler, Lucerne.

p. 254 c. Aeroplane.
Photo: Publisher.

p. 254 b.l. Arms of Flüelen on a Swiss locomotive.
Publisher.
Photo: Robert Tobler, Lucerne.

p. 254 b.r. Locomotive of the Swiss Federal Railways.
Publisher.

p. 255. Model of the royal yacht Sophia Amalia.
Copenhagen, Orlogsmuseet.
Photo: Museum.

p. 256 a., l. to r.
– Engraved silver box.
New York, Metropolitan Museum of Art.

– Chocolate jug.
Boston, Mass., Museum of Fine Arts.

– Plate.
London, Christie's Collection.

– Augsburg tankard.
Photo: Author.

– Beaker.
New York, Metropolitan Museum of Art.

p. 256 c., l. to r.
– Plate.
Gothenberg, Historical Museum.

– Queen's Ware Plate.
The Trustees of the Wedgwood Museum, Barlaston, England, GL 1473–1.

p. 256 b., l. to r.
– Pendant, in private hands.
– Seal ring with Neubecker-Lippe arms of alliance, with impression.

– Armorial ring.
Photo: Firma Bucherer, Lucerne.

– Blind embossing on a visiting card.
Author.

– Armorial letterhead.
Author.

p. 257 l. Bookplate of Bengt Jönsson Oxenstierna.
Stockholm, Royal Library.

p. 257 r. Two bookplates.
Author.

p. 258 a.r. Casket.
Nuremberg, G.N.M.

p. 258 l. Door knocker.
Lübeck, sacristy of the Church of St. Peter.
Illus. from H.A.

p. 258 b.l. Armorial shield of the English Jones family.
Pub.: Der Herold, Vol. l, 1940, pp. 63 to 71.
Photo: Author.

p. 258 b.r. Chest with representation

of a jousting exhibition.
Berlin, Museum of Applied Arts.
Pub.: Recueil du IVe Congrès International de Vexillologie, Turin, 24–27 June, 1971, pp. 181–186, 2 color pls.
Photo: Ba.Pr.Kb.

p. 259 l. Double-doored cupboard.
Hannover, Kestner Museum.
Photo: Hermann Friedrich, Hanover.

p. 259 a.r. Chandelier from the parish church of Wildpoldsried.
Photo: Lala Aufsberg, Sonthofen.

p. 259 b.r. Bedstead with the arms of Death.
Woodcarving by Peter Flötner.
Illus. from Die Kunst des deutschen Möbels. Heinrich Kreisel. p. 121.

p. 260 a. Seton Armorial, property of Sir David Ogilvy, Pencaitland.
Deposited in the National Library of Scotland, Edinburgh, Dept. of Manuscripts, fol. 16.
Photo: Tom Scott, Edinburgh.

p. 260 b.l. Detail of a Burgundian mille-fleurs tapestry.
B.H.M.; Ref. No. 14.

p. 260 b.c. British coat of arms.
Publisher.

p. 260 b.r. Tammany Hall, New York, Lithograph 49 183.
Courtesy of the New York Historical Society, New York City.

p. 261 Mille-fleurs tapestry.
London, Montacute House, National Trust.
Identified through Jean-Bernard de Vaivre, in Archivum Heraldicum 1973.

p. 262 c.l. Hans Neuerburg, cigarette pack designed by O.H.W. Hadank (d. 17 May 1965).
Photo: Christiane Marchesi, Zurich.

p. 262 b.l. Tenth World Cup Final (football); Federal Republic of Germany vs. The Netherlands; Munich, 1974.
Photo: Erich Baumann, Ludwigsburg.

p. 263 c.r. Cadillac Seville radiator badge, General Motors Corporation.
Photo: Cadillac, New York.

pp. 262 and 263, others. Applied heraldry.
Publisher.
Photo: James Perret, Lucerne.

p. 264 a. Armorial window of Peter Bubenberg.
Zurich, S.L., ref. no. 6921.

p. 264 l. Window of Glarus.
Ibid., No. 29264.

p. 264 r. Guild window, October, Watermen's Guild.
Ibid., repository of the Watermen's Guild, No. 3099.
In 1933 the Zurich guilds bought it back, together with seven other windows in the series, from the possession of the princes of Fürstenberg at Schloss Heiligenberg. A ninth window (June, Butcher's Guild at the sign of the Ram) is in V.A.M.

p. 265. Armorial window of Willisau and design for armorial window of Sursee (below).
Stained glass: Eduard Renggli, Lucerne.
Photo: James Perret, Lucerne.

p. 266. Official window of Bern.
Zurich, S.L., No. 8783.
From Schloss Wildegg, Aargau.
Stained glass: Jakob Brunner, from Brugg (Aargau).

p. 267. Armorial window of L\
Stained glass: Eduard Renggli, Lucerne.
Photo: James Perret, Lucerne.

INDEX

285